PRACTICAL REASONING

LARRY WRIGHT

University of California, Riverside

under the general editorship of

Robert J. Fogelin

Dartmouth College

HARCOURT BRACE JOVANOVICH, PUBLISHERS

San Diego   New York   Chicago   Austin   Washington, D.C.
London   Sydney   Tokyo   Toronto

For M H W

and a thousand kindnesses

ISBN: 0-15-571041-9
Library of Congress Catalog Card Number: 88-82145
Printed in the United States of America

Copyrights and Acknowledgments appear on pp. 431–32, which
constitute a continuation of the copyright page.

Preface

Practical Reasoning was developed to provide a practical reasoning course with systematic content. Since beginning the project, I have worked over the topic in a quarter-long course forty times. From a very difficult, shaky start, the course has evolved into a solid, well-received offering that is actually fun to teach, and whose main benefit is in helping students read and write argumentative essays— essays that establish or support a point of view. In this way, the course does help underpin much of the educational enterprise, and it actually fulfills the role such courses are sometimes given in the curriculum.

The course is essentially a skills course. It presumes a modestly orthodox level of perception and understanding of things in general, and a slightly higher level of reading and writing skills. Together these are forged into a systematic treatment of argument analysis, focusing special attention on the evaluation of evidence. The book begins with a treatment of paraphrase, out of which the notion of structured reasoning and schematized arguments develops naturally. A relatively orthodox induction/deduction distinction then leads to a systematic treatment of inference to the best explanation.

There are, of course, a number of different ways to use this text. But since my classroom procedure has varied very little over the forty attempts, and since the book evolved in those peculiar conditions, it might be valuable to share my procedure with instructors using the book for the first time. It is one way through the material that has produced a successful large course, and all manner of variation on it is possible.

The course meets three times weekly: two lectures and a discussion that I sometimes do myself and sometimes turn over to teaching assistants. Because the material is so nearly cumulative, I have organized the course around weekly quizzes. Typically 15 to 20 minutes long, they are designed to exercise the new increment of apparatus or understanding, usually together with much that has gone before. Each of the exercises at the ends of the first five chapters has been used—some several times—as a regular Friday quiz. At the beginning of class the following Monday I review the quiz, giving what I take to be the best response, together with some comment on systematic misunderstandings. Often the review leads directly into the new week's work.

I usually grade with two teaching assistants (for 70 to 100 students), and we have found that we are reasonably "intersubjective" if we limit ourselves to four general levels of quality. We give the numerical values 0, 1, 2, and 3 to the four levels, reading "0" as hopeless and "3" as perfect, with the intermediate values most commonly assigned. We do resort to half-points for tough cases. Part of the review is to announce the class mean (long term about 1.8) for the quiz.

This format gives students some sense of their performance both against an absolute standard and relative to everybody else in the class. The grade in the course is determined by some sort of curve or by performance-level groupings. I also offer a low-pressure final for those who think the time constraints of the quizzes have discriminated against them. It uses the same kind of problems and questions, but allows twice as much time per question. Graded generously, fewer than ten percent of those taking the final improve their grade. The weekly exercises turn out to be a good indicator of competence.

I have never tried using a midterm and a final. Doing so might work if the pedagogic value of the weekly quizzes could be found in something else. But since the course involves performance skills as much as recognition skills, getting students performing early and often has great value. The quizzes also provide early detection of serious misunderstanding—common in a course like this—and an opportunity for remedy as well.

Nearly every theme in this textbook may be pressed to levels of subtlety and detail inaccessible to the typical beginning student. Occasionally, however, such detail is not wholly wasted if the student is struggling with an exercise to which it may be made relevant. I have taken advantage of this in providing, in Appendix B, answers to the even-numbered exercises from the chapters. Some of those answers, especially the sample essays for the last two chapters, actually supplement discussions in the body of the textbook. They may be exploited in a variety of ways.

The study guides provided for the first six chapters were written by an especially conscientious teaching assistant. They are a revision of notes he circulated to his discussion groups. The contrasting idiom seems particularly helpful to some students.

Appendix A contains three good-sized chronological articles about the extinction of dinosaurs. Students may use the reasoning skills they have learned in the textbook to examine the pieces diagnostically—individually and as a continuum. This appendix contains a handful of additional, shorter news articles on various other recent topics in science for further practice in examining arguments.

The Instructor's Manual to accompany *Practical Reasoning* contains comments useful for teaching a course based on the textbook. It also provides comprehensive answers to the odd-numbered exercises in the textbook.

Acknowledgments

I thank Michael Brown, Creighton University; Harold Kincaid, University of Alabama, Birmingham; Rita Manning, San Jose State University; and Victor Vitanza, University of Texas, Arlington, for their reviews of the manuscript. I am grateful to Robert Fogelin for his editorial advice and support of the project. This text has also benefited from the comment and conversation of Dwight Furrow, Jim Hearne, Jeff Johnson, and Rita Manning. I am especially indebted to David Harrah for his careful reading of early versions of the manuscript and to David Barlow for providing the study guides. Many of the best ideas to be found here derive from work I did with Michael Scriven when I was his student and teaching assistant. The typescript was superbly prepared by Clara Dean.

LARRY WRIGHT

Contents

= 1 =

ARGUMENTS

Providing Support

Overview

Most of this text (Chapters 1–6) examines the human activity of GIVING REASONS: reasons for doing something or for thinking something is true. In this chapter we begin the examination by getting some practice determining just when, in our everyday reading, reasons are being given in support of some position or conclusion. Our main goal will be to develop a three-part routine: to see whether a passage can be broken up into reasons and conclusion; to put the ones that can in standard schematic form; and to express each component as clearly as possible in the context.

VOCABULARY

The first part of this text examines the concept of argument. As used here, the verb "to argue" refers to the activity of *offering reasons*: reasons in support of a statement someone makes or a conclusion he or she has reached. An argument, then, is simply the product of that activity.

> "I hear that administration economists have projected another year of low inflation. Have you been able to discover their argument for that projection?"

In this example, *argument* refers simply to the reasons themselves ("What reasons do they have for that projection?"); the conclusion being supported (the projection) is not part of what is being called

1

"their argument." It is quite natural, however, for *argument* to cover the entire process, including the position being supported.

> "What did you and Dad decide about the trip?"
>
> "Well, he argued that it might be a good time to try the scenic route along the coast because the snow level makes mountain driving too risky. I'm inclined to buy the argument."

Here the recommendation being supported—taking the coast route—is part of what is referred to as "the argument." So what is being called "the argument" in this case has two parts: a conclusion (let's try the coast route) and some support (the snow level is low, and the coast is scenic). In this book, *argument* will typically be used in this broader, more inclusive way; we will be treating the relationship between the two parts and will refer to them together. But the other use is correct too, sometimes, and will cause no confusion if you are aware of the context in which it is being used.

Either way, an argument involves providing support for a statement, offering reasons for reaching a certain conclusion. In this use *argument* contrasts with its employment in other contexts, such as the one in which it means, roughly, *fight*.

> Two men got into an argument in the parking lot outside Joe's Bar and Grill last night. Police had to be called when one of them drew a gun and began firing as the other fled in his car.

Here, in a reasoning text, we do not "get into" arguments in this sense at all: They need not even involve disagreement. Here, *argument* is simply meant to capture a very basic form of reasoning: the (often dispassionate) marshalling of support for a conclusion.

Closely related to the concept of argument is the sometimes tricky notion of inference. The verb "to infer" is often confused with the verb "to imply," and this confusion is worth avoiding. You may keep the distinction straight by remembering two things. First, inferring is always done by people, not by facts or statements; and second, when we infer, we always infer *from* something, usually from facts or statements. "From the wreckage strewn about the room, Holmes inferred there had been a struggle." Holmes did the inferring, and he did it *from* the fact that the room was a mess. By contrast, facts and statements imply things, and of course they do not imply them "from" anything: the expression "imply from" is nonsensical. "The wreckage in the room implied that there had been a struggle." The condition of the room is what does the implying here. We do sometimes speak of people implying things, but only when we are indirectly referring to their statements.

Keeping all this in mind, we may use either verb to talk about arguments. It takes somebody to infer the conclusion from the support claims, but the support claims themselves, if they are good enough, imply the conclusion. Philosophers have a jargon for talking about inferences, and they speak of our inferring *from* the support claims (sometimes called *premises*) *to* the conclusion. So when philosophers say they are examining an inference, they are examining what we would call an argument, using the words *argument* and *inference* almost interchangeably.

PARAPHRASE AND THE PRINCIPLE OF CHARITY

The eventual aim of our examination of arguments will be to evaluate them—to say whether they are any good and why. For our evaluations to be worth anything we must first be clear about some important preliminaries.

To this end, consider a passage of prose—a newspaper article, say, or a paragraph in a book, even a letter to an editor—that we would like to analyze as an argument.[1] Something about the passage suggests that it is intended as an argument or at least *contains* one. Perhaps it is just the contentious tone of the piece, or something it says that offends you, or even something about it that you rather like—but in any case something like this will get you wondering about the kind of support being offered for a particular statement. This is enough to get us involved in argument analysis and launch the first project of this book.

Of course, a revolting sentiment, even one expressed abrasively, does not have to be part of an argument: It could be simply the abrasive expression of a revolting sentiment, with no attempt made to defend it. This happens all the time in letters to editors. Before we can evaluate a passage as an argument, we must first be clear that it is intended as one, and just which one: What are we to take as the

---

[1]Most of what we are about to do will apply equally to constructing arguments of your own, but it is best to begin by considering someone else's arguments.

conclusion and what as the support? These are sometimes very difficult issues. In fact, if an author has anything very interesting to say, these preliminaries—what we might call matters of clarification—will frequently *dominate* an analysis. Sometimes the hardest part will be finding the conclusion and summarizing the support. After that, evaluation might be easy, or we may have shown it to be impossible without further information, or something in between. But even in cases that do not appear difficult on the surface it will be helpful to explicitly set out the pieces, getting a good grip on them and the relations among them. It is a waste of time to plunge into an evaluation when clarification is still required.

The notion of paraphrase is important to our reasoning because it is the vehicle of clarification. Any sentiment—position, proposition, conclusion, view—may be expressed in many different ways. Which way is best will depend on the circumstances: on the people involved (e.g., author and audience) and on their backgrounds, activities, institutional connections, expectations, and purposes. When author and audience know each other well, and the topic is commonplace, we can generally expect complete, effortless understanding. But the less familiar the participants are with one another, and the more difficult the topic, the more likely it is that matters of simple *expression* will get in the way of understanding. Just how something is put will determine whether the point is made.

Paraphrases are different ways of saying the same thing. In an easily imagined context[2] the following sentences are paraphrases of each other.

> The weather has been bad lately.
>
> We've had nothing but rain and fog for weeks.
>
> I haven't had to water the lawn for some time now.

To express the sentiment behind these sentences you would choose one or another, depending on your purpose and whom you were talking to. You might, of course, construct an entirely different one too. The point is that which sentence says it best depends on (sometimes tiny details of) the circumstances.

---

[2]Context is everything for a paraphrase, which should become clear as we go along.

Sometimes it might be just fine, for example, to say something in a bit of doggerel:

> The folks in Mojave tell the time of day by the Atchison, Topeka and Santa Fe.

But often a more prosaic paraphrase would be clearer:

> In Mojave, people sometimes tell the time by what's coming through town on the railroad.

Sometimes we make a point in technical jargon:

> Every juvenile benefits, both physically and socially, from periodic engagement in extra-domestic peer group activity.

But in another context a more everyday rendering is better:

> It is good for kids to play together outside.

Paraphrases like these may be helpful, clarifying in all sorts of ways and for all kinds of purposes. In analyzing arguments, however, our interest in paraphrasing will be very specific. We will be looking for the central, organizational points and principles: What's the author driving at? And this will involve paraphrasing—rewriting, recharacterizing, revising—for a number of different reasons. To begin with, you and an author may share so little in background and interest that you would naturally express yourselves very differently, making the same point through substantially different sentences. This is a common source of misunderstanding, and because of it you may have to work very hard to render what has been said into terms that are clear to you.

But even when the prose is clear, its gist may not be. And even when the gist is clear as you read it, it may be difficult to hold in mind as you ruminate on it. For these reasons it is valuable here to introduce the concept of a "bare-bones" paraphrase: a brief but clear statement of the major themes and issues in a piece. It should display the central point or points and, if there are several, show the relations among them. But it will not say much about these points. The guiding principle of bare-bones paraphrasing is economy, succinctness. Get it down to the bare bones so that the point—or the structure if there is one—can reveal itself. Eliminate the padding.

> Dear Editor,
>
> As far as I'm concerned all politicians are crooks. They may smile and kiss babies and say pleasant things at election time, but when they get back to Washington, or the state capital, or into their offices at city hall, you can trust them as far as you can throw a piano. They're all out for themselves.

In such an uncomplicated case, the bare-bones paraphrase could be

> Politicians are not worthy of our trust.

or

> Politicians in general are not worthy of our trust.

If more detail could be justified by the context, we might expand our paraphrase a little:

> The motivation of politicians is essentially selfish: They cannot be trusted.

Padding is anything we leave out so that we may see the main points—the structure, as we are calling it. We can usually leave out much that is essential to the flow of the prose, for example, introductory material, anecdotes and illustrations, humor and sarcasm. Even explanation and helpful redundancy will usually not show up in the paraphrase, so long as the understanding they permit does.

The following illustration is somewhat richer in padding than the one above.

El Niño Chances Diminish
The Associated Press

> SAN DIEGO—Climatologists say early signs of an ocean warming condition that could spawn tremendous storms have all but disappeared, meaning another El Niño, similar to the one that ravaged coastal areas three years ago, probably won't happen this year.

"At this point, it looks rather unlikely that we'll get anything this year," said Eugene Rasmusson of the federal Climate Analysis Center in Maryland.

"It's not out of the question," he said, but explosive changes in the ocean would have to happen this month for an El Niño to occur this year.

An El Niño is an unusual weather pattern that warms the Pacific Ocean temperatures and creates heavy storms. It occurs every few years and its effects last about two years.

This article, too, has a single, simple point:

El Niño is unlikely to return this year.

Everything else in the article relates to this main point as introduction, explanation, definition, or helpful restatement. (See if you can satisfy yourself that this is so, by running through every sentence in the article yourself.)

Charity

Recall that the purpose here of paraphrasing is to make a passage clearer. The clarity may be for ourselves or for others, but the point of the exercise is to get a better grip on the meaning. And for peculiarly human reasons we must constantly remind ourselves that the meaning on which we are trying to get a grip is *what the author had in mind*—as best we can determine it. This is an introductory version of the Principle of Charity that will underpin our whole analytical enterprise. It is called the Principle of Charity because of the great exertion and generosity required of us, not just to get past poor expression, but to put ourselves in the shoes of someone for whose views we may generally have nothing but contempt, in order to figure out just what those views are.

Just to be clear about this point, in contexts other than that of this textbook, paraphrases may be given for all sorts of purposes— purposes other than clarifying an author's intent. One might be given to draw a parallel with something else, or to point out an irony or create a certain impression. None of these needs to be faithful to an author's intent. Just the opposite. In political journalism, for example, the point of a paraphrase may be to be *critical*: to show how silly a passage is. So a paraphrase can be uncharitable—even a caricature—in the proper circumstances.

But not here. We use paraphrasing here as a preliminary to evaluation or criticism. So it will be as uncritical as possible.[3] Bend over backwards to make sense of what is said, erring when necessary on the side of generosity.

Subordination

Almost any interesting passage will contain more than a single point worth mentioning; and this is where the notion of structure begins to be valuable. One common but relatively uninteresting type of paragraph will contain a number of more or less independent and equally important issues. For example:

> The two-liter Rover 820 has an efficient sixteen-valve engine, designed and made by Austin-Rover, driving through a Honda five-speed manual gearbox. Equipped with single-point fuel injection, the four-cylinder produces one hundred twenty horsepower. With multipoint Lucas injection it produces one hundred forty horsepower.

The paraphrase here can be a simple list.

> The Rover 820 engine has
>   4 cylinders
>   16 valves
>   either 120 or 140 hp
> The transmission, by Honda, is a 5-speed.

Far more interesting are passages in which a main point is attended by dependent, subordinate points, the latter being there *in the service of* the former.

> ASPIRE, a Philadelphia automotive training facility, recently introduced "dial an expert" assistance for independent repair shops and service stations needing help in solving a service problem. The program, called ACCESS (ASPIRE'S Comprehensive, Computerized Education and Support System), uses a computer data bank of vehicle manufacturers' technical service bulletins, supported by a staff of consultants in various automotive systems.

---

[3]Except editorially, of course. Editorial criticism—editing—is *charitable* reworking: tidying up expression and revising to make the point sharper, more coherent, possibly more forceful. This is just the sort of revision we will make in our paraphrasing for clarity and understanding.

Here the main point is the announcement of a novel telephone assistance program for car repair. Everything else—the name, technology, and staffing—is there to help out: to provide explanatory detail, in this case. That is what is meant here by "subordinate" or "dependent." The secondary material is mentioned only because it is relevant to the main point.

The paraphrase, then, will have some rudimentary structure, some internal relationships:

> Main Point: Auto mechanics can now get expert assistance in solving service problems simply by picking up the phone.
>
> Secondary Points:
>> a. This resource is named Aspire.
>> b. It provides computer access to manufacturers' technical data.
>> c. It also provides access to trained consultants.

The original announcement was so short that the paraphrase improves on it very little in conciseness. And this allows us to see that the ability of a paraphrase to display structure is something over and above mere economy of expression. Both virtues are important here, but it is crucial to see their independence.

Subordination, and the structure it creates, is the central reason that paraphrasing is important to the analysis of arguments. Statements subordinate to a main point often contain the support being offered for that point. They are "reasons in favor of" the main point, and they are dependent (and hence subordinate) because they are there only to support that main point. They would not be mentioned otherwise.

Anti-Litter Bill

As a private citizen I wholeheartedly support the current method of recycling used in California. In my living room there is a stack of Times newspapers which is given to a neighbor when it reaches three feet high; on the back porch are bags of aluminum cans and glass containers which are taken to a recycling center at a local high school.

However, as a retailer and franchisee of a 24-hour convenience store, I am against Proposition 11. It will require retailers to become recycling centers. It will require me to take back all empty soda and beer containers brought into my store; however, I cannot call the distributor for a pickup of these empty containers unless I have at least *25 cases of each brand* sold in my store.

I currently have available to the consumer 20 different brands of soda and 10 of beer. I carry some because of a small contingent of customers who will buy them, but they are not fast sellers. If this proposition is passed, I can assure one and all that I will limit the number of brands available at my store to only those items that will sell quickly enough and be returned quickly enough to ensure me the required 25 cases for a pickup by the distributor.

I will also have to cut down on the selling space of other items that I carry in order to provide storage space. Additionally, I will be forced to have my store serviced more often by the fumigator to ensure that whatever "crawly" items are returned inside these empty containers do not infest other merchandise.

An additional problem with Proposition 11 concerns its enforcement provisions. Who is going to enforce the law and levy the fine?

HARRIET MARKMAN
Alhambra

Here the central sentiment is opposition to proposition 11. So the Main Point of the paraphrase would be something like

Proposition 11 should not become law.

or, perhaps,

Proposition 11 would be a bad law.

The rest of the article is a collection of dependent, secondary points offered in support of this central sentiment. A paraphrase could display the structure of—the internal relationships within—this article as follows:

Main Point: Proposition 11 should be defeated.

Secondary Points:

1. It would hurt small convenience stores.
    (a) by restricting the variety of stock.
    (b) by reducing shelf space.
    (c) by increasing fumigation expense.
2. We already have a functioning recycling system.
3. The enforcement apparatus is not clear.

Of course, as we have already seen, not every subordinate point is offered as a reason for a main point. Subordination should act as a *flag* to indicate that reasoning may be in progress and to signal the form it might take.

SCHEMATIZING ARGUMENTS

The purpose of this chapter is to begin the discussion of arguments. To this end it will be useful to restrict our use of the word *argument* in a slightly artificial but very useful way. What we will call "the argument" will virtually never be a normal passage of prose like a paragraph, but always its bare-bones paraphrase. What we will be discussing, analyzing, and evaluating will be an economical statement of a conclusion and whatever statements are marshalled in its support. Remove the padding and consider only the statements having a "reasons for" relationship among them (or within them). We do this to separate, as much as possible, the analysis of arguments from the complicated questions of reading and interpretation we looked over in the previous section on paraphrase. This separation will enable us to talk more systematically of different kinds of argument and strengths of support in isolation from other distractions.

Accordingly, it will be useful to introduce a stylized form of bare-bones paraphrase especially for arguments. Call this the *schematization*, or schematic picture, of an argument.

$$S_1$$
$$S_2$$
$$S_3$$
....

$$C$$

This should be read, "Statements S_1, S_2, and S_3 are (collectively) offered in support of conclusion C." This form will adequately capture the reasoning in many simple passages. Conversely, anything that can be paraphrased in this way contains an argument. The form can easily be compounded to represent more complex reasoning.

Consider the litter-bill letter we examined on pages 9 and 10. We already have a bare-bones paraphrase; it is a simple step to put it into our stylized form:

S₁   Proposition 11 would hurt small convenience stores by restrict-
      ing the variety of stock, reducing shelf space, and increasing
      fumigation expense.

S₂   We already have a functioning recycling system.

S₃   Proposition 11's enforcement apparatus is unclear.

C   Proposition 11 should be defeated.

This would be the schematic representation of the argument offered
in Harriet Markman's letter. It will be this setup we will be speaking
of when we speak of an argument.

Flag Terms

We have already seen that subordination is an indicator or "flag" that
should alert you to the possibility that an argument is being offered
and may even hint at its components (S's, C). Certain words (call
them *flag terms*) help us in much the same way. Words like *since, if,
because, therefore, so, hence,* and *thus* and phrases like *it follows
that* are good indicators that schematizable reasoning is taking place
in a passage. The first three (*since, if, because*) typically precede
supporting statements; the rest ordinarily indicate that the conclusion is coming up.

> Since proposition A on the November ballot contains a provision
> allowing the City Council to alter any part of the proposition on a
> majority vote, it follows that those who think this proposition
> would be a disaster must have a very low opinion of our City
> Council.

Phrased this way, a passage almost schematizes itself. The support
claim and the conclusion fall in the proper order, are separated by the
only internal punctuation, and are each flagged by an appropriate
expression. To schematize would require merely dropping the flags,
writing the first clause above the second, and drawing separating
lines between them. (Try it, just for practice.)

Very seldom are the support claims *and* the conclusion both
flagged by characteristic terms, however: Usually one or the other is
all you get. Even in the "proposition A" illustration, the second flag
("it follows that") is a bit forced and the passage would read better
without it. (Read the passage out loud without the offending phrase,

just to test your ear.) But dropping the second flag raises no real difficulty. One flag is usually enough even in examples much more complicated than this, and there also is so much else to go on.

Flag terms become slightly more important when the order of the components is inverted or jumbled.

> Those who think the passage of proposition A would be a disaster must have a very low opinion of our City Council, because that proposition contains a provision allowing the Council to alter any part of it on a majority vote.

This is, of course, exactly the same argument, with *because* signalling that this time the support comes last, not first. This flag makes it particularly easy to see that the schematized form should be exactly the same as in the first version.

Thoughtful writers and speakers will scatter flag terms throughout complicated passages to help the reader or listener follow the flow of reasoning: to help us schematize as we go. How they do it depends on the case and the context, of course; but just seeing the possibility can be of great help in your own work.

Compound Arguments

Sometimes the structure, the support relations, will be more complex than the two-part schematics discussed so far. There may, of course, be a number of independent arguments in a passage, but that is neither very common nor usually very interesting. Far more commonly we will find that, although there is a single main argument, the passage contains secondary arguments bolstering the weak or controversial parts of the main argument's support. The flow of reasoning will be more like a river with tributaries than a single, isolated stream.

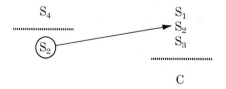

Here S_4 is clearly relevant, clearly part of C's support, but its role in the main argument is covered by S_2. If we schematized the main argument simply, S_4 would be left out as redundant. But often a more detailed representation of the reasoning is useful. So we may want to compound the schematization.

Consider the following article.

A New Use for a Well-known Drug

Aspirin, which has long been known by doctors and laymen alike to have many uses, may have yet another: It may be able to play an effective part in weight loss. When combined with the allergy relief medicine ephedrine, aspirin is believed to have, at least theoretically, the ability to help people lose weight.

Researchers at Harvard Medical School and the University of London recently published the findings of their aspirin-ephedrine studies in the *American Journal of Clinical Nutrition*. In one study, laboratory mice were fed a combination of the two drugs, and their metabolic rates increased as a result. This is important news at a time when interest in using metabolic-rate increase to reduce weight is being rekindled.

The researchers think it's possible that a mixture of the two drugs could be used to help humans control obesity. They think the active ingredients in aspirin and ephedrine should be safe for such use by humans, if only because doctors have been using them in standard, everyday medicine for centuries.

The reasoning might be represented simply in this way:

S_1 A mixture of aspirin and ephedrine raises metabolic rates in mice.

S_2 Raising metabolic rates is an established means of weight reduction.

S_3 The aspirin–ephedrine mixture is probably safe for humans.

C A mixture of aspirin and ephedrine may be useful in treating human obesity.

This representation may be criticized for omitting the second part of the last sentence, however. Our long experience with the two drugs is clearly part of the reasoning, but it is not covered in the schematic paraphrase. This violates our basic rule.

We might simply add it to S_3, of course.

S_3' Our long experience with the aspirin–ephedrine combination provides good reason to think it is safe for humans.

But then S_3' itself has the form of an argument: One statement is offered in support of another within a supporting statement. We should always try to avoid this, because the whole point of schematic form is to display the structure of reasoning by boldly separating support from what it supports. Reasons-for relations should not occur within the reasons. So the best way to handle this passage is to represent it as a compound argument. Its main argument would be represented as above, with a plain S_3, but it would have a tributary or adjunct-argument offered in support of S_3.

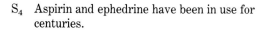

S_4 Aspirin and ephedrine have been in use for centuries.

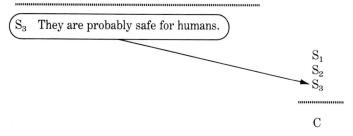

Compounding arguments is a standard technique in structuring paraphrases. Handled with care it can be immensely helpful.

Charity in Schematizing

There is, of course, no reliable, purely mechanical way to schematize arguments using the devices we have examined: subordination, order of presentation, punctuation, and typical indicator terms. These devices are *very* useful, but only against the background of our general understanding of what an argument is: statements being offered in support of a conclusion. So, much of the work will be done by our reading skill, our ability to empathize with another human struggling to articulate reasons for something. And this sharpens the point of our charity principle in its application to argument. We must look not just for the most plausible reading of a passage, but for the most plausible *reasoning* to attribute to it.

This very general advice actually yields some practically useful questions to ask in checking your perception of an argument.

1. A question that does not get asked often enough is simply whether it is plausible to suppose that the author intended the passage as an argument—as opposed, for example, to a simple expression of dismay, an attempt at humor, or unstructured sarcasm.

We are occasionally so convinced that an offensive opinion *must* involve faulty reasoning that we read a bad argument into the passage simply to be able to criticize. But speculating on what somebody's reasoning might have been is very different from analyzing a passage, and it is important to keep that difference in mind. The "all politicians are crooks" example we paraphrased on page 6 is a case like this. It cannot plausibly be broken into two sentiments with one being a "reason for" the other. It is just the slightly hysterical expression of a cynical opinion. The El Niño article on pages 6–7 is longer and more complicated, but it also lacks internal argumentative structure. It is a more interesting article for our purposes because so much padding can be omitted. But look at it again to reassure yourself that nothing we omitted from the bare-bones paraphrase bears a "reason for" relationship to the main point. Note also that this analysis refines our concept of padding, specifically for argument analysis: *Add it to your list of criteria.* (If you don't have a list, go back to page 6 and make one up.)

One of the toughest judgment calls in argument analysis concerns how to treat cases that come close to being pure expressions of opinion but contain a hint of argument. The author is obviously trying to provide support but, perhaps in the heat of the moment, garbles the formulation—just puts it badly. Charity requires that you patch up the reasoning as best you can while you schematize, to find the best argument in the neighborhood. There will usually be a lot of argumentative raw material; it just won't be clear how the author intended it to be organized. Your job will be to organize it as best you can—into the strongest argument you can think of.

Editor,

I wonder if the employees of the Department of Motor Vehicles could stop complaining about having to work on Saturdays long enough to realize who is footing the bill for their paychecks.

As a taxpayer, I'm getting more than a little tired of government—federal, state, county, and city—employees who are too busy thinking of themselves to give a "tinker's dam" about the general public for whom they are supposed to work.

If hospital services can be available 24 hours a day, 365 days of the year, I would hope the DMV could stay open 4 hours on Saturday. They certainly get more than enough holidays to compensate.

A charitable schematization of the argument hinted at here might be

S_1 The DMV is a public service wholly supported by taxes.

S_2 Keeping the DMV open on Saturday would be a substantial convenience for many taxpayers.

C   The DMV should be open on Saturdays.

With a little more imaginative effort we might be able to work in the hospital analogy more explicitly, but the version above displays the general sense of the reasoning well enough. It is patched up enough to read like an argument.

At the other end of the spectrum, when reasoning is difficult to discern because it is *complicated*, schematizing will increasingly involve trial and error. And sympathetic reading will become all-important. The best strategy is usually to first choose a good-looking candidate for the conclusion and then see if you can sensibly account for the rest as padding or support. (Reread this last sentence and underline the three key words in the second clause—*sensibly, padding*, and *support*—to give yourself a handy schematization checklist.) Until you have had a lot of pratice in charitable reading you should probably not trust your initial judgment of plausibility, sensibility, or coherence. Extending our list of questions will help check and develop that judgment.

2.   Have you left anything out?

3.   Have you called something padding that sounds like a "reason for"?

4.   Does the order of presentation and the subordination make sense on your reading?

5.   Are there awkward flag terms (e.g., is one of your supporting statements flagged in the passage with a conclusion flag)?

6. Does the support contain any internal reasons-for relationships? (If so, compound form may be necessary.)

These last five questions simply offer a different perspective on the checklist mentioned above, something to help you see the point of the list in specific application.

Let's look again at Harriet Markman's letter on the anti-litter bill (pages 9–10) and apply the checklist as we go along. Remove the padding (mostly anecdotal illustration) from the first paragraph and we have S_2. (So we've accounted for paragraph 1 as S_2 and padding.) The first sentence of the next paragraph is a version of the conclusion; the rest is a general introduction to the consequences of Proposition 11 that make up S_1. (So we've accounted for paragraph 2 as C + padding.) The next paragraph is a detailed presentation of the "variety" part of S_1. (So we've accounted for paragraph 3 as included in S_1.) The two sentences of the next paragraph provide the other two items in S_1, and the final paragraph gives us S_3. This is what it is like to show that a schematization can account for an entire passage at a middling level of complexity.

If you find yourself really struggling, you can generalize trial and error into a decision procedure, rather like a computer program. Run through the passage one sentence—or one clause—at a time, trying each one as the conclusion. Find the best schematization for each one, and, of these, choose the one that most plausibly organizes the passage—the one that best answers questions like the five on pages 17–18. Sometimes, doing this will lead you to distinguish more than a single argument. A passage may contain two independent arguments (even the author may not see their independence), or it may contain serial arguments with the conclusions of earlier ones forming support for later ones. The same general themes will organize these cases, too, but will require more of your own ingenuity and reading skill. In later chapters we will develop techniques to help with more complex structures.

Presuppositions.   Even simple reasoning will exhibit one further complication, however, one further aspect that will exercise our plausibility judgment and reading skill. Sometimes an important part of the schematic picture is simply understood or presupposed, not explicitly stated in the passage. You must figure it out and formulate it yourself to complete the schematization.

Sometimes the conclusion itself is implied but not stated:

> Beneath all the hype and hullabaloo surrounding the recommis-
> sioned battleship *New Jersey*, one fact stands out: It will never be
> more than an expensive ornament. It will be an irresistible target if
> hostilities ever erupt and will be very easy to put out of action
> unless we squander an entire fleet to protect it. Certainly the
> Department of Defense could find better uses for the money this
> project has and will cost.

The conclusion—the view being supported—is obviously something
like "The *New Jersey* should not have been recommissioned" or
"Recommissioning the *New Jersey* was a waste of money." No such
statement occurs in the passage, however, because the author doubtless thought it unnecessary. The sentiment is clear, the second
sentence offers "reasons for" it, and the schematization should be
very easy.

In other cases, an important part of the support is left unstated:

> Current economic indicators are so bad that the wise investor will
> stay out of the stock market until there is a substantial change in
> the climate.

The conclusion here is that now is not a good time to buy stock, and
the support offered is that the indicators are down. But the argument takes for granted that the indicators in question have characteristics that make the support offered reasonable. Those indicators
must be relatively stable, not volatile, and must be tied to the
economy in a sensible way. Statements that are taken for granted
are called *presuppositions*, because even though they are not explicitly stated in the argument, the strength of the argument depends on
them: If they are challenged, the argument itself is challenged. Here
these are things that *can* (reasonably) be presupposed, at least for
the moment, until something about them causes a question to be
raised. But if a question is raised, they would have to be included
explicitly among the supporting statements.

Occasionally (but not as often as we sometimes think), simply
digging out a presupposition will all by itself raise a question. Sometimes, just thinking of a presupposition will raise a difficulty that we
had not noticed before. For example, it is sometimes argued that the
price of petroleum should be held at an artificially high level because
doing so would encourage further exploration and hence increase the

petroleum supply. Among other things, this argument assumes that it would make economic sense for an oil company to plow increased profits back into the oil business. But it might be that oil companies would be better off using their profits to diversify by purchasing fast-food operations or a struggling airline company. Most of us at whom this argument is aimed would not have much reason to prefer the presupposition to the alternatives offered. So the argument, as it now stands, does not provide us with very much support for its conclusion.

Digging out presuppositions is one of the first tricks we learn when we begin to think about reasoning and arguments. But doing it well requires care and judgment (and practice!), so a couple of precautions are called for. The first is charity, once again. But this charity rule is more than simply a matter of keeping the reconstruction plausible. It is a strong, negative rule: Don't stick the author with a needlessly weak or flawed version of the argument. If you disregard this rule you end up criticizing an argument that is easily patched up. You waste a lot of time and energy, and you even risk misleading yourself about the strengths of the arguments you examine. Charity is in your own interest, here; it is an investment in the quality of your reasoning. (Of course, if you are just having fun making somebody mad, or are just reproaching the arguer, then the principle of charity is not clearly relevant—and what you are doing is not argument analysis.)

In the stock market example, it is tempting to saddle the arguer with a number of presuppositions that are easy to attack. The zealous critic might charge the author with assuming that *all* the economic indicators are bad (which is almost never the case) or that bad indicators *always* presage lower stock prices (which is doubtful). But the argument does not require anything so sweeping (and hence vulnerable) in order to make its point. In the first place, it may well be that only *some* economic indicators are relevant to stock market prices, and it is possible that it takes only a few of these to guarantee a bad market. Second, the wise investor will worry about bad economic indicators even if they are only *usually* a reliable guide to the fortunes of the market: By the time he or she has a guarantee it is too late to do much good. The principle of charity requires taking this sort of thing into account. And taking it into account requires in turn both an acquaintance with the subject matter of the argument and, frequently, a practiced imagination. As we explore argument analysis it will become increasingly clear that education and imagination are *the* indispensable requisites of this activity. Learning how to better use what we already have, and how to discover what else we need, is the major project of this book. For now it is important simply to understand the role of charity in reconstructing arguments: It helps you avoid wasting time in lightweight posturing when there is serious work to do.

A second caution for enthusiastic presupposition hunters concerns the simple judgment of when to stop. Nearly any argument will allow presuppositions to be dug out almost without limit, although they quickly become trivial and uninteresting. The stock market example presupposes that there is a stock market and that investors care about its future and that the world won't be obliterated tomorrow, among other things. But these are boring distractions: In most contexts they are *simply* understood, and mentioning them misses the point of the argument. Knowing when to stop, knowing when all the useful presuppositions have been disinterred, requires a lively awareness of the context and plain good sense. These too improve with practice.

Summary: The Role of Charity

The Principle of Charity is important in our reasoning because we are human. Our natural defensiveness in the face of disagreement often subverts our judgment, and, even when we're in friendly surroundings, we need guidance in organizing the immense discretion we sometimes have in paraphrasing arguments. Both these considerations offer the same advice: To maximize the payoff of the exercise, always construct the strongest version of the argument you can think of. When you have some discretion, choose the best-looking alternative; avoid wasting time on straw men (more on those in Chapter 6). This will sometimes (again, not as often as you might think) lead us to view the result as *our* argument as much as the author's. But usually the author would approve, and in any case, it is a small risk worth taking to gain enormous benefit.

The Nature and Function of Argument

One prevalent picture of argument is forensic: The idiom is of doing battle, or dueling, or defending a fortress, with winners and losers and cutting one's losses. This picture is obviously at odds with the spirit of the enterprise sketched here; and part of this chapter's

burden has been to display the flaws in that picture. The contempt
and hostility between opponents in conflict almost guarantee against
the productivity of reasoning. Defensiveness is the enemy of co-
gency; it undermines our judgment, our sense of plausibility. It
sends us in search of strategy instead of understanding. It is entirely
the wrong picture if we seek to learn anything. Productive argument
is part of conversation and so requires civilized forbearance if not
always generosity: interlocutors, in any case, not antagonists.

Perhaps the most instructive observation about defensiveness
and the human mind can be gleaned from the history of philosophy
and high school debate teams. The fact is simply that a clever person
can come up with a decent sounding defense of anything at all, no
matter how silly it is. Reasoning takes on the quality of a game;
confident judgment seems arbitrary, even capricious. The contest
model is attractive because it is relatively tidy and is rule-governed.
But human reasoning is more a matter of skill than explicit rules, and
what rules we find are hints and mnemonics, a crazy quilt of helpful
oversimplifications—anything but tidy.

Another way of putting all this is to say that much that is worth
reasoning about has merit too subtle to withstand rough treatment.
The aim of argument should be to display the merit of a conclusion as
clearly as possible, to allow that merit to dominate the enterprise.
This yields a picture of argument modeled on explanation, investigation, and demonstration rather than battle. Human reasoning requires guidance and instruction, not strategy and tactics.

None of this should be particularly surprising if we remind
ourselves that we will often develop an argument for our own consumption. Much of our reasoning consists in our thinking through the
reasons for something simply to assure ourselves of the virtue of a
belief or a choice we are considering. We are usually not as careful in
our private rumination as we are when we have an audience—we
won't actually sketch a schematization, for instance—and this is
sometimes a flaw. But the point of the activity is to *display the
support as clearly and understandably as possible*[4]; and this simply
is the model of argument being developed here: not a duel, just
guidance.

So when the object of reasoning is not to assure ourselves but to
persuade somebody else, the nature and spirit of the enterprise

---

[4]This explains why the word *cogent* applies so naturally to reasoning. Look it up. It
will make a good addition to your vocabulary.

remain the same; *all* that has changed is the object. Certainly, if I am to take your argument seriously, I must have the sense that you are trying to display the merits of your position, not deceive me about them. If I sense that your primary motive is to win a victory, not extend understanding, my perception and posture will be radically different. I will naturally become defensive and dramatically reduce the chances that any reasoning will take place at all.[5]

The Principle of Charity may thus be viewed as a way to win the respect of your audience—any thoughtful audience. It certainly does have this use; and if you wish to call it a "strategy" for this reason, you may, so long as you grasp the end toward which the strategy is aimed. That end is what underpins every other application of the principle as well: understanding.

The Pragmatics of Evaluation.   We cannot, of course, say very much about evaluating arguments this early in the discussion. But some preliminaries are now in order, and they will help us close our examination of the paraphrase and reconstruction of arguments.

We may take the two primary functions of argument to be those introduced in the last few paragraphs: to assure ourselves and to persuade somebody else. Most other uses of argument are parasitic on these. Notice right away that *what* we assure ourselves or persuade somebody else *of* is not always that the conclusion of the argument is true. Arguments provide support for conclusions; our evaluation will be to determine *how much* support has been offered (or how *good* that support is). And to the question "How much?" there is a range of answers from "conclusive" to "a lot," "some," "a little," "virtually none." How much is needed or useful depends on the case. On a tough theoretical question in physics a very little bit of support is not only useful but cherished, justifying enormous effort and expense. But that amount of support in the day-to-day matters of our lives—whether the food is spoiled or the brakes will hold— would be wholly useless for most purposes.

However, the most important point to make about the two functions of argument mentioned above (assuring and persuading) is that they suggest practical criteria for determining when an argument

---

[5]Obviously, again, winning may be valuable in other ways: to your ego or your standing in a social or professional group. But these functions of argumentative prose are not under study here.

has been adequately dissected. For your own assurance, you must analyze an argument far enough for it to be clear that the judgment of support strength is one *you* can *reliably* make. This, of course, requires a lively awareness of your own biases, weaknesses, and limitations, and sometimes these are very difficult to detect. The explorations in this book should both test and sharpen your judgment in these matters.

When the object of an argument is to persuade someone else, the analytical criterion is altered; how much it is altered depends on the similarities of the protagonists. The analysis must proceed until they reach common ground; the end comes only when each can make a satisfactory judgment. This rule is actually just a rudiment of civil conversation: If other people's views are important, differences in judgment must be resolved by the protagonists working from areas of agreement. This resolution takes patience, imagination, empathy, and (as always) practice, but it is the only civil recourse in a world in which different backgrounds yield widely varying perceptions.

STUDY GUIDE FOR CHAPTER 1

1. In this chapter, we are interested in how we argue in speaking and writing, with an emphasis on how we argue in writing.

    (a) Although the verb "to argue" and the noun "argument" have other uses (angry conversation, for instance), we want to restrict them here to the activity of giving reasons for a statement or a position.

    (b) We must begin by developing certain reading and writing skills, which we all have but which usually benefit from attention and exercise. For our purposes, the most important of these skills is the ability to read, say, a passage of prose, and *paraphrase* it. In paraphrasing the passage, we want to distinguish its main point and its secondary point(s).

    (c) When we paraphrase an argument we try to eliminate all of its *padding* and give the most reasonable reconstruction we can of the point the author is trying to make. Padding is everything we can omit from a clear and succinct statement of the conclusion and of the reasons offered for it. Introductory material, examples and illustration, definition of terms, humor, sarcasm, helpful restatement, even explanatory asides will usually be omitted as padding.

    (d) The *Principle of Charity* guides us in our paraphrasing. This principle tells us to give the passage the most plausible reading we can; or, to put it negatively, it tells us not to unfairly stick the author with a silly and weak restatement of his or her point.

(e) A paraphrase should have these three properties: (1) It should be briefer than the original passage; (2) it should (when possible) be clearer than the original passage; and (3) it should accurately reflect the intention of the original author.

2. An *argument*, then, is the giving of reasons in support of a conclusion.

(a) An argument has a special structure: The secondary points are (always, in a way) subordinate to the main point. They support the main point; they offer reasons for it.

(b) To capture this structure in a schematic form, we *schematize* the argument. We distinguish the *support statements* (secondary points) from the *conclusion* (main point). We put the conclusion at the bottom and the support on top:

$$S_1$$
$$S_2$$
$$S_3$$
$$\text{\tiny iiiiiiiiiiiiiiiii}$$
$$C$$

(c) *Flag terms*, like *so, thus, therefore, if, since*, sometimes help us to sort out the support from the conclusion, but usually we have to rely on our reading skills.

3. The author of a passage does not always explicitly state all of his or her argument. We must supply the missing pieces when we schematize the argument. The principle of charity requires that we do this as plausibly as we can: that we use our discretion to strengthen, not weaken, the argument.

EXERCISES

1.   Arts Center's Empty Seats

Dear Editor,

We went to see "Big River" at the stunning new Performing Arts Center and thoroughly enjoyed the spectacle, the acoustics and the lush splendor of the theater.

However, it is deplorable that half the seats were unoccupied. I asked an attendant, and she verified my guess. Of course it is expensive—$70 for the two of us in the second tier.

But why not give those empty seats to senior citizens, who deserve a break living on social security?

One call to a senior citizens center would cause a lot of happiness and entertainment for an appreciative audience.

Or, as a former high school teacher, I know the drama teacher would value having tickets for students so that they could better learn their craft and thus benefit us all one day.

Certainly all students could learn from seeing Huckleberry. And wouldn't the performers rather play to a full house? What a waste.

PATRICIA FROSTHOLM
Fullerton

a. Paraphrase this letter as economically as possible. (Hint: Try for a single main point and one or two secondary ones.)

b. Try arranging the material in your paraphrase in a different way that yields a paraphrase nearly as good as your first.

2.   Beneficial Effect of Alcohol Questioned

BOSTON (AP)—The apparent beneficial effect of drinking on cholesterol levels is questioned by a new study, which concludes that people should not substitute alcohol for exercise to protect their hearts.

Many studies have found that people who drink moderate amounts of alcohol have less heart disease, and the latest research does not dispute that belief. Instead, the researchers showed that the specific way experts assumed this protection worked in the body is wrong.

The new study came to the unexpected conclusion that alcohol has no effect on the particular blood protein that experts believe prevents cholesterol buildup on the walls of the arteries.

a. Paraphrase the complex sentiment of this article as economically as you can.

b. What makes it so difficult to capture the sense of this passage briefly?

c. If you had to decide on a single, simple main point (something simpler than what you gave in a), what would it be? How would you justify leaving out what you did?

3.   "Free Speech"

Dear Editor,

Phil Kerby ("Reagan Administration Betrays Its Fear of Free Speech," Times, Sept. 29) is up in arms against government restrictions requiring some public employees to submit their writings to an official review before publishing. He says this "directive's potential for censorship has no parallel in history."

Many, like Kerby, who are concerned about censorship and civil liberty find it curiously hard to accept the realities of the atomic bomb and the new age it ushered in. In a world that contains nuclear weapons and the new missiles, is it seriously possible to believe that we can continue with the same 18th-century freedoms we used to dream were to be ours forever?

Back in the '30s some of us laughed at Father Caughlin, a vigorous advocate of U.S. isolation, as he spoke on nationwide radio in favor of what was called "Fortress America." His mix of message and media simply did not compute. Radio was one of the new inventions that knew no national boundaries and, with other revolutionary technologies, was working hard to shrink the world to its present more convenient but also more dangerous size.

The nuclear breakthrough was only one technological change that spelled a reduction in liberty. With the dangers inherent in nuclear weapons it seems a sure bet that nothing is going to stop change to more powerful government and fewer personal freedoms. This will come about, I believe, no matter who is President or how much we may deplore it.

R. CARNEY
Los Angeles

This letter may be read in two subtly distinct ways, one of which is best paraphrased in a single sentence with no subordination, the other of which yields a main point and a secondary one. Paraphrase it both ways.

4. Which of the following passages contain an argument? Identify the support and the conclusion of the ones that do. Rewrite the argument in schematic form, omitting the padding.

   a. (Background: Take this passage to be a comment by an air safety official investigating a midair collision.) Since the pilots of both planes unemotionally acknowledged the presence of another aircraft in their vicinity, and made no attempt to avoid each other, they each must have seen a third plane, rather than each other. There was plenty of time between the acknowledgment and the collision to avoid hitting each other.

   b. On his way home from work, Ivan Potter lost control of his car, which crashed through a freeway guardrail and rolled into an adjoining soybean field. Examination of his corpse at the crash site by a qualified physician revealed no broken bones or external injuries. So it is reasonable to think that Ivan's death caused the accident rather than the other way around.

c. Dear Editor,

I resent the advertisement on page C36 of your Sunday edition. I don't take my kids to video stores because of the smarmy posters, and now I find them in my newspaper. If you plan to include such advertising regularly, I will simply have to find a less offensive source of news and information. I will not bring such rot into my house.

d. Most items imported by AJS, Inc., are fountain pens of one kind or another and are invariably defective. Nevertheless, because most of what AJS imports is from China, eccentric Beverly Canard buys something from every shipment. Among other things, we may glean from this that at least one fountain pen from China is defective.

e. Dear Editor,

There's not a dime's worth of difference among all the major-party candidates currently campaigning for president. It would be a step back toward meaningful democracy to add a space on the ballot marked "none of the above." It might encourage a little well-earned humility among our elected officials.

5. The movie lasted nearly to midnight. Joe and Sue, among those last to leave the theater, walked slowly down the street toward his parked car, stopping along the way to admire some window displays. When they got to the car they immediately noticed that the front window on the driver's side had been smashed in. Broken glass covered the seat. Suspecting the worst, Joe opened the door and turned on the interior lights. The tape deck had been wrenched from the dashboard and all the tapes were gone. Some travelers checks were missing from the glove compartment and his ornate gearshift knob was gone too. Even his parking change had disappeared from the ashtray on the console. From all this Joe inferred he had been burgled, and he called the police.

Schematize Joe's argument: Extract his argument from the paragraph, eliminating the padding.

6. On a dark and stormy night Inspector McSweet was called to the scene of a dreadful murder. The body, which was found at the stroke of midnight in the library, had been bludgeoned brutally, cruelly, and thoroughly. In the course of his inquiries McSweet discovered that the butler, Bligley, had been seen exiting surreptitiously from the library shortly before the body was discovered. Needless to say, McSweet's suspicions were aroused. When he saw a bloodstain on Bligley's cuff, which the frightened butler said was acquired in the course of culinary preparations, McSweet arrested him on the spot, on the charge of murder in the first degree.

Schematize the best argument you can find in this passage for Inspector
McSweet's evident conclusion. Eliminate the padding, but include all
relevant detail.

7.   Punish or Perish

Dear Editor,

Proposition 15 will get my vote the minute that crimes committed
with the use of a gun become a capital offense. When a life is
threatened during the commission of a crime, the perpetrator
should be subject to the death penalty.

Most of us don't personally know a person who committed a
felony. Felons are rare in public, but they populate our state and
federal prisons. Our good State Senator Presley has proposed
increasing the jail facilities at a cost of $280 million. There is an
alternative.

Suppose that we offer all felons, except those up for murder,
the opportunity for an early release. This release based on a promise to go straight with the understanding and agreement that a
repeat conviction would bring the death penalty. This proposal
should make some room in our prisons. . . .

Convicts are getting tougher while law-abiding citizens are
standing idly by and being victimized. We either get tough or we
perish.

                                    ROBERT E. PIERCE
                                    Riverside

  a. Schematize Mr. Pierce's argument for the revision of the penal code
     he suggests.
  b. Show how you can account for each of the four paragraphs by appeal
     to your schematization and the padding checklist on page 6.

8.   Move by Bell and Connally to Limit Term of President
                  Rejected a Long Time Ago

                   David S. Broder

In the space of 24 hours, late last month, two men of judgment and
experience in serious statecraft who share a conservative bias on
constitutional questions recommended to the consideration of their
fellow citizens a constitutional amendment of great consequence.

John Connally, the former governor of Texas and present
candidate for the Republican nomination for president, and Griffin
Bell, the former federal appeals court judge and current attorney
general of the United States, endorsed the proposal for granting
future presidents a single six-year term, with no possibility of re-
election.

The idea is not a new one. As Bell noted in his University of Kansas lecture, it was discussed at the constitutional convention, proposed to Congress as an amendment in 1826 and has been reintroduced some 160 times since then.

That history does more than suggest the antiquity of the notion; it also hints at its frailty. One would presume that if this particular change in the Constitution were really needed, it would have been made before now.

But this is a time when many are eager to rewrite the Constitution. Half a dozen proposed amendments are bumping into each other on their way to and from the legislatures, and given the eminence of Connally and Bell, it probably would be a mistake to ignore their notion.

In both cases, the avowed purpose of the proponents is to liberate the president from politics and incline his thoughts toward more elevated matters than re-election. As Bell put it, "The single, six-year term would permit the long-term, steady planning and implementation that our government needs plus saving a fourth year now lost to campaigning."

Or as Connally argued in his own announcement of candidacy, "Nothing . . . would be more conducive to the restoration of the confidence of the people in our form of government . . . than the knowledge that an American president from the day of the assumption of office has fulfilled his political role and has no future except as the historians view him as a statesman.

The operative assumption in both arguments is that it is politics—specifically the calculation of strategy for re-election—that demeans the presidency and undercuts the leadership potential of the office.

But that argument is buttressed neither by the experience of history nor the test of common sense. The Connally–Bell amendment would not strengthen the president's leadership, nor would it increase his accountability for the exercise of his power.

By arbitrarily lopping 24 months off his maximum term of service, it would limit his capacity to move policy in a sustained direction. By taking him off the ballot in all congressional elections held during his tenure in office, it would reduce his influence with the legislative branch and make him even less able to resist the encroachment of Congress on his prerogatives.

The proposal would also eliminate the use of the re-election campaign as a source of discipline on the exercise of presidential authority. By immunizing the president from receiving the voters' judgment on his stewardship in office, it would encourage him to ignore public opinion.

It is, in sum, exactly as bad an idea as Alexander Hamilton thought it was when he wrote in Federalist 72: "Nothing appears more plausible at first sight, nor more ill-founded upon close inspection than a scheme which . . . has had some respectable advocates— I mean that of continuing the chief magistrate in office for a certain time and then excluding him from it. . . . These effects would be for the most part rather pernicious than salutary."

a. With an eye toward schematizing Broder's argument, paraphrase each of the paragraphs in this column.

b. Schematize the argument.

c. Account for each paragraph.

9. As Steve hiked across the barren Nevada desert one cool autumn afternoon, he was increasingly impressed by the number of bleached and weatherbeaten animal bones littering the trail he had been following since morning. To his anthropologically trained eye, they seemed to be the bones of large domestic mammals—horses and cows mostly. Farm animals! What could it be, he thought excitedly, but an ancient pioneer route to California? Thousands of families must have traveled this trail before railroads connected the coasts. Steve's heart raced as he squinted into the setting sun at the mountainous barrier ahead. What must it have been like for the first wagon through!

a. What conclusion does Steve reach?

b. What reason does he offer? (That is, schematize his argument.)

10. Uninsured Free Ride Ends

We are pleased to see the Legislature has approved and sent to the governor a bill that will require motorists to produce proof they have auto insurance when stopped for traffic violations.

The bill further provides uninsured motorists will be fined and reported to the Department of Motor Vehicles, which could suspend the driver's license.

It is time for the state to get tough with scofflaws like this who are contemptuous of the rights of other motorists.

They drive merrily along, causing loss and injury to others, expecting someone else to pick up the bill for the damages they cause.

The "someone else" who gets stuck for the costs are all the law-abiding insured drivers whose rates are increased to cover the costs of accidents caused by the uninsured motorists.

It is time to tell the deadbeats of the highway the free ride has ended.

Charitably schematize the argument in this passage.

11.   Holdout Juror Halts Porno Trial

LOS ANGELES (AP)—A mistrial was declared yesterday in the trial
of Catherine Stubblefield Wilson when a single juror refused to
convict the woman labeled by prosecutors as the nation's top child
pornographer.

U.S. District Judge Richard Gadbois declared the mistrial
after a jury deadlocked 11–1 to convict Wilson of distributing
obscene material and exploiting children, said the prosecutor, U.S.
Attorney Joyce Karlin.

Gadbois set a Jan. 17 date for a new trial.

"One of the jurors apparently made up his mind before he
joined the deliberations," Karlin said outside the courtroom after
she interviewed the jurors.

"He was consistently late for court and he referred to witnesses who never testified. He said he didn't believe law-enforce-
ment officers," Karlin said. "He made up his mind he wasn't going to
vote guilty, no matter what."

Other jurors confirmed portions of what Karlin reported.

One juror, Rick Oland, said of the holdout juror: "It wasn't that
he refused to deliberate. He just said there was something in his
convictions that didn't allow him to vote guilty."

Schematize Attorney Karlin's argument as economically as possible.

12.   Man Suspects Dogs Were Set on Him
                         for Fighting Practice

CINCINNATI (AP)—A man who was attacked by two terriers, the
type often used in illegal dog fighting, says the animals may have
been set on him for practice in fighting.

Lee Dorsey, who has been hospitalized since he was attacked
Dec. 13, told police the dogs seemed to obey an unseen trainer's
commands during the incident near a Cincinnati high school football
field.

Dorsey said the dogs attacked and drew blood, seemed to back
away, then attacked again.

"For a moment, they backed off and looked toward the school
as if somebody was there," he said. "I got the feeling they heard
somebody else come along, or somebody else was up there signaling
with a whistle."

The dogs were captured by the Society for the Prevention of
Cruelty to Animals the day after the attack and are being held as
evidence. Their ownership has not been determined.

a. What conclusion does Dorsey draw?

b. What support does he explicitly offer for this conclusion?

c. What plausibly relevant fact is mentioned in the article but not explicitly attributed to Dorsey?

d. Schematize the strongest argument plausibly attributed to Dorsey.

13. Free Agents

Dear Editor,

Aside from the odd sight of conservative George Will siding with labor ("Free Agency Made Baseball a Hit," Op-Ed Page, Sept. 27), his argument that free agency has somehow brought about parity and attendance records just doesn't fit with the facts.

Consider the top teams this year. Toronto, Detroit, Minnesota, St. Louis, New York, Montreal, San Francisco. Every one of these teams built themselves up the old-fashioned way—trades and/or their own farm system.

Not one of these teams has a high-priced free agent, and you'll find no direct correlation between a team's standing and its payroll. These teams would have won had there been no free agency.

Trades have been part of the game almost from the very beginning, and Branch Rickey some 50 years ago incorporated minor league teams under the control of a major league club to properly train the players of the future.

I'm all for players to make a good salary (no more Black Sox scandals, please), but when salaries increase 700% in a decade, one has to wonder how much is enough for today's players.

There probably was collusion among the owners to restrict free agency but was it really so horrible that Kirk Gibson had to settle for $4 million in three years with Detroit and Tim Raines $5 million in three years with Montreal?

RICHARD BLUE
Hollywood

Schematize the argument in this letter.

14. On the Road

Dear Editor,

Isn't it time we get the trucks out of the fast lanes? Ever since the 55-mph speed limit came into effect, the center lanes of the free-ways have been clogged with trucks. And with the inexplicable craze for pickups and vans that has been going on since about that same time, it seems like the number of trucks increases constantly. The multi-axle long-haulers usually keep to the right, but anything smaller is likely to be right out there, front and center.

If I were king, this would be The Law: All trucks must confine themselves to the two right lanes of any freeway. If a freeway has only two lanes in each direction, trucks must drive in the right-hand lane except when passing a single other vehicle.

Actually there are two valid reasons for reserving the left lanes for passenger cars—safety and economy. The old nonsense about a small car being unsafe in a collision with a big car will soon be put to rest because we'll all be driving small cars. But the trucks are as big as ever, and worse, there seems to be no end to the craze for tippy off-road 4-wheel drives with bumpers at the height of a car's windows. These trucks have very poor braking and no evasive capability whatsoever, and God help the small car that gets in one's way.

Most vans and trucks get horrible mileage, and driving one fast makes the mileage atrocious. A pickup I used to own got 14 mpg at 45 mph and 9 mpg at 65. Why should the gas lines get longer just so truckers can ride in the fast lane?

THOMAS M. CONDRAN
San Bruno, California

a. Schematize the argument in this letter as accurately and charitably as possible.

b. Account for everything in the letter as part of the schematization or as some particular kind of padding.

= 2 =

INDUCTION
AND
DEDUCTION

Overview

In this chapter we divide arguments into two different kinds: inductive and deductive. They are evaluated differently and are useful in different contexts. The key notion of RIVAL CONCLU- SIONS, which plays a central role in later chapters, is introduced as a way of distinguishing inductive arguments from deductive ones.

THE USE OF A TAXONOMY

How many different kinds of argument are there? Before we can address this question we must look briefly—perhaps just as a re- minder—at what it is to distinguish different kinds of things. Why do we care whether two things are of the same kind or not?

When we divide things into kinds, we are grouping them by similarities—by properties they share. Things similar in a certain respect are of a kind; things not like them in that respect—not having that property—are of a different kind. Volcanoes are one kind of mountain: they share the property of being built up through lava ejections from the earth's mantle. Mountains not having *this* property, but sharing *others* (arising through the buckling of the earth's crust, for instance) will be a different kind of mountain. The Sierra Nevada and the Cascades are different kinds of mountain in this sense. But even mountains share all sorts of properties. So what counts as being the same or of a different kind depends on just what properties we use to form the groups, and the properties we choose will depend on our purpose: our motive for grouping things together in the first place. Mountains of both of the above kinds group themselves into ridges, most running roughly north–south, but some running east–west. For some purposes, *this* grouping would be interesting and nature of origin would not. The Sierras and Cascades would be of the same kind for this purpose (both running north–south), in spite of their different histories.

In other words, speaking of different *kinds* of things is useful for us precisely because (and when) it is useful to group things by their similarities and differences. So how we distinguish different kinds will depend on what similarities and differences are important to the task at hand.

Investigating the different cultural roles of women, for example, we may gather statistics on Hispanic females. Sex and ethnicity would be central to our purposes, so all Hispanic women would be similar in the two relevant respects: They would be the same for our purposes and would be grouped together in our data gathering. But if our interest were in voting patterns as a function of socioeconomic status, poor Hispanic women would be grouped with other individuals of low income—male, female, Hispanic, and Anglo—and distinguished from rich Hispanic women among others. In this case, Hispanic women would not be relevantly similar, would not be all of the same kind.

If you understand this point clearly it will nevertheless be a good exercise to extend your understanding to a different kind of example. If you do not yet understand, perhaps another example will make things clear. Consider our talk about automobiles.

If I say that my brother and I drive the same kind of car, I am probably distinguishing cars by manufacturer: We both drive Fords. But if a salesman asks what kind of car you are looking for, he is usually talking *not* about manufacturers, but about something else. The basic division in this context would be among sporty cars, luxury cars, and more utilitarian vehicles. In another context, you might be trying to explain why different cars have different handling characteristics, and a fundamental division will concern engine placement. Again, there will be three basic kinds: front-engine, rear-engine, and mid-engine. But for slightly different purposes it is common to distinguish just two basic kinds: front-engine and rear-engine. The previously separate mid-engine cars are then divided up and put into one or the other of these categories depending on whether the driver sits in front of or behind the engine. So for some purposes all mid-engine cars would be different in kind from front-engine cars, whereas for others only *some* of them would be.

This digression on kinds has been presented to help you understand the taxonomy of arguments we will develop in this text. We will want to organize our discussion around different kinds of argument, and, as always, what will count as a difference in kind will depend on our purpose in drawing the distinction. What is our purpose? To make our reasoning clearer, to display the merits of an argument perspicuously. We will make distinctions solely to aid in this task.

The point may be helpfully related to our discussion in Chapter 1. We need distinctions to fit our skills: We need distinctions *human beings* can make in practice, and we need to pick out arguments that human beings can evaluate in practice. Human abilities and interests will provide the underlying rationale when we group arguments into fundamentally different kinds in the next three chapters.

FORM

Recall the basic form of an argument:

$$S_1$$
$$S_2$$
$$S_3$$
$$\overline{}$$
$$C$$

This diagram may be read, "S_1, S_2, and S_3 are offered as reasons for C" (they bear the relation "reasons for" to C). Anything that can be put into this form is an argument. In our sense, this form is just what an argument is.

The metaphor of form (or shape or structure) is useful here as elsewhere because of its contrast with content or subject matter. Whether a collection of statements is an argument depends not on its content or subject matter, but on whether or not its parts can be put into this characteristic form, whether all together they have the required structure. Such a distinction, which depends on form rather than content, is called a *formal* distinction. So whether something is an argument or not is a formal matter. We shall shortly see other distinctions like this.

What drives us to make further distinctions is our interest in evaluating arguments, in trying to understand how good the reasons are. For this purpose let us introduce another metaphor: "link." The dashed horizontal line in the schematic diagram above may be taken to represent the *link* between support and conclusion. So the evaluational question may be put: How strong is the link? To this end we will distinguish different *kinds* of link (different kinds of support); and the distinction will once again be formal.

Notice at the outset that we can sometimes evaluate arguments (reasons) without refining our concept of link. We can sometimes judge reasons to be good or bad, a link to be strong or weak, without consideration of what *kind* of link it is, without a taxonomy of reasons. The combination of the low snow level in the mountains and the scenic beauty of the coast sometimes provides a stunningly good reason to choose the latter, longer route without any further analysis. We can all recognize the reasons as good no matter what formal kind they turn out to be. Similarly, we can all see without further analysis that a mother's testimony to the effect that "My son is a good boy. He could never kill anybody" is not, by itself, a good reason to think her son innocent of all those murders he has confessed to.

But when it is unclear, or controversial, whether the reasons are any good, we have to look more closely at the link to see which of its properties might clarify or settle the issue. What is it that makes a link strong? What makes reasons good? In order to attack this question we must begin to distinguish different kinds of link, because links may be strong in different ways. Support can be like the legs of a table or like the strands of a cable, like the buoyancy of water or the links of a chain—or like the solidity of terra firma. Good reasons come in different forms.

DEDUCTIVE ARGUMENTS:
THE SEMANTIC CONNECTION

Picture a prosecuting attorney trying to trap a defendant into admitting his guilt. The charge is embezzlement. She gets the guy to admit that, while he had authority to disburse company funds for certain purposes, the checks he wrote to himself for his vacation in the Bahamas did not qualify under any of those purposes and were not otherwise authorized. He also allowed that he was not an officer in the company and had no authority himself in such matters. He did add that he thought the money was no less than he deserved for years of loyal service, but that he was terribly sorry for any trouble he had caused.

How the jury ruled in the case is not relevant. What is important for our purposes is to see that the prosecutor succeeded in trapping the defendant into admitting his guilt, even though he never used the term *embezzle*. Understanding the "trap" will help us understand what a *deductive* argument is.

Recall that when we attribute a property like "deductiveness" to an argument, we are always addressing a schematization—assuming for the discussion that it adequately captures the reasoning in the passage from which it was derived. So let us schematize the prosecutor's argument:

S_1 The defendant had limited authority to write checks on his company's funds.

S_2 That authority did not extend to using company funds to cover his personal expenditures.

S_3 He did direct company funds into his private account for the purpose of vacationing in the Bahamas.

C   The defendant embezzled money from his employer.

Now we need to notice that this schematization does have the properties of a trap. If the defendant admits S_1, S_2, and S_3, he has *thereby* admitted that he has embezzled money from his employer; the conclusion merely recharacterizes the admission in different terms. The conclusion is in this sense "contained" within the supporting statements: trapped, like the defendant. Arguments with this property are called *deductive* arguments.[1]

Whether an argument is deductive, then, is entirely a matter of characterization, of understanding what has already been said. If you affirm the supporting statements of a deductive argument, you

---

[1]The jargon varies somewhat. Sometimes these arguments are called "deductively valid"—contrasting with "invalid" ones not having the trap property. But there are good reasons to avoid the invidious implication of this terminology, reasons that will become clear as we proceed. For now just note that "deductively valid" will be redundant here: "Deductive" is the word we will use for passing the trap test. Arguments failing the trap test will not all be *bad* arguments, just arguments of a different kind.

have *already affirmed* the conclusion, though perhaps in different words. In this sense, deductiveness is a matter of language, of semantics. How you phrase the support is crucial to whether you have captured the conclusion within it. A small variation in terminology can set it free.

So perhaps the clearest way to put the criterion of deductiveness uses the familiar semantic notion of self-contradiction.

In a deductive argument, if you affirm the support and deny the conclusion you have contradicted yourself.

This is what it is to discover that an argument is deductive. You find that you have already asserted the conclusion, C, in asserting the support; if you then deny C, you have said that something (namely C) is both true and false, which is to contradict yourself.

Although the contradiction test is probably the best way to appreciate the abstract concept, the trap test, modeled on the courtroom example, will often prove more helpful in practice. The trap test will be easier to use in deciding whether an argument is deductive. The two tests should come to the same thing, of course. But given the rough and ready nature of human language skills—the skills we use to make this distinction—it should not be surprising that one formulation engages those skills better than another. So we will concentrate on developing the trap test for practical application.

A good rule of thumb about human thinking is that the more fertile an insight, the greater the ways in which it can be misunderstood. A rich insight may nevertheless be valuable enough to justify the extra care required to have it available. Such is the trap test. It risks misunderstanding precisely because "trap" is so rich a metaphor. But the guidance we require in its use can be taken from the contradiction criterion. We have to remember that the trap is a *semantic* trap.

Not all traps are semantic, even in a courtroom. You might trap somebody into *practically* admitting his guilt—admitting it for all intents and purposes—but that would not count. He might, for instance, admit that he entered the room intending to kill the victim, chatted briefly with her, fired the gun in her direction at close range, and watched as she dropped motionless to the floor. He could even concur that the fatal bullet had ballistic markings characteristic of the gun mentioned above—and yet not be trapped semantically. The prosecutor might reasonably think she has established her case (established who killed the victim, if not the degree of the crime), that it is strong enough for the jury. And there is a sense in which the accused's testimony does amount—practically, effectively—to an admission of guilt. But practical, effective admission is not enough to qualify, because it depends on our judgment of plausibility, about which we will hear more next chapter. A semantic trap depends only on our linguistic skill, our ability to characterize.

So if there are any describable circumstances—no matter how implausible—that will allow the accused to avoid the charge, then the trap is not semantic and the argument for guilt is not deductive. In practice, what we need are circumstances that will show just how it is that we can accept the testimony (support) and consistently deny the charge (conclusion)—some conceivable way out of the trap. In the murder case we are considering, the testimony does not rule out the possibility that the accused's shot missed, somebody else shot at the same time with a ballistically indistinguishable gun, and the latter shot actually killed the victim. There are thousands of conceivable but implausible possibilities like this, and one is enough to show the trap is not semantic. These possibilities are all ways in which the accused could get out of it: show that the charge is not semantically contained within the testimony.

In a deductive argument, you can't get out of the conclusion without giving up something in the support.

Because we will occasionally want to schematize an argument *as* deductive, it will be useful to add to our schematic picture of an argument some way to explicitly represent the deductive link. The usual device is a single solid line separating support from conclusion.

Deductive Form

$$S_1$$
$$S_2$$
$$S_3$$

_____

$$C$$

Here S_1, S_2, and S_3 are offered not only in support of C, but as containing it semantically.

Applications

Some arguments will be obviously deductive to anyone with normal language skills and will not need even the modest recharacterizing of the embezzlement example. The most common illustrations are the standard syllogisms that for millennia have been used to illustrate deduction.

S_1 All men are mortal.

S_2 Socrates is a man.

_____

C   Socrates is mortal.

It is easy to see that Socrates' mortality is contained in the mortality of men if, indeed, he is one of us. It is perhaps worth noting that it is wholly irrelevant whether S_1 and S_2 are true, or whether we accept them as true. All that matters is that the link be semantic: *If* we do accept them then we have already accepted Socrates' mortality.

In other words, perfectly silly statements can form perfectly good deductive arguments:

S_1 All dentists are bald.

S_2 John is a dentist.

_____

C   John is bald.

C is trapped within S_1 and S_2; it doesn't matter that nobody would actually accept S_1.

Another kind of argument that is obviously deductive is one in which the conclusion occurs *explicitly* above the line.

S_1 John is bald.

_____

C   John is bald.

In practice, of course, nobody would count this as an argument, count S_1 as a reason for C. But it is formally deductive; it has the form of a deductive argument, and that fact will be valuable to remember when things get complicated later on.

The most interesting kind of obvious deduction, however, is the one illustrated by the prosecutor's trap with which we began. The recharacterization required in order for us to see the semantic connection is straightforward enough to suggest itself as we read. It is interesting because it begins to exercise our linguistic skill a bit, perhaps causing us to reflect more than we normally do on familiar words and phrases. Another example of this type would be

S_1 Peter dented the front fender of the family car on the way home from the prom and was sure his father would kill him if he found out.

S_2 He parked at the curb facing the wrong way, so that the dented fender was exposed to traffic, and went to bed.

S_3 In the morning Peter pretended nothing was wrong, until his father discovered the dent on his own. Peter then told him that he had no idea how the fender got banged and that it must have been hit while parked during the night.

C Peter lied to his father about what happened to the car.

The conclusion, once again, is a simple recharacterization of what was already said in the supporting statements; and it is a relatively easy recharacterization for any competent speaker of English.

A deductive link need not be obvious, of course. At the next level of difficulty, the deductiveness will not be obvious—at least not to everybody—but can be made clear (demonstrated) through some manipulation or calculation, some semantic unpacking. Consider,

S_1 Most Americans have plenty to eat.

S_2 Anyone with plenty to eat runs some risk of an unhealthy cholesterol intake.

S_3 Most Americans own a television set.

C At least one person with a television set runs some risk of an unhealthy cholesterol intake.

The semantic link here is obvious to some, not to others. For those who don't see it, it might be made clear enough by the following unpacking.

If just half of the population have plenty to eat, and half own a TV, it would be barely conceivable that nobody does both, the well-fed half being exactly those not owning a television set. But since "most" means at a minimum "one more than half," then the semantics allow no escape: At least one person must share both properties (accepting S_1, S_2, and S_3). And since *everybody* having plenty to eat runs some risk of an unhealthy cholesterol intake, the overlapping person must share that property too. You can't get out of it: You already affirm the conclusion by affirming S_1, S_2, and S_3.

The amount of explanatory detail that must be provided would vary from person to person, just as in the next case.

The number I'm looking for is 108×51.

The number is 5508.

This one involves arithmetic unpacking, for example, a binomial expansion:

$$
\begin{aligned}
100 \times 50 &= 5000 \\
100 \times 1 &= 100 \\
8 \times 50 &= 400 \\
8 \times 1 &= 8 \\
\hline
& 5508
\end{aligned}
$$

But some would understand it only if we did this:

$$
\begin{array}{r}
108 \\
51 \\
\hline
108 \\
540 \\
\hline
5508
\end{array}
$$

And some would need even further detail, such as

$$108 + 108 + 108 \ldots 51 \text{ times}$$

Others might need the addition reduced to counting. How much you need depends on what skills and background you bring to the computation.

Sometimes the display value of a special notation is helpful:

S_1 A is greater than B.

S_2 C is less than B but greater than D.

_____

C   D is less than A.

If we use $x > y$ for x greater than y, and $x < y$ for less than, we may write

$$S_1 \quad A > B$$

$$S_2 \quad \begin{cases} C < B \\ C > D \end{cases}$$

_____

$$C \quad D < A$$

And since $x < y$ is the same as $y > x$, we may do it all in terms of ">".

$$A > B$$
$$B > C$$
$$C > D$$

_____

$$A > D$$

When it is written this way, most of us would find the deductiveness obvious.

Algebraic notation and rules are designed explicitly for this display value, which makes algebraic manipulation an inexhaustible source of deductive arguments to unpack.

$$S_1 \quad 2x - y - 12 = 0$$

$$S_2 \quad 7x + y + 3 = 0$$

_____

$$C \quad y = -10$$

The following steps would be adequate unpacking for most people acquainted with the rudiments of algebra:

$2x - 12 = y$ (adding y to both sides of S_1)

$7x + 2x - 12 + 3 = 0$ (substituting the above expression for y in S_2)

$9x - 9 = 0$
$x = 1$ (rearranging the above)

$y = 2 - 12$ (substituting for x in S_1)

$y = -10$ (by subtraction)

It should be clear by now that there will, at any stage of human history, be deductive arguments that nobody knows how to display in a convincing, intelligible way. Mathematics and formal logic are constantly finding new ways and inventing new notations to aid in that process. We will return to this topic briefly later in the chapter, but we have developed deduction far enough now to look at other kinds of arguments.

INDUCTIVE ARGUMENTS: THE WEIGHT OF EVIDENCE

Recall that we are beginning to classify arguments by how they connect their support with their conclusion. When there is some question about whether the reasons offered for a conclusion are any good, we must look at the nature of the link between them. There will be different kinds of links and hence different methods of evaluation.

For our purposes, it will be most useful to make the basic distinction in our taxonomy of arguments simply between deductive arguments and all the rest: One kind is deductive; the other is non-deductive. All arguments are one or the other. It will also be useful to introduce another jargon term for the non-deductive kind: inductive. The word *inductive* is sometimes used more restrictively, but for our taxonomy an inductive argument is any argument that fails the semantic trap test, any argument in which the support does not semantically contain the conclusion.

The prosecutor's argument that failed the trap test is a good example of an inductive argument.

S_1 The defendant entered the room intending to kill the victim.

S_2 He fired at the victim at close range.

S_3 The victim died immediately afterward.

S_4 The bullet that killed the victim had on it ballistic markings characteristic of the defendant's gun.

C   The defendant shot and killed the victim.

In this case the alleged killer is able to get out of the accusation semantically (as we saw on page 41); but the ways out are not very plausible. The first shows that the argument is inductive (not deductive); the second shows that the inductive link is a pretty strong one.

This example clearly illustrates the two distinguishing features of inductive argument that will occupy our attention. The first is that the inductive link will have degrees of strength, unlike the deductive one. The deductive link is a successful semantic trap (no *degrees* of containment are possible), whereas the inductive connection may be strong or weak or in between. The second feature, closely related to this, is what gives us the different degrees: Inductive arguments depend on our plausibility judgment, not just our linguistic skill. A semantic trap is either successful or not; plausibility, by contrast, has infinitely many gradations, and this fact will be reflected in the strength of the inductive link.

Just how plausibility judgments fit into an evaluation procedure will not become clear until the next chapter. For now we will have our hands full exercising the formal distinction: looking at very basic, contrasting properties of inductive and deductive form. To aid in this task we will need another piece of schematic notation.

$$S_1$$
$$S_2$$
$$S_3$$
$$\overline{\overline{}}$$
$$C$$

Double solid separating lines will represent an inductive link, an inductive argument. So the latest argument (about the shooting) could be schematized with a double solid line.

A simpler example of an inductive argument would be

S₁   As I'm driving along, my car sputters to a stop.

S₂   The gas gauge reads "empty."

=====

C   The car is out of gas.

This is also a pretty strong argument—the reasons are good ones—but it is clearly inductive. There are all kinds of ways to get out of it and still accept the support. The car could have suffered an electrical failure that disabled both the gauge and the ignition. Or the gauge may have quit working just as the fuel-line filter finally filled up with dirt and plugged the line. These ways out show that the conclusion is not semantically contained (already asserted) in the support. And that is enough to show that the argument is inductive.

Having a distinction between deductive form and inductive form will be valuable enough to justify taking care with another peculiar consequence. Recall that an arrangement of statements may have deductive form even though nobody would call it an argument or take it seriously as offering reasons (conclusion explicitly stated among the support-claims, for instance). Similarly, arrangements may have inductive form without looking much like arguments.

S₁   My coffee is cold.

S₂   Pi is approximately 22/7.

=====

C   Napoleon Bonaparte had little to do with the American Civil War.

It is pretty clear that C is not contained semantically in S₁ and S₂, so this arrangement has inductive form. We might be forgiven for saying it is *formally* an inductive argument. At the same time, it is not what we would normally call an argument: Nobody would seriously offer S₁ and S₂ as reasons for C.

Argument Strength and Link Strength

A deductive argument can be a bad, weak argument, can fail to provide much support for its conclusion, but in only one way: by having support-claims that are implausible, clearly false, or just plain silly (recall the bald dentist example). If the support in a deductive argument is true, then so is the conclusion: There is no way out of that. If the support is seriously flawed, then the conclusion *may* still be true, though this particular support provides no reason for us to think so. Deductive arguments provide weak or worthless support if (and only if) the supporting statements themselves are weak or worthless.

Inductive arguments, on the other hand, may be flawed in two distinct ways. They may, of course, be weak in the same way as deductive arguments: because the supporting statements are weak, implausible, false, or silly. But because the strength of the inductive *link* can vary, the conclusion may end up badly supported even if there is nothing wrong with the supporting statements themselves. We can sometimes say of an inductive argument that it would not provide much (or, perhaps any) support for its conclusion *even if* the supporting statements were true. The statement above, concerning Napoleon's role in our Civil War, is an example of this: true support claims providing no support at all.

This fact naturally gives the impression that inductive arguments are intrinsically second rate; that deductive arguments are always better, stronger, to be sought first. We might feel that an inductive argument should be accepted only with regret, only if we cannot find a deductive one after a serious search. As natural as this feeling is, giving in to it is the biggest mistake you can make in understanding your own reasoning. There are two reasons.

First, some inductive arguments are so strong that you have nothing at all to gain by trying to find a deductive substitute. The gas gauge example discussed above is one like this. But there are even stronger inductive links—ones allowing even less plausible escape. The best ones rest on our best perceptions (our best plausibility judgments) and are easier to do in class than in a book. Try to imagine the details of the following demonstration as they would normally occur.

I walk to the board, pick up an eraser, and hit the board sharply with it. When I lift the eraser from the board a powdery white, eraser-shaped mark appears on that spot, where none had been before. I then allege that the eraser made the mark, and I schematize the allegation's support as follows:

S_1 I hit the board with an eraser.

S₂ A powdery white, eraser-shaped mark appeared where none had been before.

S₃ The mark appeared just where I hit the board with the eraser.

C   The eraser made the mark.

Under the normal conditions easily demonstrated in a classroom (nothing up my sleeve . . .), this is as strong an argument as you will ever find, of whatever type. If anything hangs on what made the mark, it would be lunatic to bet against the eraser.

Nevertheless, the argument schematized is formally inductive: you can get out of it without giving up anything above the double line. It might be that the eraser, despite appearance, was brand new, absolutely innocent of chalk dust; that this particular kind of chalkboard develops white, eraser-shaped age spots more or less randomly; and that that is what happened in this case. Stunningly implausible (which is a sign of inductive strength), but semantically consistent with the support. We can get out of the trap.

The second reason to avoid an unsympathetic view of induction stems from an earlier observation about human reasoning skills. Sometimes the statements required to construct a plausible semantic trap are not available to human beings in practical contexts. If we limit ourselves to plausible statements, we often cannot trap the conclusions we wish to support. Inductive arguments allow us to bring our perceptual and judgmental skills to bear in ways that would be ruled out if we were restricted to deductive form. The possibility of using induction dramatically expands the class of statements we have access to in our reasoning. The point is actually much stronger than this and will be developed more fully in the following section.

CASTING ARGUMENTS

Recall that "inductive" and "deductive" are properties of *schematizations*, not passages of prose. Very seldom does an article or a paragraph contain enough formal detail to force you to schematize it one way or the other. A passage may contain enough detail to allow the following inductive representation, for instance:

S₁ The oldest people today are about the same age as the oldest people of any period in recorded human history.

S₂ Dramatic advances in medical technology have had little impact on normal longevity. As we overcome some problems, others take their place at an increasing rate as we age.

S₃ Joe appears in every way a normal human being: behavior, history, physiognomy.

C   Joe is mortal.

But you may wish to compress the whole thing into a version of our earlier Socrates syllogism, which is *deductive*.

S₁   All men are mortal.

S₂   Joe is a man.

C   Joe is mortal.

The circumstances in which you might want to do this are tricky and will be discussed further shortly. For now it is important to see only that the two representations above show what it is like to cast an argument into our different forms, to paraphrase it differently for perhaps different purposes.

This illustration was chosen partly for the naturalness of the deductive recasting. We will find, however, that most practical inductive arguments are not so plausibly recast, because the very general statements needed to complete the semantic trap are not so readily available. We can always recast them, just not so plausibly. Our earlier inductive argument about running out of gas may be recast deductively thus:

S₁ As I'm driving along, my car sputters to a stop.

S₂ The gas gauge reads "empty."

S₃ Whenever a car sputters to a stop and the gas gauge reads "empty," the car is out of gas.

C   The car is out of gas.

Nobody would reason this way because S₃ is clearly false (remember it must be read very strictly to make a semantic trap). But this could be the sort of recasting available to us.

This provides another perspective on the "access" issue raised in the last section. Even with great effort, we usually cannot find deduction-licensing generalities that are clear enough to evaluate and that do not go far beyond the evidence we have to support them; so it is usually safer to formulate arguments around the evidence itself and avoid very general statements. And this will typically yield an inductive argument, like the original version of the running-out-of-gas argument. So we can begin to see that casting a schematic representation as inductive or deductive is just a practical choice we must make. It will be worth our while to examine the basic considerations relevant to that choice.

As you might expect, the dominant consideration is charity: Cast the argument whichever way seems best, strongest. The last few pages have been explicitly designed to prepare us for this sometimes complicated assessment. We have seen that, prior to our deciding on form, the overall strength of an argument depends on two things: the plausibility of the support-claims and the tightness of the link between them and the conclusion. And since the deductive link is semantically tight, an inductive rendering will always have a weaker link. Sometimes the difference will be very small, sometimes very big, depending on the case. On the other hand, the inductive support, not requiring the great generality of a semantic trap, will sometimes be more plausible than the support in the deductive version. So the question of charity may be put like this:

Is the plausibility of the inductive support enough better than the deductive support to compensate for the weakness introduced at the link?

If it is, then choose the inductive one. Schematically, you compare the two versions on their scores for A (support plausibility) and B (link strength),

$$
\left.
\begin{array}{c}
S_1 \\
S_2 \\
S_3
\end{array}
\right\}
\quad \leftarrow A \rightarrow \quad
\left\{
\begin{array}{c}
S_1 \\
S_3 \\
S_4
\end{array}
\right.
$$

$$
\underline{} \quad \leftarrow B \rightarrow \quad \overline{\underline{}}
$$

$$
\qquad C \qquad\qquad\qquad\qquad C
$$

and take the one with the highest combined score. Obviously there is no way to get an exact score, but this is the general idea; there will be clear-cut cases. If the comparison is too close to call, however, you will have to decide which form to use by appealing to something besides strength.

Some sample applications will refine our understanding and develop our skill in making this comparison. Deductive arguments containing a silly, absurd, or just plain false supporting statement will be weaker than just about any inductive argument with clearly true or very plausible support.[2] The deductive argument on page 42 attempting to establish John's baldness by appeal to the generalization that "All dentists are bald" provides no support whatever for its conclusion. Any middling tight inductive argument offering uniformly plausible support would be stronger.

S_1 Baldness has run in John's family for generations.

S_2 John is middle-aged.

___

C   John is bald.

We could find a case in which S_1 and S_2 adequately capture what we know about John; and in that case this very modest inductive argument would more strongly support this conclusion than the deductive one did.

What happened in the gas-gauge case is similar, but more typical of our actual options. We converted the strong inductive argument

S_1 As I'm driving along, my car sputters to a stop.

S_2 The gas gauge reads "empty."

___

C   The car is out of gas.

into a worthlessly weak deductive argument

S_1 As I'm driving along, my car sputters to a stop.

S_2 The gas gauge reads "empty."

S_3 Whenever a car sputters to a stop and the gas gauge reads "empty," the car is always out of gas.

___

C   The car is out of gas.

---

[2]Of course, the deductiveness must depend on the flawed support-claim; but that is presumed in talking of an argument's "having" or "containing" such a statement.

because we tightened up the link using an obviously false general statement. The generalizations we find to generate deductive connections in cases like this will usually be risky, even if we do not actually know them to be false.

It turns out that, in practice, conclusions interesting enough to become the object of an argument are very seldom simple reformulations of our data. So practical reasoning is usually best cast inductively. Deductive schematization of everyday, substantive arguments is quite usually uncharitable.

Even in the battle between attorneys in a courtroom, the eventual argument is seldom a simple deduction. The categorical claims about intent, responsibility, authority, and knowledge—the ones required to make the trap semantic—are precisely the ones the defense will attack as untrue. Knowledge is incomplete, intent confused, authority vague: just the things that make it tough on the generalizations needed for deductive arguments. So the task of a judge or a jury will seldom consist simply in *recharacterization*; it will normally involve assessing data several semantic removes from the eventual verdict.

None of this damages our introductory discussion of the prosecutor's trap. That was concerned with showing that admitting one thing simply came to the same thing as admitting another, as a matter of language, semantics. This is essential to understanding deduction, and it required the creation of a rather pure, abstract context. The preceding paragraph, by contrast, drags in all the dirty, practical details of an actual case. In normal courtrooms, self-indicting admissions are hard to come by. And even when they occur, a clever defense attorney can often blunt their force through conflicting testimony and the help of psychiatric expert witnesses. All this is irrelevant to understanding what a deductive argument *is*, but it is crucial to understanding where we might hope to use one and where not.

The Structural Utility of Deduction

What roles, then, does deduction play in our reasoning? One role, which we've touched on lightly a number of times already, is that of tracing consequences of a particular sort. Deduction examines semantic commitment: When we agree to something, what else are we committed to simply as a matter of language? This question is useful in sketching a prosecutor's strategy or thinking through the defense of any position. But its richest applications are in mathematics, where the rules of reformulation and consequence-drawing are explicitly designed for this purpose. If we know some things, we can sometimes find out what else we must accept that is not immediately obvious. And the discovery process is a form of semantic manipulation—unpacking, we have termed it—that yields deductive connections. If $x = 2y$ then we are already committed to $y = \frac{1}{2}x$. Ditto for more complicated equations.

More valuable to our everyday reasoning, however, is the role deduction can play in organizing complex arguments. When the support being offered is complicated, making explicit some of the internal semantic connections will sometimes help us evaluate the argument. An overall inductive argument may be viewed as a compound argument with deductive parts. The embezzlement example we looked at earlier may be viewed in this way. We have introduced all manner of data—documents, depositions, and testimony—attempting to establish the charge. But the evidence may be very hard to evaluate if it is simply piled up in a schematization without any internal structure:

$$S_1$$
$$S_2$$
$$S_3$$
$$S_4$$
$$S_5$$
$$S_6$$

$$C$$

If we break it up into sub-arguments, all arranged around a deductive core, the picture may become clearer. Some evidence will bear on the defendant's authority, some on his intent, and some on his behavior. *These* we may simply recharacterize as embezzlement:

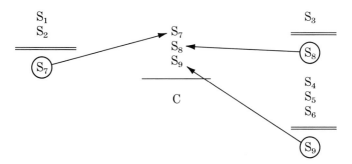

So although the overall support-picture is inductive, a deductive step will be an important part of it.

Because of these two virtues (organization and consequence-drawing), a deductive sketch can also help guide an investigation. It does this by organizing the statements we might try to find evidence *for* into a pattern, perhaps like the one above. Investigators poking around in the debris from a plane crash may explicitly seek evidence for a variety of things, such as whether

1. the plane collided with another before crashing;
2. the collision damage was adequate to seriously impair the plane's airworthiness;
3. anything else occurred, independently of the collision, that might explain the crash.

They might seek such evidence with the following deductive arrangement in the back of their minds.

S_1 The plane crashed after colliding with another plane.

S_2 The collision is a possible cause of the crash.

S_3 No other possible causes were present.

S_4 The crash was caused by something.

_____

C   The collision caused the crash.

This would organize the investigation into four areas, with the fourth not requiring any attention unless something really weird turned up.

But the author of the eventual report would be wise to avoid this form, because the notion of a possible cause, which is just the sort of categorical device we need to create a semantic trap, is too slippery to hang support on. It is slippery because we may interpret it strongly (as a real possibility) or weakly (as a mere possibility). And if we interpret it weakly, S_3 is certainly false, destroying the deductive argument's value as support. If read strongly, however, S_1 and S_3 will bear a reasons-for relationship to S_2, making the deductive arrangement a muddled representation of the support relations. How to best represent such evidence will not become clear until the next chapter, but the simple, linear deduction is much less helpful in structuring support than it is in structuring an investigation.

Other Manifestations of the Semantic Link

This is an optional section for those of you overly tempted by deductive schematizations.

The deductive link can appear in basically inductive reasoning in other ways too. Sometimes the support offered in a deductive schematization

$$S_1$$
$$S_2$$
$$\overline{}$$
$$C$$

is not strong enough to withstand being linked to a particular conclusion. A semantic connection requires us to accept C unless we give up something in the support. But the evidence against C may be so strong that we end up rejecting the support rather than accepting the conclusion. This often happens in science and results in an inductive argument.

S'   Evidence against C.
$$\overline{\overline{}}$$
C'   Something is wrong with S_1 and S_2 taken together.

The semantic connection merely allows us to bring the evidence against C to bear on those support claims. It does not provide the structure of our reasoning.

If we are desperate to throw *something* into deductive form, there is one possibility open for *any* good evidence, a possibility that also offers a grotesque caricature of our reasoning in most cases. If we can competently judge an inductive argument

$$S_1$$
$$S_2$$
$$\overline{\overline{}}$$
$$C$$

to be a strong one, then we may formulate that fact as a sentence and add it to the argument as a strong support claim. Doing so yields a deductive argument, with strong support not for C but for the closely related conclusion that C is well supported.

S_1
S_2
S_3 (That S_1 and S_2 provide strong support for C.)

C′   (C is strongly supported.)

We might object that this is not a genuine recasting of the original argument because it has a different conclusion. But that is not the real problem in representing our reasoning in this way; it is only a symptom. The real problem is that this recasting is as trivial as it is cheap, and it obscures what is important in our reasoning. No gain, big loss. For this move works only when and because we are good at evaluating *inductive* arguments. Our ability to evaluate inductive arguments is what gives us S_3, and this is what requires our skill, effort, and attention here. If a trivial reformulation obscures that fact it is not just a waste of time, it is pernicious. This trick shows once again how silly it is to force reasoning into forms for abstract reasons. The *only* reason to schematize is to make our reasoning clearer, to understand it better. This need for clarity is the only reason to have different forms. And in practical, everyday matters it will generally result in a structure of inductive form.

One final manifestation, very difficult to treat this early in the book, is worth mentioning nevertheless. When the semantic connection itself is at issue (unclear, say, or controversial), then a deductive argument can once again appear in the middle of some inductive reasoning. Unless a semantic link is obvious, reasoning may be represented deductively only if the semantic connection can be displayed using rules everybody has agreed to (algebraic unpacking, for example). But outside mathematics we find few rules for semantic unpacking that are adequate for such a display. How do we show that a controversial link is indeed semantic when we have no unpacking rules to follow? The only recourse is to a normal kind of investigation of the properties of the language: how the language operates in the relevant contexts, what job the words are doing, and how these jobs overlap. And this investigation will typically be emphatically inductive reasoning. The case *for* a semantic link will be an inductive argument.

This manifestation cannot profitably be discussed any further here, but the issues surrounding it will become clearer as you progress through the text. What an inductive investigation looks like will be treated in detail in the following chapter, and arguments about characterizations are what Chapter 7 is all about. When you have mastered the arguments in Chapter 7 you will be able to return to this section and flesh out the argument yourself.

RIVAL CONCLUSIONS

To justify concentrating on certain aspects and features of arguments, instead of others, we have occasionally relied on the fact that human beings have particular skills and specific interests. Our examination of argument has occasionally been shaped by the fact that we care about science and law, cause and effect, understanding our lives, and anticipating the future. Now, however, these things will begin to dominate our analysis. The most powerful tools for constructing and evaluating arguments will come from studying the context of practical argument. In this section we develop the first of those tools.

Notice that in the abstract, outside a particular context, any group of sentences will constitute an argument when cast in our schematic form. Any sentences may be offered as reasons for another. But in normal circumstances most such arrangements would not be serious arguments—that is, would not count as sensible (even if mistaken) reasons for something.

S_1 Jack and Jill went up the hill.

S_2 The neutron's half-life is 30 minutes.

C   Some pianos just will not stay in
    tune.

In normal circumstances this would be a nonsensical arrangement of sentences, not an argument.

The qualification "normal circumstances" is important. An imaginative work of fiction could provide these sentences with special significance (code value, for instance) that would suddenly allow S_1 and S_2 to make sense as reasons for C. The point is that sentences do not fall easily into sensible argument patterns and intelligible reasons-for relationships: making them do so requires effort, and certain conditions must be satisfied. The context must fit them together in a special way, which is why reasoning sometimes requires hard work. Examining this fit, the conditions of intelligibility, will provide the promised analytical tool.

What distinguishes a practical argument from an abstract arrangement of sentences is its purpose: It arises in a specific context, for a certain reason. And, with a little effort, we can always formulate the reason as a question that the argument is trying to answer. So, for

$$S_1$$
$$S_2$$
$$............$$

$$C$$

to be not just *formally* an argument, but one of genuine practical interest, there must be a question lurking in the context to provide its rationale, to make this arrangement of sentences intelligible. And C will provide an answer to that question. The argument schema may then be read, "S_1 and S_2 recommend C as the answer to this question." So the intelligibility criterion is simply whether or not S_1, S_2, and C make sense in this sentence. Does C answer the question? Might S_1 and S_2 be thought of as supporting that particular answer? These are judgments we can make in a usefully large number of cases.

The intelligibility criterion itself is not our primary interest here. Our interest will be in the questions and answers that meeting the criterion guarantees. These questions and answers will be the fundamental elements in our understanding of argument in its native habitat: the practical concerns of our everyday life.

The underlying question an argument is trying to answer—the one that its conclusion answers—will be called the argument's IMPLICIT QUESTION, implicit because it will seldom be stated anywhere, but rather will be something we will have to dig out ourselves. Implicit questions in some recently examined arguments could be "Why did the car stop running?" "What caused the plane to crash?" "How did that mark get on the board?" You will usually have some discretion in formulating such questions; shortly we will discuss how to best use that discretion.

If S_1 and S_2 recommend C as the answer to our implicit question (I.Q.)—as the *right* answer to that question—then there are other answers, statements that might well have been the answer, that the argument implies are *wrong* answers. We have even more discretion in forming this list than in formulating the I.Q., but often an important part of the list will be obvious. We have already begun the list in our sputtering-car example: exotic electrical failure, simultaneous plugged line and duff gauge. We can extend the list by imagining other possibilities, from realistic ones coupling a duff gauge with other engine failures to bizarre ones involving Martians with lasers or local failure of the laws of nature. It will turn out to be very important to exercise your imagination in making up these lists, but not because it will ever be useful to take Martian lasers seriously. Argument analysis will *always* require confidence—thoughtful, justifiable confidence—that we have considered all the live possibilities. And that requires us to develop our ability to think of possibilities in general, from which we may sort the live ones. Some live possibilities are as hard to think up as bizarre ones and require the same imaginative skill. Developing that skill is part of the project of this book.

As the title of this section suggests, the competing answers to the implicit question will be called RIVAL CONCLUSIONS. They are the competition C must defeat to win its position as the right answer; the rival conclusions are what S_1 and S_2 recommend C as better than. In saying that C is right, the argument is saying the rivals are wrong, and this gives us the fundamental logical property of the list—the property that will organize the next two chapters.

To avoid confusion, notice that the expression "the rivals" can mean, as it does here, C's rivals: the list of answers to the I.Q., excluding C.

	The Rivals
S_1	
S_2	C_2
....	C_3
C	C_4
	C_5
	C_6
	.
	.
	.

But "the rivals" will sometimes naturally refer to the whole list, including C (in this case, including C on the list as C_1), as follows:

S_1	The Rivals

S_2

....

C_1

The Rivals

C_1
C_2
C_3
C_4
C_5
C_6

.
.
.

Now, taking "the rivals" to mean the whole list—all the answers to the I.Q. we care to consider, including the original C—we may put the fundamental logical property of the list as follows:

The rival conclusions are mutually exclusive, incompatible with one another.

This simply means that only one of them may be true; if one is affirmed the others are automatically denied as a matter of language, semantics. They contradict each other in the sense that that notion was explained earlier in the chapter.

This, of course, does not mean that we cannot perfectly well give to the implicit question answers that overlap and include one another. It means only that for the answers to *count as rival conclusions* in our technical sense, they must not overlap and include one another. They must exclusively stake out some share of the area covered by the I.Q. so that we have an unambiguous way of referring to each part of that area. We then have a clear way of saying where the right answer lies.

This need for separateness imposes a restriction on our discretion in making up the list. It does not remove our discretion—far from it—but it gives us a condition that the list must satisfy, however we make it up. The rivals must exclude each other, must not overlap. Consider the list we began earlier:

S_1 As I'm driving along, my car sputters to a stop.

S_2 The gas gauge reads "empty."

....

C   The car is out of gas.

C_1 The car is out of gas.

C$_2$ The car has suffered an exotic electrical failure, disabling the gauge and the ignition.

C$_3$ The fuel filter became plugged just as the gas gauge packed up.

C$_4$ Martians did it with lasers.

The point of the mutual incompatibility of the rivals is that whatever the Martians did with lasers could not simply have been to empty my gas tank. For that would include C$_4$ under C$_1$. There are all sorts of ways to run out of gas: forget to fill up, develop a leak, or have Martians steal the gas with lasers. But C$_4$ cannot simply be a way of doing C$_1$. It must be incompatible with C$_1$.

Accordingly, C$_4$ must be understood to cover only those things Martians might do that are not already on the list. Sometimes it will be important to say so explicitly:

C$_4$ Martians did it with lasers, but not by emptying the tank or creating the exotic electrical failure or . . .

Of course, the mutual exclusiveness may be achieved in other ways too. Running out of gas *may* be included in C$_4$ if the Martian option is withdrawn from C$_1$. C$_1$ would then have to read (or be understood to read), "My car is out of gas, but the Martians had nothing to do with it." The latter possibility would be transferred to C$_4$.

This is just one example of how our discretion in making up the list survives the mutual incompatibility restriction. We must still decide how to distribute the various possibilities on the list of rivals. Which way is natural, or most productive, will depend on the case and the task at hand. Proper distribution is another judgmental skill to develop, but it will come along with practice.

Consider another example:

S$_1$ Parts of the plane that crashed were found miles from the crash site.

S$_2$ Some of them bore colored scuff marks.

S$_3$ Another plane had crashed nearby at about the same time.

S$_4$ The second plane was partly painted in the color of the scuff marks mentioned above.

C_1 A collision between the two planes caused the first one to crash.[3]

Rival Conclusions
("the plane" = "the first plane")

C_2 The crash was caused by a hydraulic failure. (The plane was plunging toward the ground, out of control, when the collision occurred.)

C_3 The crash was caused by an explosion, which blew off the plane's tail. (The scuff marks were from a previous incident on the ground.)

The parts of C_2 and C_3 in parentheses are included to help us see how those rivals might meet the intelligibility criterion. They will have a larger role to play in the next chapter.

On the surface, incompatibility is not much of a problem here: The rivals seem clearly distinct. But as soon as we begin to think of other possibilities, problems of overlap appear. Consider the possibility of minor contact between the two planes, which sets off an explosive device in the baggage compartment. Here the collision caused the crash, but by way of an explosion that, let us say, blows off the plane's tail. It could be included in either C_1 or C_3, or we might create a separate rival for collision-caused explosions and exclude it from both. We simply have to decide; it cannot be in more than one.

None of this should suggest that all possibilities must be considered and divided up before we can proceed. The vast majority of them will be beyond our interest and will never arise at all. The point is only that the possibilities we *do* consider might overlap in subtle and unexpected ways, and we must be alert to avoid this. Rivals that include each other can disrupt our entire argument.

Lumping and Splitting

These preceding few paragraphs should suggest another way in which we have substantial—and valuable—discretion in making up the list of rivals. We must decide how specific to make them, how much detail to provide. The crash investigators may be wise to begin with very general rivals, awaiting guidance from the data for further detail.

---

[3]It would be reasonable to conclude that the collision caused *both* to crash; but it will simplify our discussion to consider a conclusion in this form.

C_1 Pilot error

C_2 Mechanical failure

C_3 Turbulence

C_4 Collision

(As an exercise, describe how C_1 and C_3 might overlap, and allocate the possibilities to avoid it.) These might be split up into more specific rivals in infinitely many ways, but it would be a waste of time to simply wade in and begin splitting before we know of some reason for splitting one way rather than another. Mechanical failure may be of the control surfaces, the hydraulic system, or the airframe itself; this category will normally cover electrical systems too. And these items may be further subdivided. There are many electrical systems and failure can occur anywhere in any of them—at any circuit junction, any length of wire, any switch, filter, resistor, or triode. Where we stop in splitting up rivals depends on our purposes, how much we know, and what we reasonably suspect. But whether and when we *start* depends on these too.

So the investigators will poke around a bit before outlining stories about what might have happened. When they find pieces of airplane far from the crash site they will have reason to think through different possible event sequences under C_2 and C_4, each of which would be a different rival. Several stories under the subheading "airframe failure" would suggest themselves, and a number of these would be under the subheading "explosion." Diagrammatically,

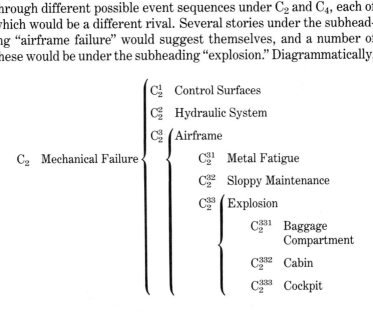

C_2 Mechanical Failure

C_2^1 Control Surfaces

C_2^2 Hydraulic System

C_2^3 Airframe

C_2^{31} Metal Fatigue

C_2^{32} Sloppy Maintenance

C_2^{33} Explosion

C_2^{331} Baggage Compartment

C_2^{332} Cabin

C_2^{333} Cockpit

Finding another plane down would suggest a splitting of C_4 much like the following:

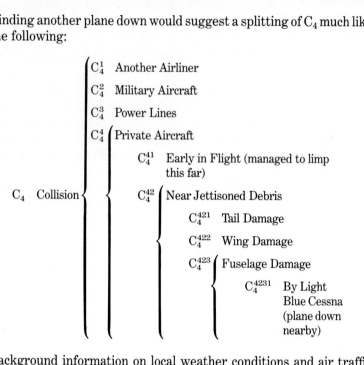

C_4 Collision

C_4^1 Another Airliner

C_4^2 Military Aircraft

C_4^3 Power Lines

C_4^4 Private Aircraft

C_4^{41} Early in Flight (managed to limp this far)

C_4^{42} Near Jettisoned Debris

C_4^{421} Tail Damage

C_4^{422} Wing Damage

C_4^{423} Fuselage Damage

C_4^{4231} By Light Blue Cessna (plane down nearby)

Background information on local weather conditions and air traffic density might recommend some splitting too. Each would result in similar diagrams or complicate existing ones.

The diagrams above graphically display the limitlessness of subdivision. Even with guidance from the context, we can still tell stories till doomsday under almost any heading. So we will have to be very careful, very selective, in deciding how much of a diagram ends up on the list of rival conclusions. The only reason to generate the conclusions here in such detail is that doing so exercises just those skills we will need in order to flesh out the rivals list in practice. Splitting rivals, providing them with helpful detail, requires a skill closely related to our normal story-telling ability. As rivals become more detailed, they are more like little stories: "Scenarios" is the common jargon. But since they must maintain the logical properties of the list, their telling requires a more sophisticated skill than the one we normally practice. We must keep one eye on the intelligibility conditions, the other on mutual exclusiveness.

So, in order to develop a skill that we may later apply discreetly, we must in practice temporarily ignore practical considerations and see what it is like to construct a list constrained by only the implicit question and incompatibility. How would we develop the list in the air crash case? We would certainly wish to include a rival attributing the crash specifically to the other downed plane; and we might want a specific explosion rival as well. One way to put them on the list while avoiding overlap would be to *substitute* them for the more general rivals they fall under.

C_1 Pilot error

C_2' Explosion in baggage compartment

C_3 Turbulence

C_4' Light blue Cessna (other downed plane) collided with fuselage near jettisoned debris.

Since they are part of mutually incompatible rivals, they will be incompatible too.

We may wish to keep the more general rivals on the list too, however. We may wish to keep open the possibility that some other mechanical failure or some other collision was at fault. To do so we must merely make sure to remove the more specific rival from its more general parent. This will avoid overlap.

C_1 Pilot error

C_2 Mechanical failure (other than explosion in baggage compartment)

C_2' Explosion in baggage compartment

C_3 Turbulence

C_4 Collision (other than the one mentioned in C_4')

C_4' Light blue Cessna (other downed plane) collided with fuselage near jettisoned debris.

If we wish to include specific rivals other than C_2' and C_4' on the list, they must meet the same conditions. They must be removed from more general rivals that we wish to keep on the list, and they must not, of course, overlap *anything* on the list. If we wish to include a slightly different scenario involving the same Cessna, we would simply have to say enough to avoid overlapping C_4', and also remove the new rival from C_4.

C″₄   Light blue Cessna (other downed plane) collided with control
surface near jettisoned debris

C₄   Collision (other than those mentioned in C′₄ and C″₄)

In this way we may elaborate on the list indefinitely, in whatever
way we find useful in specific circumstances. (For exercise, continue
the list by adding other specific collision rivals and by developing
entries under a fifth general rival of your choosing.)

Practical Implicit Questions

We have been assuming that the implicit question will be obvious,
and often enough it is. But many times there will be several different
possibilities, which will generate different lists of rivals, and it is
important to choose wisely among them. In the aircrash case, instead of "What caused the crash?" we might have used "What made
this mess?" or "What happened here?" pointing to the mess in each
case. If we knew what we thought we knew, we were wise to choose
the first of these, because, as a rule, *the most helpful I.Q. is the most
specific one that does not ignore any live possibilities*. If the I.Q. is to
be helpful to us, it must narrow our focus; so it will ignore many
possibilities—reject them as uninteresting. But we have to be confident that none of the rejected possibilities is a live one. In normal
investigations, "What caused the crash?" is fine on this score.

It is perfectly proper, however, to change an implicit question if
it becomes a hindrance. This need for change happens all the time. If
we poke around in the mess on the ground and find nothing typical of
an airplane—no riveted aluminum, wheels, seats, baggage, or the
like—we must begin to seriously consider that the wreckage was not
after all the result of a plane crash, in spite of what witnesses said.
That conclusion means we need to change the I.Q., and good candidates for the new one would be "What made this mess?" or "What
happened here?" "What caused the crash?" would ignore (now) live
possibilities.

The whole point in digging out an implicit question is to aid in
generating a list of rival conclusions. There will be times when we
have no trouble generating rivals without appealing to an implicit
question; when we do use one, we will usually need to check back and
forth between the question we choose and the rivals we want to
include. The two concepts of rivals and I.Q. are valuable tools be-

cause they can be modified to fit each case. They help organize our discretion, but they do not remove it.

Consequently, there is one more caution worth noting. If we were lazy we could use the same I.Q. for every argument: "Is C true?" Since the support is recommending C, we could simply lump all alternatives to C together in one super-rival, not-C. This rival is always possible, and there are circumstances in which we will have to fall back on this austere position in our analysis. But it is seldom helpful. Lumping all of C's rivals together obscures just those distinctions that help us come to grips with an argument. So the best advice is to avoid the ultimate fallback I.Q. if you can. Hard work at the beginning will usually make things easier later on.

Let us apply all this to a different sort of example. The police respond to a 911 call and find a service station attendant dead amidst signs of a scuffle, the cash register open and empty, and a trail of blood leading to Joe's body in a nearby alley. On Joe's body is $185, mostly in small bills, and a recently discharged gun. Their initial reasoning might schematize as follows:

S_1 Emergency call from service station.

S_2 Attendant found dead.

S_3 Cash register open and empty.

S_4 Bloody trail to Joe's body.

S_5 Money and recently used gun found on Joe's body.

C   Joe did it.

The implicit question is obviously "Who did it?" with the presumption that there was a robbery and that it and the attendant's death were part of the same event. It is natural to think of implicit questions as rival-story generators, as we did in the air crash example. The story suggested by the data is that Joe robbed the station and killed the attendant, but was fatally wounded in the process. This story makes the presupposition mentioned above, so it is natural to look for rivals meeting the same condition. We may easily relax the presupposition if we need to.

Since the question is "*Who* did it?" the different rivals will simply be different suspects. This means that different stories with the same protagonist will all yield the same rival. It does not matter how (or when or why) Joe did it. All those possibilities collapse into the same rival: Joe did it. So the list might begin something like this:

C_1 Joe did it.

C_2 Sam did it.

C_3 Sue did it.

.

.

.

And we could continue it as far as we have suspects. But notice that the mutual exclusiveness requirement demands that we immediately make a decision about the possibility of multiple perpetrators. Joe and Sam may have done it together. Where does that go on the list? If it is included under "Joe did it," then it cannot be included under "Sam did it" or we will have unpermitted overlap. We simply have to decide whether to put it one place or the other, or perhaps somewhere else. It cannot go in more than one place.

The natural way to handle this problem systematically is to let "x did it" mean "x did it acting alone" and include teams separately on the list. That is, after exhausting the list of individual suspects, continue with

C_{49} Joe and Sam did it.

C_{50} Joe and Sue did it.

.

.

.

and later, perhaps,

C_{97} Joe, Sam, and Sue did it.

.

.

.

Often enough, this much will be simply understood and raise no problems. But it is good to be alert to difficulties that might arise and know what to do about them if they do.

We introduce another level of complexity by relaxing the presupposition that the death and robbery were a single event. The I.Q. would read "Who killed the attendant and who took the money?" This would give us two lists, which could be combined in a variety of different stories. For example, Sam killed the attendant and, later, Sue took the money. Since we are just *relaxing the presupposition* that it was a single event, not *supposing* that it was not, we may include the first list in this one by having the same name in both places, the same answer to both questions.

For the next complication, focus on the attendant (the first of the two questions) and forget about the robbery. We might wish to take seriously the possibility that he died of natural causes or by accident—that *nobody* did anything to cause his death. That is, we look down at the bottom of the list and find the rival "nobody": nobody did it. This is not so much an answer to the implicit question as a rejection of it. Asking "Who . . . ?" presupposes it was somebody, so to take "nobody" seriously we must ask a broader, more general question: "What happened to the attendant?" for instance, or "How did he die?" The new list will include all the old suspects, of course (it still might have been somebody), but we may now add old age, a freak accident, drug overdose, and flawed arteries as well.

The broader I.Q. opens up other possibilities on the old list of suspects. Under the whodunnit I.Q. there was just one rival per suspect or group of suspects. But if we ask "What happened?" instead of "Who did it?" then we open up the possibility of having many different rivals that involve Joe acting alone. Every distinct story, every different way in which Joe might have done it acting alone, may now be put on the list separately. We are not *forced* to split up the old rivals; it is just that the new I.Q. allows us to do so if we wish. The underlying principle of the entire enterprise is to find the I.Q. that does what you need to have done—the one that gives you the rivals you need to organize your thinking. We have developed these examples in such detail in order to provide a clear sense of how the possibilities change with a change in the question and to exercise our understanding of the constraints on the process.

INDUCTION AND DEDUCTION REPRISED

Recall that the rivals are simply answers to a certain question. They are linked to the support only very indirectly, through one of their members and by way of the intelligibility conditions. So it should not be surprising if, occasionally, one or another of the imagination-generated rivals finds itself in direct, semantic conflict with something in the support.

S_1	Dead attendant		Rivals
S_2	Trail of blood	C_1	Joe did it.
S_3	Joe's body	C_2	Sam did it.
S_4	Perpetrator is short and fat.	C_3	Sue did it.
		C_4	The tall, thin man seen leaving the scene did it.
C	Joe did it.		

This example has been oversimplified to display a semantic conflict between S_4 and C_4. In a case like this we usually want to keep S_4 in spite of the conflict, and if we do keep it then C_4 is eliminated from consideration semantically, as a matter of language, not because of our ability to judge plausibility. C_4's impossibility is part of what we have already accepted in the support. When this conflict happens we call C_4 "semantically eliminated." It is still an answer to the I.Q., still a rival to C_1, but it is semantically eliminated from consideration as long as we have these supporting statements. Diagrammatically,

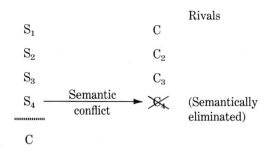

Of course, more than one rival may be eliminated in this way, and elimination may involve combinations of support claims, not just a single one. For example,

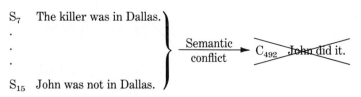

Now, by various devices we may make the list of rivals complete, covering all the possibilities. In the service station robbery,

C_1 Joe did it.

C_2 Sam did it.

C_3 Somebody else did it.

C_4 A group of people did it (two or more).

C_5 Nobody did it (something else happened).

We usually have no need to do this, but it can be done, and it allows us to make the following point:

If the support semantically conflicts with all rivals but one, then it can be cast into a deductive argument for the uneliminated conclusion.

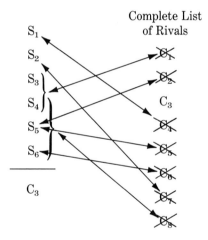

If this result is not obvious we can make it so by recalling that if we have *all* of C_3's rivals, they may be lumped together in the super-rival not-C_3. The I.Q. in this case is the normally unhelpful one: "Is C_3 true?" There are only two answers: "yes" and "no"; that is, either C_3 is true or not-C_3 is true. And since not-C_3 has been semantically eliminated, C_3 must be true by the very criterion we use to identify deductive arguments: It has already been affirmed in our accepting the support.

The main reason to display deduction in this way is to refine the can-you-get-out-of-it test. The original version of this test required us to think of "conditions under which" the conclusion might be false and the support still true. And you could be forgiven the thought that the notion of such conditions was not transparent, was sometimes more puzzling than helpful. The semantic elimination of rival conclusions is designed to give clearer substance to that notion. The "conditions under which" are simply *uneliminated rival conclusions*. So the induction/deduction distinction may now be formulated

> If you can find one rival to the argument's conclusion that is not eliminated semantically—that is compatible with the support— then the argument is inductive. If you can show there is no such rival, you have shown that the argument is deductive.

Since we have developed a procedure for thinking up rivals, and only one of them can be true, we have a procedure for thinking up conditions under which the conclusion is false. This should make the test easier to apply, should allow the formal distinction to be made more easily.

The difficulty of casting practical arguments deductively appears here, altered but recognizable. The problems lie in finding the very general devices needed to complete the lists and in coming up with plausible support claims to conflict with those devices. None of the earlier points changes, except perhaps in idiom. The purpose of this section has simply been to present the basic formal distinction between induction and deduction in clearer and more tractable form.

DETAILED ILLUSTRATION

It will be useful to apply the apparatus we have developed in the first two chapters to a real and slightly more complicated example.

> On the evening of January 24, 1978, several residents of a barren area of the Northwest Territories reported a spectacular fireball over Baker Lake, a body of water just west of Hudson Bay. For several weeks U.S. tracking stations had been warning that a Soviet satellite, possibly containing a nuclear reactor, had dropped very low in its orbit and was likely soon to fall into the atmosphere. Its orbit would have taken it over northern Canada about the time the fireball was reported to have occurred. Later that same week the Russians admitted losing a nuclear-powered satellite, but added that the danger of nuclear contamination was remote. Shortly following this announcement, two geologists hiking down a

river just east of Baker Lake discovered radioactive debris, of clearly human fabrication, poking out of a crater in the ice.

From all this, Canadian government officials concluded that the Soviet satellite had in fact returned to earth, burning up in the atmosphere in the vicinity of Baker Lake and showering that part of the Northwest Territories with radioactive debris.

This passage is inferentially complex, but we may extract from it the following argument:

S_1 A Soviet satellite, possibly containing a nuclear reactor, was observed dropping dangerously close to the atmosphere.

S_2 Observation of the fireball over Baker Lake by local residents occurred at about the time the fireball's orbit would carry the satellite over that part of northern Canada.

S_3 Man-made radioactive debris was found the same week near Baker Lake, in a place the material could not have occupied for very long.

C   The fireball over Baker Lake was the returning Soviet satellite.

The natural implicit question, the one the conclusion seems obviously to be answering, is "What was the fireball over Baker Lake?" So the list of C's rivals would simply be the list of other things the fireball might have been, a reasonable beginning of which would be

C_1 Meteorite

C_2 ICBM test

C_3 Failed rocket launch

C_4 Exploding aircraft

C_5 Some other falling satellite

C_6 An atmospheric phenomenon (St. Elmo's fire, aurora borealis, etc.)

C_7 Exploding swamp gas

C_8 UFO from an alien civilization

These rivals have been constructed to be easily read as incompatible with each other and with C. If there is a problem with C_2 and C_3, we might change C_3 to read "Failed rocket launch that is not part of an ICBM test." C_2 might be altered instead, of course. Notice also that the argument's conclusion, C_1, taken together with C_5, forms the general rival "falling satellite." So, by the convention introduced in section 6, we might change C to C_5'.

The argument is pretty obviously inductive from almost any point of view. But if asked to explain why you thought so, you might select any rival on the list and offer it as, again pretty obviously, compatible with the support. You could even provide more detail if you thought it might help. For example, nothing conflicts semantically with the possibility that the fireball was a meteorite that came along at about the same time as the satellite and that the satellite is still up there. The radioactive debris would then have to be from some other source—a joke, perhaps, or an accident, or something else coincidental. These possibilities, though long shots, are not in semantic conflict with the support. All S_3 says is that the debris could not have been there very long; it could have come from anywhere. Nothing in the support is *contradicted* by our saying that it was dumped there by somebody with a waste-disposal problem.

Now suppose that something in the story, or in the ensuing investigation, made us want to take seriously the possibility that the fireball reports are a hoax. Perhaps the boredom of an Arctic winter drove local residents to entertain themselves in this way. To take this hoax idea seriously would require a pair of changes. First, "hoax" does not answer our implicit question, which simply presupposes there was a fireball. To add "hoax" to the list we would need an I.Q. innocent of that presupposition, something like "What provoked all those fireball reports?" We could then keep the rivals listed above (a meteorite might have provoked them) and simply add "hoax" to the list. The boredom of an Arctic winter would then be a possible story.

The story would be in direct semantic conflict with the support as it now stands, however. S_2 commits us to a fireball. So if we have reason to take seriously the possibility that there really was no fireball, just reports of one, then we have reason to change S_2 to allow it. Remember, you are designing the schematization. You will usually have a great deal of discretion, many choices to make. Make them wisely. You will never want a simple turn of phrase to rule out rivals you have reason to consider seriously.

It will be useful to conclude this chapter by discussing another kind of example. The tightness of the deductive link sometimes encourages students of reasoning to force reluctant arguments into deductive form in spite of the cautions of this chapter. A good example of the temptation can be found in the following paragraph.[4]

> Some criminal robbed the Russell mansion. Whoever robbed the Russell mansion either had an accomplice among the servants or had to break in. To break in, one would have to either smash the door or pick the lock. Only an expert locksmith could have picked the lock. Had anyone smashed the door he would have been heard. Nobody was heard. If the criminal who robbed the Russell mansion managed to fool the guard, he must have been a convincing actor. No one could rob the Russell mansion unless he fooled the guard. No criminal could be both an expert locksmith and a convincing actor. Therefore some criminal had an accomplice among the servants.

This paragraph was contrived to yield the following deductive schematization:

S_1 Some criminal robbed the Russell mansion.

S_2 Whoever robbed the Russell mansion either had to break in or had an accomplice among the servants.

S_3 To break in one would have to either smash the door or pick the lock.

S_4 Only an expert locksmith could have picked the lock.

S_5 Anyone who smashed the door would have been heard.

S_6 Nobody was heard.

S_7 If the criminal who robbed the Russell mansion managed to fool the guard, he must have been a convincing actor.

S_8 No one could rob the Russell mansion unless he fooled the guard.

S_9 No criminal could be both an expert locksmith and a convincing actor.

C   Some criminal had an accomplice among the servants.

---

[4]Example taken from I. M. Copi, *Introduction to Logic*, 2nd ed. (New York: Macmillan, 1968), p. 334.

Now if we recharacterize the substance of the paragraph in a more plausibly idiomatic way, we can arrange the support into a pretty good inductive argument.

S_1' The Russell mansion was robbed.

S_2' Nobody heard a violent entry.

S_3' The usually reliable and alert guard saw nothing suspicious.

C_1 It was an inside job.

The implicit question is something like "How did it happen?" so the natural rivals would be

C_2 The robber (somehow) got past the guard and got into the mansion quietly.

C_3 The robber got past the guard and broke in, but the noise he made in doing so was obscured by other noise or distraction.

C_4 The robber got past the guard and broke in, but nobody was within earshot to hear him.

Notice that at least three other rivals are semantically eliminated:

C_5 The missing valuables were removed noncriminally.

C_6 The guard was in on the plan, observed the break-in, and lied about it.

C_7 Somebody else heard the break-in but lied about it.

These are, of course, super-rivals, naturally split into a number of subrivals. Each of these is, naturally, eliminated too.

Now, in ordinary inductive arguments, there are usually a number of bizarre possibilities not clearly covered by (that is, included in) any rival on the list. They are so implausible that we automatically and rightly ignore them. If some consideration later recommends that we take one of them seriously, it may easily enough be formulated at that time; but in normal circumstances they all may be safely ignored. The first difficulty in a deductive casting of substantive arguments arises at this point. In order to eliminate semantically all of our conclusion's competition, we must make sure all possibilities—

even bizarre ones—are covered by the rivals we eliminate. In the Russell mansion robbery, we must be sure the support claims conflict with possibilities such as somebody's living undetected in the mansion for twenty-five years, taking the valuables, and then teleporting herself out of the solar system, all without the complicity of a servant. To make sure everything of this sort has been semantically eliminated requires some terminological artificiality; but we can manage it if we are careful.

The trick is to begin with logically exhaustive super-rivals (typically, C and not-C) and then subdivide them into exhaustive subrivals in a way that allows our support claims to bear directly on them. This will, of course, usually take us some distance from the natural diagnostic rivals. In the Russell mansion example, the most convenient beginning (given the support claims) is to divide the (super) rivals into break-ins versus everything else:

$$C = \text{Robber broke into the mansion.}$$
$$\text{not-}C = \text{Robber did not break into the mansion.}$$

In this context not-C is naturally taken to include all the possibilities not covered by C.

Both C and not-C may be exhaustively subdivided in the following way:

$$
C =
\begin{cases}
C_1 & \text{Robber broke in by smashing the door.} \\
C_2 & \text{Robber broke in by picking the lock.} \\
C_3 & \text{Robber broke in in some other way.}
\end{cases}
$$

$$
\text{not-}C =
\begin{cases}
C_4 & \text{Robber did not break in but had an accomplice} \\
    & \text{among the servants.} \\
C_5 & \text{Robber did not break in but had no accomplice} \\
    & \text{among the servants.} \\
C_6 & \text{Robber did not break in but had several accomplices among the servants.}
\end{cases}
$$

C_6 is included here merely because the conclusion we seek refers to a single accomplice. We might take the conclusion as an idiomatic way of saying " . . . at least one accomplice . . . ," but it is simpler to keep it literal; and nothing much hangs on this. C_2 must be further subdivided to allow the elimination we seek:

$$
C_2 = \begin{cases} C_{2A} & \text{Robber broke in by picking the lock and fooled the guard.} \\ C_{2B} & \text{Robber broke in by picking the lock and did not fool the guard.} \end{cases}
$$

And since the deductive argument's first support claim (S_1) characterizes the robber as "some criminal"—that is, semantically eliminates everybody but those properly so characterized—we may safely adopt this characterization in the list of rival conclusions. (It will shortly be clear why this is convenient to do.) So the complete list looks like this:

C_1 Some criminal broke in by smashing the door.

C_{2A} Some criminal broke in by picking the lock and fooled the guard.

C_{2B} Some criminal broke in by picking the lock and did not fool the guard.

C_3 Some criminal broke in in some other way.

C_4 Some criminal did not break in but had an accomplice among the servants.

C_5 Some criminal did not break in but had no accomplice among the servants.

C_6 Some criminal did not break in but had several accomplices among the servants.

Now, looking down the list of support claims (S_{1-9}) in the argument, we can see the following semantic conflicts:

S_5 and S_6 together eliminate C_1, since they explicitly reject any smashing that was heard and any that was not.

S_8 eliminates C_{2B}.

S_3 eliminates C_3 by explicitly ruling out all "other" ways of breaking in.

S_2 eliminates C_5 by direct conflict: S_2 says the robber either broke in or had an accomplice among the servants; C_5 says "no, neither."

S_2 also eliminates C_6, if we take "several" to conflict with "an" accomplice, as we have here. Interpreted this way, C_6 says "no, neither" too.

Finally, S_4, S_7, and S_9 together eliminate C_{2A}, because S_4 and S_7 require that the criminal in C_{2A} be both an expert locksmith and a convincing actor, while S_9 conflicts directly with this.

We have thus semantically eliminated all but C_4; some criminal did not break in but had an accomplice among the servants. Since the original conclusion, "Some criminal had an accomplice among the servants," is explicitly contained in C_4, it is an obvious deductive consequence of C_4. So the overall argument is deductive.

What is wrong with casting the argument this way? On the sort of evidence we would normally have in a robbery investigation, many of the deductive argument's support claims (S_{1-9}) would be pretty shaky. Together they would provide very little support for the conclusion. This is due almost entirely to the peculiar nature of the statements we require to eliminate substantive rivals semantically. They must often be indefensibly categorical, such as S_8 and S_9; or offer peculiar combinations, such as S_2; or both, such as S_3. The peculiar device of referring to the robber as a "criminal" was probably employed for just this reason. If "no criminal" in S_9 were replaced by "nobody" or even by "no robber," the argument would probably sound more ridiculous than it does in its present form. Only because *criminal* severely restricts the group of people we must consider does S_9 have the little surface plausibility it does. And that is not very much. Furthermore, what little plausibility accrues to S_9 through this artifice is doubtless lost to S_1 in the exchange. For S_1 is plausible only if *criminal* is *not* very restrictive: only a slightly hysterical deprecation of the robber. If restricted to "career criminal" or "someone with a criminal record" to comport with our reading of S_9, then S_1 becomes far less plausible.

The peculiar behavior of the word *criminal* here is typical of what happens when we try to force everyday arguments into deductive form. The formal requirement of constant meaning is so much at odds with our normal use of language that we fall easily into equivocation. When we consider S_1 and S_9 separately, the Principle of Charity virtually guarantees that we will read *criminal* one way in one and another way in the other. But that is easy to forget when we are embroiled in semantic elimination: There the presence of the same word in each dominates our perception. We are easily seduced, with devastating effect on our reason.

So the rule to follow in casting substantive arguments is simply to do it the most natural way in each case. Sometimes we will naturally eliminate all competing rivals by semantic means alone; but only in very special circumstances should we *expect* to do so. Usually the argument we get will naturally be inductive. We should then make the best of it, because if we try to force it into deductive form we are likely to end up with a weaker argument and open ourselves to much semantic risk along the way.

THE USE OF FORM AND STRUCTURE IN THINKING ABOUT REASONING

This chapter has introduced some basic argument forms and hinted at more elaborate structure and apparatus to come. As the apparatus emerges, you should find yourself working hard to exercise it, to practice making the key distinctions in the messy circumstances of everyday life. Only in this way will it be of any value to you. But in our devotion to the exercise, it is easy to come to the wrong perspective on all this and develop an unhealthy attitude toward the apparatus.

The formal apparatus is simply a tool to organize and guide your reasoning whenever you feel the need. It is not magic, which is why you must sometimes think and work hard to learn how to use it. But it is also not sacred: Once you master it, you should use it or abuse it however you see fit. To do this competently, you would do well to bear in mind the viewpoint from which the apparatus is being developed.

On the model of argument presented in Chapter 1, the whole point in digging out reasons for a conclusion—in thoughtfully representing support-relations—is to display the merits of a conclusion: to state as clearly as possible what virtues it is supposed to have, what good it is supposed to be. And we need this clarity specifically for the sake of three overlapping activities: to understand the reasoning, to evaluate it (see if we can improve on it), and to articulate it (explain it to somebody else). The formal distinctions and structure are being created to assist in this task and these activities. That is why our taxonomy is so dependent on human skills and interests.

So the entire apparatus—from paraphrase, implicit questions, rival conclusions, induction, deduction, and charity to the diagnostic algorithm of Chapter 3 and the elaborate compound schemata of Chapter 5—may be thought of as a collection of *guides, suggestions,* and *reminders*. In one way they are like *maps*; in another they are *mnemonic devices*. They are like maps in that they can guide us through the staggering complexity of the matters we wish to reason about, can show us ways of viewing daunting terrain. Their mnemonic function, on the other hand, is to draw our attention to possibilities, limitations, and temptations. We constantly need reminding of the possibilities and limitations in our skills and the temptations of our humanity.

Suggestions will always be of the form TRY THIS. When you are stuck or worried, a bit of apparatus, a formal distinction, some self-conscious charity will often get you over the hump. The initial task is to internalize the analytical process so that helpful suggestions occur to you, automatically, at the right time. It is in this spirit that you should plunge into the chapter that follows.

STUDY GUIDE FOR CHAPTER 2

1. We make several formal distinctions in this chapter (a formal distinction is a distinction based on the form of something rather than on its content). One distinction we have used already is the one between an argument and other things: A passage of prose contains an argument if it has secondary points (support claims) that are offered in support of a main point (conclusion). Another distinction we want to make is between two different kinds of arguments: *inductive* and *deductive*.

    (a) The top and bottom parts of a schematized argument are *linked*. If the support claims are good reasons to believe the conclusion, then we say that the link is a strong one. If they give some reason, but not good reason, to believe C, then we say that the link is weak.

    (b) One type of argument has a link that is absolute—the *deductive argument*. A deductive argument is one in which the conclusion is semantically guaranteed by the support (that is, the support-claims, taken together, *mean* that the conclusion is true). There are a number of ways to test for the deductiveness of an argument: (i) If you accept the support, you are trapped into the conclusion; you can't get out of it; (ii) if you deny the conclusion and affirm the support, you contradict yourself; (iii) the conclusion is contained in the support.

    (c) An *inductive argument* is the opposite of a deductive argument. If an argument is not deductive, if it has failed the above tests, then it is an inductive argument.

    (d) We normally want to avoid schematizing arguments as deductive because doing so requires support-claims like "If the gas gauge reads empty as your car sputters to a stop, the car is invariably out of gas." This kind of support-claim is very risky, if not obviously false. To unfairly stick an author with such a claim goes against the principle of charity outlined in Chapter 1.

(e) The strength of an inductive link will vary: Different inductive arguments will have different degrees of strength.

2. An argument is usually given for some specific reason. And this reason can be helpfully formulated as a question. Someone who gives an argument for some conclusion thinks that the conclusion answers a question he or she finds interesting and sees the support as offering reasons for accepting this particular answer.

   (a) We call this question an *implicit question*. It is implicit because the author rarely states it explicitly and the schematizer (that is, the reader) must formulate the question. Implicit questions will be of the form "Why did X happen?" "Who did that?" "What should I (we) do?" "What should we expect?" and the like.

   (b) The most important point about (a) above is that the conclusion(s) *must answer the implicit question*. If the conclusion does not answer the implicit question, then either the implicit question or the conclusion has been badly formulated.

   (c) The implicit question should be formulated so that it can have several different answers. An implicit question of the form "Is C true?" has only two answers ("yes" and "no") and so is called the *ultimate fallback question*. Since it has only two (very uninteresting) answers, it must be avoided.

   (d) The answers to an implicit question are called the *rival conclusions*. Rival conclusions are the *different* possible answers to the implicit question. And since they have to be different, they will always be *mutually exclusive*; they cannot overlap. For example, if the implicit question is "How did she die?" we might be tempted to make C_1 "She died of natural causes" and C_2 "She died of a heart attack." But we cannot do this, because C_1 and C_2 would not then be mutually exclusive. To die of a heart attack *is* to die of natural causes; so C_1 and C_2 here would not be rivals.

3. The fact that there are competing rival conclusions for an inductive argument, but only one conclusion for a deductive argument, gives us another test for whether an argument is deductive. If all but one of the rival conclusions is in semantic conflict with (one or more of) the support-claims, then the argument is deductive. (Semantic conflict means that the support-claim and the rival conclusion contradict each other.) Alternatively, we can see that an argument for some conclusion C is *inductive* if so much as one of C's rivals is semantically compatible with the support offered.

EXERCISES

1. S_1 Sally Robinson will be graduated from Millard Fillmore College next term, with a grade-point average just below 3.0.

   S_2 Medical schools have never admitted a Millard Fillmore graduate whose grade-point average was below 3.5.

   ───────────────────

   C Sally will not be admitted to medical school.

   This argument is pretty obviously inductive (see if you can explain why in a sentence or two). It can be recast as a deductive argument simply by expanding S_2 to read

   S_2' Medical schools never have and never will admit a Millard Fillmore graduate whose grade-point average is below 3.5.

   a. Explain why the revised argument is deductive by showing that denying C contradicts S_1 and S_2'.
   b. In normal circumstances, which argument better captures the reason Sally might have for thinking she will not be admitted to medical school? Why?

2. S_1 All the important economic indicators are good.

   S_2 When all the important economic indicators are good, the future of the economy will always be rosy, at least in the short run.

   C The short-run future of the economy is rosy.

   a. Is this argument inductive or deductive?
   b. Cast it the other way as plausibly as you can.
   c. Suppose that once, many years ago, all the important economic indicators were good just as the economy was plunging into a severe recession. Explain the difference between the impact of this fact on the inductive version and its impact on the deductive version. That is, how would it affect the support provided for the conclusion in each case?

3. Schematize Joe's argument in exercise 5 of Chapter 1 in the most natural way.
   a. Is this argument inductive or deductive (is there any consistent way out)?
   b. How strong is the support this schematization offers for Joe's conclusion? Explain (briefly).

4. S_1 Johnny Dilworth is a Republican, running in an over-whelmingly Republican district that has elected only Republicans for years.

C   Johnny will be elected on Tuesday.

  a. Is this argument inductive or deductive?
  b. Briefly explain why (use the "Can you get out of it?" test).
  c. Cast the argument the other way as plausibly as you can.
  d. Which version is stronger? Why?

5. S_1 The news media have been filled with reports of the U.S. naval presence in the Persian Gulf.

  S_2 When an issue is reported as widely as this, every college student knows about it.

  S_3 Joe is a college student.

C   Joe knows about it.

  a. Is this argument inductive or deductive?
  b. Cast it the other way.
  c. Which argument provides greater support for the conclusion?
  d. Explain.

6. Schematize attorney Karlin's argument in exercise 11 of Chapter 1 (if you have not already done so).
  a. Is the argument inductive or deductive as you have schematized it? Explain why. (Can you tell a story that gets you out of accepting C without abandoning any support?)
  b. Cast it the other way.
  c. Which form is stronger? Why?

7. Consider the following inductive argument.

  S_1 Driving along in his car, Joe heard a loud *pop!*

  S_2 The vehicle's ride immediately deteriorated, as did steering control, and the car executed a series of distracting wobbles, ending only when Joe managed to bring it to a stop on the shoulder of the road.

  S_3 Examination revealed the right rear tire to be half way off the rim, grotesquely shredded, and too hot to touch.

C   The *pop* was a blowout.

   a. Cast the argument deductively by simply adding a general S_4. (Don't rewrite the whole argument.)

   b. Suppose the following:

   Just last year Joe's brother, after driving for several miles on a flat tire, heard a truck backfire just as he entered a badly paved section of Interstate 5. The lurid wobbles caused by the pavement were exacerbated by the flat and he pulled off the road. There he found the right rear tire in shreds, half way off the rim, and too hot to touch.

   Explain the difference in the effect this episode would have on the inductive and deductive versions of the argument above.

8. Schematize the argument directly attributed to Lee Dorsey in the article used for exercise 12 of Chapter 1.

   a. Is this argument inductive or deductive? Explain why.

   b. Cast it the other way as plausibly as you can.

   c. Which version is stronger? Explain.

9. "There was a loud crash in the kitchen, and when I looked in there I saw a broken glass on the floor. Nothing else seemed out of place, so the noise must have been caused by the glass breaking."

   a. Schematize the argument in this paragraph.

   b. Is it inductive or deductive? How can you tell?

   c. Cast it the other way.

   d. Which is stronger? Why?

10. Schematize the argument in exercise 6 of Chapter 1.

   a. What is this argument's implicit question?

   b. Is the argument inductive or deductive? (Use the compatible rivals test.)

   c. Cast it the other way.

   d. Which casting provides the conclusion with better support? Why?

11. The wind woke me from a sound sleep at about 4 a.m. I could hear it howling through the trees and across rooftops. In the morning, when I took out the trash, our large, metal garbage can was not in its usual spot next to the garage. I finally found it wedged under a bush on the other side of my car, which had been parked in the driveway. The car itself had new scrapes and scratches, down low on the side facing the can's normal location.

   a. What answer does this passage suggest to the question "What caused the new scrapes and scratches on the side of the car?"

b. Schematize the support that may be found for this answer in the passage.

c. Give another answer (that is, a rival conclusion for the schematization) that is compatible with the support offered.

d. What does your answer to c tell you about the argument you schematized?

12. S_1 For the past decade little Johnny has had difficulty breathing, has tired easily, and has been thought to be asthmatic.

S_2 Recently, physicians discovered, lodged in one of Johnny's lungs, a toy brick apparently ingested years before.

S_3 When the brick was removed, Johnny's breathing difficulty vanished almost immediately.

C   Johnny's breathing problem was due to the toy brick in his lung.

Take the implicit question to be "What caused Johnny's breathing problem?"

a. State some rival conclusions.

b. Are any rivals (semantically) compatible with the support?

c. Is this argument inductive or deductive?

d. Recast the argument as the other kind.

e. Is the new argument better than the first? Why or why not?

13. During a series of operations on the surface of Mars, the scoop arm on *Viking I* stopped responding to commands. When the *Viking* simulator on Earth (a near twin to the mechanism on Mars) was subjected to the same series of operations, a pin malfunctioned and jammed the arm. Subsequently, a simple operation on the simulator caused the pin in question to fall out, freeing the arm. Delighted with this turn of events, the scientists in charge of *Viking I* on Mars commanded it to perform the same operation. When it did, the *Viking I* arm once again functioned normally. A television camera on board *Viking I* was then trained on the ground directly beneath the scoop arm; a pin just like the one that had jammed the simulator arm was observed lying in the Martian dust.

Take this to be an argument for the conclusion that the scoop arm of *Viking I* had been jammed by a malfunctioning pin. By the rival-conclusions test, show that this argument is inductive on its most charitable reading.

14.   W. German Landlord, Deep in Debt, Kills Self

COLOGNE, West Germany (AP)—Guenter Kaussen, a financially troubled landlord with extensive property holdings in West Germany and the United States, hanged himself in his apartment here, officials reported Monday.

A government statement said Kaussen's body was discovered Monday morning. No suicide note was found, but authorities ruled out foul play.

Kaussen, 57, owned between 16,000 and 20,000 apartments throughout West Germany, officials said, and was considered the country's biggest landlord. He also owned several thousand apartments in San Francisco and Atlanta, and had been under investigation for suspected improper business practices.

The statement quoted Kaussen's tenants as saying he had been behaving strangely recently. Last weekend, Cologne police rescued some of Kaussen's employees after he locked them in his office.

He was believed to be $133 million in debt, with $45 million owed to creditors in the United States. His real estate investments in the United States were believed to have resulted in heavy losses. Although he reportedly earned about $1.3 million annually from rents in West Germany, it was not enough to pay off mounting debts.

It was not immediately clear who would take over Kaussen's holdings, which in San Francisco included 25 properties with more than 1,500 apartments.

Schematize the best argument you can find in this article for the conclusion that Guenter Kauseen's death was a suicide.
a. What is the implicit question?
b. Provide two rival conclusions compatible with the support.
c. Provide one rival incompatible with the support.
d. Is your argument inductive or deductive? Explain why you think so.

15. Schematize Steve's argument in exercise 9 of Chapter 1.
a. What is this argument's implicit question?
b. Provide two rivals to Steve's conclusion.
c. Is Steve's argument inductive or deductive? Why?

16.   Skeleton, Car Wreck Found in Mountains

An innocent outing to local snow-covered mountains turned into a grisly find for a couple of Air Force men and their families Sunday afternoon as they came upon a skeleton in a wrecked car.

Steven Zarate of the coroner's office said the skeleton is that of a 54-year-old man from Rancho Mirage. The man's name has not been released pending notification of his family.

Sgt. Jay Jones of the Banning Highway Patrol station said the man was reported missing on July 7, 1986. The missing person's report indicated that the victim had left Escondido en route to his home in Rancho Mirage prior to being reported missing.

Jones said the skeleton, hanging over the car's door, was mostly covered with snow. The wrecked car was situated about 250 feet down a steep cliff off the north side of Highway 243 north of Allendale Station and south of Lawlor Park, said Jones.

Jones said the location where the car left the roadway is far enough from a populated area that no one may have heard the crash. The roadway opposite the crash area is popular for people playing in the snow but the other side "is so steep hardly anyone goes down there," said Jones.

Jones said the highway patrol is assuming that the incident is a traffic accident and unless the coroner's autopsy finds something it will be investigated as an accident.

a. Schematize the argument offered in this passage for the conclusion that the unnamed Rancho Mirage man (URMM) died in an automobile accident. (Hint: To cull support from the passage, ask "What would lead you to think the URMM died in an auto accident?")

b. What rival conclusions might Sgt. Jones have in mind in the last paragraph? (List at least two.)

c. What implicit question does this recommend?

d. Give a rival in which the incident was a traffic accident.

e. Are any of your rivals in b or d compatible with the supporting statements?

f. What does your response in e tell you about the argument?

17. The radio crackled madly and we lost radio contact with Flight 544 just as it entered an ominous-looking storm cell about six hours ago. It is now four hours overdue at its destination, and we've had no word from it. The terminal staff is doing its best to cheer the people in our waiting room, but I think the worst has happened.

a. Give two plausible implicit questions that could organize this passage into an argument.

b. Provide three plausible answers (rivals) to each.

c. Schematize the argument around the most helpful of the questions developed in a and b.

d. Is your argument inductive or deductive? Explain why you think so.

18.
Pilot May Have Failed to Set Flaps
Inadequate Check Prior to Takeoff Indicated in Crash

ERIC MALNIC
Times Staff Writer

ROMULUS, Mich.—Failure by the pilot to deploy the wing flaps of his aircraft may have caused the crash of Northwest Airlines Flight 255 in which at least 154 people died, federal investigators indicated Wednesday night.

John Lauber, head of the National Transportation Safety Board [NTSB] investigating team, said that the "black box" flight data recorder recovered from the aircraft indicated that the flaps and slats were in an "unusual" retracted position when the plane attempted to take off.

He also said that the pilot and first officer may have omitted a mandatory preflight check designed to make certain the flaps and slats were working properly.

Preflight Check

Cockpit conversations taped by the voice recorder recovered from the wreckage indicated that, when the pilot and first officer went through their preflight check, they omitted mention of the flaps and slats, which are included on the checklist, Lauber said.

There was no explanation for those omissions.

Pilots have to rely on instruments to make such checks, because the wings are not visible from the cockpit. Thus, it is not known whether any failure to deploy might have been a deliberate decision on the part of the flight crew, an omission, or some mechanical malfunction possibly overlooked during the flight check.

Flaps and slats are large metal surfaces that normally are extended during takeoff to provide a plane with extra lift.

a. The NTSB spokesman is addressing several questions here. For one he offers some rival answers in the next to last paragraph. What is that question?
b. Write out the suggested answers as rivals (use complete sentences).
c. One rival naturally splits into two. Which is it and how does it naturally split?
d. The article continues with the following paragraph:

On Wednesday night, Lauber stressed that, although the flight data recorder *indicated* the flaps and slats were not deployed, further evidence is needed to prove this conclusively.

     i. What revision of the implicit question is suggested by this paragraph?

    ii. Give a rival (answer/conclusion) allowed by this question but not by the earlier one.

= 3 =

EVIDENCE (1)

Diagnostic Induction

Overview

One kind of inductive argument employs our understanding of
things so directly that it deserves to be singled out as basic. This is
diagnostic induction, and a systematic treatment of it is worked out
in this chapter. The nature of our diagnostic skill naturally divides
evidence into two distinct kinds; and this division helps organize an
evaluative apparatus.

INTRODUCTION

Evaluating inductive arguments requires us to make judgments
about plausibility: The tightness or strength of an inductive link
depends on how plausibly you can get out of it. It depends on the
plausibility of the story you must tell to escape the conclusion. This is
a good place to begin, because judging the plausibility of such stories
is something human beings can all do pretty well sometimes. In a
whole range of everyday circumstances we are all competent to say
how plausible various possibilities are. If your watch is not where
you remember leaving it, your experience in the circumstances will
often allow you to intelligently estimate the likelihood of various
suggestions: The watch was stolen, you lost it, somebody moved it,
or you just forgot where you put it. And *no* experience you have had
will make it plausible to suggest that it has disguised itself as your
shaving mug or has been teleported to a distant planet by aliens.
These are judgments we practice every day: Our lives depend on

them. So an argument-form that employs such judgment skills should be just what we are looking for, should fit nicely into our taxonomy. We also have a well-developed sense of how to improve our judgment if we need to. We know what information, experience, and training are required to make it better. If we're new to the area we may not have any idea how safe it is to leave watches lying around, and so may not be confident of our judgment about theft. But we know how to find out. Ask the locals, check police records. Run a test if we feel it's that important. We are seldom at a loss for ideas. From this connection with plausibility estimates, inductive arguments derive two of their essential features—features that dramatically distinguish them from deductive arguments.

1. The first, which we have already seen, is the matter of degree: An inductive link may be practically as strong as a deductive one, just so-so, very weak, or anything in between. Furthermore, we shall see, an inductive argument may be valuable anywhere within that range. A weak link will not always be worthless.

2. The second feature stems from the fact that plausibility estimates always depend on a vast, unarticulated understanding of how the world works in relevant respects. An understanding of larceny, living quarters, habit patterns, my own personality, and life itself weigh in my thinking about what happened to my watch. Inductive arguments, quite unlike deductive ones, lean on the world for support. If the world were vastly different—if, say, chalk and erasers and blackboards had wildly different properties than they actually do—our earlier argument about the eraser-shaped white spot would naturally lose some of its strength. It might not support its conclusion at all. Everything depends on simple facts about the familiar objects of our everyday experience.

These two features are responsible for much of the complexity and difficulty we will encounter in analyzing inductive arguments. But they also account for the central role such arguments play in our reasoning. So our exploration of induction will usefully begin by examining them in greater detail.

RELATIVE PLAUSIBILITY JUDGMENT

The skill that does most of the work in evaluating inductive arguments is actually even more modest than suggested in the introduction. This skill is the ability to say which, of two (rival) stories, is the *more* plausible. Normally, doing this is far easier than estimating just *how* plausible the stories are. We can often say that theft of the watch is less likely than simple memory lapse, but not have much idea just how likely either suggestion is. The ease with which we naturally apply and develop our relative plausibility judgments opens for us a truly enormous range of cases in which we can create inductive arguments and evaluate evidence. Because the skill is so modest, it should be no surprise that human beings have it and can apply it so broadly. What is impressive, and will require this chapter to demonstrate, is now powerful a tool we can create using this modest judgment capability.

Relative plausibility judgments are not just easier to make than absolute ones; they are usually more refined as well. When we can reliably give absolute plausibilities, they are typically very crude. The scale we use has four or five divisions: certain, very plausible, 50/50, not very plausible, and surely false:

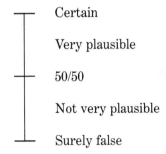

Occasionally we can be a bit more precise than this, but not often. Even a statistician's numbers, when applied to everyday events, are usually best rounded off to these categories. But using relative plausibility judgments, one at a time, we can often produce among the rivals a ranking with several more distinctions than this. Or we may find many levels of relative plausibility but not be able to fit them on the above scale at all.

As a consequence of all this, our basic evaluative procedure will be *comparative*. It will not directly yield degrees of strength, but just some sort of ranking among the rivals. We will often be able to find the *best* answer to the implicit question while remaining uncertain of how good that answer is.

But this is not a drawback. It is simply a consequence of the way human skills engage the world. Moreover, in many cases the best bet is precisely what we want. We realize information is limited, but we must make a decision and wisely look for the best among uncertain alternatives. Most tough decisions are like this: which school to attend, job to take, car to buy, investment to make. Should I go into the service, join the Peace Corps, or go to law school? The major decisions in life are made with a fragmentary and impressionistic grasp of the relevant data. All we can do is the best we can do—that is, make relative plausibility judgments, not absolute ones.

Even when we do make firm absolute plausibility judgments, the investigations we employ in reaching them are *based on* relative plausibility judgments. We begin with uncertain best bets and refine the list by gathering more information on *them*. We need guidance on which leads to run down, because there are always too many possibilities. Guidance is provided by our relative rankings. This is simply a principle of experimental procedure in science: Design the experiment to test the most plausible alternatives first. It is silly to check out the alien teleportation thesis before looking at larceny and memory failure. In this way we can build absolute plausibility judgments out of relative ones by gradually raising difficulties for the competition, by gradually making escape less and less plausible. But the relative judgments are basic: They underpin the process.

We should now have a better grip on this "matter of degree." And part of this is an improved understanding of how inductive arguments can be valuable even when link-strength is not great: Even weak inductive arguments provide rational guidance when information is limited. If we must act on sketchy data, they give us best bets. If we gather more data, they guide the process. These are just two aspects of the same thing. Typically, we begin investigations with only limited information. We determine the best-looking rivals simply so that we may know what to do next, what data to gather. This is true even when the entire collection of serious rivals together does not constitute a very good bet. We often begin with clues and hunches. But they are enough to give the procedure direction, to distinguish reasonable beginnings from the infinite possibilities. Relative judgments are all we need to begin.

LEANING ON THE WORLD

A moment's reflection on any strong inductive link will reveal how dependent its strength is on much that is outside the argument, on things we (reasonably) take for granted. In the argument about the eraser-shaped mark, for example, that strong link would be weakened if chalk dust did not readily jar loose from erasers struck against a solid surface; it would be eroded severely if the dust, once jarred loose, did not mostly stick to the board but rather fell into the chalk tray. An indefinitely large collection of facts about the world—some simple, some grand—bear like this on the strength of every inductive argument.

The question naturally arises, "How can we get away with leaving things out of the argument that are clearly relevant to its strength?" Why don't we include everything? How do we distinguish the explicit support from what we take for granted? This is a basic, common, and understandable worry, but one we can easily remove by looking at the practical features of our reasoning.

First, we obviously cannot include everything that is relevant because there is an infinite amount of it. All the properties of chalk and chalkboards, shockwaves, atmospheric viscosity and turbulence, local seismic stability and temperature variations, and uncountable other things bear on the connection between what I did with the eraser and how the mark got on the board. If we had to write everything down, we couldn't use inductive arguments. Fortunately we don't have to write it all down. We do actually, rightly, understand much about how the world works. The boring commonplaces we count on as we lead our lives really are boring commonplaces. Grass is green; when you trip you fall down and not up; it hurts to be run over by a bus; every room in the house seems to have air in it. There are billions of things like this that we seldom need even to mention, much less write down in an argument. The obvious, stable regularities of the world that allow us to make our way about are the sorts of things inductive arguments take for granted. The rule is this: Mention only important, useful things in the support—omit the boring parts.

None of this means that any specific thing must always remain unstated, that any particular fact is always boring. What will be useful to mention will vary from context to context. Include in the support anything you have reason to draw attention to. If your audience knows nothing of automobiles, you will have to add something to the "sputtering car" argument of Chapter 2 about the engine's dependence on finite injections of fuel. Schematizations are paraphrases. Their major function is to emphasize what is important, to make it stand out against the background of boring detail that is reasonably taken for granted. If you can paraphrase, you can make the distinctions necessary to get inductive arguments started.

From all this it is easy to see how deeply our evaluation of inductive arguments depends on our range of understanding of how the world works. This means, of course, that each of us will be able to evaluate the arguments better on some topics (when we have a lot of experience) than on others (when we do not). But we do already have a lot of experience, and we know how to find out more if we need to. A general understanding of how the things in our environment work is something we all achieve naturally, because it is closely linked to our survival. Our ability to understand is one of our better skills. And this is why inductive arguments play such an immense role in our reasoning.

KINDS OF INDUCTION

Recall that the basic distinction in our argument taxonomy is between induction and deduction. Deductive arguments form a rather neat category, defined by the way we evaluate them. Inductive argument, by contrast, is a broad, amorphous, catch-all category: everything else. We have been able to say a few things about the whole category, but to go any farther we will have to make some distinctions within it. As we distinguish different *kinds* of inductive arguments, patterns will begin to emerge that will make it easier to comprehend this whole category of arguments. Complicating our taxonomy will enable us to see better how our understanding functions in our reasoning.

DIAGNOSTIC SKILL

Our understanding of "the way things work" is best, most sure-footed, when it concerns the perception of the ordinary objects and events of our everyday lives. We have a pretty good grasp of what is going on around us through both our direct observation of things and our more general understanding of how things work behind those direct observations. We are at our best in simply *recognizing* the things that pass before us in the course of our lives—the colors, shapes, sizes, sequences, and types of things we see, hear, taste, feel, and smell. We know people, houses, cars, and cows when we see them; can distinguish music from highway noise; can tell a bad cold from a good night's sleep. In basic but crucial ways, we are very good at recognizing what is going on around us. If we confine our attention to arguments in which we use this skill, we know ahead of time that we will find there the strongest inductive arguments money can buy.

We can call these "diagnostic inductive arguments," because our skill here is in *diagnosis*, in telling what's going on. The central skill is, of course, simple perception—seeing, hearing, etc.—in which we in some sense directly confront what's going on and "read it off." The skill is simply recognizing houses, trees, people, and the like. But often we are just as good at telling what happened even though we were not there to see it. We can tell by the puddles that it rained, tell by the broken screen that your brother forgot the housekey again. This skill is not perceptual so much as generally diagnostic. This more general skill, which *includes* direct perception but is not limited to it, will ground diagnostic induction.

DIAGNOSTIC FORM

A useful, rough and ready way to identify an argument as diagnostic is to look at its *implicit question* (I.Q.). Is it asking for something that might be called a diagnosis? The most general diagnostic questions are "What's going on?" "What happened?" "What was that?" More specific derivatives would be "What caused that?" "Who did it?" "Why did this happen?" and the like. Inductive arguments with I.Q.s like these are the typical diagnostic arguments we will examine in this chapter. This is enough to get us started; we will refine the criteria as we go along.

It should now be obvious that many of the arguments we discussed in Chapter 2 are diagnostic. The I.Q. of the sputtering car argument was "What caused the car to stop?" And of the eraser-shaped mark we were asking "What made the mark?" (a version of "What caused this?"). In either case we could have fallen back on "What's going on here?", perhaps the most diagnostic-sounding of all the diagnostic I.Q.s.

What sort of I.Q. is not diagnostic, then? Besides the usually trivial "Is C true?", which has only two answers and hence is largely unhelpful, "diagnostic" contrasts with two other basic kinds of I.Q.

"What will happen?" requests a prediction, and "What should we (or I) do?" requests a recommendation. Either of these may involve a diagnosis as part of the argument, but each requires something beyond plain diagnostic recognition. So treating arguments for recommendations and predictions is better left until we have mastered the easier diagnostic ones. It should now be clear that some of the arguments we looked at in Chapter 1 are *not* diagnostic. The introductory argument concerns the government's inflation forecast and is accordingly predictive; the bottle-bill case and the DMV example concern recommendations. (To practice making this distinction, re-read the arguments offered as exercises at the ends of the last two chapters and see if you can confidently identify the diagnostic ones.)

A second important feature of diagnostic arguments flows directly from the first. If the underlying question always has the form "What's going on?" or "What happened here?", then the answers will have to tell, or perhaps just sketch, a story about what went on. So, for diagnostic arguments, the rival conclusions will all be EXPLANATIONS of a certain sort. They will all attempt to explain what is going on or what happened. This is enormously important because explanations are the natural expression of our *understanding*, which is precisely the recognition skill we wish to exploit here. Diagnostic arguments register our understanding of the various possibilities in a list of RIVAL EXPLANATIONS.

The air-crash example we discussed in the last chapter illustrates all this in some detail. The implicit question could be "What happened?" or perhaps "What caused the (first) plane to crash?" The first list of rivals gives very general explanation sketches, perhaps just explanation categories. Pilot error, mechanical failure, turbulence, collision: These are the most general propositions we might reasonably call "rival explanations" of the crash. Increasingly specific rivals give greater and greater explanatory detail. Airframe failure due to an explosion in the baggage compartment, for example, or control surface damage due to a collision with a light blue Cessna. Every list of rival conclusions in that case is a list of rival explanations of what happened there. Rival explanations will consequently have all the properties and uses that we found rival conclusions to have. Most important, they will be mutually incompatible, not overlapping.

We are now in a position to create the first piece of our evaluative apparatus, take our first step toward saying *how good* an inductive argument is. We do this by simply applying our skill in making relative plausibility judgments to the list of rivals generated by an argument's implicit question. Applying this skill will allow us to rank the list of rival explanations in the order of their plausibility. We will use the expression PLAUSIBILITY RANKING to refer to this ordered list.

We begin with an argument and an *un*ordered list of rivals:

$$
\begin{array}{ll}
S_1 & \qquad C_1 \\
S_2 & \qquad C_2 \\
S_3 & \qquad C_3 \\
\overline{\qquad\qquad}\; d^1 & \qquad C_4 \\
\qquad ? & \qquad C_5 \\
& \qquad C_6
\end{array}
$$

Our relative plausibility judgment then provides the list with its order. We simply appeal to our understanding to rank the rivals from most plausible, through less plausible, to, perhaps, wholly incredible. Where our understanding is good, the ranking will be as objective as our best perceptions. Perhaps it will look like this:

$$
\begin{array}{c}
C_4 \\
C_1 \\
C_5 \\
C_3 \\
C_2 \\
C_6
\end{array}
$$

This order would say that C_4 is more plausible than C_1, C_1 more plausible than C_5, and so on. But we might not be able to discriminate clearly among all of them; there may be ties in the ranking:

$$
\begin{array}{c}
C_4 \\
C_1 \; C_5 \\
C_3 \\
C_2 \; C_6
\end{array}
$$

Here we would be saying that, on our current understanding, C_1 and C_5 are equally plausible and cannot be confidently distinguished (similarly for C_2 and C_6, of course).

---

[1]A lowercase "d" will be used to indicate that an inductive argument is diagnostic, when that fact is important.

To illustrate both this procedure and our competence in a hypo-
thetical case, consider a fictitious Joe Smith who leaves the New
England coast in a rowboat with the goal of rowing across the
Atlantic to Europe. A week later a violent storm crosses his planned
course, and a few days later his boat is discovered, intact but empty,
about a hundred miles from the mentioned intersection. What happened to Joe? This question serves to organize a diagnostic inductive
argument around the very general evidence just offered. The rival
conclusions would be the different things that might have happened
to Joe, a useful cross-section of which are listed below:

S_1 Joe Smith left New England in a rowboat on a course for
      Europe.

S_2 A week later a storm intersected his course.

S_3 A few days later his boat was found, empty, near that point of
      intersection.

_____ d

C   ?

Rivals

C_1 Joe fell out of the boat and swam to shore.

C_2 Joe is out there somewhere treading water.

C_3 Joe drowned in the storm.

C_4 Joe rendezvoused with a Soviet submarine on an espionage
      mission.

C_5 Joe was picked up by a passing ship.

C_6 Joe was rescued by aliens in a flying saucer and is now living on
      Mars.

Based on what we know so far, the plausibility ranking would be

$$C_3$$
$$C_5$$
$$C_4$$
$$C_1 \quad C_2$$
$$C_6$$

or, perhaps,

$$
\begin{array}{ccc}
 & C_3 & \\
 & C_5 & \\
C_1 & C_2 & C_4 \\
 & C_6 &
\end{array}
$$

It is pretty clear that drowning is most plausible, Martians least, and the others somewhere in between. We could all agree on this much at least.

When we have an argument with one rival clearly at the top of the plausibility ranking, we can say the same thing we did in our discussion of intelligibility criteria in Chapter 2. The supporting statements in such a case do in fact recommend one particular conclusion as the best answer to the implicit question. That is how we would read the schematization if the top rival were taken to be its conclusion. When an argument meets this condition, when its conclusion is the best of the rivals, we will call it "sound."

Sound Inductive Argument

$$
\begin{array}{ll}
\begin{array}{l}
S_1 \\
S_2 \\
S_3 \\
\hline
\quad\quad\quad d \\
C_3
\end{array}
&
\begin{array}{c}
\text{Ranking} \\
C_3 \\
C_5 \\
C_1 \ C_2 \ C_4 \\
C_6
\end{array}
\end{array}
$$

The Joe Smith rowboat argument is sound if we use the drowning rival as its conclusion.

NEW INFORMATION

Diagnostic inductive argument is often called "inference to the best explanation." When we understand how things work, we are diagnostically competent; and part of that competence is an ability to explain things, to judge the relative plausibility of various explanations. This use of our judgment gives us a plausibility ranking and, sometimes, a best explanation. But our diagnostic skill has another component, one that often plays an even larger role in our reasoning. Sometimes we know just what to go looking for that would *change* (or firm up) our plausibility estimates. We know what new information would have an impact on the plausibility ranking.

Call this component of our diagnostic skill "relevance judgment" (the other one, recall, is plausibility judgment). Relevance to what? You might say "relevant to the argument," but that is misleading because when you add new data you get a different argument. "Relevant to (answering) the implicit question" would be better. The best would be "relevant to the plausibility ranking." New information is relevant, in this sense, if it has any impact on the plausibility ranking. If it would change the order, break ties, increase the size of gaps and even subtler things, it is relevant. It would change our understanding of the particular case.

There are times, of course, when we are content to rank the rivals on the information we have and accept the result: the best bet. The first argument we create may be strong enough; or, if it is not, we may have no idea what to go looking for to make it better. Far more frequently, however, we know all kinds of things that would change our plausibility estimates, all kinds of information that would, if discovered, tip the balance from one rival to another. For the Coast Guard to report pulling an unconscious man from a swamped rowboat in the North Atlantic helps the rescue rival (C_5) in the Joe Smith argument. For his wife to get a letter from Moscow in Joe's handwriting helps the espionage rival.

We also have a good grasp of what is clearly not relevant. The weight of the Washington Monument, or the fact that most mountain ranges run north-south, would, by itself, have no impact on the ranking. Something might come up to connect such things with Joe's fate: Anything might be made relevant by weird circumstances. But it would *take* weird circumstances, something quite beyond our normal expectations. We are right to ignore outlandish suggestions until outlandish circumstances arise.

Our ability to judge relevance turns arguments into investigations. The first component of our diagnostic skill (plausibility judgment) gives us leads to chase down; this one directs the chase. The original context will set a problem (What happened to Joe Smith?) and give us an initial plausibility ranking (with leads to chase down at the top). New information will generate a series of arguments with different plausibility estimates. Sometimes the ranking will change; sometimes new rivals will appear; often old rivals will drop from serious consideration.

Investigation Pattern

Stage I

S_1
S_2
S_3
$=\!=\!=\!d$
C_3

Ranking

$\left.\begin{array}{l}C_3\\C_5\end{array}\right\}$ leads to chase down

$C_1\ C_2$

$\left.\begin{array}{l}C_4\\C_6\\ \cdot\\ \cdot\\ \cdot\end{array}\right\}$ not serious possibilities

Stage II

S_1
S_2
S_3
$\rightarrow S_4$
$=\!=\!=\!d$
C_5

Ranking

$\left.\begin{array}{l}C_5\\C_3\end{array}\right\}$

$C_1\ C_2$

$\left.\begin{array}{l}C_4\\C_6\end{array}\right\}$

Stage III

S_1
S_2
S_3
S_4
$\rightarrow S_5$
$=\!=\!=\!d$
C_5

Ranking

C_5

$\left.\begin{array}{l}C_3\\C_1\\C_2\\C_4\\C_6\end{array}\right\}$

Stage IV

S_1
S_2
S_3
S_4
S_5
$\rightarrow S_6$
$=\!=\!=\!d$
C_5

Ranking

C_5

$\left.\begin{array}{l}C_3\\C_1\\C_2\\C_4\\C_6\end{array}\right\}$

The new information that a Coast Guard cutter has pulled an unconscious man from a swamped rowboat near the point where Joe's boat is later discovered creates a Stage II argument with C_5 (rescue) at the top of the plausibility ranking. It still might have been somebody else, but Joe is a decent bet. If Joe's wife then meets the cutter when it docks, and identifies Joe, everything but C_5 falls from serious consideration in Stage III. The argument for C_5 is not just sound, it is strong when the wife's identification is added. And it can be made stronger still. If the rescued man recovers consciousness and talks convincingly with friends and relatives about intimate details of their past, from Joe's idiosyncratic perspective, Stage IV is overwhelmed with relevant data. The case is closed.

This is how we turn relative plausibility judgments into absolute ones, weak inductive arguments into strong ones. But it is also an important insight into the nature of diagnostic argument. Diagnostic inductive arguments are always, at least potentially, part of the dynamic process of investigation and discovery. They are what you get when an investigation pauses to evaluate its progress. But for us it is more important to notice that diagnostic inductive arguments also *start* investigations. When the evidence is unclear or controversial, one thing to do is *go get more*. Knowing what to get is part of our diagnostic skill.

LUMPING AND SPLITTING AGAIN

As we gain information we will naturally want to split up the rivals in the way set out in Chapter 2. The lead we chase down will not be simply "rescue by a passing ship," but "rescue by a particular Coast Guard cutter." We will be down at the dock waiting for this particular boat, not boats in general. So, as we did in the last chapter, we may simply replace C_5 with this new, more specific C_5'. But we may wish to keep the more general rival, simply removing the particular one from it. We will have to make some adjustments to maintain mutual exclusiveness while pursuing our interest. As a result, the Stage II rankings will probably look like B or C below, not A.

Stage II

S_1 Joe Smith left New England in a rowboat on a course for Europe.

S_2 A week later a storm intersected his course.

S_3 A few days later his boat was found, empty, near that point of intersection.

S_4 A Coast Guard cutter reported pulling an unconscious man from a swamped rowboat near the point where Joe's boat was found a few days later.

=== d

Ranking

A	B	C
C_5	C_5' (cutter)	C_5' (cutter)
C_3	C_3	C_3
C_1, C_2, C_4	C_1, C_2, C_3	C_5 (some other passing ship)
C_6	C_6	C_1, C_2, C_3
		C_6

Each of these rankings is right in its way: Each gives a different aspect of S_4's impact on the previous ranking. Which one you will use depends on your interest at the time. Usually it will be closer to B or C.

EXPLANATION

We may articulate our diagnostic judgment in a helpful way if we recall that diagnostic rivals are rival *explanations*. When we judge the rivals to be more or less plausible, we are estimating how well or badly they explain what happened, or what is going on, given what we know about it. In areas of our competence, our understanding of how things work shows up as a skill for estimating explanatoriness. We judge how easy (or hard) it is for the various rivals to explain what went on, against the background of our understanding. My familiarity with cars—especially *my* car—tells me that being out of gas explains the vehicle's sputtering to a stop, with the telltale gas gauge reading, more easily than does an exotic electrical failure. It would be silly not to chase the gasoline lead first.

We try to fit the different rivals in with everything else we know about the subject. This is why diagnostic rivals so easily become *stories*: The stories do the fitting. On the initial data in Joe Smith's case, the espionage story just does not fit as well with what we know as drowning or even innocent rescue does. Drowning, unfortunately, explains Joe's disappearance most easily.

Judging relevance employs exactly the same skill. The arrival of a letter from Moscow in Joe's handwriting has an impact on the plausibility ranking precisely because it is easier to explain on one rival than on the others. The espionage rival explains it easily; naturally, it is much tougher to explain on the drowning rival or any of the others. The idiom we often use in such a case is "explain away." The drowning rival would have to explain away the letter by telling some story about its being a hoax or a coincidence. This story then becomes part of the drowning rival, which lowers its plausibility somewhat, unless and until some new information surfaces that can prop up the story. Being harder or easier to explain is one way new information can change the plausibility ranking.

But it can change it in another way too. Were we to find that Joe worked for a sensitive defense industry, had recently stolen some classified material, and had had extensive secret correspondence with the KGB, that too would be relevant. It would have clear impact on the plausibility ranking; but its impact would take an entirely different form. This new information is not something for the rivals to explain (or explain away). They need say nothing about why he worked where he did or how he got involved with the KGB. People in touch with the KGB can drown like anybody else; no special story needs to be told. No, the relevance of all this background on Joe lies in the fact that *it makes the original data easier to explain* on the espionage rival. It alters our understanding and allows us to see that an otherwise outlandish explanation is, in this particular case, not so outlandish. The ranking has been shaken up—and once again by explanatory relations. Not because there is anything new to explain, however, but because we have a new appreciation of what is available to do the explaining.

TRACES

These two ways in which data may be relevant to a plausibility ranking apply to the original evidence too, not just to new information. The original data may either be explained itself or just help to explain something else. So we may speak of there being, in general, two different *kinds* of evidence, two different kinds of support in diagnostic inductive arguments. This distinction will provide the final important feature of diagnostic form.

The best way to make the distinction between kinds of evidence is to focus on one particular diagnostic question; generalizing to the others will be easy once the point is developed. Perhaps "What happened?" is most representative. A diagnostic argument with this implicit question will naturally begin with information suggesting (even dramatically) that something did happen. A swamped row-boat, a sputtering car, an empty cash drawer, a streak through the sky—something like one of these will raise the question "What happened?" Such an occurrence or object suggests that something happened because it appears to be *part* of the "happening," an *aspect* or *consequence* of whatever happened: evidence of something beyond itself. It is natural to call these things "trace data": They are traces left by something we want to find out more about.

If we now recall that the rivals here are explanations, attempts to explain what happened, it will be clear that the traces are something the rivals will try to explain. In explaining what happened, the respective rivals will inevitably explain why the boat was swamped and empty, why the car sputtered to a stop, what happened to the money, and what caused that streak in the sky. Trace data are something for the rivals to explain.

Not all diagnostic support is like this, however, as we saw in the last section. Some support will just be useful, relevant background that helps in the explaining but does not itself get explained by the rivals. In Joe's case, the rivals will not explain why the Atlantic was stormy, even though the storm is clearly relevant to ranking the rivals. A robber's motive is clearly relevant to his rank among the suspects; but to understand his plausibility as a suspect we need not explain *why* he has that motive: We need only know that he has it. His motive is not a trace as the empty cash drawer was.

Traces always involve explanation *by* the rivals; but the best way to express the relation will vary from application to application. Sometimes it will be clear enough to say that a bit of trace is something the rivals are trying to explain (empty rowboat). Sometimes it will be weaker than this: A trace will be explained naturally as part of the story if it is important enough to be pursued (exact location of the rowboat). Sometimes it will be stronger: A trace will be something the rivals *must* explain if they are to be taken seriously (letter from Moscow). And some rivals will try to explain the trace away, by adding an adjunct story, rather than taking it on directly. So in general all we can say is that traces are whatever gets involved in explanation by the rivals in one or another of these ways. Other information that is not a trace may be a relevant part of the argument by playing a background role in the explanatory process. Non-trace data become relevant to the plausibility ranking when they help (or hurt) another rival in their attempt to account for the traces.

With this understanding we may now give a more specific characterization of diagnostic inductive arguments: They are *arguments containing trace data.* Any argument offering data for rival conclusions to explain will be diagnostic. This is a stronger criterion than the I.Q. plus rival explanations together, for whenever it is met the other two will be also, but not the reverse.

Typical diagnostic arguments will have support of both trace and non-trace kinds, of course; and the trace data can come in any of its various explanatory forms. The Baker Lake fireball investigation, for example, eventually produced an argument schematizable as follows.[2]

---

[2]This schematization does not comport perfectly with the one given at the end of Chapter 2. The changes are minor and help illustrate the issues of this section.

S_1 On the evening of January 24, 1978, a fireball lit up the sky over Baker Lake in the northern reaches of Canada.

S_2 For weeks, tracking stations had been reporting that a Soviet satellite was in a dangerously low orbit.

S_3 Radio contact with the satellite was lost the evening the fireball was sighted.

S_4 The satellite was due to pass over northern Canada, from west to east, at about the time the fireball was sighted.

S_5 The fireball traveled from west to east.

S_6 Fireballs are typical of satellites re-entering the earth's atmosphere.

S_7 Radioactive debris of plausibly human fabrication was found poking out of a crater in the ice of a frozen river.

S_8 The river was east of Baker Lake.

S_9 The Soviets reported that the satellite in S_2 was powered by a nuclear reactor.

═══ d

C   The fireball was the returning Soviet satellite.

The original natural rivals (meteorite, space debris, some other satellite, etc.) would be trying to account for the fireball: Why did the sky light up like it did? So S_1 would be trace data. And so would S_3. C would naturally explain loss of radio contact; the others would have to explain it away, perhaps with a story about radio failure. S_7 would have exactly the same status, except that stories about where the radioactive debris came from would be generally less plausible. S_5 (direction of the fireball) the rivals would *have* to account for, if they wanted to be taken seriously. It would be very central, strong, controlling trace data.

The rest of the support is naturally taken to be non-trace data, relevant not because it gets explained but because it helps one or another of the rivals explain the traces. In this case they all (S_2, S_4, S_6, S_8, and S_9) help C account for the trace data that the investigation turned up. S_2 and S_6 make the satellite story antecedently plausible; S_4 helps C explain the location and direction of the fireball, S_8 the location of the debris, and S_9 its radioactivity.

INVESTIGATIONS:
EVOLUTION IN UNDERSTANDING

When we add information to a diagnostic argument, creating a series of arguments on the same topic, the most common result is happy, rapid convergence on a best rival and the rapid drop from serious consideration of all the rest. We find the watch where we now remember leaving it, recover Joe Smith's body, identify the radioactive debris as Soviet. Yet because successful, rapidly converging investigations are so much a part of our lives, they draw little notice. We naturally neglect them in favor of the much rarer intractable or inconclusive ones that fascinate us, perhaps frighten us, simply because they do not fall in line effortlessly. Our understandable, very practical, preoccupation with the tough cases may therefore mislead us about the quality of our reasoning skills. In the tough cases our memory of events is filled with confusion and inconclusiveness. We forget that the vast majority of our reasoning *is* effortlessly successful, undeniably competent if not very interesting. Tough cases are attention-grabbing—maybe a little scary—just because they contrast so boldly with our usual experience and disturb our usual competence.

It is worth bearing all this in mind as we examine diagnostic arguments in the worst of circumstances. When we start off on the wrong foot, badly misunderstand what is going on, or encounter a genuinely weird case, we can make sense of it in the same way, can mobilize the same apparatus—only progress is slower. How fast we converge on an answer depends on how far it lies from our original understanding.

In general, when we add new information to an argument and alter the plausibility ranking, we change our understanding of the matter, a little or a lot. The new information may just firm up our old understanding, as discovering Joe Smith's body would. We were pretty sure he had drowned; now we know. But adding information can shake things up too, turn the barely possible into a live consideration. The letter from Moscow in Joe's handwriting would do just this: make us suddenly take seriously something we had previously dismissed as outlandish.

The further new discoveries depart from normal expectations the more our understanding of the case will change. And a discovery may completely scramble our original picture of what happened; every aspect of the schematization and diagnostic apparatus is open for modification as the result of such changes. We have already examined investigations that have forced us to relax an implicit question. What looked like an air crash stopped looking so much like one, so we had to stop asking "What caused the crash?" and try "What made this mess?" But the changes can go far deeper. Data that originally seemed to be traces of a single event may, on further study, turn out to be unrelated. If the Baker Lake investigation had gone differently, and the suspect Soviet satellite had begun broadcasting from orbit again the week after the fireball was sighted, our view of the radioactive debris sticking out of the river ice would be radically altered. If no other satellite candidate was uncovered, the debris and the fireball would begin to look like traces of different things. What looked like central trace data in the fireball investigation could be made irrelevant by new information.

When a trace loses its relevance, so ordinarily does the background information that serves it. If the satellite ceases to be a serious rival account of the fireball, then all the background on its orbit and recent history can be omitted from the support, too. Of course, it is always possible that data losing its original relevance can gain it back from a new quarter. A freak coincidence can provide a new rationale for keeping it in the argument. Were the Soviet satellite to record a close brush with a meteorite on the evening in question, for example, its orbit would suddenly become relevant to the meteorite rival. That information could make the orbit relevant as long as the meteorite was a live possibility. Without a new rationale such as this, however, the background on the Soviet satellite would fade into irrelevance with our new understanding of what happened.

DIAGNOSTIC COMPOUNDING

It should be clear that the information gathered in an investigation can itself result from subsidiary diagnostic investigations. This is especially true when we're educating ourselves about relevant background, but it can apply to traces too, depending on how we wish to characterize them. When we say that a reactor-powered satellite was due to pass over northern Canada on a certain evening, we may do so as the result of considerable weighing of evidence, considerable diagnostic rumination. So it will occasionally be important to represent a diagnostic investigation as a sequence of *compound* arguments, rather than simple ones.

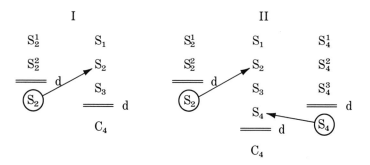

And sometimes the secondary arguments, the diagnostic tributaries, will require more of our attention than the main branch does.

Establishing that Joe Smith was actually in contact with the KGB might be the trickiest part of the rowboat investigation. We may have nothing very direct—just unusual radio equipment, strange patterns of behavior, missing documents, and the like. But these may be treated as trace data in a tributary diagnostic argument, and we may conclude that the best explanation of those traces is that Joe was in contact with the KGB. This item may now become part of the main branch in support of the submarine rendezvous rival.

Similarly for trace data. Simply identifying the retrieved rowboat as Joe's can be a diagnostic investigation. The boat might have characteristic markings, color, fabrication, or defects (all traces). And these, together with Joe's well-publicized travel plans (background), form a model diagnostic induction. Prime conclusion: The boat is Joe's.

DETAILED ILLUSTRATION

The value of the apparatus introduced in this chapter lies in its organizing the application of our diagnostic skills. In focusing our understanding of how things work to answer specific questions, we are able to weigh the evidence for competing conclusions. To see the scope and power of this way of organizing things, let us apply the apparatus to a more complicated and arcane case. Let's consider an event about which our information is sketchy and our background not very good and monitor how the procedure gradually refines our perception of the event, develops our understanding of what happened.

A useful example is the sinking of the *Titanic*. Recent exploration of the sea bottom off Newfoundland has focused attention on that event in just the right way for this study. Interested lay-spectators all had somewhat the same idea about what the search team was looking for: a nearly 900-foot-long, four-funnelled, steel ship, possibly still upright, perhaps resting on its side, undoubtedly corroded and banged up, but recognizable. This common perception is partly due to a naive but serviceable picture of what happens when a ship sinks. Derived from experiences with toys in the bathtub and accessible wrecks like the *Andrea Doria*, the simple story of the *Titanic* angling gracefully toward the bottom and settling, uncomfortably, into the mud is not a stupid one. And it is easily refined. So let us use it to begin a diagnostic investigation.

The event being investigated is the *Titanic*'s more than two-mile dive to the bottom of the Atlantic. The question is "What was the trip like?" "What happened to the *Titanic* after it slipped from sight?" The "naive" account is one rival story, but many others are easily imaginable. The ship may have landed upside down, tumbled down a steep underwater slope, disappeared into a giant crevasse, or been carried off by a complicated iceberg. We may use the casual spectators' impressions to form Stage I of an investigation.

Stage I

S_1 The liner *Titanic* struck an iceberg and sank, nose first, in a part of the North Atlantic about two and a half miles deep.

S_2 It disappeared from view at a surprisingly steep angle.

$\overline{}$ d?

C_1 The ship sank gracefully to the bottom, nose first, leaving behind unsecured objects on exposed decks and suffering some structural damage on impact with the sea floor, but settling upright.

Rival Conclusions

(Same general story, except that the ship . . .)

C_2 Landed upside down.

C_3 Tumbled down a slope.

C_4 Fell into a crevasse.

.
.
.

The question mark after the small *d* above signals that the argument is diagnostic only in the weaker of the two senses we distinguished. It has a diagnostic I.Q. and diagnostic rivals, but there are no traces for the rival stories to explain. Yet. It clearly hints at possible traces and thus makes a perfectly good starting point for a diagnostic investigation.

Venerable but unpublicized information, including our first bit of trace data, will move us toward Stage II. As the *Titanic* slid below the surface, survivors in nearby lifeboats reported hearing an incredible crashing noise, like metallic thunder, coming from the direction of the disappearing ship. (This, as part of the event, is something for the rivals to explain: a trace.) Some who knew details of the *Titanic*'s design speculated that the noise came from ninety-ton boilers tearing from their mounts and tumbling out through the bow as the stern heaved high in the air before plunging out of sight. See the drawing below.

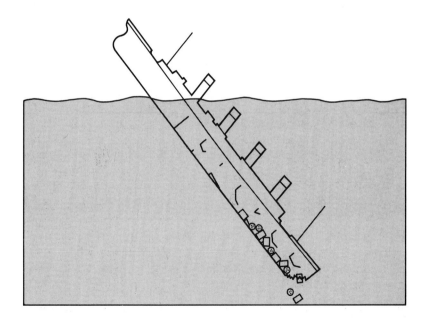

This speculation is clearly not intended to be part of any of the Stage I rivals, so we could simply develop it as a separate rival account (C_5), with the understanding that none of the others be read as involving the business with the boilers. But there is a more helpful strategy. Since the ship could go on to do the things mentioned in C_1, C_2, etc., after jettisoning its boilers, we might split this new rival into a parallel series. C_{1b} would be "settled gracefully into the mud, right side up, after jettisoning boilers through the bow." And so forth.

Stories could also be easily added to the original rivals to help them account for the metallic thunder. The boilers could tumble around inside the hull and *not* come out, for instance. It would not be so implausible to think that even massive boilers might be slowed by the forward bulkheads braced by water-filled compartments. See the drawing below.

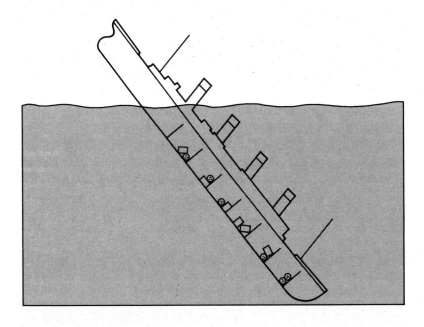

We might mark these additions by putting the subscript a next to the original conclusions: C_{1a}, C_{2a}, etc. So Stage II would look something like this:

Stage II

S_1 The liner *Titanic* struck an iceberg and sank, nose first, in a part of the North Atlantic about two and a half miles deep.

S_2 It disappeared from view at a surprisingly steep angle.

S_3 The ship's engines were powered by twenty-nine boilers, weighing ninety tons each.

S_4 Observers on the surface reported a tremendous metallic clangor coming from the ship as it sank.

$$================================== \text{d}$$

C_{1a} ?

C_{1a} still seems most plausible, but the thought of internal catastrophe so disturbs the naive model of a ship's sinking that our judgment of link-strength is weaker than before. Many new possibilities now seem live. If the shape of the bow is substantially disturbed by objects coming out through the steel plates, the picture of graceful descent becomes less compelling. It is less clear now what to expect of the exploration, but our education is progressing.

First visual contact with the wreck, seventy-some years later, reveals the liner in two pieces, a considerable distance apart, on a placid expanse of mud plain. The larger, bow half, is found upright and relatively intact. This provides immensely significant new trace data, as well as background about the sea floor that is nearly as important. (Check to make sure you know which is which.) Given the location, none of the graceful-descent stories can plausibly account for the great separation of the pieces. The ship had to have broken up long before it hit bottom. This devastates our earlier picture and drops those stories from serious consideration. Plausible accounts now must be of rending trauma and pre-trauma agonies, possibly beginning at the surface.

Two plausible mechanisms of rupture give somewhat different trips to the bottom. The liner might have broken up at the surface if the hull was not strong enough to support the stern when lifted entirely clear of the ocean by the water-laden bow. On the other hand, if the *Titanic* was intact when it disappeared below the surface, the immense pressure of the sea, even at modest depths, might crush the long, flat sides amidships if much air were trapped inside. Before the stern had completely disappeared, pressure on the flanks would have reached ten tons per square foot.

Breakup at the surface would make the image of rolling boilers far less clear. But the breakup itself, without the boilers, would doubtless have been noisy enough to account for reports of metallic thunder. So we would probably want to seriously consider only three rival stories at this stage.

C_6 Ship broke up at surface, its bow angling down steeply, shedding loose objects from exposed decks and severed hull; stern and debris settled more or less vertically.

C_7 Ship sank intact, boilers rolling out through bow; pressure then broke hull in two—rest of story like C_6.

C_8 Ship sank intact, boilers rolling around inside; rest of story like C_7.

The support picture would look like this:

Stage III

S_1 The liner *Titanic* struck an iceberg and sank, nose first, in a part of the North Atlantic about two and a half miles deep.

S_2 It disappeared from view at a surprisingly steep angle.

S_3 The ship's engines were powered by twenty-nine boilers, weighing ninety tons each.

S_4 Observers on the surface reported a tremendous metallic clangor coming from the ship as it sank.

S_5 The *Titanic* was found in two major pieces, both upright, about a third of a mile apart, on a large plain of sediment.

=== d

?

Given the information at Stage III, it would be hard for us (that is, nonexperts) to distinguish among the three stories.

When the wreck was explored more fully the following year, new traces helped rank the rival stories. Virtually all of the debris was clustered around the stern, including the few visible boilers. The bow, much of which was visible above the sediment, was intact except for the point of contact with the iceberg, where the plates were still bent inward (N.B.). These traces practically eliminate C_7, leaving C_6 and a version of C_8 in which rupture occurs very near the surface. Since this revised version of C_8 requires a relatively (!) low-pressure collapse of the hull, it leaves C_7 as at least slightly more plausible. (Write out Stage IV as an exercise.)

To further separate (or reverse) these rivals would require us to learn more about the forces involved, but we are now armed with some specific questions that will make research efficient. How much bending should the hull have been able to withstand? Could much air have been trapped in the hull? How much pressure could the steel plate withstand? Answers to these questions would provide enormously helpful background education: non-trace data that might be enough to settle the matter. But further trace data could be useful too. Digging around in the sediment might reveal the order in which the debris was ejected, which might tell us just how the hull broke up. This would in turn make relevant further (background) data on the location of various objects within the ship.

We have now pursued this example far enough to sketch typical features of diagnostic investigation. The symbiotic interchange between trace and background displayed clearly here is the key characteristic of such investigations. Background helps us look for traces; traces indicate needed background, education. This interchange is what focuses a search, allows convergence on a single story. And we can begin with *divergence*. First results of investigation can, as here, merely vandalize our first picture without providing much help in finding a substitute. It can be some time, in a tough case, before we regain the certainty of our original perception.

ARTICULATION

The goal of this chapter has been to better understand one of our basic skills, to come to see in some detail just what we do when we evaluate evidence in the best, clearest cases. Of course, the aim has been not only to understand what we do, but to firm and extend its application as well. The hope has been, in part, that our better understanding might naturally lead us to see other good uses of the same skills and procedures.

A third and thus far neglected aim has been to help us become more articulate about our reasoning. The apparatus of this chapter should help us *explain*, to others and sometimes ourselves, *why* we reason as we do. It should help us make our reasoning clear even when it does not need improving. This aim has lurked just below the surface of the discussion and doubtless has been partly achieved. But we are now in a position to address it directly and so complete our general discussion of diagnostic induction.

Trace Data

Isolating trace data streamlines our articulation by giving us a way to refer to everything we are trying to explain, provides a handy way to express our judgment of soundness. If we think the argument is sound with C_5 as its conclusion, we do so because

C_5 is the best account of the trace data.

If we wish, we may qualify this understanding by referring to the other support.

C_5 is the best account, given what we know.
or
. . . all things considered.
or
. . . given what we have recently discovered.

We may similarly explain the impact of a specific trace on the plausibility ranking.

S_4 elevates C_5 because C_5 explains S_4 effortlessly, whereas S_4 represents a considerable hurdle for C_4.

This much is pretty straightforward and has been elaborately illustrated throughout Chapter 3. Articulating the role of the rest of the support—relevant information that is *not* trace data—is more difficult and complicated, however.

Non-Trace Data

Information not explained by the rivals is relevant to a diagnostic inquiry if it helps or hurts a rival in its attempt to explain the traces. So a statement articulating this role in a specific case would read something like this:

S_3 is relevant because it helps C_5 explain S4.

This formula is both rich and deceptively simple because "helps" covers so many possibilities.

The fact that the Russian satellite contained a nuclear reactor (S_9) helps the Russian-satellite rival (C) explain the radioactive debris (S_7). It shows how C could explain it. But "showing how" can be much more complex than this. When the scoop-arm of the *Viking I* Mars lander malfunctioned (see exercise 13 of Chapter 2), one rival account was that a pin had jammed the mechanism. The elaborate experiment on the simulator in Pasadena was performed simply to show how the pin rival could explain the trace data on Mars. In science this kind of "showing how" can involve teams of mathematicians and weeks of computation.

But helping a rival can also consist simply in removing (or lowering) a hurdle. We might have thought that the yellow marks on the fuselage constituted a hurdle for the collision-with-a-blue-Cessna rival. Not being able to explain the color of the marks lowered its ranking. But we may find out (S_{24}) that the jetliner was involved in a minor collision with a yellow plane on the ground some time before takeoff this morning. This "showing how" simply removes an obstacle: We may proceed on the presumption that the yellow marks are irrelevant to the crash.

Each of these "helps" has a parallel "hurt." Non-trace data may show that a rival *cannot* account for a certain trace, at least not without great difficulty. If the satellite's orbit was from east to west across Canada that evening, it is virtually impossible for the satellite to account for the fireball, which went in the opposite direction. And elaborate scientific calculations can show that a theory gives the wrong answer: The theory cannot account for the data as we have it.

These are some of the more common ways to articulate aspects of a diagnostic argument or inquiry. But we may use the resources of this chapter for even subtler articulations. If somebody does not understand why we take one thing to be a trace of another, we may explain it by supplying some background linking the two: *that background* is why we chose this explanation as best. I look out the window and see fresh oil drippings on the driveway. I infer that the garbage has already been collected. A friend wants to know why I infer this, why I take the drips to be a sign (trace) of garbage collection. I can explain it by filling her in on relevant background— for example, that I keep the driveway fastidiously clean and know there was no oil there last night; that the oil is in the exact place where the garbage truck was parked when my garbage was loaded into it; that the truck has leaked occasionally in the past; and perhaps that today is garbage day. Against this background my account of the trace seems quite plausible. I have explained why I take the oil to be a trace left by a garbage truck.

Articulating Our General Understanding of How Things Work

In explaining why we make the connections we do, why we see things the way we do, we very quickly reach the limit of our ability to articulate. We run out of helpful things to say. I can explain why I take the oil drips to be signs of a garbage truck, but I cannot say anything very helpful about how looking at the driveway reveals the drips to me. "I can tell drips when I see them. I'm good at that; trust me." In the normal course of our lives, explanation ends in un-analyzed perception. We get to our basic understanding and stop. And fortunately this is almost always good enough: Much of our basic understanding of things is broadly shared. We don't have to explain why we think the bulk in the next seat is a person or the fire truck is red. When someone does not follow us *here*, we may just be stuck. For we have no systematic way of talking about basic perceptions. If we have to explain them to somebody, we must *invent* ways of talking. We must fall back on our intellectual resources: lots of metaphor, imagination, and hope. Or we simply fail: "I don't know how I know, I just do."

All basic skills are like this: inarticulate. Walking, driving, or swinging a bat we simply learn how to do by watching and trying. The talk that accompanies learning (especially when it is done well) does not describe the skill or explain what to do so much as it hints and prods in certain directions. ("You're rushing your swing: You've got to wait on the ball." or "Don't start slowing down yet: You'll really confuse that poor guy waiting to turn left. You may even tempt him out in front of you.") At bottom you simply develop—develop balance in walking; develop a feel for clutch engagement and braking distances in driving; develop a swing, and a sense of when to start swinging, in batting a ball. Certainly we talk about these performances; but the talk usually demeans the performance (we're better than we can say). And we have no vocabulary at all to describe how we keep our balance or when to start swinging the bat.

So let us invent a little. Because philosophers are always wrestling with this sort of difficulty (articulating the inarticulable), they have developed a vocabulary we can exploit here and modify for our purpose. The key notion is that of a *disposition*. We will sometimes be able to articulate our understanding by appeal to what things are disposed to do in certain circumstances. We can usually specify the things, often even the circumstances. We just need to agree on a way to describe what they are disposed to do. This description is what sometimes requires effort and imagination. So let's begin with an easy example and work our way up.

Simple dispositions—and explanations based on them—are part of our normal conversation. (This is why they prove a useful resource.) Fragility, for example, is a dispositional concept. Part of our understanding of things is the realization that some objects are fragile, that they are disposed to break when treated roughly. Here we have all three elements in the equation. We can specify an object (glass statuette), circumstances (rough treatment), and a disposition to do something (shatter). Everybody understands these character- izations well enough for them to provide helpful explanations. It is easy for me to explain my gentle treatment of an object by appeal to this dispositional property of fragility. And it's easy even though what counts as "shattering" and what counts as "rough treatment" are not exhaustively (or even interestingly) specifiable in advance. We understand them well enough to understand what sort of special treatment is required and why.

The whole point of appealing to dispositions here is to give us a way to articulate things that are difficult to say anything about at all. We must resist the temptation to belittle them for not being able to say everything we would like them to. Dispositions allow us to express coarse but useful patterns in our complex and subtle under- standing of things. And this is a distinct improvement on the inar- ticulateness that often prevails otherwise.

Other features of dispositions also arise from their role in articu- lating subtle perceptions in complex circumstances. These features are also sometimes misperceived as flaws, weaknesses. One of the "flaws" is that dispositions allow exceptions. We've all dropped a genuinely fragile object and had it not break, due simply to luck of the fall. We thank our stars: We do not even think of bouncing the object again to see if it is *really* fragile. Part of our objective under- standing is the distinction between luck and misdiagnosis: Some- times we are effortlessly reliable at making this distinction. And that is what is captured by our using *fragile* dispositionally. We cannot say exactly which rough handling will break the vase and which will not. But we can say something coarse, dispositional, and *not* exact that is nevertheless objective and immensely useful: fragile.

We can, of course, discover that we were wrong in attributing a disposition—wrong, for instance, in thinking that the vase was fragile. But not just any failure to break would *show* we were wrong. To do that would take certain kinds of failure (such as the vase surviving serious attack with a hammer) or systematic failure (its surviving several different falls). The perseverance of dispositional attributes in the face of failure is not random or capricious. It is disciplined and selective. The patterns, though coarse, are clear and objective.

Putting the matter this way shows how deep a role diagnostic induction plays in our reasoning. For we may reconstruct the support for our dispositional picture as a diagnostic argument. The reason to say that the dispositions are there is that they are the best explanation of certain features of our experience.[3] Our experience with things like the vase is that they react to rough handling in a complex but systematically disappointing way. The best explanation of this experience is that those things have a property: a disposition to react in that way. We call it *fragility*.

But why call this an explanation? Isn't it too trivial to explain anything? These two questions are part of a natural reflex, but one we must resist. For how trenchant an explanation seems depends wholly on how hard it is to impart the understanding the explanation contains. And the understanding in our basic perception usually imparts itself without ever being formulated in explanation. So it seems trivial. But if articulating it is ever important, then it will *not* be trivial. Articulating our basic understanding will have the *form* of an explanation; and how explanatory it seems will depend on how useful it is at the moment. If we are stuck, it will seem brilliant.

Conversely, the strength of a diagnostic argument depends on how good, how plausible, how uncontroversial the best explanation is. If the explanation is so clear that it seems trivial, that yields the strongest possible argument: The evidence is conclusive.

Dispositional explanations are contrast-explanations,[4] and the contrast here is quite modest, of course. *Fragility* simply means that some property of the vase is involved in the pattern of breakage. The contrast is with all *extraneous* factors: someone lurking in the shadows, using inaudible shockwaves to break vases whenever I get the slightest bit rough, for example. That would account for the pattern too, but with little plausibility. *Fragility* merely says it is the vase's fault: No excuses are lurking in the shadows. If the vase were different in this respect the pattern would be too. Some objects have

---

[3]If you are following closely you will realize that dispositions will function as background in other diagnostic inferences. So what we are doing here can be viewed as constructing a diagnostic tributary supporting some non-trace data in other diagnostic arguments.

[4]It may be argued that all explanations have a contrast component. Dispositional ones may have nothing else.

it, some do not. For this we have overwhelming evidence: Some patterns demand one explanation, some demand another. We can be so certain in part because the claim is so modest. But such modesty does not diminish the value of the articulation.

We may actually schematize all this in diagnostic form. The patterns would be trace data, and much else would be relevant background (our ability to distinguish rough handling from gentle, for example, or to recognize objects as similar in relevant respects). So we might distinguish two general support claims:

S_1 Patterns of breakage in our experience with objects of a certain kind, appearance, or history.

S_2 General relevant background.

$$=== \quad d$$

C   Those objects are fragile.

Rival conclusions would be all the various (though implausible) ways in which the patterns might occur with objects that were not fragile. Coincidence, conspiracy, and incompetent identification of conditions would be examples.

Fragility is what we might call a passive disposition: The object is disposed to have something happen to it. But some things are disposed to more elaborate, more active behavior: wild animals to flee when approached, some tame ones to come when called. Our understanding of human personalities may be partly rendered as dispositions to respond one way or another to greetings, requests, demands, and various conversational gambits. "Oh, that's just Charlie: He always talks like that. What a sourpuss!"

Of course, he doesn't have to *always* talk like that (*always* is normally innocuous hyperbole here). Being a sourpuss can manifest itself selectively too, on particular occasions. And sourness can be an objective feature of our understanding of Charlie even if we cannot say much about what those occasions are. This is another feature of dispositions that makes them well suited to articulate patterns in the enormous complexity of our perception and our lives. We can reliably recognize all manner of things in conditions we cannot describe. And these recognitions may be used in explanation. Groping around in the pre-dawn darkness, for example, I know it takes special light for me to see whether the socks I have in my hand are dark blue or black. I cannot say much about what the light must be, but I will know it when I find it. Very minor changes in the light suddenly allow me to see that they are blue. I just move around until I can see it. We recognize personalities in somewhat the same way. Charlie doesn't have to be sour when asleep or eating or even always in conversation. We have some idea what brings out the episodes of sourness—can even expect them sometimes—but, like the light conditions, we need not specify them to make the diagnosis.

For a perfectly useful explanation, it is enough to make explicit two of the three dispositional elements—(1) the object and (2) what it is disposed to do—as long as the manifestations are systematic and recognizable. "If you move it around in the light you will eventually see the color" explains one aspect of your perceptual competence: articulates part of what you understand. We may similarly express our understanding of a person. "He'll always exaggerate the bad aspects if he has the opportunity." We might not be able to do more than give an example of "an opportunity," but that example would still usefully spell out a significant part of our understanding. The fact that it would be nice to have more detail should not dim our appreciation of what we have.

The objectivity of our understanding simply concerns getting it right: the socks and Charlie. And getting it right is a straightforwardly diagnostic maneuver. But doing so is not the issue here. Human beings are quite generally competent in perceptions of color and personality. The question here is what it would be like to articulate those perceptions.

Trace Data, Again

This excursion into dispositions has been aimed at deepening the level at which we can articulate our reasoning. We may appeal to a coarse-grained, dispositional rendering of our perception of things, for example, to explain why we take certain phenomena to be trace data: why we take them to be traces of what we do. Somebody, sitting on a bench just off the street, arises purposefully and casts an interested gaze up the street. I take this action to be trace data: evidence of an approaching bus. I can explain why, to those not sharing my perception, by providing background either on the circumstances (benches by curbs being typical of bus stops) or on what people waiting for buses are disposed to do as a bus approaches.

The first of these is easy because notions like "bench," "curb," and "street" naturally suggest themselves. The dispositional part is harder because characterizing the behavior in understandable ways takes some imagination. But once we have fallen on notions like "purposeful" and "interested," the explanation may proceed as in the easier case. For our common experience with people allows us to draw attention to features of human behavior in this way. A recognizable way of getting up and a familiar way of casting a gaze suggest a bus as the best explanation in these circumstances. Distinguishing and articulating these notions represents some advance over "I don't know how, I just know."

The features of the bus-stop example are typical of the diagnostic inferences we constantly make in the course of our lives. When we get to basic perceptions we can usually say a little something about the circumstances, but the underlying causal patterns take some effort to articulate. Dispositions help. When we judge that the eraser made the mark on the board, the properties of erasers, chalk, shockwaves, and blackboards that conspire to produce it are obviously very complex. But for that case all we need is a very coarse dispositional appreciation: Used erasers are disposed to leave particular marks when struck against blackboards. This much we know, which is why we rank the explanation so high.

ACCUMULATING MNEMONICS

It is good to remind ourselves, as we come to the end of this chapter, of the spirit in which the entire diagnostic apparatus should be taken. It is a series of suggestions and reminders to guide us in our evaluation of evidence. We need to remember that our best evaluative skill lies in making judgments of *relative* plausibility, and that our perceptions and diagnoses organize themselves around certain characteristic implicit questions. In general, the diagnostic model provides a way to marshall our estimable understanding of things in an evaluative and exploratory enterprise. We divide what we understand into three categories: trace data, non-trace data, and explanations. The hard part comes in actually *expressing* that understanding in explanations, splitting them up, keeping them incompatible, and keeping them distinct from non-trace data. Doing all this takes some practice, but it is a valuable tool to master. We will refine it further in the next chapter.

STUDY GUIDE FOR CHAPTER 3

1. There are two main ways in which an argument can be bad or good: (1)
    The support claims can be false or true, and (2) the link between the
    supports and the conclusion can be weak or strong (for a deductive
    argument, of course, only the first way matters). In evaluating induc-
    tive arguments, we want to concentrate for now on the second of these.
    We will be judging the relative strength of the link between the support
    and the rival conclusions. We will be addressing the question "How well
    are the various rivals supported by the data or information provided in
    the argument?"

    (a) This judgment about which rival is supported better than the others
        is called a *plausibility judgment*, and the ranking of the rivals
        according to this judgment is called a *plausibility ranking*.

    (b) A plausibility ranking of five rivals, C_1, C_2, C_3, C_4, C_5 (numbered in
        the order in which they were formulated—the numbers have *noth-
        ing* to do with plausibility), might look like this:

$$C_3$$

$$C_1$$

$$C_2, \ C_4$$

$$C_5$$

    This means that C_3 is the most plausible (given the support claims of
    some argument), C_1 is second, C_2 and C_4 are tied for third, and C_5 is
    the least plausible.

    (c) A plausibility judgment has three important features: (1) It is
        comparative: We cannot always (or even usually) say just *how* good a
        conclusion is, but only that one conclusion is better than some other
        conclusions, that this one looks pretty bad compared to these two,
        and so on. (2) The judgment depends on what we already know—on
        our *background knowledge*. To take a simple example, if I do not
        know the slightest thing about how a car works, then I will not be
        able to judge the relative plausibility of various conclusions about
        why it won't start. I won't be able to say that the problem is more
        likely with the fuel than with the battery or vice versa. (3) The
        judgment also depends on our *diagnostic skill*—our ability to un-
        derstand how things work (or why they fail to work). Items (2) and
        (3) are not entirely separable: Our diagnostic skill depends on our
        background knowledge.

2. All of this applies only to what we will call *diagnostic inductive argu-
    ments*. (Non-diagnostic inductive arguments will be discussed later.)
    Diagnostic inductive arguments inquire about the things going on in the

world around us; and their rival conclusions offer competing possibilities.

(a) Diagnostic inductive arguments have *diagnostic implicit questions*: "What happened to my ice cream?" "Why won't the car start?" These questions ask what's going on or what happened.

(b) The rival conclusions of diagnostic inductive arguments will be (should be, must be) *explanations* of what happened or what is going on: *Somebody ate* my ice cream; the car won't start *because* the battery is dead.

3. Let us analyze the following example: Kaussen, a man who was $133 million in debt, is found hanging dead in his apartment. (See exercise 14 of Chapter 2.) Our immediate conclusion is C_1, that he committed suicide. (The support would be simply S_1 Kaussen was $133 million in debt and S_2 Kaussen was found hanging dead in his apartment.) Suppose we want to consider the following rival conclusions: C_2 Kaussen was murdered by a Mafia hit man, C_3 Kaussen was murdered by his wife, C_4 Kaussen was murdered by a hyper-dimensional being who happens to look like a rope in this dimension. The plausibility ranking would be

$$C_1$$

$$C_2, C_3$$

$$C_4$$

(a) The first thing we should ask ourselves is, What is the implicit question? It should be something like "What happened to Kaussen?" or "How did Kaussen die?" Second, ask, "Do all the rivals answer the I.Q.?" and "Are they explanations of what happened (to Kaussen)?" Yes, that he committed suicide explains why he's hanging there dead. That he was murdered doesn't explain it very well, but we can fix that: His wife, or the Mafia hit man, murdered him and faked a suicide. The existence of the rope-like being explains why it looks like there is a rope around his neck.

(b) Given what we know about Kaussen, our diagnostic skills tell us that our ranking is right: Suicide is most plausible because we know that being $133 million in debt sometimes leads to depression, and depression sometimes leads to suicide. On the other hand, we do not know anything about Kaussen's relations with the Mafia or his wife, so murder by either of them is less plausible than suicide (and both are more or less equally plausible). And since we have no reason at all to suspect that hyper-dimensional rope-like beings feel any hostility toward humans, C_4 is obviously the least plausible of the four rivals.

4. Another important skill in evaluating arguments is the ability to deter-
    mine the relevance of new data. Our plausibility ranking may be tenta-
    tive and may change as new data is provided or found. New data is
    relevant to an argument *if it has any impact on the plausibility rank-
    ing*, that is, if it makes any of the rivals more or less plausible (it doesn't
    have to change the ranking, though).

    (a) For the Kaussen case, suppose we found the following information:

    S_3 Kaussen owed the $133 million to the Mafia and had been
         receiving threatening letters from them.

    S_4 Kaussen's wife loved him deeply.

    S_5 Kaussen loved chocolate chip ice cream.

    S_3 is relevant because it makes C_2, that he was murdered by a Mafia
    hit man, more plausible (though perhaps not more plausible than
    C_1). S_4 is relevant because it makes C_3, that he was murdered by his
    wife, less plausible (though not less plausible than C_4). S_5 is obvi-
    ously not relevant as things now stand.

    (b) This last qualification, that S_5 is not relevant, is important (as things
        now stand). Because relevance judgments involve plausibility judg-
        ment, they also will depend on our general understanding of things.
        Consequently, *anything* may *become* relevant to a list of rivals if our
        understanding of things changes in the right way. We will return to
        this point shortly when we discuss non-trace data.

5. As we have already seen, conclusions in diagnostic inductive arguments
    are explanations, or accounts, of what happened or what's going on or
    the like. They answer the implicit question by giving an explanation of
    whatever the I.Q. is asking. We have also seen that what the I.Q. is
    asking is usually part of the support (the hanging corpse, missing ice
    cream, silent car). And so rival conclusions are explanations of the
    support (or at least some of it). This feature is definitive of diagnostic
    induction, so be sure not to get it the wrong way around: Conclusions
    explain support, not vice versa.

    (a) Support claims may be distinguished by their relation to the rival
        conclusions. Since only some of the support claims contain details of
        what happened, or what went on, only these particular claims are to
        be explained by the rivals. Support claims that are explained by the
        rivals, should be explained by the rivals, or must be explained by the
        rivals are called *trace data*. (They are called trace data because they
        are usually actual traces of what happened or what went on: Finger-
        prints are traces of someone's presence; ashes are traces of a fire.)

    (b) *Non-trace data* are support claims that are not in need of explana-
        tion, but are relevant to the argument. They are relevant because

they help (or hurt) some particular rival's explanation of the support that does need explanation: They make it easier or harder for a rival to explain what it must. In the above example, what needs explaining is Kaussen's death and his being found hanging. His debt does not need explaining (at least not in this particular argument), but it is relevant because it makes the suicide rival more plausible. The fact that his wife loved him doesn't need explaining, but it is relevant because it makes the rival that he was murdered by his wife less plausible.

(c) Suppose, for example, that a light has gone out, and we want to explain why it has gone out. Suppose further that the light bulb was an old one. The argument would be

S_1 The light went out.

S_2 The bulb was old.
$$\overline{\hspace{7cm}}\ d$$
C_1 The light bulb burned out.

Rivals

C_2 There was a power failure.

C_3 The fuse in the fuse box blew out.

Initial Plausibility Ranking

C_1

$C_2\ \ C_3$

Notice first which support claims contain trace data and which do not. We need to ask ourselves what in the support is explained, or should be explained, or must be explained, by the conclusion (and the other rivals). The fact that the light went out is what the argument is about, so its going out is obviously something that needs to be explained and thus is trace data. Do the conclusions need to explain why the light bulb was old? No, of course not. And none of the rivals can explain why the light bulb was old. So S_2 is non-trace data. (We should notice, though, that the concepts of trace data and non-trace data are relative to the argument we are pursuing. In another argument, the age of the light bulbs in a house could be a trace, to be explained by various rivals concerning the history of the house.)

(d) Suppose we are given a new piece of data, S_3: The light came back on a few moments later. Is this trace data? One might not think so at first, since the I.Q. is "Why did the light go out?" and not "Why did the light come back on again?" But S_3 is trace data because some rivals would have trouble explaining it, and they would *have* to explain it. If someone gave the argument above, the first thing one would say in response is "If you think the light went out because the bulb burned out, then how do you explain that it came back on?" Clearly the light's coming back on should be explained by the conclusions. So it is trace data.

(e) S_3 is what is called an *explanatory hurdle (for C_1)*. It does not conflict semantically with C_1, but it makes it very hard to believe that the light went out because the bulb burned out. S_3 is also an explanatory hurdle for C_3 (an explanatory hurdle is always a hurdle *for some particular rival conclusion*), because it is hard to believe that a light could go out because of a blown fuse and then come back on a few moments later. It is not a hurdle for C_2, however, because local power failures are often of short duration. So if C_2 is what happened, the light's coming back on by itself is easy to explain.

(f) If we still want to hold on to a conclusion that is confronted with an explanatory hurdle, then we must *explain away* the hurdle. We must find new support that shows that the hurdle is not really a problem for our conclusion. For instance, we might find (S_4), that the bulb in the lamp is self-repairing—the first few times the bulb burns out it spontaneously generates a new filament in a few minutes. This regeneration would explain away the hurdle for C_1 and put C_1 back at the top of the plausibility ranking.

EXERCISES

1. S_1 Several people have reported seeing a large, hairy creature roaming the woods of Northern California. They describe it as being part ape, part human, and having very large feet.

   S_2 Enormous human-like footprints have been found in roughly the same area.

   —————————————————————————————— d

   C   There is some previously unidentified, near-human creature living in the woods of Northern California.

   a. Provide two rivals for this conclusion.
   b. What is the plausibility ranking of these three conclusions based on the data given?
   c. Provide one piece of new data that would clearly change the plausibility ranking.

    d. What is the new plausibility ranking?

    e. Which conclusion may be soundly drawn from the data you now have?

2. The philosophy department secretary duplicated 100 copies of a Philosophy 7 homework assignment this week and entrusted them to the teaching assistants. Yet the last few students to leave class on Wednesday found that all the homework sheets had already been taken: None was left for them. Since only 81 students have registered for the class this term, it must be the case that the teaching assistants cannot be trusted to carry a handful of papers across campus without losing some of them.

    a. What is this argument's implicit question?

    b. What conclusion (answer) is offered?

    c. State two rival conclusions (explanations), one of which is clearly more plausible and one of which is clearly less plausible than the conclusion offered.

    d. What does your response to c tell you about the soundness of the original argument? Why?

    e. Provide (make up) some new information that, if discovered, would clearly change the plausibility ranking of these three conclusions. What would the new ranking be?

3. The radio crackled madly and then we lost radio contact with Flight 544, just as it entered an ominous-looking storm cell about six hours ago. The plane is now four hours overdue at its destination, and we've had no word from it. The terminal staff is doing its best to cheer the people in our waiting room, but I think the worst has happened.

    a. Schematize.

    b. What is the implicit question?

    c. Give a rival that is less plausible than C.

    d. Provide some new data that would change the ranking of C_1 and C_2.

4. In 1963 Sweden introduced nationwide automobile inspection. At that time the average life of an automobile in Sweden was just over ten years. During the first eleven years of the inspection program the average life of an automobile increased to over fourteen years. Swedish government officials have inferred from this that the inspection program has increased vehicle life.

    a. What is the conclusion of the (diagnostic) argument in this passage?

    b. What (against your background) is the best rival to that conclusion?

    c. Is the argument in this passage a sound one? Why?

    d. Describe some new data that, if discovered, would change the plausibility ranking of the two conclusions you have given in a and b above. How would it change the ranking?

5.   Wounded Man's Note Leads to His Dead Wife

DESERT HOT SPRINGS—The body of an elderly woman was discovered in her apartment yesterday after her husband was found lying shot beside his car, with a note nearby saying he had killed his wife, authorities said.

Evelyn Thompson, 79, was found dead in her apartment with several wounds in her back and a cord around her neck, according to Desert Hot Springs police. It was not immediately determined how she died. An autopsy is scheduled for today.

Her husband, Harold Thompson, also 79, who was found lying beside his car at about 8:20 A.M. on a road just outside the city limits, had a gunshot wound in his head.

Deputies said a small-caliber handgun and an apparent suicide note written by Thompson, saying he had killed his wife, were found.

Take C_1 to be that Harold Thompson killed his wife and the implicit question to be "What happened to Mrs. Thompson?"

a. Provide two further rival conclusions detailed enough to be explanatory.

b. Rank all three rivals on the data provided in the newspaper clipping.

c. Provide a new discovery that would change the order in b.

d. What would the new ranking be?

e. If these are the most plausible rivals, what conclusion would be soundly drawn after c?

6. During a series of operations on the surface of Mars, the scoop arm on *Viking I* stopped responding to commands. When the *Viking* simulator on earth (a near twin to the mechanism on Mars) was subjected to the same series of operations, a pin malfunctioned and jammed the arm. Subsequently, a simple operation by the simulator caused the pin in question to fall out, freeing the arm. Delighted with this turn of events, the scientists in charge of *Viking I* on Mars commanded it to perform the same operation. When it did, the *Viking I* arm once again functioned normally. A television camera on board *Viking I* was then trained on the ground directly beneath the scoop arm; a pin just like the one that had jammed the simulator arm was observed lying in the Martian dust.

Take this to be an argument for the conclusion that the scoop arm of Viking I had been jammed by a malfunctioning pin.

a. Schematize the argument.

b. Give two rival conclusions.

c. Rank all three conclusions.

d. Provide some new support (something you might discover) that would reduce the plausibility of your number one rival, but would not change the ranking.

e. Now provide some further data that would change the ranking.

f. What is the new ranking?

7. Smoke-Filled Air Said Hazardous to Non-Smokers

PITTSBURGH (AP)—A comparison of cancer records at a hospital serving the Amish helps show that non-smokers who breathe smoke-filled air have a higher rate of lung cancer than those with little contact with smokers, a new study says.

The study in the February issue of the *Journal of the Indiana State Medical Association* concludes that a "negligible" incidence of lung cancer among the non-smoking Amish gives "additional evidence that passive smoking is associated with increased incidence of lung disease."

Dr. Gus H. Miller, a psychologist and mathematician who heads the Studies on Smoking clinic at Edinboro, surveyed 348 lung cancer cases at Lancaster General Hospital between 1971 and 1977.

The hospital serves Lancaster County, which has the nation's highest concentration of Amish, a strict religious sect whose members rarely smoke or mingle with outsiders.

The hospital's Cancer Registry, which records all cancer deaths and religious affiliation, shows only one of the 348 people who died of lung cancer during the period was Amish, and that person "was related to a cigar-smoking Amish man," Miller said.

Miller said Lancaster County physicians also have noticed that, unlike the general population, the Amish are almost free of lung disease.

"The most noticeable difference among the two populations was in the exposure to cigarette and tobacco smoke," Miller said. "Since the Amish lived in a closed society noted for its non-smoking behavior, there is nearly a complete absence of tobacco smoke contaminants in their houses and work places.

"This condition is in contrast to the non-Amish who, whether smokers or non-smokers, are constantly exposed to cigarette and tobacco smoke contaminants in their houses and places of employment," Miller said.

"Thus," he concluded, "the smokeless environment appears to be the most likely reason for the extremely low incidence of lung cancer in the Amish population."

Schematize Dr. Miller's argument with the same care and sensitivity that he shows in presenting the data.

a. What are the most interesting rivals? (That is, what other explanations of Dr. Miller's data might you want to consider?)

b. What new data would make you want to take one of these rivals seriously?

8.   Study Time Affects Grades by Very Little, Study Finds

The Associated Press

STATE COLLEGE, Pa.—College grades will suffer more from cutting classes than from cutting study time to a minimum, according to researchers.

The researchers, writing in the June issue of *Social Forces*, said they found little correlation between the amount of time spent studying and a student's grade point average.

"I guess I really don't want to believe that studying doesn't pay off," said Edward Walsh, associate professor of sociology at Pennsylvania State University, who assisted in the series of studies conducted by University of Michigan sociologist Howard Schuman.

Schuman was on sabbatical and could not be reached, his secretary said.

In the first study in 1973, researchers interviewed 424 students in Literature, Science, and Arts College about their study habits and grade point averages.

Students who reported studying less than two hours each weekday had an overall grade point average of 2.94. The average grade point was 2.91 for students studying two to three hours a day, 2.97 for those studying three to four hours, and 2.86 for students hitting the books four to five hours a day.

The grade average jumped to 3.25 for students studying five to six hours a day, but dropped to 3.18 for those going at it six or more hours.

Several subsequent studies yielded similar results, the researchers said.

The first study also found that grades went up steadily with the percentage of classes attended regularly by students. That finding was supported in a later study, the researchers said.

a. What conclusion do the researchers reach concerning study time and grades?

b. What evidence is offered in support? (Summarize it in a single sentence.)

c. The implicit question that professors Schuman and Walsh seem to be addressing is "Why do grades change so little with such large differences in study time?" Accepting this I.Q., provide a rival conclusion (explanation).

d. One interesting kind of possibility is ruled out by using this I.Q. What is it?

e. Reformulate the I.Q. to allow this rival.

9.   Man Suspects Dogs Were Set on Him for Fighting Practice

CINCINNATI (AP)—A man who was attacked by two terriers, the type often used in illegal dog fighting, says the animals may have been set on him for practice in fighting.

Lee Dorsey, who has been hospitalized since he was attacked Dec. 13, told police the dogs seemed to obey an unseen trainer's commands during the incident near a Cincinnati high school football field.

Dorsey said the dogs attacked and drew blood, seemed to back away, then attacked again.

"For a moment, they backed off and looked toward the school as if somebody was there," he said. "I got the feeling they heard somebody else come along, or somebody else was up there signaling with a whistle."

The dogs were captured by the Society for the Prevention of Cruelty to Animals the day after the attack and are being held as evidence. Their ownership has not been determined.

a. What conclusion does Dorsey draw about why the dogs attacked him?

b. What support is offered in the article for this conclusion? (Schematize the argument.)

c. State one (reasonable) rival to Dorsey's conclusion.

d. Which conclusion is more plausible on the support provided?

e. Provide one piece of new data that would clearly change the plausibility ranking (that is, change which one is more plausible).

f. Which conclusion may be soundly drawn from the data you now have?

10. Late one night, on a fog-shrouded stretch of rural interstate highway, a chain-reaction collision involving several trucks and dozens of cars touched off a spectacular blaze that eventually engulfed nearly all of the vehicles. In the investigation the following day, police were at first unable to locate the driver of one of the cars. She was later found at the bottom of a very steep embankment bordering the crash site, dead apparently of injuries suffered in the fall. Police theorized that the woman, distraught over wrecking her brand new car, committed suicide by hurling herself over the guardrail against which her car had come to rest.

a. What conclusion do the police draw about the woman's death?

    b. Based on the data provided in the paragraph, state two rival conclusions (explanations), one of which is clearly more plausible than the one given in a, and the other clearly less plausible.

    c. Assuming that this paragraph contains all the information the police had relevant to the woman's death, what does your response to b tell you about their inference?

11. S_1　For the past decade little Johnny has had difficulty breathing, has tired easily, and has been thought to be asthmatic.

    S_2　Recently, physicians discovered a toy brick, apparently ingested years before, lodged in one of Johnny's lungs.

    S_3　After the brick was removed, Johnny's breathing rapidly improved, becoming nearly normal in a few weeks.

    == d

    C　Johnny's breathing difficulty was due to the toy brick in his lung.

    a. What is this argument's most natural implicit question?

    b. Provide two rival conclusions.

    c. Rank the three rivals on the data provided.

    d. Describe a discovery that would have a substantial impact on the ranking.

    e. What impact would it have, and why?

12. Dear Editor,

The article about the potential evils of TV recalled a personal experience.

    I am an employer in a service profession, who has conducted job interviews with recent graduates for many years. About 10 years ago, I began to notice a change in the focus of questions from these graduates. Until 1975, among the first questions asked were almost invariably those dealing with the type of work the graduate would be doing, the responsibility he or she would be given and the degree of autonomy involved; starting salary and opportunities for advancement would normally come up later in the course of the interview.

    Starting in the mid-1970s, however, a shift in emphasis occurred which continues to this day. Among the first questions now usually asked by prospective employees are: What's my starting salary? How much vacation will I get? What benefits do you offer? How long before I have to start work?

    While none of these questions is itself unreasonable, the discernible shift in the priority and emphasis led me to reflect on something: television.

It was during the period of 1950–1955 that TV became generally available to consumers; by 1955 the majority of U.S. households had a TV. Studies show that in the average household the TV is turned on five hours a day. Even if there are only two commercials every half hour, that still means four per hour, 20 per day, 140 per week and at least 7,280 commercials bombarding that household each year.

What's the message from these TV commercials? "You've arrived when you drive a BMW." "You're a better person if you wear Calvin Klein jeans." "It's great to fly United to beautiful Hawaii." All materialism; all creating a desire to have; never extolling substance; never mentioning that in order to have these things one must go to school and then *work* to get them.

My mid-1970s-and-following graduates now represent the first generation in the work force which has been raised from infancy in a household with a television.

J. C. GARRETT
Costa Mesa

a. What bit of trace data is Garrett trying to explain?
b. What explanation does he offer?
c. What background information (non-trace data) supports his inference?
d. Schematize his argument.

13. Through the rain of embers and fly ash from a nearby brush fire, Herman scrambled up a ladder onto his roof, carrying a hose.

a. Accept this as the sole support claim in an argument answering the question "Why is Herman doing that?" What conclusion may be soundly inferred? (That is, what is the best explanation?)
b. State two rival conclusions.
c. Give some data that is *not* trace data but that would (if discovered) clearly elevate one of these two rivals to the top of the plausibility ranking.
d. Give some trace data that would now (that is, including c) elevate the other rival to the top of the list.

14. Rat's Bone Is Clue in Hunt for Columbus' Fort

The Associated Press

GAINESVILLE, Fla.—A rat's jawbone, a pig's tooth and other artifacts found on the northern coast of Haiti could help pin down the location of Christopher Columbus' first settlement in the New World, a University of Florida researcher said.

"We discovered deep in what looks like a well the jaw of a European rat and the tooth of a European pig," Kathleen Deagan, an archaeologist at the Florida State Museum on the UF campus, says in the November issue of National Geographic. "Before Columbus, both of these animals were unknown in the New World."

A team of archaeologists and other specialists have been analyzing some seven tons of remains found on the northern coast of Haiti at a site believed to be La Navidad, the fort Columbus built after his flagship, the *Santa Maria*, ran aground on a coral reef in 1492.

Columbus left 39 men at La Navidad. Upon his return a year later, he found the fortress burned and his men dead. The site was abandoned and its exact location lost to history.

"We are excited and expectant that, as the 500th anniversary of Columbus' journey approaches, we may be able to shed some light on what happened to the first settlement in the New World," Deagan said.

The team, which visited Haiti in June, is trying to uncover conclusive evidence that the small Arawak Indian village is the site of La Navidad. Charcoal from a European-style well was carbon dated to the late 1400s.

Zoo archaeologists Karla Bosworth and Erica Simons, working under museum curator Elizabeth Wing, identified the rat jaw and pig bones, which were sent to the University of California at Irvine for further analysis.

"Jonathan Ericson analyzed the tooth for the stable isotopes of carbon, nitrogen and strontium," Deagan said. "Strontium reflects the composition of the soil and plants that grew in it. Since the pig ate these plants while its bones and teeth formed, Ericson was able to show that the pig grew up in Spain and not Haiti.

"By comparing the amount of these elements in various Spanish soils with the pig tooth, he concluded the pig grew up in the vicinity of Seville, not far from Palos, the port from which Columbus set sail," Deagan said.

Deagan and colleague Maurice Williams have been digging on and off for seven years with funding from UF, the National Endowment for the Humanities, the Organization of American States and the National Science Foundation.

Efforts this summer, however, were hampered by a general strike in Haiti which forced the team to leave the country.

a. List all the trace data offered in this article (that is, everything the UF researchers think they can explain by their hypothesis).

b. What explanation (hypothesis) do the UF researchers offer?

c. What rival explanations might be important to bear in mind? (List at least two.)

d. What bit of information is offered as both a trace *and* an explanation?

e. Construct a tributary argument to reflect this role, and schematize the best argument you can find in the passage for the UF hypothesis.

f. Which supporting statements contain non-trace data? Explain.

15.   Sheriff's Canine Sniffs Out Burglary Suspect

SUNNYMEAD—A sheriff's dog led deputies to one of two men suspected of burglarizing a home on Locust Street yesterday afternoon, deputies said.

The dog helped deputies find Lewis Randall Strong, 20, of Sunnymead. A second man, Darrell Earl Howard, 18, of Sunnymead, was arrested at a friend's house yesterday evening.

Arko, the sheriff's dog, was called in after R. Warner came home and found Strong and Howard inside the house around 3:30 P.M., deputies said.

Howard, who was armed with one of two guns he had taken from the home, allegedly pointed the revolver at the homeowner and told him to stand still. The man ran down the hall, and Howard allegedly fired two rounds at Warner but missed, deputies said.

Howard and Strong were seen running into the hills behind the house. In the one-hour search that followed, Arko led deputies to Strong, who was hiding in brush about 100 yards from the house, deputies said.

Neighbors and onlookers cheered and clapped when Arko found Strong, who was not armed, the sheriff's department said.

Howard was arrested around 9:30 P.M. at a friend's home on Via Del Sol. He was booked in the County Jail on suspicion of burglary and attempted murder. His bail was set at $25,000.

Strong was booked in the County Jail on suspicion of burglary and possessing stolen property. His bail was set at $10,000.

Deputies recovered one gun.

a. From this article construct an inductive argument for the conclusion the police obviously reached concerning what was going on in Mr. Warner's house that afternoon. Use everything relevant.

b. What are the trace data? Explain.

c. Provide a rival conclusion. Show how it could explain (or explain away) the trace data.

d. Provide some new evidence that would substantially raise the plausibility of your rival in c (without semantically eliminating the original conclusion).

16. Exercise 4a of Chapter 1 offers an argument about a midair collision.
    a. Provide some rivals to the conclusion stated in that exercise.
    b. What are the crucial trace data these rivals must accommodate? How do they do it? (Sometimes, "it's obvious" will be a satisfactory answer to this last question.)
    c. What new information would clearly elevate one of your rivals past the one offered in the exercise?
    d. Is this new information trace data? Explain.

17. Professor Robinson, the most popular instructor on campus, was found one sunny morning slumped over his office typewriter, with a bullet hole in his temple. His fifth floor office door was locked and could be opened from either side only with a key which was found in his pocket. The detective assigned to the case concluded that Robinson's death was a suicide.
    a. State two alternatives to the detective's conclusion, i.e., rival accounts of the matter.
    b. Rank these three rival conclusions in order of plausibility.
    c. State some new information that would alter your ranking. Explicitly state why it would change your mind this way.
    d. Do it again. (That is, state a bit of data which, if discovered, would alter your ranking in a new way.)
    e. Was any of the new information you provided trace data? Explain.

18. S_1 A Southern California youth contracted bubonic plague while staying at the Silent Valley campground.

    S_2 An unusual number of blow-fires, which feed on dead rodents, have been noticed flying in and out of ground-squirrel tunnels in the area around the campground.

    S_3 It is well known among epidemiologists that rodent fleas can transmit bubonic plague.

    Taking these three statements to be support for the conclusion that the rodents in the Silent Valley campground area are infested with bubonic plague, answer the following:
    a. Is the argument inductive or deductive? Why?
    b. Is it diagnostic or nondiagnostic? Why?
    c. Which statements provide trace data? Why?
    d. What relevant information is not trace data? Why?
    e. Give a rival account of the trace data.

19. Man Injured During Burglary at Santa Ana Gun Shop

Santa Ana police, responding to a silent burglar alarm Sunday afternoon, surrounded a closed gun shop and found a burglary suspect injured on the building roof, Lt. Bob Jordan said.

Jose Alvarez Sanchez, 20, of Santa Ana was arrested on suspicion of burglary and rushed to Western Medical Center . . . to treat severe gashes to his right arm and fingers of his right hand, Jordan said.

Stanley's Gun Room . . . was surrounded and a police dog team called in to search for additional suspects, but none was found. Jordan said a box of "25 to 30 handguns" that had been pushed out a small hole made in the building's outer wall was recovered.

Police said the suspect apparently climbed onto the roof of the gun shop . . . , crawled into a ventilation shaft and cut a hole in the sheet metal to enter a crawl space between the roof and ceiling. It was in cutting the metal that Sanchez cut himself, Jordan said.

Consider the argument in this article that would have the implicit question "What was Sanchez doing in Stanley's Gun Room?" Then entertain the following rival conclusions.

C_1 He was burglarizing the store.

C_2 He fell through the roof and was trying to attract attention without breaking too much stuff.

C_3 He was punishing his father (Stanley) who had just disinherited him.

C_4 He was repairing the ventilation when he fell into the shop.

C_5 It was a fraternity prank.

a. What are the trace data in the article? Explain why they are traces.
b. Provide some new information that would elevate one of the other rivals (your choice) in the ranking. Is it trace data or not? Why? Explain very briefly why you think it elevates your rival.
c. What assumption about the time and circumstances of Sanchez's activity does the article seem clearly to make?
d. Which rival would benefit most if this assumption turns out to be false?

20. Consult the schematization you provided in exercise 6 above. (If you have not worked the exercise, provide a schematization.)
   a. Which support claims contain trace data?

   b. In each case, explain why as articulately as you can.

   c. Explain similarly why the others do not contain trace data.

   d. Provide a rival to C; give ranking.

   e. Provide an explanatory hurdle that would change the ranking.

   f. How might the lower-ranked rival explain this away?

21.   Blast Levels Camarillo Packing Plant

CAMARILLO, Calif. (AP)—An explosion in the tomato-ripening section of a packing house leveled much of the building and critically injured one man Thursday night.

"There was no fire. We know ethylene was involved, but we don't know how," said Ventura County fire dispatcher Shonna Matthews.

The explosion rocked the Milton Poulos Corp. plant in the 300 block of East 5th Street at 5:25 P.M. The explosion occurred in the tomato-ripening area where a gas process is used to prepare the vegetables.

"Basically what we've got is a building that came down. We're about five miles away and it hit us like a sonic boom," Matthews said.

A 45-year-old man, assumed to be an employee, was hospitalized in critical condition with multiple injuries, Matthews said.

Investigators did not know the cause of the blast.

This article attempts to begin a diagnostic investigation.

   a. What is the initial bit of trace data?

   b. What qualifies it as a trace?

   c. What relevant non-trace data is offered?

   d. Why is this not trace data?

22.   4 Skinned Carcasses Turn Out to Be Coyotes

Lee Harris
Times Staff Writer

The deftly skinned animal carcasses that have been turning up in Lakewood are the remains of coyotes—not dogs—that apparently were caught in steel traps and killed for their pelts, SPCA officers said Thursday.

An autopsy performed on the last of the four carcasses that have been discovered since December showed that the animal had fed on small animals and possibly a bird, according to Cpl. Vicki Young of the Los Angeles Society for the Prevention of Cruelty to Animals.

"This is typical coyote food," Young said.

This article offers a diagnostic inductive argument.

a. What is its implicit question?

b. What two rivals are offered?

c. Which seems best on the data given?

d. Why? (Note: Write out this answer carefully; this is an important test of articulateness.)

23. ### Dogs May Have Eaten Dead Woman's Body

HESPERIA (AP)—The skull and one foot of a woman whose body apparently was eaten by her pet dogs were discovered in her home by her nephew, authorities said.

"We think the dogs completely chewed up the rest (of the body) or buried it in the back yard," said Dave Hammock, a San Bernardino County deputy coroner. "We dug everywhere, but with the rain and everything, it's hard to locate anything."

Hammock said he believes Mary Ethel Hessey, a 61-year-old cancer patient, died naturally and her body later was eaten by the dogs.

"There is no visible trauma to the skull, and no indication what caused her death," Hammock said, adding that with the few remains it will be impossible to determine how the victim died or whether she was dead when the dogs attacked her.

San Bernardino County sheriff's deputies believe the woman died inside her home and was dragged outside through a broken sliding glass door by the dogs when they became hungry.

The woman had been dead between three and four weeks before the remains were discovered Tuesday by her nephew, Raymond Nuccil, Hammock said.

He said the dogs, described as medium-sized mongrels, "looked in pretty good shape to me—not like they were starving or anything."

The dogs were to be destroyed by San Bernardino County Animal Control Services.

Schematize the coroner's argument in this article in standard diagnostic form.

a. What are the trace data?

b. Provide a rival that is less plausible than the coroner's.

c. Provide some new evidence that would elevate your rival over his.

d. Is it trace data? Why?

24. S_1 It's Monday, around 11:30 A.M.

S_2 The T.A.'s office hours are 11 A.M. to 12 P.M. on Mondays and Wednesdays.

S_3 The T.A.'s office door is open.

S_4 The T.A. is not in the office.

S_5 The T.A. was in lecture class earlier this morning.

S_6 There is a nearly full cup of steaming coffee on the T.A.'s desk.

=== d

C_1 The T.A. is around somewhere and will be back momentarily.

a. What is the implicit question?
b. Which support claims are trace data and which support claims are background information?
c. One rival conclusion is C_2, that the T.A. went home early. Which support claims are explanatory hurdles to C_2?
d. If the T.A. has indeed gone home early, tell us a story about how C_2 might get over the hurdles you just listed.

25.   Disease Link Seen to Water Heaters

COLUMBUS, Ohio (AP)—Lowering temperatures in water heaters to save energy may have touched off the sudden outbreaks of Legionnaires' disease nearly a decade ago, a researcher says.

An Ohio State University study concludes that lowering the temperature of water heaters in hotels, hospitals and other buildings to conserve fuel probably created a near-perfect environment for the bacteria, *Legionella pneumophila.*

Joseph Plouffe, associate professor of medical microbiology and immunology, said that in the 1960s most buildings, including hospitals, kept their hot water at a temperature of about 140 degrees. But in the 1970s, energy conservation measures coupled with rules by the Joint Commission on the Accreditation of Hospitals caused thermostats to be turned down to 110 degrees.

"When they brought it down to 110 degrees Fahrenheit, they provided the ideal temperatures for the growth of the organism," Plouffe said.

The organism is known to flourish in both large and small water systems and causes an often-fatal form of bacterial pneumonia.

The study's conclusion is based in part on a survey of six buildings in the Ohio State University Hospital's complex. Researchers compared water temperatures to the presence of the *Legionella* bacteria in the buildings.

Because of special requirements, two of the six buildings maintained their water temperatures at 135–140 degrees. The other four lowered their water temperature to 110–120 degrees in the 1970s.

The first two buildings showed no bacterial colonization, while tests on the water supplies in the other four did turn up the bacteria.

In one building, researchers killed the *Legionella* by flushing the system with water heated to 160 degrees, Plouffe said.

This newspaper article, written in 1983, offers a diagnostic argument for the conclusion roughly sketched in its headline.

a. Schematize the argument (it will be useful to make explicit one connection that is only implied in the article).

b. Which of the support claims contain trace data? Why?

c. How do the others bear on the evaluation of evidence-strength in this case?

26.   Nest in Flue Blamed in Marine's Asphyxiation

CAMP LEJEUNE, N.C. (UPI)—A bird's nest that jammed a furnace flue and caused an apartment to fill with carbon monoxide was blamed Saturday for the death of a Marine. It may also have caused the earlier death of his wife.

Richard A. Talada, 21, of Chenung, N.Y., died only weeks after the mysterious death of his wife, Ester. He was found dead Tuesday in the apartment by his commanding officer. Authorities said he had been dead for two days.

His wife died Jan. 20. Her cause of death was listed as pneumonia, but medical sources told the *Raleigh News and Observer* it probably was the result of carbon monoxide poisoning. An autopsy of Talada disclosed that he died of carbon monoxide poisoning and pneumonia.

Military investigators examined the Talada home and dismantled the furnace. They found the bird's nest in the flue and decided the nest had blocked the emission of poisonous carbon monoxide, a byproduct of LP gas, allowing the gas to enter the apartment.

Talada had recently requested that the furnace be examined by Camp Lejeune maintenance personnel because it was not providing enough heat. Camp Lejeune spokesmen said they could not determine what maintenance workers found when they checked the furnace.

One medical source said that if the wife's blood had been checked for carbon monoxide levels after her death, Talada might have been warned of a possible danger.

Talada's father has hired Elmira, N.Y., lawyer Robert Miller to investigate the deaths of his son and daughter-in-law. Miller said he would fly to Camp Lejeune today to begin his investigation.

Cmdr. Steven S. Sohn, chief of laboratory services at the Naval Regional Medical Center at Camp Lejeune, conducted the autopsies of both Taladas. "There was no indication for checking for carbon monoxide (poisoning) at the time" of the woman's death, Sohn said.

He said that after Ester Talada's death, he examined Talada and the couple's 2-year-old son and found no problems.

Sohn said one reason he ruled out carbon monoxide poisoning was that children are more susceptible to such poisoning than adults. If carbon monoxide had been the cause of the mother's death, he reasoned, the child also should have died.

He said he had done everything possible to determine the cause of her death.

The Talada's infant daughter died of leukemia Dec. 5.

a. List the support offered in the article for the conclusion that the nest blocked the flue enough to cause a carbon monoxide buildup in Talada's apartment.

b. What are the trace data? Explain.

c. What explanatory hurdle for the bird's nest story is found in the article? Carefully explain why it is a hurdle.

d. What possibility is raised by this hurdle? How serious is it? Explain carefully.

27. The Santa Ana wind howled around the house as Rita sat reading in her living room. Suddenly her reading lamp dimmed and went out. After waiting a few seconds to see if it would come back on, she got up and crossed the room to her study. The light in the study refused to come on with the switch. On her way out to check the fuse box, a small light in the kitchen caught her eye. The clock on the stove was functioning perfectly. When Rita returned to the living room she found the reading lamp burning once again. It must have been a general power loss, she thought, perhaps due to the winds.

a. Schematize Rita's investigation as a diagnostic inductive argument. (It will take some care to preserve all the traces.)

b. What are the trace data? Explain.

c. One rival to Rita's conclusion is that the reading lamp went out due to a blown fuse. Call this C_2. What bit of trace data constitutes the most obvious explanatory hurdle for C_2?

d. What new information would help C_2 clear this hurdle? (That is, what would help C_2 explain it or explain it away?)

28.   Lessons of Life

Dear Editor,

It just could be that the belts men are wearing to hold up their pants are interfering with their digestive system.

When men wore suspenders they lived as long as women did. Just about 25 years after they quit wearing suspenders and started wearing belts, they began dying nine years younger than the women. Is it just a coincidence that in the Middle West, where more men wear bib overalls, people live longer?

The only statistics I have are my own family, having been born on the farm in northeast Kansas. Naturally all us boys wore bib overalls. All four boys have worn bib overalls to this day. Our average now is 84 years with two still alive. Our three sisters' average age now is 84 years with one still alive.

I should add that there were never any smokers in our family and that we all went into the parlor every night at 9 o'clock where we formed a circle and told God how we loved Him for being so good to us.

For long life for men I would say: Don't wear belts, don't smoke and do your best to keep the Commandments.

                                        ERNEST ANDRUS
                                        Homeland

a. Schematize Mr. Andrus' diagnostic argument as economically as possible (accept what he offers as data, for the sake of argument).
b. Which supporting statements contain trace data? Briefly state why in each case.
c. What complication is introduced by the final two paragraphs? How does this affect the argument?
d. What new information (compatible with the support) about men from the Midwest would weaken the argument? Is this trace data or not? Explain.

29.   Medfly Officials Suspect Hoax

LOS GATOS (AP)—There is a "strong suspicion" that pesticide spraying over part of San Mateo County may have been extended unnecessarily due to a hoax, a Mediterranean fruit fly project official says.

"There's a strong suspicion in my heart that spraying there is unnecessary. But we just can't be sure," deputy project manager Dick Jackson said yesterday. He said a hoax may have been responsible for the extension.

On at least three occasions, someone is believed to have placed Medflies in traps used to determine the spread of the infestation, Jackson said. The outbreak has been centered to the south and east of San Francisco Bay.

The flies could have been planted by someone who doesn't like the project, Jackson speculated, or by a project employee trying to prolong his job.

"Whoever it is, we're pretty sure that someone's been playing jokes on us," he said.

One of the incidents involved the discovery of flies in traps near Loma Mar, an isolated community in the mountains south of San Francisco.

Six fertile flies were found in one trap in an area where only a single sterile fly—one of billions released by project officials—had been found before.

"The chances of something like that happening are just too remote to believe," Jackson said.

Other suspicious finds occurred last week in south San Jose and Oct. 29 in Sunnyvale, where a fly with notched wings was trapped, indicating it might have been handled with a forceps.

"Those flies were so desecrated we know they had to (have been) put in there," Jackson said.

More than 28,000 traps designed by Jackson are spread throughout the San Francisco Bay area.

Jackson, a U.S. Department of Agriculture entomologist, said he doubts the hoaxer will be caught—if there is a hoax.

But he said it will be easier to detect planted flies from now on.

"We're catching so few flies now that we can have the trapper bring them in here and take a careful look at each one," he said.

a. Cast the argument in this passage as a diagnostic inductive argument for the conclusion suggested in the headline.

b. What are offered as trace data?

c. Provide a rival account of these data.

d. What splitting of the original rival is discussed in the passage?

e. What new evidence would make this division useful?

f. Is this new evidence trace data or not?

30.   Probers Say Adapter on Electrical Outlet
                   Caused Plymouth Tower Fire

                        Emanuel E. Parker
                     Press-Enterprise Staff Writer

Riverside Fire Department investigators have concluded that a problem with an adapter caused the electrical short that started Tuesday's Plymouth Tower fire, which killed an elderly woman and forced the evacuation of 146 elderly tenants.

In repairing the fire damage, Plymouth Tower officials are considering installing a sprinkler, but the cost may be too high for the non-profit group that operates the building.

The Fire Department may recommend the installation of smoke detectors in the individual units, Fire Chief Richard Bosted said.

Fire Department Investigator Albert Plaxco said the condition of the adapter's metal parts, all that remain after its plastic exterior melted, is evidence it caused the short.

"The . . . metal parts are pitted and burned away," Plaxco said. He said it takes temperatures of about 2,000 degrees Fahrenheit to disintegrate copper, the metal used in the adapter.

"The fire did not generate that kind of heat," he said. "Temperatures in that range can only be created by the intense electrical currents caused by shorts."

a. Schematize the diagnostic argument contained in this article.

b. What are the traces? What identifies them as such?

c. What useful background is provided? What distinguishes it as background?

d. State a rival that would have to explain away the traces in paragraphs four and five.

e. What new information would make it relatively easy for the rival to explain away these traces?

= 4 =

APPLICATIONS

Overview

The interplay between trace and background underpins much of
our reasoning and can help us better understand many cognitive
activities. This chapter exploits our model of diagnostic argument
to cast light on reasoning in several different contexts.

INTRODUCTION

Everyday conversation is filled with diagnosis. Often enough the
diagnostic detail is right on the surface, but occasionally some keen
paraphrasing is required to make it obvious.

Smith: "Look at those two birds out there. I can't figure whether
they're fighting or mating."

Jones: "They must be fighting because they aren't the same kind of
bird: One's a raven, I think, and the other's a mockingbird."

Here it is right on the surface. Smith offers two different (rival)
accounts of the birds' behavior, thus casting it as trace data in a
diagnostic enterprise. Jones' observation then provides some non-
trace data that clearly helps one rival and hurts the other. (Less
barbarous idiom would have it that Jones offers a consideration
clearly favoring one of the two accounts.)

Like everything else in life, the diagnostic inferences we commonly encounter tend to fall into certain patterns. Some of these

patterns will be clear enough, and interesting enough, to justify our calling them a particular *kind* of diagnostic argument (cf. pages 35–37 of Chapter 2). Sometimes whole ranges of arguments will have enough in common to make separate treatment of them useful, make it valuable for us to accumulate reminders about those specific patterns.

So in this chapter we will substantially complicate our argument taxonomy. The next four sections will introduce four different kinds of diagnostic induction: correlational, testimony, sampling, and enumeration. Each category is defined by a characteristic kind of trace data: a correlation, a statement, a sample, and a list, respectively. In every case our task will have three main components:

(1) to identify the (sometimes disguised) trace data,
(2) to develop the automatic instinct—the reflex—to ask "What's the best explanation of this?"
(3) to lump and split the rivals in the most helpful way.

Not surprisingly, this third component will require the most of us. We will also be dividing *rivals* into kinds, for the first time, which will take some subtlety and imagination.

The last two applications (in the last two sections) do not offer new *kinds* of argument, but rather just topics on which our accumulated insights cast some light: the nature of circumstantial evidence and the structure of science. There is, of course, much more to say about science than we have room for here. The brief discussion will be valuable, however, if it provides some guidance in your thinking about scientific procedures and institutions and their relation to more mundane reasoning.

CAUSE AND CORRELATION

In many of the diagnostic arguments of Chapter 3 the conclusions were causes. The rival accounts of the air crash, the fireball, and the car's sputtering to a stop were all causes. A plausible implicit question in each case was "What caused this?" And each of the accompanying arguments was of the same, very standard form: We were given the effect and asked to come up with the cause. Typically,

S_1 Effect   Rival cause
S_2 Circumstances   candidates
S_3 Background

$\overline{\qquad\qquad\qquad\qquad} = $ d C_1
                                          C_2
C   Cause C_3
                                          C_4
                                          C_5
                                            .
                                            .
                                            .

Arguing for a causal connection has another common diagnostic form, however. It derives from a much more specific pattern in our diagnostic reasoning, but one which our apparatus can help us explore. Its close relationship to arguments we have already examined makes it a good place to begin our applications.

In this second pattern the crucial trace is not simply an effect, but a correlation between two things[1]—call them A and B. Things like sunspots and radio interference. Instead of having to come up with a cause, we are being asked whether there might not be some causal connection *between* these two things. Might one be causing the other, for instance? So the major difference from the earlier cases is that the originating trace data will contain not just an effect, but hot candidates for both cause and effect. And the I.Q. will not be an open-ended "What caused this?" but a much more pointed "Might A and B be causally related, and if so how?"

The word "correlation" here is meant to cover a large, loosely related collection of things, the nature of which will emerge more clearly as we proceed. We may capture it crudely at the outset by saying that A and B correlate in this way if they simply "go together" in a recognizable sense—like sunspots and radio interference. And we will restrict our attention initially to cases in which "going together" refers to a sequence of some sort. A and B correlate if they go together regularly or, at least, in a long sequence.

A Standard Case

The reason it is useful to talk about correlations is that we can sometimes explain them. We think we know, at a very general level,

---

[1]Two *some*things: more on this shortly.

why the two things go together[2]: They are connected, *causally* connected. We usually even have an intelligent suspicion of the *way* they are connected. Intense sunspot activity always seems to be accompanied by (that is, to go with) radio interference. We think we know why: Sunspots cause radio interference. Since we have a trace and an explanation, we may formulate all this as a simple diagnostic inference:

S_1 Intense sunspot activity always seems to be accompanied by radio interference.

————————————————————————————————— d

C Sunspots cause radio interference.

S_1 is offered in support of C; and indeed part of the reason we think sunspots cause radio interference is that they go together, correlate. But as in any diagnostic argument, much else may be relevant to our estimate of C. Here, relatively minor additions can substantially strengthen its support. Consider two.

A. Other Trace Data. We may notice that the amount of interference varies with the intensity of sunspot activity. C would help us explain this too, making the argument stronger. We might wish to say that the co-variation is part of the correlation itself. So C explains not just that A and B go together, but explains specific features of the correlation as well. The same kind of point could be made if the interference accompanying sunspots were always (or even typically) of a specific kind or character.

B. Non-Trace Data. We may, of course, know other things bearing on the correlation. We may know, for example, that turbulence in the earth's magnetic field interferes with radio transmission. Finding a strong correlation between sunspots and turbulence in the terrestrial magnetic field strengthens our support for C: We begin to understand the underlying causal mechanism of sunspot interference.

Finally, concerning the original trace, it is worth noting that it does not matter whether we take the "going together" to be in A's

[2]Explanations in this section will all be pitched at this very general level for the reason specified in the introduction: This is the level at which the patterns emerge.

always accompanying B or in A's *seeming* to always accompany B. We may explain either by a causal connection. The second of these allows a slightly broader range of compatible rivals, and having that extra range will sometimes be important. This issue will be treated in greater detail shortly, along with other possibilities.

The General Rival: Chance

The focus of this section is on the diagnostic arguments arising from our attempts to explain why A and B go together, or correlate. One general-level explanation is that they are causally connected. What are the rivals? At this level there is only one: coincidence, accident, chance, blind luck. A and B just might happen to go together by accident, by the chance confluence of unrelated factors. It is doubtless just coincidence, for example, that recently all my teaching assistants have had names ending in the letter *w*.

A more useful example is again provided by sunspots. For decades, around the turn of the century, sunspot intensity also correlated almost perfectly with share prices on the New York stock exchange. Here the causal connection rival gets no help at all from non-trace data; so in the absence of some other trace, chance coincidence is the best account of the correlation.

Correlations

For our purpose we need not restrict "correlation" to uniform regularity. Any sort of "going together" that might be explained by a causal connection will be of interest. So we will adopt the common practice of calling any differential frequency a correlation. If A's go with B's just slightly more than they do with non-B's, we may say there is a correlation between A and B. There is something to explain.

Both smokers and nonsmokers die of lung cancer. But more smokers do than nonsmokers: There is a small but quite reliable difference in the frequency of lung cancer in these two groups. So we say there is a correlation between smoking and lung cancer.[3] Some correlations are dramatic, others more subtle. But anywhere on the

---

[3]Since lung cancer is virtually always fatal, there is also a correlation between smoking and dying of lung cancer.

spectrum a correlation may be explained by a causal connection. Any correlation may function as trace data in a diagnostic argument.

Correlates

Some writers on this topic have, for a variety of reasons, urged that the correlates, A and B, cannot be just any old thing; they must always be of a specific logical type, usually events. The correlation would then be not simply A correlates with B, but, for example, events of kind A correlate with events of kind B. And usually we can force our talk about correlations into any of the suggested forms. But doing so will often require force and will generate barbaric new ways of speaking about things we already have a perfectly good way of speaking about.

For our purposes, there will be no point in forcing our expression into any of these narrow molds. The diagnostic model can handle correlations between states, activities, properties, objects, and conditions, as well as events. The *activity* of smoking correlates with the *condition* of having lung cancer. The significance of this statement is transparent to anyone modestly competent in English. Nothing is to be gained by burdening our expression here with abstract restrictions. The best advice is to express a correlation in the most natural way and to work for clarity with all the resources at your disposal, including paraphrase, of course.

Directions of Causal Influence

Since we will need the generalized notion of a correlation very frequently in the remainder of this section, it will be useful to introduce an abbreviation:

$$A/B$$

This will stand for any correlation between A and B of the kind we have discussed: any regular going together that we might use as trace data in a diagnostic argument for a causal connection.

A/B = A correlates with B
Smoking/lung cancer
Sunspots/radio interference
Sunspots/stock prices

In this section our interest is in representing some useful patterns in the diagnostic arguments that take A/B as their characteristic or originating trace data.

$$\frac{\text{A/B}}{?} \quad \text{d}$$

The general-level implicit question is "Why do A and B go together?" or "What is the best explanation of A/B?" We have already split the rivals into two large groups:

C_1 A and B are causally connected.

C_2 A/B is the result of mere chance (which is to say merely that the two parts are *not* causally connected).

These may be thought of as rival categories, within which we will find specific stories of how or why A and B have come to correlate as they have. But sometimes an explanation at this very general level is interesting without further detail. Simply showing that the sunspot/ stock market correlation could not be the result of chance would be a very big deal, for example, even if we had not a clue as to what story to tell about their causal relationship.

Nevertheless, we find the promised patterns only by dividing up C_1 in a certain way. C_1 says that A and B correlate in the way they do because they are causally connected. There are, obviously, all sorts of different ways A and B might be connected, and lumping these "ways" into three different categories turns out to be particularly useful. If all we know about A and B is that they correlate in some sense, then there are three different patterns into which the causal stories might fall. A might cause B; B might cause A; or some other thing, X, might bring A and B about independently of one another. In other words, the *direction* of causation may be from A to B, from B to A, or from something else to A and B independently. This third possibility has been called "common cause": A and B have a common cause; neither directly causes the other. The perfect correlation between eclipses and high tide is an example of common cause. Eclipses don't cause tides, nor tides eclipses. They are both brought about, independently, through the alignment of the sun and moon.

Because we will want easy access to these three possibilities, it will be convenient to adopt a special notation for them too; we will use an arrow ($\rightarrow$) to indicate direction of causal influence:

C_{1a} $A \rightarrow B$ (direct cause)

C_{1b} $B \rightarrow A$ (reverse cause)

C_{1c} $X \nearrow^{A}_{\searrow B}$ (common cause)

So the general diagnostic picture of correlational inferences will look like this:

S_1 A/B		Rivals
S_2 Circumstances		C_{1a} $A \rightarrow B$
S_3 Background		C_{1b} $B \rightarrow A$
============== d		
C		C_{1c} $X \nearrow^{A}_{\searrow B}$
		C_2 Chance

Illustration.   Most of the time our general understanding of things will make one or two of the four general rivals too implausible even to consider. How could radio interference cause sunspots ($B \rightarrow A$), for instance, or death by cancer cause smoking at an earlier age? But there will be many cases in which our preoccupation with one possibility—one mechanism—will blind us to the possibilities from another direction. So it is important to think through all the options in any subtle or complicated case. Giving us some practice in doing this, and a formal reminder of what to do, will be the major value of this section.

Several studies have shown a strong correlation between television watching and obesity in pre-teenage children. The more television they watch (A) the more overweight they tend to be (B). Accepting the results as genuine, it is still possible that the correlation is a freaky quirk of the population that, like the sunspot/stock market patterns, signifies no connection between A and B at all. That is, the best account of this A/B may be C_2: chance. That possibility is neither very likely nor very interesting, however. The value of this example is in our displaying the various directions of causal influence that are possible in a single case.

For example, the correlation might be due to (explained by) the fact that kids eat more and exercise less the more they sit in front of the tube. This would be C_{1a}: A → B. Watching television is the culprit. On the other hand, maybe obese kids are, *because* of their weight, less social or less inclined toward sports and, as a consequence of this, naturally gravitate toward passive, isolated activities like watching TV. This would fall under C_{1b}: B → A. Television would not be the culprit in, but the beneficiary of, obesity. Finally, the whole phenomenon may be traceable to the underlying makeup of kids at some level. It might be that the correlation arises from a developmental link (X) between low metabolism and passive personalities. Kids tending to be overweight also tend to watch more television, but the two are independently brought about by a common antecedent. The kids would tend to be heavy even if there were no television around to watch, and vice versa.

In complicated circumstances such as these, you often want to tell a complicated story: one with components from more than one direction. Some of the correlation may be due to A → B, some to B → A, and some to a number of common causal factors. This obesity/ television example is useful because nothing in it or our experience makes any of these possibilities silly or outrageous at the outset.

Stories and Plot Lines.   The amount of detail we require in a diagnostic story will depend on the context. As we saw in Chapter 3, sometimes something as simple as "The collision caused the crash" is adequately explanatory; but sometimes we need much more. It all depends on our interest: the question at hand, the progress of the investigation, other very practical matters. So, given a need for detail, the four generalized rivals of our correlation scheme are actually just categories, within which many different (rival!) stories may fall. All the different ways in which watching television can lead to obesity would come under the heading C_{1a}.

We may think of the generalized rivals as organizing the stories by plot line. All the stories having plots in which A leads to B fall under C_{1a}. Those plots in which B leads to A fall under C_{1b}. All those attributing A and B independently to a common antecedent fall under C_{1c}. And, finally, C_2 contains all those stories telling us that A and B have been found together simply by chance or coincidence and are not connected at all. Complicated rivals may contain elements of each of these, of course, in the same way teams of perpetrators got on our list of rivals in criminology arguments. The same precautions about avoiding overlap apply.

Again, how much detail you want will depend on matters of interest and context. So occasionally the generalized categories will be adequate rivals without further specification. Sometimes a simple "A causes B" will be a useful conclusion, as it is in the smoking/cancer correlation. But if one of the generalized rivals is adequate as it stands, quite frequently the others will not be, even in the very same case. If someone disagreed with the Surgeon General's account of the smoking/cancer correlation, and offered as a rival simply "Cancer causes smoking," we would not know what he had in mind. The statement would not yet be a rival explanation; it is at best a promissory note that might be redeemed with one. As it stands it is just baffling.

Not that it cannot be redeemed. Our dissenter may have a story in mind:

> Look, I think cancer is basically genetic and develops much more slowly than researchers think. The early stages of lung cancer, which usually occur during adolescence, produce a slight discomfort which is relieved by smoking. So future lung cancer victims enjoy smoking more than the rest of us and get hooked more easily.

Though not very plausible, this would at least go some way toward explaining the correlation. The story, in the context, would probably be the least detailed proposition to count as a genuine rival in this B → A direction.

Isolated Pairs

A closely related kind of trace data falls into the same explanatory pattern we have been examining, and we will expand our notion of correlation to cover it too. This is the single occurrence of an A/B pair. The earthquake and the cracked stucco on the garage correlate in this sense: The stucco was not cracked before the quake, but it is now. This too is a "going together" that might be interesting to explain. And it may be explained by causal influence of various directions.

So a correlation, for diagnostic purposes, may be a long sequence of A/B pairs; but it may also be a single A/B pair that draws our explanatory attention in the right way. Whether a single pair counts as a correlation will simply hang on whether explaining it is diagnostically fruitful. The fact that my watch battery died the day the Statue of Liberty turned 100 is boring. The question "What explains the fact that they happened on the same day?" is pointless. So this will not be a correlation for us: There is nothing to explain.

There are a truly enormous number of mundane pairings that will count, however: much of our daily lives. The fact that the pain occurred just as the bee settled on your hand will count, for instance. So will the drip in the bucket and the rain outside. The evidence we have for much of our causal understanding arises from the obvious significance of isolated pairs of events.

> punch/loose tooth
> racket/nearby plane
> draft/open door
> out of gas/car won't run

Correlations like these are not just obviously significant, they are usually transparent. The "going together" is causally explainable, and we know which way the causal influence runs. They are normally so obvious we never think (or need) to set out a diagnostic argument on their behalf.

But the causal link between single pairs is not always obvious; and when it isn't, the same resources are available that we used in the diagnostic treatment of more literal correlations. Most interesting are cases in which it is not clear whether A or B occurred first. This uncertainty allows us to consider seriously rivals of various directions and makes a wide range of information relevant to settling the matter.

The careful investigation of a racing-car crash illustrates all the possibilities about as well as can be expected in a single example. We begin with a crash and a crumpled car: The crash (A) correlates with many broken pieces (B). The breaking of the various bits may relate to the crash in each of the four possible ways. Some surely broke in the crash (A → B). The failure of one may have caused the crash (B → A). Some may have broken in a preceding incident (e.g., collision with another car), which independently caused the crash (common cause). And some might have been broken all along and were not involved in the crash at all (chance).

To establish one of these relationships requires the same understanding, imagination, and resourcefulness we would use in any diagnostic investigation. A broken hub-carrier may be implicated by trace data turned up in the search: fresh scrapes and gouges in the track surface, characteristic of dragging metal, just where the car left the road. We may explicitly appeal to background information to make our rival plausible. We know what happens when a hub-carrier breaks. And the subsequent collapse of the suspension makes scrapes and gouges easy to explain. What our background provides familiarity with here is a *modus operandi*[4]: We know how things like this work, and that knowledge allows us to explain what happened. So we have the focused relationship among traces, background, and explanations characteristic of a diagnostic enterprise:

S_1 Crash (A)/Broken hub carrier (B).

S_2 Scrapes and gouges.

S_3 Modus operandi considerations.
$$\overline{\qquad\qquad\qquad\qquad\qquad\qquad} \text{ d}$$
C_{1b} $B \to A$

Other discoveries could change our view of the crash, of course, but this is one way in which the investigation could go. We might find an account of the scrapes and gouges that would make $A \to B$ a better account of the correlation. It all fits the general diagnostic picture.

Chance.   Evidence that A and B are *not* connected—that they occurred together by chance coincidence (C_2)—usually does not fall into a nice, neat, diagnostic argument like those above. The evidence is normally indirect, negative. Where a causal connection is initially plausible (crash/broken hub-carrier), we may become persuaded that A and B are actually *not* connected, simply by eliminating the C_1 rivals. We begin with serious causal possibilities and dismiss them all by finding insuperable objections to them one by one. On the other

---

[4]The Latin for "way of operating" used prominently in criminology: We recognize a specific burglar's modus operandi.

hand, even when a causal connection is unlikely at the outset (sun-spots/stock prices), the argument for C_2 will often be negative too. It may simply point to the absence of any reason to think better of a causal connection we thought outlandish to begin with: no special circumstances, perhaps; no other traces to explain.

In some cases, however, there is a more direct way to establish the chance rival. If we know which part of a correlated pair occurred later in time, we can sometimes show that it was brought about by something *wholly unrelated to* the other correlate. Diagrammatically,

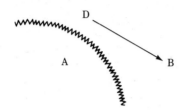

We call this a bypassing causal account, and it usually involves finding a $D \rightarrow B$ account that is simply much more plausible than the $A \rightarrow B$ account or any common cause. So it works best with A/B correlations that do not have strong C_1 rivals. As I leave my office one night I routinely flick the light switch (A) and, instead of the usual result, all the lights visible in the corridor and other offices go out too (B). $A \rightarrow B$ is not very plausible, but the coincidence is impressive and, lacking any other explanation, I am tempted to accept it. On my way home, however, I hear on my car radio that the entire downtown area (where my office is located) has been plunged into darkness by a failed transformer (D).

This is a pretty clear case. $D \rightarrow B$ is much more plausible than $A \rightarrow B$; and D is pretty clearly independent of A. Common causes are also not much of a threat. But in tougher cases the common-cause issues must be addressed. The bypassing diagram above is some-times confused with one of the following:

$$D \rightarrow A \rightarrow B \qquad\qquad A \rightarrow D \rightarrow B$$

$$D \overset{\nearrow A}{\underset{\searrow B}{}} \qquad\qquad X \overset{\nearrow A}{\underset{\searrow D \rightarrow B}{}}$$

But to establish C_2, D must be *independent* of A. In each of these diagrams D and A are causally connected, not independent of each other.

Illustration. To develop your skill in using the apparatus, it is good practice to work out genuine (if implausible) rival stories from all four categories in some difficult cases. Doing so will give you some skill at using the apparatus when your imagination needs stimulating. Suppose a rancher finds a small outbuilding collapsed (B) the morning after a mild earthquake (A) has shaken the area. The building had been fine the day before. The most natural account of A and B occurring on the same evening is A → B: The quake collapsed the building. Next most natural would be chance: Vandals, say, knocked the building over; the quake just happened to occur on the same night.

C_{1b} and C_{1c} take more imagination. For B → A we might construct a story like the following. Say geologists have discovered that keeping the groundwater level artificially high in an unstable region can prevent the rock along a fault from slipping much longer than if normal fluctuations are permitted. High groundwater locks the fault. Now suppose the outbuilding in question contained control equipment for an elaborate hydraulic system that maintains the groundwater level. In that case, the collapse of the building could disrupt the control and let the groundwater level drop, triggering an overdue earthquake: B → A.

For common cause we might employ the same groundwater control, this time not in the building but next to it. Then a runaway tractor might smash first the control and then the outbuilding. The rampant tractor would then be a common cause of both A and B. It brought them both about, but independently. There are many other stories that would have the same causal structure. Exercise your imagination and think of some.

The Diagnostic Nature of A/B

The reason to devote a section of this book to cause-correlation arguments is to explore the diagnostic patterns arising when the traces contain a pair: A/B, two things that go together. Consequently, for our purposes, a correlation is any pairing (of two things) that generates those patterns. A and B correlate if anything about their relationship raises the right questions, generates a diagnostic argument or investigation.

So we may say about correlations just what we did about traces in general, except that they are pairs. The nature of traces is to be explained; so correlations are simply *pairs* to be explained. A correlation, then, is any pairing that demands explanation or suggests an explanation: one that somehow or other allows or encourages rival accounts of the pair. As with traces in general, whether it is useful to treat something as a correlation depends on our understanding of how things work: what we know about the world. This, again, is typical of diagnostic arguments.

One consequence is that we will encounter many borderline cases. Whether to think of a certain pair as a correlation will sometimes be unclear. Usually the best strategy is to throw it into standard cause-correlation form and see how it works. One way to read C_2 is, It turns out that there was nothing to explain. We thought the cracked stucco correlated with the earthquake, but all that correlated with the quake was my *noticing* the crack. The crack did not pair with the earthquake: All that needed explaining was my noticing it (which *did* correlate with the quake).

A good rule for schematizing correlational arguments may be gleaned from this strategy. Since very minor differences in A and B can have such a great effect on how the argument develops, it is important to understand just what an author takes to be correlated with what. And sometimes this pairing will not be clear until you see what *gets explained* in the argument: until some particular A is connected causally to some particular B. So the procedure will sometimes work backward. To determine the crucial trace data, we may have to first look at the rivals to see what pair they are trying to explain.

Summary

The purpose of this chapter is to add detail to our diagnostic apparatus. In this section the detail concerns what to do when the traces contain a correlated pair. The main effort has been devoted to determining the level of generality at which useful patterns develop and to lumping rivals together to display those patterns. The next three sections—testimony, sampling, and enumeration—follow this same form, with other kinds of characteristic trace data.

TESTIMONY

Genetic Arguments

Arguments asking us to "consider the source" of a statement have a bizarre and checkered history. Sometimes called "genetic arguments," they offer the *source* of a statement—the person, the circumstances—as an *argument*: as a reason for or against the statement itself. Discussions of genetic argument have generated deep, ambivalent tension, due largely to the impulse to cast such arguments deductively. Vaunted human fallibility makes them particularly implausible candidates for a deductive rendering, yet we seem to use them all the time. Accepting a genetic argument is called *taking somebody's word* for something, and it is hard to imagine getting through life without doing so. We constantly accept statements when all we know about them is their source: where we found them, who said them. And it is seldom foolish to do so.

In fact, genetic support is sometimes the strongest support we can find, in many circumstances the very best argument for accepting a statement. Why do we think the flight will be late? The man at the check-in desk said so. Why do I think there was a toxic spill on Interstate 10? The newscaster said so. Why do we think the soloist is Ashkenazi? The program says so. Why do I think the bank opens at 9 a.m.? The recorded telephone message says so. "Saying P" can be a very good reason for P, depending on who says it and where: depending, that is, on the source.

All this suggests that we try to find some inductive way to represent genetic arguments, and our diagnostic apparatus is available to accept the challenge. What is required is to think of statements as trace data, to be explained in one way or another. Different explanations will appeal to, or reflect on, the *truth* of the statement in different ways. So we can begin to see how a statement can occur in an argument for itself, which is nevertheless not deductive. A statement may, in a way, be evidence for itself:

$$S_1 \quad \text{Somebody said "P."}$$
$$\rule{5cm}{0.4pt} \text{ d}$$
$$C \quad P$$

That is why we call arguments of this basic form "testimony arguments." The model instance is accepting someone's testimony. Sometimes the best explanation of somebody's saying something is—or presupposes—that what they said is true. Part of the reason the newscaster said there was a toxic spill is that there was a toxic spill. This is how these explanations can get at the truth of what they explain.

The rest of the argument will be standard diagnostic fare, except that it will be laced with source considerations. The circumstances may include where we looked or who we called, as well as tone and expression. Background will include our understanding of institutions and people, perhaps including what we know about the person making the statement. But the notion of a statement's being evidence for itself is formally peculiar enough that it will be worth our effort to place it in a clear context.

Behavior as Evidence

Saying is doing; talking is behavior. And behavior raises no special problems as trace data. When we explain behavior, we explain what happened in a perfectly orthodox way, and hence we generate perfectly orthodox diagnostic arguments. Viewing talk as a special kind of behavior will help us understand testimony as a special kind of evidence.

Consider first the behavior of animals. When I was growing up in rural Pennsylvania, we could always tell when something had gotten into the neighbor's turkey pen in the middle of the night. There was a characteristic, hysterical racket. And the inference is plainly diagnostic: The best account of that racket, in the middle of the night, was some stranger—human or animal—in the pen. I was led to understand that someone with long experience could frequently tell the nature of the visitor from characteristics of the sound. One level of stridency was best explained by "weasel," for instance. Even subtler perceptions are sometimes possible with house pets. Our familiarity with a dog or a cat can allow us to diagnose mischief from guilty looks and behavior. The best account of the animal's slinking or hiding behavior is a chewed-up slipper (as well as the lonely partner left in the closet).

Human behavior may be read in the same way, with even greater subtlety and detail. The face of the person I am talking with distorts with terror as her eyes fix on something over my left shoulder. It might be that she's having a heart attack or is play-acting, but the best account is that something awful is going on behind me. My instinctive turning to look is quite reasonable. Verbal behavior (talk) may be evidence too, while not yet (literal) testimony. Sometimes the evidence is in the manner of speech. My friend's clipped, cold tone tells me he is angry: That is the best account of it. A novel inflection or a raised eyebrow may be significant too. But the diagnostic value of Uncle Ned's bum knee is more to the point. The conditions surrounding a nearby weather system make Ned's arthritis act up painfully. So when Ned says his knee hurts, we all infer (diagnostically, as the best explanation) the approach of a local storm front. Years of reliable weather forecasting support this account.

We can bring out the structural peculiarity of testimony by comparing this case with a weather report on the evening news. Uncle Ned says one thing and we infer another. Schematically,

$$\frac{S_1 \quad \text{He says, "knee hurts."}}{C \quad \text{Storm is approaching.}} \ d \qquad \frac{S_1 \quad \text{Says "Q"}}{C \quad P} \ d$$

When we draw the same conclusion from a television forecast, on the other hand, what the forecaster doubtless said was simply that a storm is approaching. Schematically,

$$\frac{S_1 \quad \text{He says, "Storm is approaching."}}{C \quad \text{Storm is approaching.}} \ d \qquad \frac{S_1 \quad \text{Says "P"}}{C \quad P} \ d$$

This is the sense in which a statement may be evidence for itself. What distinguishes testimony from other behavior as trace data is that P occurs both above and below the line, in both support and conclusion. But the argument is not deductive because of the *way* P occurs in the support: as behavior, as somebody's saying it. And somebody could say "P" even if P were false. So the support does not (deductively) commit us to the *truth* of P at all. Saying "P" is only evidence for P; and evidence only in some circumstances—when the best explanation of saying it underwrites its truth.

Rival Explanations

The standard way to undermine testimony—to attack its value as evidence—is to explain it away. We show it to be motivated not by its truth but by a wish to deceive, for instance, or, perhaps, to stem from incompetence or error. The guy in the next seat may have said it's 10:15 because his watch is wrong. If his watch is wrong, the value of his information is destroyed. We can't take his word for it. If someone tells you what you want to hear because she is afraid of you, what she says is worthless as data. Her statement may even be true. But because she's motivated by fear, her making the statement doesn't provide any evidence for it, any reason to believe it to be so. In another case, the windows rattle and I say the rattling is caused by an earthquake. But if I am legendarily incompetent at distinguishing earthquakes from sonic booms and these from nearby construction blasts, my testimony is undermined: My incompetence breaks the connection between my statement and its truth.

Whenever the explanation of somebody's making a statement—the reason they said it—is bad judgment, fear, hope, pity, illusion, or simple mistake, the statement is undermined as testimony. For our purposes in this section, we will lump together all undermining rival explanations of a statement under the heading "C_2." C_2 may be read: "The statement was made for reasons other than, and unrelated to, its truth." We can explain why the statement was made, without appeal to its truth.

The other generalized rival of interest, C_1, is the underwriting rival. C_1 includes all accounts of a statement that reject C_2 and make the *saying* of P in some way dependent on its *truth*. To explain why a statement is made we presume its truth or appeal to that truth in some other way. Sometimes the appeal will be explicit: Truth will *be* the offered explanation. "I wonder why she said it was cold out when she came in earlier." (Reply.) "Perhaps because it was cold out then." Here, saying P is explained by P.

$$\frac{S_1 \quad \text{She said "P."}}{C_1 \quad P} \text{ d}$$

C_1 may be read here, "She said it because it was true." All C_1 accounts have a component of this form.

The explanation of why we say things, like the explanation of anything else, responds sensitively to context, however. So C_1 explanations will often not be simply "said it because it was true," but rather something more complicated that presupposes the statement to be true. The lady on the telephone time recording does say it is 10:15 simply because it is 10:15. But if *I* tell you it is 10:15, it might be because you asked me to let you know when it was 10:15, for example, or because it was getting late and I thought we should go. Offering something like one of these as the explanation of why I said it simply takes for granted that I got it right: Part of why I said it was 10:15 is that it actually was.

None of this means that I might not misread a clock or exaggerate the lateness to prod you along. But my doing one of those things would be part of why I said what I did; it would be part of the explanation. The explanation (in *this* context) would have to include mistake or disingenuousness and hence would fall under C_2, not C_1. That is the force of "the explanation" here. The explanation can stop with "thought you ought to know" or "because it was important" only if deception and incompetence are not factors, are not part of why you said it. So the general form of testimony arguments may be represented thus:

S_1 Somebody (or something) says "P."

S_2 Circumstances (who said it, where, how it was said).

S_3 Background (including institutional and biographical).

$$=== \quad \text{d}$$

C $(C_1 \text{ or } C_2)^5$

There may be several distinct, live possibilities under either C_1 or C_2 (or both), and we would have to lump their plausibilities to decide whether the testimony supports P. This can, of course, be so messy as to be undecidable. But it is fairly common, in our listening to testimony or accepting somebody's word, that the possibilities under each heading are limited and coherent. It is overwhelmingly likely that the woman on the phone said that the bank closes at 3:30 simply because she wanted you to know—a version of C_1. But even the long-shot C_2 possibilities are limited: first day on the job and robbery in progress probably exhaust the normal ones. Since C_1 is clearly the best account, the schematization would look like this:

---

[5] If C_1 is "said it because true" and C_2 is "said it for reasons unrelated to truth," there remains the possibility that the explanation is "said it because it was false" (C_3). But this possibility is usually unimportant and may be neglected. For when people say false things they do so almost never *because* they are false, but rather *in spite of the fact* that they are false. Falsity may fail to prevent a liar from saying what he does, but it seldom explains why he said it. The explanation will usually fall under C_2: hope, fear, embarrassment, and the like. In the few cases in which C_3 is useful, it ends up behaving more like C_1 than C_2. We end up with some support, but for the opposite of the statement made (not-P).

S_1 Somebody said, "Bank closes at 3:30."

S_2 That person answered the phone at the bank.

S_3 Background on banks and commerce.

$$\overline{} \; d$$

P   The bank closes at 3:30.

Saying "P" provides support for P, and fairly strong support too, because the C_2 rivals are such long shots.

Separating Basic Issues

Often enough the simple schematic picture above will be adequate for our purposes. But since incompetence and insincerity are such radically different ways to undermine testimony, it is sometimes useful to consider them separately, in two different arguments. The natural way to do this is to create a weird compound argument of two stages. The first determines whether the message is sincere; if it is, the second determines how much weight we should attach to the sincerity in the circumstances.

Diagnostically, we begin with the characteristic trace: Somebody said "P." but instead of trying to explain the trace directly by appeal to its truth, we first try to explain the statement in terms of sincere belief. And if we are successful in this, we may then try to explain the belief by appeal to its truth. Instead of saying, "She said it because it was true," we will expand to "She said it because she believed it, and she believed it because it was true."

Each argument will obviously be diagnostic, with the conclusion of the first (a genuine belief, or confidence) being the organizing trace data for the second. So for good testimony, the expanded schematic would look like this:

S_1 Somebody (say, Smith) says "P."

Stage One S_2 Circumstances bearing on sincerity.

S_3 Background bearing on sincerity.

$$\overline{} \; d$$

C_1' Smith really believes P.

S_4 Smith thinks P. ($= C_1'$)

Stage Two S_5 Circumstances bearing on competence.

S_6 Background bearing on competence.

$$\overline{\rule{10cm}{0pt}} = \text{d}$$

C_1 P

Stage-one rivals (C_2') would have to explain why Smith said "P" in spite of not believing it. The categories would be the ones mentioned earlier: fear, embarrassment, hope of gain, or joke. C_2' would explain the statement as dishonest, duplicitous, deceitful, or disingenuous. And if C_2' is the best account of stage one, we cannot go on to stage two because we lack the key trace, S_4. The testimony will have been undermined without our considering questions of competence.

Stage-two rivals (C_2) will include all the other ways in which testimony can go wrong. C_2 will explain, in a way that breaks its connection with truth, how Smith could come to believe P. Smith really thinks P but, in the circumstances, his thinking so carries no weight with us. What we are calling incompetence, then, comes in many guises. Genuine incompetence is something like not being able to tell time. "He thought it was 10:15 because he still can't reliably tell which hand is which." And if I try to estimate the speed of an airplane overhead or the Richter scale reading of a felt earthquake, I may test the limit of my competence: My belief in certain things may be best explained by my lack of skill. But C_2 will also include bad luck and simple mistake, like relying on a slow clock or misreading the newspaper. These may not be literal incompetencies, but they undermine testimony—sincere testimony—in the same way. So we will lump them all together in stage two of our diagram.

Illustration

Mr. Farnsworth: Rob, would you drop the car off at Turner's sometime this morning? I'm having him overhaul the engine—he said he'd get you a ride home if you got there by noon.

Rob: Overhaul the engine!? Why do you want to do that?

Mr. Farnsworth: Fred said it needed an overhaul, and he'll do it for me if I can leave the car all week.

Rob: Gee, Dad, I know Mr. Turner's an old friend, very honest and all that, but this is way out of his league. He runs a very good gas station, but changing oil and fan belts is about as complicated as it ever gets there. I doubt he owns a compression gauge. I'd never tear into a motor on his say-so. He must not understand the limits of his own expertise.

Here Rob Farnsworth and his father disagree about whether to take Fred Turner's word for something. Rob's argument against it illustrates the value of an expanded, two-step schematic. He contends that everything is fine with stage one, but problems arise in stage two: Fred says what he does because he believes it, but his believing it is not best explained by its truth.

S_1 Fred says the engine needs an overhaul.

S_2 Fred runs a gas station.

S_3 Fred is a long-time family friend with a reputation for honesty.

$$\overline{}\ d$$

C_1' Fred thinks the engine needs an overhaul.

$S_4 = C_1'$

S_5 and S_6 Fred's work has involved nothing more complicated than changing oil and fan belts.

$$\overline{}\ d$$

C_2 Fred believes the engine needs an overhaul for reasons not closely related to truth.

We may use this example to illustrate the various trace and background considerations relevant to each step. Background for stage one would typically be reputation for honesty or carelessness with the truth. In general we will need to estimate how much motivation a speaker needs before something besides truth will explain what he says. Circumstances (S_2) may provide motivation, among other things. If Fred were in desperate financial trouble, that might make a C_2' account of what he said more plausible (said it because he needed the money). Needing the money might explain some of the circumstances too (the touch of panic in Fred's voice, his anxiousness to do the job this week) and hence make them trace data for stage one.

Background for stage two would center on experience in the perception or diagnosis being made, sometimes extending to an actual track record when available. If Fred had recently been a dealer's main diagnostician, and had a reputation for unerringly spotting those engines whose symptoms could be treated by minor replacements and adjustments, stage two would be dramatically altered. His background would provide strong reason to think him competent: It would be non-trace data in support of a C_1 account of Fred's belief.

One other second-stage possibility is worth mentioning before we leave this discussion. The hopes and fears relevant to stage one sometimes also undermine our competence: Our motivation can affect our judgment. We may wish for something so much that we talk ourselves into a belief we would reject immediately any other time. Fred may be in such desperate financial straits that he imagines the sounds he hears to be piston slap and bearing knock when, in less stricken times, the noises would seem perfectly trivial to him. Such motivational pressure may lead us in stage one to suspect deception. In stage two it will appear as *self*-deception. Motive can undermine testimony at either stage, albeit in very different ways.

Checklist for the Two-Stage Schema.

Stage-one rivals

C_1' Statement made, at least in part, because author thinks it is true. (go on to stage two)

C_2' Statement explained by motivational factors independent of belief in P. (stage two impossible)

Stage-two rivals

C_1 Author believes P because it is true.

C_2 Author's confidence in P due to mistake or misjudgment.
  (a) Incompetence
  (b) Simple error
  (c) Self-deception

SAMPLING AND STATISTICAL INFERENCE

We frequently find ourselves needing to know about something, but in a position to examine only a small part of it. Sometimes the object of our knowledge is simply too vast or expensive or otherwise diffi-cult to inspect directly. We wish to know the sentiments of the voting population on the upcoming election, but we haven't the time or the resources to ask everybody. A magazine may want to tell its readers about the new Toyota Camry, but can afford to test only one or two. Other times the obstacle lies in the destructiveness of the test. To test a car's crashworthiness we have to crash it; to see if the soup tastes right, we must taste it. But if we crash all the cars or taste all the soup, the test loses its point.

So we sample. We sample the soup, take a sample of the voting population, obtain a sample Toyota. If the sample is typical, or representative, we can learn a lot about what we are interested in from examining the sample we have. But what kind of reason can we have to think that the sample is representative of the rest? No matter what we do, a sample will be unlike the unsampled part in some respects. Just the fact that we ended up with *it* makes it different, and that difference *may* be linked to other differences. For cases like the electorate and the soup, the sample is different in size too. Representativeness is never absolute. So what we must assure ourselves of is that the sample is representative *in the right respects*: typical in the aspects we care about.

But, again, how do we do that? We must fall back once more on our basic understanding of things, the understanding that grounds diagnostic induction. We understand enough about soup to know that if we don't stir it up, its contents tend to settle in layers. So, for example, a sample scooped from the bottom will contain more rice than one scooped off the top. Which represents the soup? Probably neither, because the sampling procedure is distorting the sample's properties. Or, to put it more diagnostically, the procedure explains the ingredients as much as the soup does. Mixing everything up before sampling will distribute the ingredients more uniformly throughout the pot. Then when we sample we will have some reason to think the sample represents the soup. We can say the sample contains the mix it does *because* the whole pot of soup does, not because of some peculiarity of our sampling procedure.

This example allows us to see how natural it is to capture repre-sentativeness diagnostically. Getting a representative sample in-volves setting things up so that the best explanation of the sample's having a property (12% rice, for instance) is simply that the thing sampled has that property. Let us adopt some familiar jargon here and refer to the thing sampled as "the population." This name fits voters and consumers better than it does soup, but we can stretch the vocabulary a bit[6] in tough cases to simplify our discussion. So the aim is to arrange things so that the sample has property P *because* the population does. The sample is too salty *because* the soup is too salty. That's what we were sampling to find out. Sometimes we can set things up so that this representativeness is true of many properties of a sample, sometimes only a few. How many does not matter, as long as the properties you are interested in are among those explained by the population, not by the sampling procedure. We will then have evidence that the sample is representative in the right respects.

The rivals will cluster in a way parallel to those in testimony arguments. All those rivals explaining P in the sample by P in the population will underwrite a sample-to-population inference, and we will call them C_1 rivals. C_1 is read, "The best account of the sample having P (e.g., excessive saltiness) is that the population has P as well." All the rivals explaining that P in the sample comes not from the population but from some peculiarity of the sampling procedure undermine the inference and are lumped under C_2. We have already seen how our general understanding of things can be marshalled to elevate C_1 over C_2 for sampling soup. Stirring will break the connection between sampling procedure and sample properties, allowing the soup itself to explain those properties. And this is how sampling works in general. We understand a lot about how a procedure can affect—can bias—a sample's properties, and we know how to learn more. The trick is to arrange the circumstance so that the C_2 explanations will be at a disadvantage—as far-fetched as possible.

So if we sample a voting population, for example, to see who is favored in an upcoming election, we must take precautions to make sure that how we sample does not bias the results. If we poll during the day on weekdays, we will miss many single working voters and families with both parents working. We know enough to worry about this: Working parents probably don't have the same political profile as the electorate in general, so removing them from the sample is like skimming soup off the top. It will bias the sample. In 1936 there was a connection between owning a telephone and voting Republican: Most people not owning a phone voted Democratic; the people in the phone book were atypically Republican. So when the *Literary Digest*

---

[6]We may think of soup as a population of bits and pieces and grains and even molecules, if that helps the imagination.

used a telephone survey for a pre-election poll, they got a badly unrepresentative sample. Voters in the sample preferred the Republican, Alf Landon, by a large margin. But in the election a few days later, the Democrat, Franklin Roosevelt, won in a landslide. The sample property of preferring Landon was due not to a preference for Landon among voters in general (C_1) but to the procedure used to select the sample (C_2). A connection between procedure and preference biased the result.

We can, of course, get an unrepresentative sample no matter how careful we are, simply through bad luck. We can take all the reasonable precautions and still end up polling only Democrats. We can shake up the jar of mixed jelly beans and still draw out seven of one color. Bad luck is an undermining rival too, but it is different enough to deserve its own heading: C_3. So we have three general explanatory headings. A sample may have property P because the population has it (C_1), because of a peculiarity in the sampling procedure (C_2), or through bad luck (C_3). The first is the one we want, and we usually get it by eliminating the other two. Eliminating bad luck is usually a matter of getting a big enough sample—and keeping an eye out for obvious absurdity.

In sampling, we are always aiming for an argument that looks like this:

S_1 Sample has property P.

S_2 Circumstances (including sampling procedure).

$$\overline{\qquad\qquad\qquad\qquad\qquad\qquad\qquad\qquad\qquad\qquad\qquad} \quad \text{d}$$

C_1 Population has property P.

We attempt to support C_1 by fine-tuning S_2. The fine-tuning will often consist largely in a direct attack on C_2 and C_3, lowering their plausibility and raising C_1's indirectly.

Illustration

Learning all the S_2 precautions that pollsters require to competently sample public opinion is a curriculum all by itself, far beyond anything we can attempt here. But we can illustrate the basic diagnostic features of the enterprise with a more familiar if crude example. We all know enough about the institutions surrounding the kitchen cookie jar to make reasonably informed judgments about samples drawn from it in various circumstances. The thing to notice is how circumstances change what we can infer from a sample. Whether a sample is representative will depend on the circumstances, the sampling procedure, *and* the property we are interested in.

Let us begin with some circumstances. The jar is opaque and I cannot see into it, but it seems to be full of something (it's heavier than it should be if empty, and my hand touches something close to the top). Suppose I sample the contents by drawing out the first thing I touch, which turns out to be a sugar cookie. What does this tell me about the contents of the jar (the population)? Against the general background of normal kitchens it does not tell me much: There are too many different possible populations that would explain getting that sample. But it does give me one very good bet: I have found a (the) cookie jar. I understand enough to know that a cookie is not usually the first thing in a jar of teabags or jelly beans. The best account of the sample is that the jar contains cookies. The sample is probably representative in this respect.

S_1 Sample = one sugar cookie.

S_2 Drawn as described, in circumstances as described (everything else presumed normal).

$$\overline{\hspace{10cm}}\ \text{d}$$

C_1 The jar contains cookies.

What kind of cookies? Here things are much less certain. But we may change the circumstances to aid representativeness even in this respect. We know something about how the jar is filled. Let us say that the person who fills the jar buys (or makes) only one kind of cookie at a time and, further, fills the jar only when the last batch is completely gone. This is like stirring the soup: we may presume uniformity. So *any* sample will be representative as to kind. If we get a sugar cookie off the top, we may infer that the jar is filled with sugar cookies.

S_1 Sample = one sugar cookie (sample property: 100% sugar cookies).

S_2 Circumstances as amended above.

$$\overline{\hspace{10cm}}\ \text{d}$$

C_1 Population has the same property (100% sugar cookies).

If we relax either of these assumptions about how the jar is filled, however, C_2 obviously rises to the top of the plausibility ranking. If assortments or layers are genuine possibilities, our sampling procedure becomes a better account of the sample property (100% sugar cookies) than a uniform population is. So it is natural to look for a better sample. For a new sample I take four more cookies off the top, and, let us say, they too are sugar cookies. The sample property, then, remains the same (100% sugar cookies), but the procedure is different (five off the top). With this sample let us first consider just the case in which assortments are possible but layers are not: The filler uses only single kinds or random assortments and fills the jar only when empty. In these conditions our new sample is again probably representative: The best account of it is that the population is all sugar cookies. For it would be very tough to get five sugar cookies in a row from a random assortment; so if layers are not an option, a C_2 account of the sample property is not very plausible. Schematically,

S_1 Sample = five sugar cookies (sample property: 100% sugar cookies).

S_2 Filler uses only single kinds or random assortments and fills jar only when it is empty.

S_3 Sample is drawn consecutively from the top.

=== d

C_1 Population is 100% sugar cookies.

Making the filler less fastidious pushes C_2 back toward the top. If the jar gets filled whenever we happen to have cookies, and perhaps with several different kinds at a time, and with assortments that are not completely random, then our sampling procedure may just be working its way through a single layer. C_2 may easily explain the sample even in a non-uniform population. So if we allow all these possibilities we must sample differently for plausible representativeness. To raise hurdles for a layer-type C_2 account, we boorishly draw cookies from several places in the jar—one from the bottom, some from the middle. Suppose, with this new procedure, we end up with the same sample: five sugar cookies. This clearly hurts the layer hypothesis. But in the circumstances we are considering, there are so many possibilities that we must begin to worry about C_3: bad luck. How likely is it that I ended up with the only five sugar cookies in the jar, for instance? If there were only two or three chocolate chip, how likely is it that one would find its way into my sample? These are difficult questions that must be treated quantitatively and are beyond the scope of this text. But the quantitative algorithm works against the diagnostic background we have just examined. Furthermore, as we have seen, it is possible to make some useful progress even without appeal to statistical theory. And if circumstances are too messy for mathematical idealization, qualitative arguments are all you will be able to construct in any case.

Randomness

One further topic deserves brief mention. The less we know about the conditions in a population and the laws and institutions governing it, the less certain we can be about how a sampling procedure might affect the properties of a sample. When we are thus uncertain, one recourse is to make the sample random. That is, we try to overwhelm our ignorance by breaking as many connections as we can between procedure and sample property—at least all those we think might have the slightest bearing on the outcome. To take a random sample of registered voters, it would not be enough to wander (even randomly!) through neighborhoods knocking on doors. People who happen to be home, or accessible, or cooperative may have systematically atypical political views. We don't know, so those connections would be a worry: The selection would be insufficiently random.

One way to randomize would be to place every voter's name on a slip of paper, put them all in a drum, spin it, and draw the sample from different places in the drum. This should be enough to break all connection between political preference and being chosen in the sample. Randomness is just an extravagant way to eliminate bias, to assure that the sample we get is no more or less likely to be chosen because of the properties we are interested in. When we eliminate bias in this way, the only undermining rivals still open fall under C_3: bad luck. So to assure representativeness we merely attend to the size of the sample. Sometimes this is straightforward. When it is not, however, it raises all those questions addressed by quantitative statistics; and they are, unfortunately, beyond the scope of this investigation. Here we are merely examining the diagnostic ground of sampling.

As a practical matter, randomizing is often pointless or impossible due to the nature of the population or features of the context.

Numbering the cookies in our cookie jar, and then tormenting slips of paper, would be a waste of time, for example. The only reasonable way to number them would be to take them out of the jar, and in doing so we would find out what kinds they are, defeating the purpose of sampling. We could, of course, shake the jar; but if (as we supposed) it is nearly full, they would not move around much. Layers and sequences would remain, and randomness would not be achieved. If we shook hard enough to break up the layers, we would also break up the cookies: Crumbs and powder would defeat the point of the survey too. Often enough a non-random sample is all we can get, and, as we have seen, it may be just right for our purposes.

COUNTING CASES:
INDUCTION BY ENUMERATION

Suppose I had studied crows for years and had, from my experience, come to conclude that all crows are black. If I had a record of every crow I had examined, I might number the individual birds and set out the following inductive argument for my conclusions:

S_1 Crow #1 is black.

S_2 Crow #2 is black.

S_3 Crow #3 is black.

.

.

.

S_{258} Crow #258 is black.

C   All crows are black.

The simple counting of cases, or instances, sometimes strikes us as a purer, less complicated form of induction than that set out in Chapter 3. Some thinkers have argued that the enumeration of cases like this is actually the basic inductive concept, underpinning the more elaborate arguments we have been examining. However, attempts to show how such an underpinning might work have not met with any success. The reason is that even the purest cases of induction by enumeration seem to presuppose the general understanding of things that complicates the more complicated cases. In fact, they turn out to be diagnostic inductions in disguise.

This is not to say that lists never support generalizations. It's just that, when they do, it is not the list itself, in isolation, but also what we know about the items on the list, and the circumstances in which the instances were recorded, that provide the support. And then we need to find the best explanation of getting that particular list in those particular circumstances. The list plays the role of trace data in a diagnostic inference. Sometimes the best account is a generalization, sometimes not, depending.

Many lists, schematizable in the same way as our list of crows, lead to just the opposite conclusion. In California, or some other seismically unstable region, we might reassure ourselves with the following argument:

S_1 Day #1: no earthquake.

S_2 Day #2: no earthquake.

S_3 Day #3: no earthquake.

.

.

.

S_{258} Day #258: no earthquake.

C   We will never have an earthquake.

But geologists tell us that, in such an area, a far better explanation of a long time passing without earthquakes occurring is that the accumulated subterranean stress is not being released and is instead building for a big quake. The longer the string of quiet days, the worse it is going to be. Similarly, the evidence of our daily lives would, by enumeration, yield immortality:

S_1 Day #1: I did not die.

S_2 Day #2: I did not die.

etc.

But we know full well that with each passing day death is closer, not more remote.

Accordingly, my thought that my list of crow observations supports the generalization that all crows are black must be partly the result of what I know about birds, pigmentation, and the range of habitats in which I have seen crows. It might be that the best account of all *those* crows being black is that all crows everywhere are black, but it is not a matter of merely counting cases.

CIRCUMSTANTIAL EVIDENCE

We are now in a position to throw some light on a common but often misunderstood notion: circumstantial evidence. Evidence drawn from the circumstances is often and obviously crucial in making a diagnosis. Many of our diagnostic schemata have parts explicitly reserved for circumstances, and often much else could be rightly so described. Sometimes circumstances contain trace data (broken screen, burning neighborhood), sometimes background (famous modus operandi, Joe Smith's planned course). Sometimes circumstances are all we have (racing car crash), and they can constitute a very strong argument (crash caused by a broken hub carrier).

Nevertheless, the term "circumstantial evidence" is commonly used derogatorily, as a way of demeaning evidence: "The suspect was acquitted because the case against him was merely circumstantial." This suggests the evidence is not very good, and not very good *because* it is circumstantial. There is something right about this. But it is a subtle point, and care is required to see how it fits with everything we have learned so far.

In a typical criminal case of the kind alluded to above, the problem usually is that nobody actually saw the defendant commit the crime. No one saw him kill the service station attendant; no one could place him at or near the scene of the holdup on the evening in question. There were no witnesses. The evidence we do have includes reliable testimony that a car just like the suspect's was in the neighborhood of the service station just before the crime and other reliable testimony that he, around that time, suddenly seemed to have more money than was usual.

Even if we add that the defendant had no alibi, the case for conviction here is rather weak, and weak because it lacks, quite specifically, evidence that is not circumstantial: direct identification of the defendant at or near the scene of the crime. So we can begin to see the point in calling evidence "merely circumstantial." If the question concerns identifying an individual—especially one who does not want to be identified—recognition by a reliable witness is an ideal kind of evidence. Our ability to recognize people, to discriminate among other human beings, is one of our best, most well-developed perceptual skills. In the right circumstances, a personal recognition can be of enormous value as evidence in an inductive inference.

By contrast, circumstances of the kind mentioned in this case are too coarse-grained to implicate a unique individual. They do not have the right kind of detail to provide a confident identification. Too many rival accounts of them are possible. So when "circumstantial evidence" is meant to refer to circumstances like these, and a personal identification is in question, there is some sense in using "circumstantial" as a derogatory term, some sense in thinking of circumstantial evidence as intrinsically weak.

But the lesson to be learned from this is a narrow, practical one about our skills and interests, not a general one about the basic nature of evidence. For as soon as we relax the constraints we have imposed on the *kind* of circumstance or the *kind* of conclusion, the contrast vanishes. We have already seen how strong diagnostic arguments can be without eyewitness testimony, when the conclusion does not involve identifying a person. But even in the criminal identification we have been examining, we might make a case from the circumstances every bit as strong as a direct observation of the crime, simply by allowing more finely detailed circumstances.

Fingerprints are as unique as faces; guns and ballistic markings are nearly so; but in contrasting with eyewitness accounts of a crime, they will all be part of the circumstances. So if we found that the fresh fingerprints on the empty cash drawer were the suspect's; that the bullet taken from the attendant's body was from the defendant's gun, which he was famous for never letting out of his sight; and that the bills he spent the evening of the crime were ones marked by the service station owner in anticipation of a robbery, such a case would be circumstantial, but easily as strong as an isolated eyewitness's identification. We could easily make it stronger still by simply accumulating more (circumstantial) detail.

So on occasions when it is natural to use the phrase "circumstantial evidence" to stand for a narrow, relatively weak kind of evidence, it would be wise to call these more detailed circumstances simply "indirect evidence." We would then make a three-part contrast among (a) the direct observation of something, (b) circumstantial evidence for it, and (c) other indirect evidence for it. In these terms we may then observe that, although direct observation is sometimes of truly enormous value in support of a conclusion, there is no general categorical difference between the support provided by direct observation and indirect evidence derived from the surrounding circumstances.

In fact, indirect evidence can be so strong that we will quite properly reject eyewitness accounts conflicting with it. Spectators testify that the victim was standing when the fatal shot was fired, but the path of the bullet through the body makes that simply inconceivable. We reject the observers' descriptions as deceived or dishonest (see pages 166–75). It is easier to explain away the direct observation reports than the results of the pathologist's examination.

Direct observation may be undermined in all sorts of ways, of course, and can be virtually worthless. Sometimes the observations will conflict with each other. One witness says the victim was standing; another says he was already on the ground. This lack of agreement suggests that circumstances have undermined perceptual competence: Perhaps both observations are suspect. All the considerations relevant to the competence of testimony are relevant here too. If there is much excitement and we are scared out of our wits, our perceptual reliability will be eroded. So too will it be affected if we have a deep emotional commitment to something or someone in the dramatic events unfolding in front of us: We let our hopes guide our eyes and see what we wish had happened rather than what did.

In short, the reliability of our perceptions *depends* on the circumstances. Even our best direct observation may be undermined by some feature of the circumstances. A perfectly normal, competent personal identification may be demolished by the existence of an identical twin. So in general the only rule is to set out all the relevant data—direct and indirect—and find the best account of it all. Sometimes eyewitness testimony can be discounted; sometimes it will be impossible to explain away.

SCIENCE AS A DIAGNOSTIC ACTIVITY

The natural[7] sciences may be thought of as general ways of treating diagnostic questions. What distinguishes them is their attempt to extend our understanding of things *in general*, rather than our

---

[7]The social and behavioral sciences are too controversial to be treated simply.

understanding of specific, practical matters of the kinds that have occupied us so far. One way to classify sciences is by the form of the implicit question they address. Basic sciences (physics, chemistry, biology) address a present-continuous tense question of the form "What is going on?" Historical sciences (paleontology, archeology) are devoted to finding out "What happened?" so the question is in the past tense. Other sciences (geology, cosmology) contain aspects of each of these.

Naturally, the various sciences are also differentiated by their subject matter: the sorts of things they apply these questions to. Physics inquires about matter at the most basic or abstract level, biology investigates organisms, chemistry inquires into the composition or analysis of matter at a certain level, geology into the development of the earth's crust, cosmology into the nature and evolution of stars, archeology into past civilizations, meteorology into the weather. Explaining different subjects always requires somewhat distinct procedures and models, rewards different approximations and idealizations, and employs different tools and apparatus. This is why there are distinct disciplines, different departments in universities. But the distinctions, though sometimes profound, are simply due to the practical problems arising from the treatment of different subject matters: They arise naturally; they are not imposed from above. So the disciplinary relations are constantly changing, evolving; and there is room for much overlap at the edges. Not only is physics valuable to cosmology and evolutionary biology to paleontology, but there are whole disciplines of overlap. Examples are biochemistry, geophysics, and physical chemistry. Paleontology might be thought of simply as the overlap between biology and geology.

In short, the *differences* among the natural sciences stem entirely from the different aims of their investigations, from their different objects of study. Even the different questions they address derive from this source. Their *similarities*, on the other hand, come from their all being diagnostic enterprises. They all generate understanding through the explanation of trace data in the arenas they have staked out for themselves. But sciences are distinguished from other diagnostic enterprises by the generality of the understanding to which they all aspire. Explaining individual traces is not an end in itself; it is part of the broader endeavor of understanding the whole slice of nature falling under the purview of a given science. When I try to explain why my car won't start, I do so simply to solve a practical problem I have. When cosmologists try to explain the puzzling supernova of 1987, they do so for the sake of a better understanding of the evolution of the universe.

Some Structural Features

Theories. We may discern a number of large-scale features of the natural sciences by applying and extending the cluster of concepts we have developed in Chapters 3 and 4. Explaining trace data is the basic diagnostic move, and it will be the most revealing place to begin. Since the grand understanding at which the sciences aim is based on explaining specific bits of data that are *not* very grand, we may think of the diagnostic activity as taking place on two different levels. Most of the science we read about in the popular press—in fact, most scientific activity—consists in attempts to fit bits of data, individual phenomena, into currently accepted theoretical frameworks. Geologists try to show how features of continental land masses (mountains, fault lines, layers of fossils) may be understood within plate-tectonic theory. Cosmologists try to understand the quantum mechanics of the supernova of 1987. Geneticists try to understand the molecular structure of a particular virus.

Except for the generality of the frameworks within which they work, these scientific activities exactly parallel the more mundane diagnostic investigations we have examined. The frameworks provide background from which various explanations derive their initial plausibility. The rest is done by how well or badly the various accounts explain details of the phenomenon in question. These accounts may be called theories (with a small *t*) in the same way I may have a theory of why my car quit on me last night or a theory about what happened to Joe Smith. We may develop a theory of plate motion along the San Andreas fault, a theory about the mechanism of supernovas, or a molecular theory of heredity. In each case the support for the theoretical account depends both on how well it fits within a working framework and on how well it accounts for the relevant traces.

Scientists will commonly devote an enormous amount of time and effort to working out the details of such accounts and to digging up traces to be explained by, or to raise hurdles for, those accounts. An example that can be understood without extensive training is the recent controversy over the extinction of the dinosaurs. The fossil record contains many instances of abundant species dying out relatively rapidly, and this poses a puzzle for paleontologists, geologists, and evolutionary biologists. What causes sudden extinctions? Because of the time intervals involved, it is possible that the extinctions occurred over a period of days, years, or centuries. Even centuries are relatively short on this scale. So a range of theories is possible—from gradual, global cooling trends to sudden cataclysms. And the mechanism could be anything from volcanoes and viruses to comets and solar aberrations. Of course, some extinctions might be traceable to one phenomenon while others result from something else. It is a complicated study.

So explaining why the dinosaurs died out sixty-five million years ago is just a small part of this general puzzle. But explaining even a small part is useful for our purposes because it illustrates the diagnostic structure in an accessible way; and it shows how much care and attention to detail are required for any progress to be made on a scientific problem. In the following article a bit of trace data is presented, along with some reason to think one particular theory best accounts for it.

Bits of Quartz Called Clues to Extinction of Dinosaurs

The Associated Press

WASHINGTON—Bits of quartz found at several sites around the world appear to confirm a theory that the extinction of dinosaurs and other forms of life 65 million years ago resulted from the impact of a large meteorite or comet, scientists said yesterday.

Researchers from the U.S. Geological Survey office in Denver said grains of quartz taken from five sites in Europe, as well as New Zealand, the Pacific Basin and elsewhere, have structural features associated with the impact of a large body striking the Earth.

Detailed analysis of the mineral debris shows that it comes from a single massive event and not from a series of volcanic eruptions, as other scientists contend, they said in a new report.

The microscopic fracturing found in the quartz is more like that associated with the pressures of a massive impact than what would result from volcanic activity, they say in today's issue of the journal *Science*.

Bruce Bohor, Peter Modreski and Eugene Foord said the so-called "shocked quartz" is found in the same sediment layers that contain unusually high levels of iridium, a metal common in asteroids, meteors and comets.

The researchers said the latest findings bolster the controversial, 10-year-old theory of Nobel Prize-winning physicist Luis Alvarez and his geologist son, Walter, that a single catastrophic event led to a great extinction of life on the Earth.

The Alvarez theory says that impact of an extraterrestrial body 65 million years ago threw up a giant cloud of debris that encircled the globe and diminished sunlight for months, if not years. The climate cooling caused by the dust resulted in the death of dinosaurs and many other types of animal and plant life, it contends.

A body 6 miles wide hitting the Earth at 45,000 mph, as calculated by the Alvarez theory, could have blasted debris high enough into the atmosphere to account for the worldwide shock quartz distribution, Bohor said.

The Alvarez meteorite theory is only one of a number of theories—some catastrophic, some not—currently being offered to explain this extinction. The controversy among them is just an extension of the moves made in this brief article: Traces are offered as hurdles; background is marshalled in support or opposition. It all looks rather like our attempt to understand the last flight of the *Titanic*.[8]

Theoretical Frameworks.   The other level at which diagnostic activity takes place is that of the general frameworks themselves. Quantum Theory, Plate-Tectonic Theory, Evolutionary Theory— theories with a capital *T*—provide explanatory frameworks within which the respective sciences try to organize their understanding. Sometimes these too find themselves in competition with rivals, fighting to gain or hold a place in the guidance of research. But the grand scale of the process at this level, as well as its complexity, subtlety, and pace, makes the pattern more difficult to discern and harder to characterize. It is interesting enough to be worth the effort, however.

The major source of our difficulty in dealing with general framework theories lies in their abstractness. This sometimes deceptive abstractness has three distinct consequences, which we will consider in turn.

[8]Further examples extracted from this controversy and other topics of interest may be found in Appendix A.

A. Form.   Framework theories provide only the *form* of the understanding at which a discipline aims, not the substance. They represent a very general insight about how practitioners have found it most profitable or productive to think about their subject. As such, frameworks say something valuable about the form that explanations must take, but by themselves they provide little explanatory detail. There are many different views within evolutionary biology of just *how* living things evolve, and different views in tectonic theory of the nature of the plates and the mechanism of their motion. To use a different kind of example, the mechanical theory published by Newton in his *Principia* provided the *form* of a gravitational account of planetary orbits. But actually working out the details of those explanations—getting the orbits right—required incredibly imaginative exertions by the greatest minds of the eighteenth and nineteenth centuries.

General framework theories *guide* research but do not dictate it. Many distinct courses of development are always possible. The details depend on how problems are resolved by small-*t* theories, grappling with the dirty details under the framework's guidance. Which interference must we take seriously and which can we neglect? What approximations work? What compounding of effects is necessary? What is available from other areas of science? Or from technology? What data have been irretrievably lost through cosmic accident? For an entire framework to fail, you must show that none of the possible developments will work.

This last observation has the most far-reaching consequences for understanding how frameworks change. For to know whether understanding can be achieved under the current framework, trained specialists must work out the technical problems of applying it to the field it covers. Paleontologists must dig out the fossil record; mathematicians must invent methods to work out the orbits; seismologists must trace fault lines and epicenters. Only if all this is going on can we make the basic plausibility judgment: How well is it going? And even then, only those who understand the detail— usually practitioners themselves—can make the judgment. Are we making reasonable progress against the technical problems? Or are our best efforts failing in such a way as to suggest that the framework—the form of the inquiry—is at fault? This is why it is sometimes hard to say in a few words just why a capital *T* theory was abandoned, and also why some theories are not given up in spite of progress disappointing to those outside science.

B. Finding a Rival.   Because framework theories are esoteric and global in their purview, it is common for them to go through long periods in which serious rivals simply do not exist. Casual suggestions may abound, but it takes a real investment to work out in enough detail a rival framework that can actually guide explanatory research as well as one that is already working. Diagnostic evaluation and criticism cannot even begin, of course, until there are rivals. So unless things begin to go so badly that someone is motivated to develop a rival, the current theory will be best because it is the only show in town.

Not that this demeans a theory: It is easy to overstate the case here. When one considers how hard it is to make *any* sense of the fossil record, the topography of continents, or the mechanism of radiation, that we have a framework successfully guiding research in such an area is remarkable. We need a special reason to invest the effort in a new one.

The relative unavailability of rival frameworks is a source of science's power to generate insight. It helps explain how mere humans have been able to make such enormous progress against the impressive complexity of nature. The lack of rival frameworks puts pressure on science to solve the tough technical problems constantly arising within the existing framework. There is incentive to take on the tough cases, to sweat over conflicts and contradictions, to devise methods and models to surmount obstacles. It is in these activities that science produces its greatest insights: the neutrino, DNA, the source of the Continental Divide. But they require hard work, commitment, imagination—sometimes genius. Were it easy to crank out new framework theories, we would many times do just that: cut and run instead of breaking our brains against the tough problems involved in making any framework grapple with details. Science, and our general understanding, would be far poorer for it.

C. Historical Scale.   Nearly all of the actual cases in which a real rival rose up, did battle with an accepted framework theory, and displaced it as a disciplinary guide are long past—part of the history of science. As a consequence, it is only with great difficulty that most of us can understand such a revolutionary episode as being a case of human reasoning. This is so for a pair of closely related reasons. First, surprisingly hard work and historical sensitivity are required to take an antique framework seriously; special training is usually necessary to appreciate its structural virtues, to understand it as a genuine option. Without this understanding, the abstract details will seem merely abstruse or quaint, perhaps irretrievably primitive. Second, we usually learn about old frameworks from partisans of the superseding ones—in science classes, not history classes. And the purpose in these classes is not to teach accurate history but to display the nature and virtues of current science. This is, of course, a perfectly legitimate pedagogic enterprise; but it is uniformly better served by a caricature of history than by a faithful recounting of the episode.

Accordingly, if we wish to understand the scientific rationale— the reasoning—of such an episode, we must ignore much of our current culture and science through which we naturally view it. We must develop something of the perspective of the participants, especially in separating the *promise* of a new framework from its eventual accomplishments. For in the adopting of a new framework, much of the weight must fall on its explanatory promise, as determined by the well-trained and informed perceptions of the practitioners at the time. Their work with available alternatives may give them good reason to *expect* a particular framework to be productive, but the actual results are something to be accumulated over coming decades through hard work and imagination. On the other hand we, looking back through history, naturally see its accomplishment, its successes, the productivity itself. The framework seems just right. It is hard to imagine why anybody would use a different one, would look at things in another way.

These three consequences of a theoretical framework's abstractness disguise the fact that when they are replaced, the procedure is basically the same as it is in choosing among small-*t* theories: a competition among rival explanations. The key judgment is the comparative ease with which the different frameworks allow us to explain phenomena within the complex, extensive network they cover. The grand scale on which this promise is redeemed, however, provides a nice contrast with the mundane investigations we have studied so far. Looking at actual historical examples will cast useful new light on diagnostic inquiry.

Copernicus. The earliest theoretical framework change to have much impact on modern science was astronomy's abandonment of the earth as center of the universe. This historical episode illustrates all the issues just discussed almost too well: It may require more historical sensitivity than the average person has.[9] Nevertheless it comes first chronologically and treats a science we all have some grasp of—justification enough to try developing the sensitivity as we go.

Looking back at the Copernican suggestion, we find it hard to see heliocentricity as anything other than a fact about the universe that astronomy simply discovered. It seems so obvious now that we find ourselves telling stories of primitive religious commitments and self-centeredness to explain why it took so long to discover. But to do so grotesquely distorts everything about the matter. It scandalously misrepresents the scientific sophistication of early astronomers and cosmologists and ignores the difficulty of developing a sun-centered astronomy that would work as well as, much less better than, the earth-centered one of the time. This natural picture makes it impossible to imagine the complexity of the competition between the two viewpoints. So we must really exert ourselves to see that competition as resting essentially on the perception and judgment of particularly trained minds as they grappled with the tough, technical problems that arose in their attempt to understand celestial motions.

The earth-centered astronomy of the fifteenth century, which Copernicus was part of, and departed from, was the product of some of the greatest minds that ever lived. The mathematical models of Eudoxus, Callipus, Ptolemy, and Hipparchus are dazzling to this day. Great sophistication is required to follow even their simpler calculations. The computation of distances and dimension by Aristarchus and Eratosthenes, among others, is as resourceful and imaginative as anything in science today. The cosmological arguments of Plato and Aristotle are harder to appreciate, but this is entirely due to our looking at them through five centuries of heliocentric accomplishment. If we can bring ourselves to read them without the concept of gravitation, without Newtonian inertial dynamics—in short, without the whole picture of the solar system and universe we have grown up with—their arguments against moving the earth are not just cogent, they are compelling. Let us look at one.

The immense dimensions of the earth were well known in antiquity. Its circumference was measured with fair precision by Erastosthenes, more than two centuries before the birth of Christ. So if the diurnal motion of the heavens was to be explained by a rotating

[9]For an accessible study, see T. S. Kuhn, *The Copernican Revolution* (Cambridge: Harvard University Press, 1957).

earth, that would mean we were rushing along at something like fifty times the speed of a horse at gallop. Yet we have absolutely no sensation of this (as we *do* on horseback). Furthermore, what is to prevent everything from being flung off into space? (The principle of the sling was known before David and Goliath.) And why are the clouds not left behind? The modern answer to these questions depends on the hard-won successes of the heliocentric perspective. But without gravity, and an understanding of inertial dynamics, it was preposterous to spin the earth. Other, subtler arguments were advanced as well, against both daily and yearly motion of the earth.

By the time Copernicus finally proposed astronomy from a moving, spinning earth, geocentric astronomy had become staggeringly complex mathematically. The paths of the heavenly bodies *are* complex, no matter how they are represented. So the system of whirling wheels, developed in the centuries before Copernicus to account for those motions, required immense geometrical competence to manipulate. It took a sophisticated mathematician (Copernicus), and all the pages of a large book (*De Revolutionibus Orbium Caelestium*), to even *propose* an alternative theoretical framework. Enormous skill and effort were required simply to take the wheels, transfer the center of their motion from the earth to the sun, and show that the paths of the planets could be generated in this way as well. It took this much simply to show that astronomy could be done from that vantage. Whether it was better or worse was another question.

What, then, motivated Copernicus' proposal? Why, after two thousand years of holding the earth fixed, did a competent astronomer exert himself to try doing it another way? Why did he decide that solutions to astronomy's technical problems should no longer be pursued within the old framework? Diagnostically, the change can have but two sources: trace data and background information. Normally this would be taken to mean that one of the following two things occurred. Some dramatic, new trace raised new difficulties for the framework; or what scientists had learned about something else in science damaged an accepted explanatory form or helped its rival. The nature of a theoretical framework provides another possibility under "trace data," however: protracted failure to make progress on an old explanatory problem. Something that initially does not appear to be much of a hurdle becomes one as more and more plausible attempts to get around it fail.

So the intractability of a technical problem, in the face of concerted attempts to solve it, may, after a time, suggest that the framework itself is at fault. This is just what happened at the end of the nineteenth century to both classical mechanics and classical radiation theory. The problems that eventuated in the abandonment of these frameworks had been known for some time. It was their persistence, in spite of heroic attempts by the best minds in physics to solve them, that resulted in the adoption of new frameworks: relativistic mechanics and quantum theory, respectively.

For Copernicus there were no new traces to account for. His motivation came from the other two areas: evolving background and stubborn implausibilities. First, scholastic mechanists, during the century preceding *De Revolutionibus*, began to develop crude conceptions of inertia and gravity,[10] which served to loosen the hold of commonsense objections to moving the earth. This loosening automatically raised the plausibility of a heliocentric framework, allowing a serious astronomer to at least consider its possibility. Second, the geocentric account of planetary motion had several unhappy features that had resisted resolution for centuries. And many of these features hinted that the problem might lie in the sun's role. The combination of these two factors was enough to launch *De Revolutionibus*. It is illuminating to look at the second of these in more detail, to develop some feel for the diagnostic nature of explanatory promise.

The most engaging trace data to be explained by astronomy, for Copernicus as well as astronomers for centuries before, were the motions of the five visible planets. The four most salient features of these motions, together with one other matter, will allow us to sketch Copernicus' argument. These features are (1) the planets' general motion westward through the stars; (2) the fact that they periodically stop and execute a little retrograde loop to the east before continuing their westward drift, as in the drawing at right; (3) that they vary in brightness in a fairly systematic way; and (4) that two of the planets (Venus and Mercury) never stray very far from the sun. The other matter is the order of the heavenly bodies, their relative distance from earth.

To account for the motions, geocentric astronomy offered a system of whirling wheels. It all rested on uniform circular motion, which, once started, would presumably continue without further

---

[10]It is hard to exaggerate how far these conceptions were from ones we hold today (see the bibliography in the Kuhn volume cited earlier for further reading). But they were enough to start our thinking in another direction.

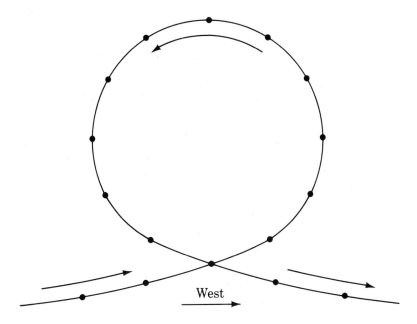

intervention. A planet moved on a circle, whose center moved on another, whose center moved on another, until, finally, one had its center fixed at the center of the earth. To generate the paths more and more accurately required merely compounding the apparatus, as shown on page 198. Any path could be traced against the starry background in this manner.

The mechanism that actually developed, however—the one required to get the gross motions right—had several features that were never really satisfactory and left the framework vulnerable to changes elsewhere in science. The major one was that the data were vastly more systematic than the explanation. Many features that looked like they should be systematically significant could be handled only ad hoc, by adding a wheel here, changing a velocity there. Some examples:

The retrogressions (item 2 of the four above) exhibited all sorts of regularity. First, their size and frequency varied inversely: Planets that executed large loops retrogressed less frequently than those that executed small ones. And the latter were dim planets, the former bright. Furthermore, retrogression always occurred when a planet lined up with the sun, and the three whose motion was not tied to the sun (Mars, Jupiter, and Saturn) were always brightest then

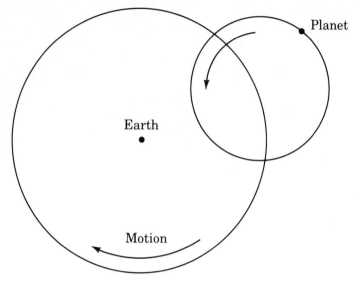

BASIC APPARATUS

too. Not a hint of why these regularities should occur could be found in the mechanism. Astronomers of the day accommodated them by adding wheels and changing velocities to make sure things occurred when they should.

Similarly for the striking fact that Venus and Mercury never wandered more than a certain number of degrees from the sun in their trip around the zodiac. This had been known since antiquity; and astronomers since antiquity had puzzled over its significance. Surely it signaled some important contrast with the other three that were free to roam the zodiac unrestricted. But the geocentric model simply added more detail to keep them in their allotted range.

Finally, the actual location of Venus and Mercury, whether between us and the sun or outside of the sun's path, was still unsettled thousands of years after the question had first been asked. The option of letting them go from one side to the other was not open, for then their earth-centered mechanisms would collide with each other and with that of the sun. This problem would make it nearly impossible to think of the mechanisms as real and explanatory.

For all these reasons the model of whirling wheels has occasionally been thought to be merely a predicting device, not an attempt to explain the motions. And some people doubtless used it in this way. But only some. For, as Copernicus insisted, if you wanted to hold the earth still in the center of the universe, the whirling wheels provided the best account of the motions that humans had come up with. Yet it still had deep, unresolved technical problems: It strained plausibility. It was only acceptable if there were no reasonable alternative.

With the modest advances of fifteenth- and sixteenth-century mechanics, a heliocentric model moved closer to reasonability. It gained enough plausibility to encourage a practicing astronomer to work out the details from that perspective. And having done this, Copernicus found that many of the unresolved puzzles simply vanished. The change was actually very small. He kept the entire whirling-circle apparatus. (What else was there to do?) He merely moved its center from earth to sun and worked out the paths from there. From this perspective, even with the old apparatus, he was able to generate easy, natural explanations for all of the above regularities left unexplained on the geocentric model.

Mercury and Venus, as interior planets, would naturally never appear more than a fixed distance from the sun, determined by the size of their orbits. They could wander from one side of the sun to the other without danger of collision because the mechanism no longer had to reach across the sun to the center of the earth. The retrograde loops simply vanished as features of the planets' actual paths: The planets just appeared to reverse directions against the starry backdrop as the earth overtook and passed an outer planet or was overtaken by a faster, interior one. Naturally this "reversal" occurred when the planets were nearest the earth and hence were lined up with the sun; the outer ones would be brightest then too, for the same reason. The size of the retrograde loops was explained by the relative distance of the planets' orbits from earth's. The large ones were for the close planets (Mars and Venus and, to a lesser extent, Jupiter), the small ones for more distant planets. And the greater distance of these latter two, Mercury and Saturn, would immediately account for their dimness, compared with the former three.

The infrequency of the larger loops would then be due to the nearby planets having orbital periods close to our own, and hence taking relatively longer to overtake one another. The greater frequency of small loops was due to much greater speed, in the case of Mercury, or much less, for Saturn.

Letting the earth move meant that many venerable phenomena of astronomy had to be explained as not really "out there," but due, at least partly, to our motion through space. A moving observer changes his relationship to many things at once. Hence the explanations become connected, systematic. This struck Copernicus—as it would strike others—as immensely promising. It held promise of a systematically better way for astronomy to work out an understanding of the cosmos.

Also promising was the new role of the sun. It had all along been taken to be the largest object in the universe, so it fell comfortably into its role as center of the major motions. This latter feature is something we now naturally exaggerate the importance of. We must restrain our critical impulse here, for we see the role of the sun through the lens of the elegant dynamics that heliocentricity allowed to develop. Copernicus could see only its promise.

But the perception of promise is everything here. It is the final piece of the puzzle, the factor that overcomes still strong objections to doing things in a new way. An established framework—and especially the original one in a field—always captures some basic plausibility: It seems just right in certain respects. Its first successes then give it genuine authority. So when paradoxes and implausibilities crop up, we naturally treat them as problems to be solved. We do not cut and run at the first obstacle, or the second. It takes a lot to abandon a working theoretical framework. When practitioners begin to think there is something wrong with the basic explanatory form, AND somebody shows *in some detail* that explanations can be given another form, which avoids the troubling implausibilities, AND that new form appears promising to the trained eyes of those struggling with the technical problems of the field—only then will a discipline open itself to the trauma of changing the framework within which it seeks understanding.

If a new framework succeeds in providing understanding it will, in redeeming its promise, become as deeply rooted in our perception as the old one was. We will begin to see it as always having had those successes built in. It will then be almost impossible to return to the original context and see the framework as merely, amorphously promising. What the Copernican shift allowed—even prompted— was the work of Kepler, Galileo, Déscartes, Hooke, and Newton, resulting in orbital mechanics and, eventually, our modern picture of the cosmos. It was explanatorily successful right away, and it continued building success on success. It is the worst sort of case to be historically objective about.

The diagnostic competition among explanations at this level requires plausibility judgments that can be reliably made only by a

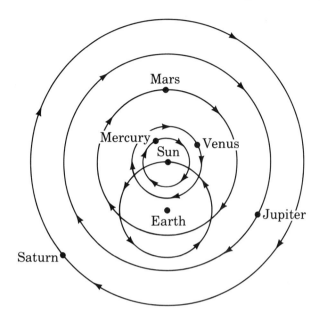

serious student of the old framework, facing the particular technical problems of the time, with the understanding then available. The best we can probably hope for is to appreciate the human complexity of those judgments, to sympathize with the trauma—and the gamble. To this end it is useful to note that an old framework never goes quietly. Its partisans invariably patch it up ingeniously in attempts to save it. The theory the new one supplants is invariably stronger than the one it attacked and better by far than the caricature we learn later. That is why the process works. No easy victories are allowed: Only genuine promise passes the test.

For heliocentricity, the severest test came a century after *De Revolutionibus*. Tycho Brahe proposed an earth-centered system in which only the moon and the sun revolved around the earth directly. The five planets were added as satellites of the sun, as in the drawing above. This system had most of the virtues of Copernicus'. But it came too late. Some of the sun-centered system's promise had already been redeemed. Tycho's student and protégé Johannes Kepler was soon to propose the first laws of orbital motion. The glimmer of promise had become the glare of insight. There was no going back.

Oxidation. A different kind of example, illustrating the same features, comes from the history of chemistry. (The same cautions

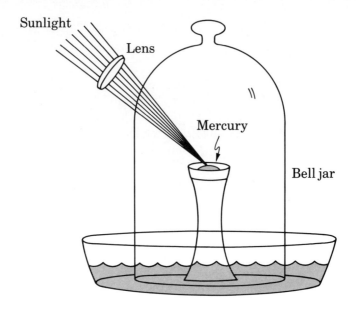

Sunlight

Lens

Mercury

Bell jar

apply.) Until the end of the eighteenth century the process of combustion, and the calcination of metals, was thought to involve the release of something from the object during its combustion or calcination. In eighteenth-century chemistry this something was known as phlogiston. It is a natural theory, for in the lighting of a match, or the burning of a log, something does seem to be given off along with the heat. It too was a very successful theory, providing the form within which chemical explanations could be given for all sorts of what we would nowadays call "reactions."[11] But toward the end of the eighteenth century, the career of phlogistic chemistry bore a striking resemblance to that of earth-centered astronomy three hundred years earlier.

It began, in the same way, with some troubling explanations. Questions raised by the theory itself were answered in a strained, ad hoc, unpromising way. Two stand out. The first derived from the fact that a sample of metal always gained weight during calcination. If pure mercury were heated in air, for example, the red mercury calx

---

[11]For a useful discussion see E. J. Holmyard, *Makers of Modern Chemistry* (Oxford: The Clarendon Press, 1931).

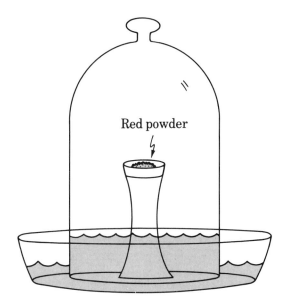

Red powder

resulting would always weigh more than the original mercury. This was troubling because calcination was the loss of phlogiston: Heat drove phlogiston out of the mercury, leaving the calx. Chemists explained this by postulating that phlogiston had negative weight. We nowadays might think this silly or obviously false; but that would be reading too much of recent science into the chemistry to two centuries ago. Repellent gravitational forces (like repellent magnetic or electrostatic ones) were not *incoherent*. It was just that this was the only place in all of science that seemed to require them. In attributing negative weight to phlogiston, simply to account for these reactions, chemistry took on a substantial plausibility burden, for a very modest payoff. It was as troubling as not knowing where to put Mercury and Venus in space. In the absence of encouragement from some other quarter (other traces to explain, perhaps), the idea of negative weight would be acceptable only if there were no workable alternative.

The other place where trouble arose was in accounting for what happened when these reactions were carried out in a confined space, with a determined amount of air. Chemists sometimes monitored their manipulation of matter by carrying out experiments in bell jars inverted in water (see drawing on page 202).

This isolation controlled some variables in an obviously desirable way. When mercury is heated and turned into the red calx in these conditions, however, the most notable result is a rise in the water level inside the jar, as in the drawing on page 203.

Because something (phlogiston) was coming *out* during calcination, this result once again required an unpromisingly contrived (if ingenious) explanation.

First, phlogiston escaped not only from the sample, but from the bell jar too, like light. Given the unsettled material nature of phlogiston, this was not terribly problematic. The mechanism of the water-level rise was more troubling, however: The water was supposed to rise because the heat and fumes of the reaction reduced the springiness of the air in the jar. This, again, was not nearly as bizarre a suggestion as it now seems. Boyle's experiments with the pressure/volume relation were known as measuring the spring of air, so the metaphor had clear scientific currency. And anyone who has squeezed a balloon or ridden in a pneumatically suspended car has experienced the parallel between metal springs and gaseous ones. If metal springs weaken when heated, why not gaseous ones? Et cetera.

Not being absolutely incoherent, however, is a long way from being promising. To take the spring metaphor seriously, with all its implications about temper, was again to shoulder an immense plausibility burden for small gain. If nothing else required this much of the metaphor, chemistry would accept it only if forced to. Only, that is, if there were no feasible alternative.

Of course, all this provides motivation to develop an alternative theoretical framework—a radically different *way* of explaining these reactions and perhaps others too. Antoine Lavoisier is famous for doing just that. He proposed that what happened during combustion and calcination was that some previously unidentified part of the air left the atmosphere and joined the original substance. There was nothing there but heat and various substances. No mysterious principles were required. This accounted for the two recondite phenomena (simultaneously!) in a natural, effortless way. And chemists of the day quickly came to see it as a promising way to treat other reactions as well.

As it was for the astronomical controversy of the sixteenth century, and for any other general framework change, the pace of the diagnostic process was slow and its scale grand. The new way of explaining reactions had a clear plausibility advantage in a few respects—and promised others. It was adopted because of its promise as a way of actually doing chemistry—guiding research. But to actually make the case for the new framework—to redeem the promise—took decades of accomplishment. We see Lavoisier's suggestion through eyes conditioned by two centuries of its success. It is understandably difficult to strip all that away and share the sense of promise without the certainty of accomplishment—that is, to share the gamble. It does no harm to bear in mind this fact: There is no record of the times that promise of this caliber bore no fruit at all.

Synopsis; and an Interesting Issue.   Episodes in which scientists change their minds about the nature of basic phenomena and processes dot the history of science. Dalton revised the way we conceive of chemical change in general; Planck and Einstein dramatically altered the way physicists think about radiation; Jason Morgan and others revolutionized geologists' picture of the earth's crust. These changes all represent the same variant of diagnostic form. They each concern our developing understanding of a vast network of things, studied in minute detail. So competition cannot even begin until an upstart rival is worked out well enough to engage our understanding at the current level. And estimating relative plausibility requires technically trained judgment, and judgment not just of explanatoriness but of explanatory potential. Nevertheless, this is just an esoteric variation on diagnostic procedure. At bottom it shows scientific understanding to devolve on perceptions and judgments honed against esoteric nature in the same way our more mundane understandings rest on ordinarily trained perceptions and judgments.

One current issue this discussion casts some light on is the evolution versus creationism controversy. Creationists argue that science texts are simply biased in not including a creationist alternative to evolutionary theory in scientific accounts of the development of life on earth. They point to deep divisions within evolutionary biology about how evolutionary theory is supposed to account for a number of awkward phenomena. And they are absolutely right in contending that there are clear inadequacies and awkwardnesses in the evolutionary account of the fossil record as we know it.

The trouble with the creationist suggestion is that there is no creationism rival. Merely pointing to problems needing work and suggesting there might be some other way to resolve them is, as we have seen, wholly uninteresting as an argument for a general framework change. What is required to even *begin* the argument is to work out a creationist rival that actually engages our understanding of the fossil record at the level of detail we are currently exploring. It needs to show biologists *how* the awkwardness can be eliminated, *how* creationism would guide research at this level of detail, and just what promise it holds.

Science is no stranger to weird forces and bizarre effects. The history of science is filled with suggestions that seemed outrageous at first but simply grew familiar with time. Action at a distance, quantum states, drifting continents, quarks, uncertainty, and anti-matter all began life under a cloud of suspicion. Each seemed vaguely subversive. But each became an orthodox part of our scientific un-derstanding by offering itself as the best-looking account of some bit of scientific detail. Before creationism can be taken seriously as a rival scientific framework, it must seriously accept this challenge.

Creationists sometimes feel that they can meet or circumvent this constraint by saying that "God can do anything He wants" *is* an account of the detail. But to take this stance is simply to trade on a misleading ambiguity. A perfectly good explanation of gaps in the fossil record, for example, might be that they are wholly random— not explained by any identifiable antecedent. This, in fact, is the account given by a quantum mechanics of unstable particle decay. But physicists did not adopt this account simply because they could not find an antecedent that would explain decay. They did so because pure randomness helped explain the details. Random decay accounts for all sorts of trace data: It made a positive contribution to our understanding.

"God made the gap" might do the same thing, of course, but only by coming to grips with the detail in a helpful way, as the random-decay thesis did. Otherwise, it is simply the cop-out available to any inadequate framework: Maybe there is no explanation (we just have to accept colliding mechanisms, negative weight, and other para-doxes and incoherencies). It is simply a prescription to cut and run when the going gets tough. But science is full of tough problems. Understanding nature is a complicated, difficult business, and suc-cess depends on sticking it out through the rough spots. The whole enterprise would collapse if we settled for easy victories.

Discoveries.   Many of science's most interesting discoveries have been characterized in a way that naturally misleads the average person about the nature of the process. The picture to which non-scientists naturally assimilate scientific discoveries is one of discovering the dog under the bed or a fly in the soup. You look, and there it is. But when scientists discover the positron, or marsupials in Antarctica, or the age of the universe, or (even more darkly) *the charge of* the electron, the role played by the developing theoretical framework bulks so large that the everyday picture obscures what is going on. Diagnostic unpacking, once again, can help.

When paleontologists announced the discovery of marsupials in Antarctica, what they had found, in the everyday sense, was part of a tiny skeleton. To infer that it once had a pouch requires substantial input from zoological taxonomy, guided by much anatomical and evolutionary theory. But even this would not be adequate to support the announcement that marsupials once thrived in that isolated, polar climate. In order for "marsupials once lived here" to be clearly the best account of finding that skeletal fragment in Antarctica, we must have some reason to think the climate was not always so harsh. Recent plate-tectonic theory provides just this. As a bonus, it also allows that Antarctica was once very likely directly linked to Australia and South America, where marsupials are found today.

A natural reaction to all this is to flagellate our diction. All we *really* discovered was a tiny fragment of skeleton; everything else is speculation, we may wish to say. But it is unnecessary, and ultimately destructive, to react in this way. If we bear in mind the diagnostic structure of scientific discovery, we may allow the significance to be part of the discovery. Given what we know of drifting continents and the systematicity of the fossil record, "marsupials once lived in Antarctica" is not just the best explanation of the fossil, it is a very good one indeed. We probably should have *expected* to find them there. The fact that other accounts of the trace data are possible (skeleton came in accidentally on somebody's sock) is simply not relevant. What we think is a fly in the soup may be a tattered raisin, too. When we characterize a discovery, a certain level of plausibility is all we can ever hope for.

Just what level of plausibility to hold out for depends on all sorts of practical features of the context. The dog under the bed *might* be an impressive hallucination (Let's see, what did I have for breakfast . . .). Any characterization is revisable in light of new information. A firm grasp of the diagnostic interplay between trace and background should allow us to make our way here.

So, in general, when scientists announce they have discovered a new particle, or the age of the Milky Way, what they have turned up is a trace that fits into an extensive explanatory pattern in a certain way. Whether they characterize the discovery as *evidence of* X, or as X itself, depends on a complex judgment of plausibility, significance, and practical features of the context.

Observation and Experiment.   A hint of the diagnostic character of scientific observation is contained in each of the last three sections. Observation of what goes on in nature provides the trace data that scientific theories explain. The conditions under which these observations are made are of special interest, however. The role of circumstances is the same as it is in more mundane investigations: Circumstances determine significance, the value of a trace. Joe's fingerprints on the cash drawer implicate him only if he did not work at the register all morning and routinely handle the drawer. Similarly, the air in the bell jar is significant to the eighteenth-century chemist only if he can be sure none got in from the outside during the reaction. The special interest in the conditions, the circumstances, under which a scientific observation is made lies in their detail and precision. Because of the level of detail science is concerned with, the surrounding conditions must often be understood very precisely, far more so than would be required normally.

Accordingly, we almost never advance the interests of science by simply looking around at nature, hoping to notice something. What they require is the pointed search for circumstances in which an observation will be significant: relevant to the short list of explanatory alternatives we have. We go looking for bits of quartz on the sea floor, marsupial fossils in Antarctica, neutrinos emitted from exploding stars.

Sometimes we can actually arrange the circumstances so that an observation will be significant. We do this when we run an experiment. We make sure the samples are pure and the temperature controlled; or we construct a cloud chamber and carefully control the magnetic field. The requirement of significance frequently makes either kind of observation—natural or experimental—very expensive. This is why the first rule of experimental design—and scientific observation generally—is to think the procedure through carefully to avoid trivial results. Nothing can guarantee significant results, but carelessness can guarantee insignificant ones. All we have to do is miss one element—proper degree of precision, a variable to control, stability of apparatus, ambiguity of a reading—to ruin an experiment. Careful planning can even make failure useful. For if we use everything we know to set the stage, then an incoherent or wholly unexpected result can conclusively indicate one thing: Our understanding is currently inadequate. That knowledge can be monumentally significant. But if we simply did not think the procedure through carefully, *that* may be all we learn from failure.

STUDY GUIDE FOR CHAPTER 4

1.   In Chapter 4 we apply the distinctions we have made so far to particular kinds of diagnostic inductive arguments. The first kind is a correlation–cause argument.

   (a)   One particular kind of trace data is a *correlation* between two things (or events, series of events, etc.). When two things happen in such a way that some sort of causal influence is suggested between them, the fact that they happened as they did is a correlation. The two things are called the *correlates* and are labeled A and B. The correlation is represented by A/B. Since the fact that they happened together is trace data, that fact is what must be explained by the rival conclusions. The basic form of the I.Q. is "Why A/B?" ("Why do people who smoke a lot get cancer?")

   (b)   We can divide the kinds of rival conclusions into two basic categories: (1) A/B because there is some causal connection between A and B and (2) A/B because of chance—the correlation is just a coincidence. The first category can be further subdivided according to the direction of causal influence so that we have four major categories:

   I.   Forward cause: A caused (or causes) B.

   II.   Reverse cause: B caused (or causes) A.

   III. Common cause: Something (X) caused (or causes) both A and B, independently.

   IV.   Chance.

   (c)   Forward cause is usually pretty straightforward. It is often the most obvious causal connection between A and B, the one suggested by the correlation in the first place. Reverse cause and common cause are usually more difficult to understand initially, and so they must sometimes be accompanied by a detailed story explaining the mechanism by which B might cause A or X might cause both A and B.

   (d)   A note on common-cause explanations: It must be very clear that A and B are caused by X independently of each other. It cannot be that X causes A which in turn causes B, or vice versa. Recall that rival conclusions must be mutually exclusive: If we give "X causes A which causes B" as a rival to "A causes B," we have dreaded overlap:

rivals that do not exclude one another so the second is not a genuine rival.

(e) The last explanation of a correlation is non-causal: A and B are not causally connected at all; the correlation is simply a matter of chance. Arguments for this conclusion (IV) are usually indirect: raising objections to or hurdles for each of the candidates in the other categories (I, II, or III). Occasionally, however, we can give a more direct argument by offering a *bypassing account* of the later correlate, when we know which one that is. If we take B to be the later correlate, then a bypassing account is just another causal account of B that has nothing at all to do with A: D causes B, and D has nothing to do with A.

2. Another type of trace data to consider is a statement or, rather, the fact that somebody made a statement. Since in testimony arguments we consider and judge the *source* of the evidence (for example, the person who made the statement), this type of argument is called a "genetic argument."

(a) The fact that somebody said P is trace data; the implicit question, then, will be of the form "Why did X say P?" And the rival conclusions will be rival explanations of why X said P.

(b) Two very general considerations in deciding why somebody says something are, first, whether he believes what he says or not and, second, whether he knows what he is talking about. Of course, if we decide that he *doesn't* believe what he says, then the second consideration doesn't even matter. If we already know that X doesn't believe P, but said it for some other reason (as a joke or a lie, for instance), then we don't really care whether he is in a position to know whether P is true. But if he *does* believe it, then we can, and sometimes need to, go on to ask ourselves why he believes it. (After all, we all believe things for various reasons, sometimes for very bad reasons—superstitions, prejudices, and misunderstandings, for example.)

(c) Since we have these two considerations, we can break up our schematizations of testimony arguments into two steps. The first step will be about the speaker's sincerity—whether he believes what he is saying. The first step starts out with the trace data (S_1), "X said P." And the I.Q. will be "Why did X say P?" (But since we are talking only about X's sincerity, the question will actually be something like "Did he say it because he believes it, or as a joke, or as a lie, or . . . ?" So we already have in mind a more or less exhaustive list of the kinds of rival conclusions when we ask the implicit question, and only the details have to be given.)

(d) We also already know the sorts of support claims that will be relevant for the first step. S_2 will give the circumstances (having to do with sincerity) in which the statement was made: X was on stage, or X was doing a TV commercial, or X was in court, or X was having a normal conversation (the first two of these leading us to believe that X was not sincere and the third and fourth leading us to believe that he was sincere). S_3 will give the part of X's biography that is relevant to his sincerity: X is a habitual liar, or X is a practical joker, or X is quite honest. And the conclusion C′ will be the best explanation of why X said P in the circumstances that he did, being the sort of person that he is: C_1', X believes P; C_2', X was joking, X was lying in hopes of cheating us out of our money; and so on.

(e) If the best explanation of why X said P is that he sincerely believes P, then we can go on to the second step to judge whether X's statement is any reason for *us* to believe P. S_4 (second-step trace data) will simply be the fact that X believes P, and the implicit question will be "Why does X believe P?" In this step, we are concerned with deciding whether X is able to judge that P is true, so this step is called the competence step. The support claims S_5 and S_6 will be about X's competence in judging P to be true. S_5 will give circumstances relevant to X's competence: X wasn't anywhere near where P was supposed to have happened, but was in Canada at the time; or X was right there on the spot; or P seems obviously false (this last one is relevant because, if P seems obviously false to the normal observer, then X will have to have some *special* competence for us to care about what he believes). S_6 will give the biography of X that is relevant to his competence: X is an expert in such things, or X is a complete idiot, or X doesn't know the language, or X is always drunk at that time of day, or . . . And the conclusion of this step will be the best account of why X believes P: C_1, he believes it because it's true; or C_2, that's the sort of thing only idiots usually believe, or it *seemed* like it was true from where he was standing, but actually he was in the wrong spot to tell; or . . .

(f) For this section, it is a good idea to *memorize* the basic form of a two-step testimony argument (on pages 172–73) and the checklist on page 175.

3. Sometimes we argue that, because one thing (or a few things) has some property, everything similar to this thing (or these things) also has this property. This is how statistical arguments work: Because 70% of the people polled (usually a very small number of people) believe X, 70% of the whole country (or the whole state, or the Democratic party, or whatever) believe X. Such arguments are called *sample-to-population arguments*.

(a) A sample-to-population argument falls under the category of a diagnostic inductive argument. The fact that some sample of the population has property P is the defining trace data, and the conclusion that the population itself has that property is offered as the best explanation of the sample's having that property.

(b) Since a sample-to-population argument is inductive, other rival conclusions can be given. That the whole population has property P is not the only possible explanation of why the sample has P. There are three basic categories of rivals for these arguments. The first (C_1) is that the population has property P. (We call this the *underwriting rival* because it underwrites (secures) the inference from the sample to the population.) The second kind of rival (C_2) is that the sampling procedure is flawed or biased (this is called an *undermining rival* because it ruins the sample-to-population inference). The third type of rival (C_3—which is also an undermining rival) is simply bad luck.

(c) So sample-to-population arguments are very simple diagnostic inductive arguments of this basic form:

$$S_1 \quad \text{The sample has property P.}$$
$$========================= d$$
$$C_1 \quad \text{Population has property P.}$$

And there are two types of rival conclusions:

C_2 Sample has property P because of some distorting feature of the sampling procedure.

C_3 Sample has property P because those who did the sampling were unlucky enough to pick out members of the population with P; but P is not characteristic of the population.

How do we rank the rivals? Sometimes we can just tell that a sample-to-population inference is faulty (that is, we have a basic and generally trustworthy sense of what is plausible and what is not). For example, if we sampled opinion on gun control at the firing range we could be pretty sure ahead of time that the results would not be representative of, say, all American adults. Similarly, it would be silly to poll a convention of Republicans to determine the popularity of a Democratic candidate. These are easy cases. For subtler ones we simply need to know (or learn) more about the population and the circumstances of sampling. As in any diagnostic endeavor, we must understand enough to rank rivals. If we are doing the sampling, and we wish for a C_1 explanation, we must arrange the circumstances with that wish in mind.

And the less we know the more we must arrange. If we don't know what procedures will affect the property in question, we must resort more and more to randomizing. We break as many systematic connections as we can between P and the sampling procedure. Put names in a hat and shake them up, for instance. But we can do this only sometimes. To give "names" to the cookies, recall, we had to take all of them out of the jar, and that defeated the purpose of sampling. In general, randomizing is often impractical and usually expensive; eliminating rival explanations of P some other way is usually a good idea.

EXERCISES

1. The Association of American Medical Colleges reports that, nationally, half of all philosophy majors who applied to medical schools were accepted, the highest success percentage of all undergraduate majors. So if you want to get into medical school your chances will be better if you become a philosophy major as an undergraduate.

   a. Schematize the above argument as an instance of inferring a cause from a correlation. (Use "A" and "B" to specify what is correlated with what.)

   b. Provide a common-cause rival explanation of the correlation.

   c. Provide some information that, if discovered, would show the common-cause rival to be *clearly* more plausible than the one in the argument.

2. Consider the argument in exercise 4b of Chapter 1. The subject of this argument is the direction of causal influence between two correlates, A and B.

   a. What are the correlates?

   b. What evidence from the circumstances is offered as favoring one direction over the others?

   c. Which direction does it favor and why? (Hint: You might employ the notion of an explanatory hurdle.)

   d. What new information would clearly elevate an explanation with a different direction of influence to the top of the ranking? Explain.

3. I awoke to the insane blare of the burglar alarm guarding the market across the street. The power in my room was off, but the night light soon flickered back on. A quick check of my clock showed the power had been off for only a few minutes. I wondered aloud whether the two things were related.

a. What two things?

b. How might they be related? (Provide one story for each of the four possibilities.)

c. Provide some new information that would clearly change the plausibility ranking of these stories from your first estimate of it.

4.   Satellite Fails

A satellite that provides weather information about the western U.S. and the Pacific failed last week. Officials think that the failure may have been caused by sun flares. The operations manager for the federal agency that oversees the satellite's functioning said that a proton particle may have shot out from the sun and struck the satellite. Ninety minutes before the satellite failed, a solar flare had occurred, and several hours after the flare magnetic disturbances occurred on earth.

a. What are A and B (the correlates)?

b. How can you tell? (What tips you off that *these* are being offered as correlates of one another?)

c. Tell a story about the causal link between A and B that is different from the one offered in the passage. Which of the four rival categories does this story fall in?

5. John Paul: "Hey! From now on I'm not going to put my name on my quizzes."

   Sally Ann: "Why would you want to do a dumb thing like that?"

   John Paul: "Well, it's pretty clear that my T.A. doesn't like me. Up to the last quiz I got nothing but zeros, but last Friday I inadvertently left my name off my quiz and I got a 2."

Take the correlates in this argument to be (A) John Paul's leaving his name off his quiz and (B) John Paul's doing well on the quiz.

a. What makes John Paul think there is a causal connection between these correlates?

b. What connection (i.e., which direction of influence) does he infer?

c. Give a reverse-cause account or a common-cause account of the correlation.

d. Provide some new information that would, if discovered, *clearly* establish the rival you offered in c over John Paul's.

6. During the night a minor earthquake rattled Jane's bedroom window enough to wake her up, but the shaking of the earth could barely be felt.

Next morning, an outbuilding Jane had been in and out of all the previous day was found almost completely collapsed.

    a. What is it about the earthquake and the collapse that suggests a causal connection between them?

    b. What connection does it suggest?

    c. What, by implication, is the correlation? (Give A and B.)

    d. Of the three remaining rival categories, which is most plausible? Why?

    e. Give a bypassing account of the collapse.

    f. What would raise chance to the top of the plausibility ranking?

7. Late for an appointment, Linda grows increasingly impatient as she slows for a red light. "Change, damn it," she yells. The light changes obediently, and Linda continues without having to downshift.

    a. Taking A to be Linda's yelling and B to be the light's changing, what direction of causal influence is suggested by the word "obediently" in this passage?

    b. What gives that suggestion the little plausibility it has?

    c. Give, in some detail, rival explanations from the other three categories.

    d. Give a bypassing account of the light's changing.

    e. What would clearly raise chance to the top of the plausibility ranking?

8. The mean income of Yale graduates is three times the national average. Apparently, going to Yale increases the amount of money you can expect to make.

    a. Clearly state the correlates A and B.

    b. What direction of causal influence is offered as explaining A/B?

    c. Provide a rival story with a different direction of influence.

    d. Provide some information that, if discovered, would clearly elevate your rival in the plausibility ranking.

9.   Schools, Post-Prayer

Dear Editor,

I was a teacher in the public schools at the time prayer was banned from the classrooms. It was in the early 1960s.

    I always began the school day by recognizing God—alternating between the 23rd Psalm, The Lord's Prayer, or a song. The students were happy, cooperative and open to learning. Each day, I left school with an appreciation of the day's progress.

    Before the end of that year I felt like something had a choke-hold on me: tensions, lack of interest, resistance to learning and behavioral problems began raising their ugly heads. Until I retired in 1977, I saw the same problem with each successive year.

According to the report published in the May 11 *Press-Enterprise*, by the National Commission on Excellence in Education: "The College Board's Scholastic Aptitude Tests, S.A.T., demonstrate virtually unbroken decline from 1963 to 1980. Average verbal scores fell over 50 points and average mathematic scores dropped nearly 40 points."

I can't help but note the correlation of the timing of the decline in classroom achievement and the removal of prayer from the classroom.

I understand this issue of prayer in the classroom is now again before the Supreme Court. Let's believe and pray that they will once more allow God to have his way in our classrooms. Within my own mind and spirit I believe here lies the answer.

ELLEN VROOMAN
Corona

a. What are A and B?
b. What explanation does Ellen Vrooman offer of this correlation (what direction of causal influence)?
c. Provide a distinct account of your own (different direction of influence).
d. What information would clearly promote her account over yours?

10.   Studies Link Coronary Artery Disease, Coffee Drinking

Boston Globe

People who drink five or more cups of coffee a day are nearly three times more likely to develop coronary artery disease than non-drinkers, according to a newly published report from Johns Hopkins University Medical School.

The heart troubles could be caused by eating foods high in cholesterol, not getting enough exercise or other bad habits that may be more pronounced among coffee drinkers, said Andrea Z. LaCroix, a disease specialist and one of the authors. But while studies continue, she advised people to assume that coffee is the culprit.

"Individuals interested in acting prudently, based on questions we raised, should be discouraged from drinking large amounts of coffee," LaCroix, whose study appears in today's *New England Journal of Medicine*, said.

Alan Dyer, author of another new study on coffee and heart disease, sounded a similar warning yesterday: "People should drink no more than three or four cups a day," said Dyer, acting chairman of community health programs at Northwestern University Medical School.

However, Dr. Daniel Levy, director of cardiology at the Framingham (Mass.) Heart Study, cautioned against overreacting. Coffee "is not the smoking gun we have for cigarettes, cholesterol and high blood pressure, but it is at least prudent to cut back on extraordinary consumption."

LaCroix' team followed 1,130 Johns Hopkins medical students for up to 35 years. Fifty-one suffered heart attacks, angina or sudden cardiac death; detailed comparisons were made between their coffee drinking habits and those of the rest of the group.

The findings were dramatic: People drinking five or more cups a day were two to three times more likely to develop coronary artery disease than non-drinkers. Heavy coffee drinkers can substantially lower their risk by reducing their daily consumption.

Dyers' study, presented last month at a meeting of the World Conference of Cardiologists but not yet published, yielded similar findings.

Men who drank six cups of coffee a day were nearly twice as likely to die from coronary artery disease as non-drinkers, based on a study of 1,910 workers at a Western Electric factory in Chicago. But while Johns Hopkins researchers found the risks of drinking coffee grew with each cup consumed, Dyer found troubles mainly in people who drank at least six cups.

Both studies factored out the effects of cigarette smoking.

a. State the correlation broadly enough to cover both studies mentioned.

b. What direction of influence do the researchers favor?

c. What general rivals are suggested in the second paragraph? Develop a detailed story of one of those types (two or three sentences).

d. Give two different *kinds* of new information (discoveries) that would make your rival plausible.

11. Study Rules Out Genetic Link in Smoking Deaths

BOSTON (AP)—The theory that smokers die younger than non-smokers because of some environmental or genetic difference—not the cigarettes they use—is disputed by an 11-year study published Thursday.

The argument, voiced by tobacco industry spokesmen, among others, was tested in a review of the habits of 4,004 smokers and nonsmokers in California. The researchers, paid by a tobacco industry-backed group, concluded they could find no evidence to support the idea.

They kept track of 4,004 middle-aged men and women for 11 years and found that the death rate among the smokers was 2.6 times higher than among nonsmokers.

"I think this adds more evidence that smoking is indeed a causal factor leading to death," sayd Gary D. Friedman, who directed the study.

A report on the research, conducted at the Kaiser-Permanente Medical Care Program in Oakland, Calif., was published in Thursday's *New England Journal of Medicine.*

In Washington, a spokesman for the Tobacco Institute declined comment on the findings. The study was paid for by the Council for Tobacco Research–U.S.A., an organization financed by tobacco companies.

The researchers took into consideration 48 characteristics of the persons' jobs, health and personalities that might have contributed to a difference in death rates. Among them were alcohol consumption, blood pressure, occupational exposure to chemicals, use of sleeping pills and complaints of insomnia and depression.

"None of them explained away the smoking–mortality relationship," Friedman said in an interview.

For example, if the smokers had emotional disturbances, their death rate was 2.8 times higher than nonsmokers with similar problems. If they did not, the rate was 2.5 times higher than emotionally stable nonsmokers.

If the smokers were exposed to industrial hazards, their death rate was 2.9 times higher; if not, it was 2.4 times higher.

a. What causal story (explanation) do the tobacco industry spokesmen seek to disparage?

b. State the correlates (A and B) clearly.

c. What direction of causal influence do the spokesmen offer as more plausible?

d. What conclusion do the Kaiser-Permanente researchers reach about all this?

e. Characterize their grounds for this conclusion diagnostically.

12.　　　Link Seen Between TV, School Test Scores

SACRAMENTO (UPI)—Children's scores in school achievement tests fall off in close relation to the amount of time they watch television each day, the California Department of Education said today.

It unveiled the results of a survey of more than half a million public school pupils, in which their scores in the state's sixth- and 12th-grade assessment tests were measured against their TV habits.

"I was not surprised that TV had the effect of decreasing their test scores, but I was surprised at how much," said Alexander I. Law, chief of the department's office of program evaluation and research. "There is a very substantial relationship."

Law insisted the survey was "not a scientific experiment," but an effort to gather information.

"It's a question of association, something like smoking and lung cancer," he said, predicting that the California survey would set off widespread research into the effect of TV on students.

The survey indicated that sixth-graders who watched TV an hour or less a day achieved scores about 7 percent higher than those who spent four hours or more daily in front of the tube. Test scores declined rapidly for all children who viewed television more than three hours a day.

For high school seniors, the scores fell almost in direct relation to the amount of time they devoted to television.

Twelfth-graders watching TV six hours a day or more got scores about 14 percent lower in all areas than those who confined their viewing to an hour or less.

The survey embraced 281,907 sixth-graders tested in May and 233,125 high school seniors tested in December 1979 under California's school assessment program. Third-graders also were tested but did not figure in the television survey. The tests, less than an hour in length, cover reading, written expression and mathematics.

The only group of TV watchers whose test scores showed slight improvement were sixth-grade children from lower income families where parents had little education. Law said that for these children, exposure to up to three hours a day of television apparently improved their language skills.

Law said it was the first mass effort to measure the effect of TV on children's school achievement. He said the results were about the same as those of tests made elsewhere with children in classroom size groups.

Law said the children tested estimated their daily TV watching time themselves. They were asked to exclude time spent viewing sports events.

a. Clearly state the correlation.
b. What causal account of the correlation is offered (that is, what direction of causal influence did the California Department of Education infer)?
c. Describe rival accounts with different directions of influence.
d. Provide some mixed information (trace and non-trace) that, if discovered, would make one of the rivals you described in c more plausible than the one offered in the article.

13.

Music Hath Charms,
Maybe Even Longevity for Its Lifelong Devotees

Harold M. Schmeck

NEW YORK—Music may have charms little considered even by the poets who write so much about it or the musicians who create it. Under the right circumstances, a life devoted to music may be a prescription for longevity.

This is the conclusion of an associate professor of medicine at the University of California at San Diego who is also a lifelong symphony devotee and amateur musician. Struck by the fact that Leopold Stokowski died in his 96th year, the professor, Dr. Donald H. Atlas, did a little epidemiological research on the longevity of symphony conductors. He published the results in *Forum on Medicine*, a publication of the American College of Physicians.

The doctor noted that Arturo Toscanini lived an active life to the age of 90; Bruno Walter to 85; Ernest Ansermet to 86 and Walter Damrosch to 88. . . .

But is this evident longevity of gifted musicians a myth based on a few famous examples, or is it real?

"The death of Stokowski prompted me to examine statistically the life span of members of this distinguished profession," Atlas said.

From several source books and his own experience, Atlas compiled a list of 35 deceased major symphony leaders and found their mean length of life to be 73.4 years. The life expectancy of American men in general is 68.5 years, he said, and the difference is statistically significant.

"I am aware that a comparison of the current survival expectancy of American men to that of European-born conductors from the last century may be open to question," Atlas said. "Nevertheless, since I have not been able to find a single death in this group at an age younger than 58, I firmly believe that these men were protected by some undetermined factors from the modern scourge of early fatal ischemic vascular disease," disease of the heart and circulatory system.

a. Carefully describe the two correlates (A and B) between which Dr. Atlas claims to have found a correlation.

b. What explanation does Dr. Atlas offer of this correlation?

c. Granting Dr. Atlas' figures, describe what you take to be the most plausible rival to Dr. Atlas' explanation of it.

d. Which of these is more plausible on the information given?

e. What new information would, if discovered, clearly promote the less plausible of these to the top of the plausibility ranking? (If you ranked them equally, promote either one.)

14. Japanese Monkeys Live Life of Riley

TOKYO (UPI)—Take a dip in a hot spring everyday and you'll stay healthy, at least if you're a monkey living in botanical gardens on Japan's northern main island of Hokkaido.

The 45 Japanese monkeys in the city Botanical Gardens at the Yukawa Hot Spring Spa in Hokkaido, about 500 miles north of Tokyo, make it a habit to take a hot bath each day, said one of the keepers recently.

Monkeys kept in cages catch colds and are susceptible to serious diseases, but the botanical animals rarely do, the keeper said.

a. What causal connection is alleged in this article?
b. (Therefore) what are A and B?
c. Provide rival explanations from the other two directions of influence (one each).
d. What new information would make one of these clearly more plausible than the allegation in the article?

15. Does Fussiness Indicate Higher IQ?

A recent Canadian study indicates that babies who are fussy may have higher IQ's than babies who are calm in comparison.

Nearly 400 children aged 4 months to about 5 years—all of them from middle- or upper-class families—were studied. Some of the fussy babies had IQ's as high as 134; the high score among the calmest babies was 120; the IQ scores for average babies, neither very fussy nor very calm, fluctuated between 118 and 120.

Dr. Michel Maziade of Laval University in Quebec recently published her study in the American Journal of Psychiatry. She found that, at least in middle- and upper-class families, parents talked to and interacted more with their fussy, temperamental babies, attempting to calm them down or change their difficult behavior. Parents who had calmer babies tended to leave the children more to themselves. Dr. Maziade feels that the special stimulation the fussy babies receive may help them develop more rapidly.

a. What correlation is offered as trace data here?
b. What causal hypothesis is offered in explanation of this trace?
c. What direction of influence does this represent?
d. Describe a common-cause rival.

e. Give a reverse-cause rival.

f. Provide a rival (to the hypothesis in b) with the same direction of influence as the one in the article.

g. What new information would clearly lower the plausibility of the hypothesis in b?

16.   Study Links Drinking to Less Heart Disease

Ronald Kotulak
Chicago Tribune

People who drink alcohol in moderation—about two to three drinks a day—may be reducing their risk of developing heart disease, according to a report in the *Journal of the American Medical Association.*

A study of 24 healthy males who normally consumed one to four drinks a day showed that alcohol increased blood levels of apolipoproteins A-I and A-II, proteins that are strongly associated with a lowered risk of coronary heart disease, said Carlos A. Camargo, Jr., of Stanford University's Center for Research in Disease Prevention.

"The results suggest that the association between moderate alcohol intake and reduced risk of coronary heart disease may be mediated in part by increased levels of serum apo A-I or apo A-II or both," said Camargo, who headed the research team.

The findings are helping scientists to understand the apparent beneficial effect of alcohol in preventing heart disease, he said.

Although adverse effects on health are "rarely" seen at these levels, the researchers cautioned that even moderate drinking has the potential for danger in its effects on unborn babies and as a cause of traffic accidents and alcohol addiction.

"Recommendations that everyone drink at even moderate levels must be seriously questioned in light of the potential dangers associated with this level of intake and the likelihood of increased consumption by some individuals," Camargo said.

Interest in the potential protective role of alcohol was sparked by earlier studies involving autopsies and coronary arteriography that showed drinkers tended to have less hardening of the arteries.

Researchers found that alcohol increased blood levels of a specific kind of cholesterol called high-density lipoprotein, which appeared to remove other types of cholesterol from the inner linings of blood vessels. These deposits are believed to build up to form fatty plaques that cause heart disease.

The study found that when the daily drinkers, who ranged in age from 30 to 60 years, abstained from alcohol for six weeks, their apoliprotein levels dropped dramatically. When they resumed their daily drinking patterns their protein levels increased significantly.

This article contains two correlational arguments: one for the conclusion offered in the headline, the other buttressing one of the first argument's support claims.

a. Schematize the first, more general argument, omitting the tributary. (Hint: It should contain one bit of trace data and some non-trace data.)

b. Which is trace and which is not? Explain.

c. Add the second correlational argument as a tributary to the first.

d. What trace data does it contain?

e. Provide a plausible common-cause rival for the tributary's conclusion.

17.   Tooth Decay Might Be Limited by Saccharin

Peter S. Hawes
Associated Press

HARTFORD, CONN.—Saccharin, one of the world's most widely used artificial sweeteners, may be a cavity fighter, according to a University of Connecticut researcher.

Dr. Jason M. Tanzer, professor of oral diagnosis at the University of Connecticut's School of Dental Medicine, said rats given saccharin had as much as 42 percent less tooth decay than other rats in two separate studies.

"It's somewhat of a surprise that the consumption of saccharin appears to fight cavities, at least in rats," said Tanzer.

Tanzer's studies suggest that saccharin slows or prevents the growth of *streptococcus mutans*, bacteria generally considered the prime cause of tooth decay.

The growth of the bacteria, a distant cousin of the one that causes strep throat, is encouraged by the presence of large amounts of sugar, for which saccharin is a substitute, said Tanzer.

He said, however, there is no data suggesting that the decline in tooth decay is more than coincidental with the increased use of saccharin.

"I can only raise the question," said Tanzer.

In the past 10 to 15 years, he said, tooth decay has declined substantially in the U.S. and other Western nations, partly because of fluoride use.

But he noted that in those same years "a lot of people have chosen to consume saccharin for whatever reasons—weight-loss notions, for example," he said.

Tanzer's research was reported in the March issue of the *Journal of the American Dental Association*.

In the sixth paragraph Dr. Tanzer says he has "no data suggesting that the decline in tooth decay is more than" coincidentally related to the use of saccharin.

a. Explain as well as you can why this is false. That is, show what data he has and why it does suggest more than this.

b. In the terminology of diagnostic induction, what *kind* of data is this? Why?

c. In what way is paragraph 4 ambiguous?

d. What role do paragraphs 8 and 9 play in the argument you began in a?

18. Link Suspected Between Hearing Loss, Crime

James Patterson
Scripps-Howard News Service

PARCHMAN, Miss.—Two researchers are studying whether hearing loss plays a role in landing people behind bars.

Because nearly half of inmates tested at the Mississippi Penitentiary at Parchman are found to have at least some hearing disorder, two University of Mississippi researchers say it is possible.

The university speech pathologists, Thomas Crowe, chairman of the department of communicative disorders, and instructor Julie Walton, say there could be a link between communicative disorders, especially hearing loss, and criminal behavior.

The two have screened hundreds of inmates at Parchman for communicative disorders since 1982, said Walton.

The effects of undetected hearing and speech language problems begin at an early age before prison is part of an inmate's life and, unless diagnosed and treated, can cause problems as he matures, said Crowe.

"These children start school, and they're already a step behind because often they are unaware of a hearing loss.

"They may not learn to read well and have difficulty communicating with teachers and peers. Often, this causes their self-confidence to drop. Once they're labeled a slow learner or learning disabled, they drop out and are more subject to unacceptable behavior," he said.

In 1982, 48.5 percent of 136 prisoners tested showed evidence of hearing loss, and in 1984 48 percent of 246 inmates displayed a marked loss in hearing, Walton said.

The educators, who have a laboratory at Parchman, conduct tests on Fridays as a service to the prison's medical staff and university research purposes.

Initially, a cross-section of the prison population was tested for research data, but last year they began testing consenting new prisoners as part of an entrance physical, said Walton.

"We found the trend continued in results of nearly half of the new inmates. About 48 percent failed hearing tests. They might have had a mild to severe loss in either ear," she said.

We haven't, absolutely, established a link between loss of hearing and criminal behavior, but the high number of prisoners found to have hearing disorders creates a question in our minds. The possibility probably needs to be investigated more fully."

Crowe added that the test results are not conclusive.

"The possibility exists that suffering from a communicative disorder could be one of the links in the chain of circumstances that lead an individual to a life of crime," he said.

"But merely having a communicative disorder doesn't necessarily or directly lead to antisocial behavior. Some of society's greatest contributors—Charles Darwin, Thomas Edison—suffered from communicative disorders."

They treat Parchman inmates found to have speech and voice disorders, such as stuttering. Many of the prisoners, he said, display articulation problems.

Walton said socioeconomic and environmental influences may be major factors in hearing loss.

"Lifestyles are key. Not wearing protective ear equipment when exposed to loud noises like gunfire, rock music or clamorous machinery can quickly disable someone's hearing," she said. "Some hearing loss is induced by trauma such as fighting, shock, hunting and other tense situations.

"Most of the new inmates have never had a hearing test and are unaware of a mild loss of that sense," she said.

a. What particular correlation are the two University of Mississippi researchers trying to explain?
b. What direction of influence do they seem to think most plausible?
c. What specific explanatory story in this direction do they offer?
d. Flesh out a common-cause account and a reverse-cause account from the possibilities suggested in the last few paragraphs of the article.

19.   Fertilizer Link to Lou Gehrig's Disease Under Study

The Associated Press

MILWAUKEE—A possible link between Lou Gehrig's disease and a fertilizer produced by Milwaukee's sewage treatment district requires investigation, an expert on the disease said Friday.

Dr. Benjamin Brooks said he was alerted to the possible link between the rare, incurable disease also known as amyotrophic lateral sclerosis and the fertilizer Milorganite by the cases of three players on the 1964 San Francisco 49ers football team who contracted the disease.

Former 49ers Matt Hazeltine and Gary Lewis have died, while teammate Bob Waters, 48, now a football coach at Western Carolina University, has been diagnosed as having the disease. The use of Milorganite on the 49ers' practice field in the 1960s has been suggested as a possible factor in their illnesses.

Patrick Marchese, executive director of the Milwaukee Metropolitan Sewerage District, said it would cooperate with any study of a link with ALS, "but we don't see a problem with our product."

The levels of cadmium and other toxic metals in the fertilizer have been reduced.

Brooks, director of the ALS clinical research center at the University of Wisconsin-Madison, said three of his patients, two from Wisconsin and one from Illinois, told him this week that they had used the fertilizer.

The *Milwaukee Sentinel* said yesterday that it had located six ALS patients who had used the product on their lawns and gardens, some more than 20 years ago.

ALS is characterized by a gradual deterioration of nerves and muscles, commonly resulting in a loss of use of the limbs and increasing difficulty in eating and speaking. Once the disease is diagnosed, victims die within three to five years on average. No cure or cause is known.

Gehrig, one of its most famous victims, was a New York Yankee baseball player who died in 1941.

Donald Wood, associate director of research for the Muscular Dystrophy Association, which studies ALS, said yesterday that no link has been shown between ALS and Milorganite.

a. What are A and B?
b. What causal connection is suggested in the article?
c. Suppose we discover that ALS is congenital. Describe first a bypassing account and then a common-cause account based on this discovery.

20.   2 Copters Lost in Island Raid, British Reveal

From Reuters

LONDON—Two British helicopters crashed on South Georgia Island while the navy was preparing for the assault that recaptured the island from Argentina last month, the Defense Ministry disclosed Monday.

Military sources said the helicopters were carrying special commandos on a reconnaissance mission. There were no injuries, they added.

The crash was kept secret for more than three weeks and announced Monday after London newspapers learned of the story.

South Georgia, a remote island east of the Falklands, was seized by Argentina on April 3, the day after the capture of the main Falklands group. The Royal Marines recaptured it on April 25.

The Defense Ministry said Monday night that the two helicopters crashed on the island in a blizzard on April 22.

The crews were rescued unhurt by another helicopter. One helicopter was destroyed, but the other may be salvaged, the ministry said.

Military sources said the helicopters were carrying teams of the Special Boat Squadron, a highly trained and secret commando group, sent to pinpoint Argentine positions on the island.

a. What correlates with the crashing of the helicopters in a way that suggests a causal relation between it and those crashes?

b. Articulate this suggestion. That is, say something about what you know that makes the suggested causal link plausible.

c. Schematize the argument you have set out in a and b.

d. Give a specific rival under one of the other three general headings (provide a bypassing account if your rival is chance). Make it as plausible as you can.

e. Provide an example of new information that, if found, would move this rival up into serious competition with C_1.

21.   Vandalism Cited in Train Derailment

EL MONTE (AP)—Vandalism caused the derailment early yesterday of part of a mile-long freight train causing injuries to the engineer and a brakeman, a Southern Pacific spokesman said.

"The information that we have right now is the cause of the accident was vandalism," spokesman Tony Adams said. "Our investigation found what is called a fair, a rail anchor, wedged into the switch mechanism. . . . It didn't get there naturally."

The westbound diesel, the "Memphis Blue Streak," was hauling 81 cars from Tennessee to Los Angeles when it derailed around 3:37 a.m. just east of Santa Anita Avenue, causing damage "well in excess of $1 million," Adams said.

The engineer and the brakeman were in the lead engine that was 80 percent destroyed in the derailment 15 miles east of downtown Los Angeles. Both men were hospitalized.

"The engine cab itself was crushed," Adams said, noting that the men had to be cut out of the cab.

a. Why is this not an inference from a correlation to a cause? Schematize.

b. What is the relation between the rail anchor and the spokesman's conclusion?

c. How could he have phrased his conclusion so that it *was* a correlation--cause inference?

d. From this perspective, which direction of causal influence does the spokesman rule out? Explain.

e. How would the rival in d appear in the schematization in a? (That is, what is the spokesman ruling out from this perspective?)

22.   Woman Made Ill; Herb Tea Recalled

DENVER (AP)—The nationwide recall of Celestial Seasonings Herb Tea Inc.'s "Comfrey" tea was ordered after a woman drank a concentrated brew equivalent to 18 cups and suffered an adverse reaction.

The recall, which forced cancellation of the company's first public stock offering, was issued last week after traces of atropine, a potentially toxic herb derived from the poison deadly nightshade, were found in the woman's tea. The unidentified Mississippi woman has since recovered, the company said.

She had brewed a concentrated cup equivalent to 18 cups of the recommended strength, and drank it as a home remedy to help mend a broken hip, company chairman Mo Slegel said.

Atropine can cause hallucinations and convulsions, according to Cheryl Montanlo of the Rocky Mountain Poison Center.

However, Slegel and Dr. Barry Rumack, director of the poison center, said at a news conference Sunday that tea drinkers should not be worried because the amount of atropine found was so minute.

a. From this passage, schematize a one-step testimony argument for the conclusion expressed in the last sentence.

b. Give a C_2 rival that might explain at least some of the trace data better than the conclusion in a. What might it explain? What non-trace data would support such an explanation?

23.   Illegal Weapons Sale

The United States' largest handgun manufacturer was recently fined $120,000 for illegally selling military equipment. Some of the 10 million dollars worth of goods Smith & Wesson sold to France has allegedly found its way to Libya—including sophisticated night-vision binoculars that can be attached to rifles, tanks, and other weapons for use at night. Bangor Punta Corp., which owns Smith & Wesson, says that, on the contrary, there is no evidence that it has done anything wrong.

    a. Formulate an argument from testimony using the statement made by the Bangor Punta official.

    b. Comment on the argument under the headings of motivation and competence.

24. Consider the following statement by a coach to her team, just before their first game:

This team has the ability to go undefeated this year.

View this as testimony for evaluation in a two-step diagnostic argument.

    a. Make up circumstances and background that would support C_1 rivals at each step.

    b. Change things so that C_2 would be a better bet for step two.

    c. Change things again so that C_2' is better for step one.

25. Consider the following statement by an oil company executive, testifying before a Senate subcommittee:

If the government will decontrol natural gas prices and allow them to seek their natural level in an open market, we will be able to recover vast quantities that are currently unavailable.

    a. Based on the testimony checklist (page 175), under what headings might the senators raise the most serious difficulties with this testimony? Describe the most plausible difficulty (rival) for each stage.

    b. Why are the other aspects of the checklist more secure in this case? (That is, why are rivals under the other headings less plausible?)

    c. What data could the executive supply that would allay the kind of difficulties you mentioned?

26. Used car salesman to prospective buyer:

This car has fifty thousand trouble-free miles left in it.

Evaluate this statement as testimony in the following way: Provide supporting statements in the first stage (S_2 and S_3) that would establish the salesman's sincerity (that is, make C_1' the best of the rivals). Then provide second-stage support that would show truth not to be the best account of the salesman's confidence. What *would* be the best account of the salesman's confidence in this case?

27. "Johnny, where have you been all morning? I've been trying to get into the garbage and you have the only key."

    "Oh, I've been desperately trying to contact my Mom in Kansas City. They've got a monster flood going on there and I had to find out if she was okay."

    "Gee I'm sorry, I didn't know. Is she all right?"

    "A little shaken: The house is under water. But she's fine physically. I finally tracked her down at a Red Cross information center. I don't know just how she got there, but it was good to finally speak to her."

    a. What evidence do we have that Johnny spoke to his mother this morning? That is, use the sketchy circumstances provided in the dialogue above to structure a two-step evaluation of this fragment of what Johnny said. Assume normalcy for everything not dealt with specifically. (Use C_1 conclusions for each stage.)

    b. Give a modestly plausible (C_2') rival to the first-stage conclusion.

    c. Give a possible, though not necessarily plausible (C_2), rival to the second-stage conclusion.

    d. What new information would raise your C_2 rival to the top of the plausibility ranking (above C_1)?

28. Suppose I have a medium-sized cardboard box, into which I can neither see nor reach my hand. I would like to know something about its contents, so I tie a small magnet on a string, drop it into the box, and examine the things clinging to it when I pull it back up. I drop the magnet in several times and each time several small pieces of metal cling to it—never anything else. I infer from my accumulated sample that the box contains only small pieces of metal.

    a. In diagnostic terms, why does the sampling procedure undermine the inference?

    b. What sort of property might the sample have that we could more securely infer in the population? That is, what else might I notice about the little pieces of metal that would be better explained as a property of the population than by the selection procedure? Explain why, in diagnostic terms.

    c. Think of a selection procedure (within the restrictions mentioned) that, if it yielded the *same* sample, would allow me to infer that the box probably contained nothing but small pieces of metal. Explain.

29. In the past ten years, just over four thousand students have taken Professor Ogden's introductory course. The grade for the course is determined by three quizzes given during the term and a final paper due the last day of class. Over this span of ten years, 284 students have come to see Professor Ogden during the last week to discuss some matter pertaining to the course. Of these conversations, 279 were prompted by the student's conviction that his or her quizzes had been graded too

severely. This statistic provides strong support for the view that the overwhelming majority of Professor Ogden's students in this course think their quiz scores underrepresent their performance.

Treat this as a simple diagnostic inference from a sample to a population. The property of the sample, which is being inferred to exist in the population as a whole, is a general dissatisfaction with the quiz scores.

a. What is the most plausible C_2-category rival you can think of? That is, describe the connection between the way the sample was selected and the sample property (general dissatisfaction) that would most plausibly explain the sample's having that property even if the population did not.

b. How plausible is this rival?

c. How would you select a sample in this case that would essentially rule out this rival as a significant possibility?

30. The Academic Senate wants to know how many students favor a tighter grading policy. So they send a simple ballot to every student asking for a simple yes or no answer to the following question:

Should a minimum of at least ten percent of the students in every class receive a failing grade?

Of the 15% returned, 76% were "no" votes, 23% were "yes" votes, and 1% were illegible.

a. What is the sampling procedure? (That is, how are members of the population chosen for membership in the sample?)

b. How might this procedure produce a higher percentage of "no" votes than the student population?

c. What does this say about representativeness?

d. How might the Academic Senate have sampled to avoid this difficulty?

31. Police officers occasionally become deeply pessimistic about the human condition: They come to think badly of the general level of civility, motivation, and self-control in the community.

Analyze this pessimistic perception as a misguided sample-to-population inference. In other words, treating a police officer's experience in the community as his or her sample, explain why this sample might be unrepresentative. (Use your imagination: There are several things worth mentioning.)

32. Consider the article examined in exercise 18 of this chapter.

a. How might the sampling procedure used there produce an unrepresentative sample?

b. What diagnostic procedure would allay these fears? Explain how in some detail.

33. While researching human longevity (how long we live), the Guinness organization found that birth and death records are kept so badly in most parts of the world that claims to great age are both generally suspect and wholly unverifiable. There was an exception, one source of a great deal of reliable data, but it, they decided sadly, could not help them determine maximum human lifespan.

   The most reliably pedigreed large group of people in the world, the British peerage, has, after ten centuries, produced only two peers who reached their 100th birthdays, and only one reached his 101st. However, this is perhaps not unconnected with the extreme draftiness of many of their residences and the amount of lead in the game they consume.

   Consider the Guinness argument here as a sample-to-population inference.
   a. What is the population?
   b. What is the sample?
   c. What is the Guinness quote saying about representativeness?
   d. Describe (in helpful detail) the connection between sample property and selection procedure on which the Guinness judgment rests.

= 5 =

EVIDENCE (2)

Secondary Diagnostics

Overview

The diagnostic apparatus may be useful even when it is not the whole story. Predictions and recommendations go beyond diagnosis, but often rely on it. In this chapter we explore some common diagnostic structures found within more complicated arguments.

INTRODUCTION

Many arguments that are not simply diagnostic may be understood as having diagnostic parts or steps. Of course, complex arguments may be compounded out of any mixture of steps—inductive, deductive, diagnostic, non-diagnostic. But the arguments of greatest interest in this chapter will be those that contain diagnostic steps (often just one) but are not diagnostic in overall form. Looking at these arguments will show us how to extend the skills and apparatus developed in the last two chapters to another group of useful arguments.

Recall that an inductive argument is not diagnostic when it contains no trace data, when its conclusion does not explain any of the support. This can happen to any conclusion, even a diagnostic one, if the support is exclusively background. The first *Titanic* argument in Chapter 3 was like this. But such arguments will be of less interest than those for conclusions that are inherently not diagnostic. Both predictions and recommendations, for instance, are about things that have not yet occurred and may not ever occur. So they may be conclusions of arguments before they have left any

traces. An argument about the future of the economy or one recommending a negative vote on Proposition 11 simply cannot be diagnostic. These conclusions do not attempt to simply explain what's going
on: They go beyond simple diagnosis.

A diagnosis may be part of the support for either kind of conclusion, however. And when it is, breaking up the argument to display
that fact will almost always be helpful. The general picture will be
something like this. We begin with an unstructured induction:

$$S_1$$

$$S_2$$

$$S_3$$

$$S_4$$

$$C$$

We have no apparatus for analyzing inductions that are not diagnostic. So, unless we can break up such an argument, our treatment of it
will fall back on our more or less unguided resourcefulness, on our
unstructured plausibility judgment. This, indeed, will sometimes be
good enough, but we will be treating the argument as though it had
no form at all, returning essentially to our earliest schematic form:

$$S_1$$

$$S_2$$

$$S_3$$

$$S_4$$

$$C$$

And we may clearly improve on this picture by showing the argument to have some internal diagnostic structure: to contain a disguised diagnostic step, for example. Then it might be broken up
something like the following:

$$
\begin{array}{c}
S_1 \\
S_2 \\
S_3 \\
S_4 \\
\rule{2em}{0.5pt} \\
C
\end{array}
\quad = \quad
\begin{array}{c}
S_1 \\
S_2 \\
\rule{2em}{0.5pt} \\
C'
\end{array}
\; d \quad + \quad
\begin{array}{c}
C' \\
S_3 \\
S_4 \\
\cdots\cdots\cdots \\
C
\end{array}
$$

To break up an argument in this way is actually to cast it in *compound form*, as a condensed version of the main argument now accompanied by a tributary.

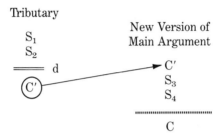

Tributary

New Version of
Main Argument

This is a clearly useful complication if the new version of the main argument is easier to evaluate than the original argument was. It is also valuable, however, if it merely displays points of contention in better detail. And, it will turn out, arguments for predictions and recommendations often do turn on differences in diagnosis that are not easily recognized. So it will be worth our while to learn how to break them up in this way.[1]

PREDICTION

Commonly, predictions are extrapolations: They extend into the future our understanding of how things have been up to now. Even our prediction of a dramatic change is typically based on our understanding of how things are. That understanding is what makes us expect a change. So we should not be surprised when the support we

---

[1]The compounding may, of course, result in arrangements of the original argument's pieces other than the one shown here. Some will be considered later. This one is typical, however, and will serve to introduce the strategy.

offer for a prediction contains a diagnostic step: a step offering an account of how things are, a step explaining some trace data.

Consider a standard election forecast. We think that Smith will win next week's primary, and the reason we think so is that he has such a dramatic lead in the polls. Our reasoning is naturally cast in a simple, but non-diagnostic, induction.

S_1 In next week's primary, Smith is favored by 64% of the eligible voters polled.

C   Smith will win next Tuesday's primary.

Our diagnostic skills, and our understanding of an enormous range of things, bear on this argument in a number of ways. Perhaps the most direct is one we examined in Chapter 4. The reason we think the poll results are relevant to the election outcome is surely that we take them to be representative of the entire voting population. So a sample/population inference is doubtless going on behind the scenes here; and this inference can be unpacked diagnostically, as we have already seen.

S_1 Smith is favored by 64% of the eligible voters polled.

C' Smith is favored by a substantial majority of eligible voters.

This then becomes the tributary of a newly formulated main argument:

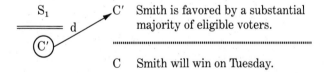

C' Smith is favored by a substantial majority of eligible voters.

C   Smith will win on Tuesday.

So we can begin to see how our diagnostic skills and apparatus may be brought to bear on prediction.

But there are other ways too. In projecting from now to Tuesday, we rely on our general understanding of people and their opinions and behavior under broadly recognizable conditions. We understand (or can easily learn) the general sorts of things that change public opinion and the conditions that aid or hinder people in going to the polls to vote. And, as we saw in Chapter 3, if this understanding requires articulation—if there is some question about it, for instance—it will rest on further diagnostic arguments.

In fairly common cases our understanding of an electorate would be good enough for a very strong projection. (Any of the usual national or state-wide elections are like this.) So let us make our understanding explicit in a very strong version of the argument and note how we would defend it. Weaker versions will be similar but easier. Consider

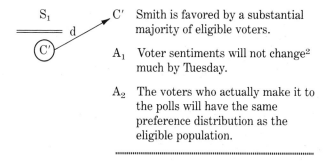

S_1 | C' Smith is favored by a substantial majority of eligible voters.

A_1 Voter sentiments will not change[2] much by Tuesday.

A_2 The voters who actually make it to the polls will have the same preference distribution as the eligible population.

C Smith will win on Tuesday.

The first thing to notice here is that while this argument is clearly very strong, it is *not* clear whether the argument is inductive or deductive. It is strong because if S_1, A_1, and A_2 are true it would be lunatic to bet against Smith. But whether Smith's winning is semantically contained in them would depend on subtle details of what would count as an election and what to construe as winning. Would C still be true if a military junta overthrew the civilian government on Tuesday and invalidated the election? Would it matter whether the overthrow occurred during the voting or after? Would it count if the world were destroyed by nuclear war or by collision with an asteroid? All the ways out would look like this, and you might want to read the words one way for some purposes and another way for others. But since none of these outlandish possibilities needs to intrude on our normal reasoning about elections, it is

---

[2]All we need here, of course, is the qualification that it won't *decline* very much. But since we understand the conditions of stability so much better than those of change, we usually predict no change in one direction from reasons for no change at all. Similar remarks apply to A_2.

best to leave the form of the main argument undetermined: It is strong no matter how these issues are resolved. That is why the separating line is dashed.

So, with that preliminary out of the way we may return to the question of how we would defend the pair of strong assumptions, A_1 and A_2, that license our projection. They will clearly be reasonable sometimes, but what makes them reasonable? In each case they represent something like normal conditions: what we should expect if nothing special happens. For Smith to die or to become embroiled in scandal over the weekend would have an impact. For Smith's supporters to be so confident that they feel no urgency in voting could destroy representativeness. So the understanding behind A_1 and A_2 would be something like this: "Look, we know the sorts of things that change voter preferences and affect turnout differentially, and we have no reason to think anything like them will happen in this case." In Chapter 3 we used dispositions to link our causal understanding to diagnostic induction (see page 121), and doing so works here too.

The stability of an electorate may be looked at as a disposition *not* to change; other properties may be viewed as dispositions to change in way or another under recognizable conditions. As in those earlier examples, the exact conditions and causal relationships are inaccessibly complex. But we can often explain what we need to by appeal to the coarse patterns sketched in disposition talk.

The parallel with earlier cases is exact. We attribute fragility to the vase because that is the best account of certain patterns in our experience. Schematically,

S_g Our general experience with objects of a certain kind, appearance, or history.
$$\overline{} = d$$
C   They are fragile.

Similar argument sketches may be generated by our experience with electorates.

S_{g1} Our general experience with public opinion polls and elections.
$$\overline{} = d$$
C″   Candidate preference is relatively stable over short periods, unless there is some spectacular occurrence or revelation.

So whenever conditions are relatively normal, and we have no reason to expect spectacular occurrences, we may add S_n as an explicit support-claim and provide a modest compound argument for A_1.

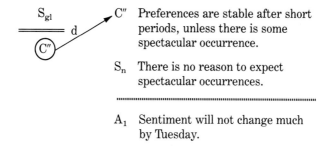

S_{gl}
$= d$
(C'')

C" Preferences are stable after short periods, unless there is some spectacular occurrence.

S_n There is no reason to expect spectacular occurrences.

A_1 Sentiment will not change much by Tuesday.

When one tributary is of particular utility in a compound, as it is here, we may streamline the schematization by collapsing the two occurrences of the first conclusion (C") and writing the tributary directly over the main argument. Instead of

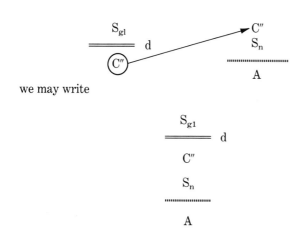

we may write

$$S_{gl}$$
$$= d$$
$$C''$$
$$S_n$$
$$A$$

This is called a *linear* compound, and it will be valuable whenever we need room for a lot of detail or a lot of structure. Other, normal tributaries may be added to the streamlined form too, of course.

In streamlined, or linear, form the compound tributary built on A would then be the following:

S_{g1} General experience with public opinion polls and elections.

$\overline{\qquad\qquad\qquad\qquad\qquad\qquad\qquad\qquad}$ = d

C'' Preferences are stable over short periods, absent spectacular occurrences.

S_n There is no reason to expect spectacular occurrences.

....

A_1 Sentiment will not change much by Tuesday.

A similar tributary may be constructed on A_2:

S_{g2} Our general experience with human motivation and voting patterns.

$\overline{\qquad\qquad\qquad\qquad\qquad\qquad\qquad\qquad}$ = d

C''' Unrepresentative voter turnout is virtually always the result of some detectable factor, such as bad weather, overconfidence, or selective apathy.

S_n There is no reason to expect any of these factors to apply in this case.

....

A_2 A representative group will vote.

So the overall schematization would look like this:

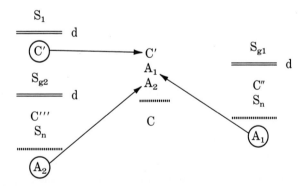

In this way our diagnostic skills and machinery may be brought to bear on a conclusion that is not itself diagnostic. This may be valuable in evaluating the support for such a conclusion. But it can also be

useful in thinking through—articulating—the case for a conclusion we are already pretty certain about.

Forecasts supported by raw data will quite typically respond to the treatment illustrated here. The ground of the projection will often be clearer if we interpose a diagnostic conclusion between the data and the prediction. This (first) tributary is so prominent here that we will commonly push it together with the main argument to create a two-step, linear compound. Instead of

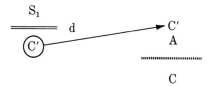

we will write

$$S_1$$
$$=====\ d$$
$$C'$$
$$A$$
$$.................$$
$$C$$

This abbreviated version allows the main diagnostic step to be written down more easily. Since streamlined, clear presentation will be our central interest here, we will adopt this version as standard prediction form. (Again, we may add tributaries to this picture too, when doing so is useful.)

Consider a typical weather forecast developed from raw data:

S_1 It is raining to the west.

S_2 Temperatures across the state have been falling in a characteristic way.

C It will rain here sometime today.

Meteorologists would point out that the best explanation of S_1 and S_2 is that a storm front[3] is moving in our direction; that would be their diagnosis. Expanding the argument to include it will make their reasoning clearer.

S_1 It is raining to the west.

S_2 Temperatures across the state have been falling in a characteristic way.

=== d

C' A storm front is moving in our direction.

A   It will develop in the normal way.

....

C   It will rain here sometime today.

A has been added to the second step as being typical of the reasonable assumptions connecting diagnosis to prediction. (Think of the parallel in a physician's prediction of the course of a disease.) And, of course, we may bring evidence to bear on A too.

The observation on which this section is based is that, even though evidence for predictions cannot contain traces of the event predicted, it may contain traces of *something*. These will, in general, be traces of the underlying process or mechanism we rely on in making the prediction. And the "underlying mechanism" may be as simple as the dispositions we examined at the end of Chapter 3. Making the underlying diagnosis explicit will often make our reasoning clearer and easier to evaluate. Furthermore, if there is disagreement—different views of how strongly the raw data support the forecast—it can usually be pinpointed in the diagnostic step or in the second-step assumptions to which it gives rise. This will increase the chances of dealing with the disagreement reasonably and may even suggest how to resolve it.

Look again at the election forecast. If someone thinks Smith will lose, in spite of the poll results, the reason will surely be found in C_1, A_1, or A_2. For if Smith does lose, it will almost certainly be due to an error in one of those three places: The poll was inaccurate, or voter sentiment changed, or the actual voting was not representative.

---

[3]Meteorologists' concept of a front is, again, a dispositional concept rather like those we have used above and in Chapter 3. Attributing a front to the atmosphere is like attributing fragility to a vase: It is simply saying that the pattern in our data is a coherent property of the atmosphere.

Undermining versus Underwriting Rivals

Just as we found in our treatment of testimony in Chapter 4, various diagnostic rivals may have wildly different effects on a prediction. The storm-front rival of our most recent example underwrites the prediction in an obvious way. It does not guarantee the prediction, but it fits congenially into a supportive argument. By contrast, if a newly emerging volcano turned out to be a better account of the rain and temperature gradient, that would, equally obviously, undermine the forecast. If the rival is not a storm front, then all bets are off. It will be good to exercise this distinction a little before going on to more complicated arguments.

A slightly more challenging election forecast will provide what we need. Headlines of the form

SMITH CLOSING IN ON JONES

suggest a more complicated mechanism than the mere stability we exploited in the earlier example. Suppose our raw data contain a change: In the last week Smith has narrowed Jones' lead from eight points to three. Smith's supporters use this change to predict that Smith will win. What does the argument look like? We begin with the simple, non-diagnostic inference:

S₁   Smith has chopped 5% off Jones' lead this week and is now almost even with him.

C   Smith will win the upcoming primary.

In order to make this inference, Smith supporters must have in mind some account, some diagnosis, of what is going on. Something or other is going on: *That* is why the gap has closed. And this "something or other" is what suggests that Smith will continue to gain until he passes Jones.[4] It is the interposed diagnostic step in our compound form.

An adequate C′ would be something like "The electorate is finally beginning to see the real Smith, and they prefer him to the real Jones, whom they know all too well."

---

[4]Obviously he must pass Jones at the right time in order to win. The example is complex enough already, however, so we will treat just Smith's pulling ahead and assume it comes at the right time.

S_1 Smith has chopped 5% off Jones' lead this week and is now almost even with him.

$=============================$ d

C'   The electorate is beginning to understand the real Smith.

A   Their perception of Jones is well developed and relatively stable.

....

C   Smith will win.

For our purpose it does not matter what you think of this argument. The point in setting it out this way is to show the various effects on C of substituting various rivals for C'.

Calling C' an underwriting rival merely says that it is relatively easy to build on C' an argument supporting the prediction, C. Undermining rivals, then, would be rivals that made it difficult to do so. For instance, C_2': "The gap's closing was a (typically temporary) result of Smith's narrow victory last week in the only state in which he was leading." Another would be C_3': "Smith's popularity has peaked early due to his imprudently exhausting his funds on an early television blitz." Many rivals to C' would, like these, point to the very opposite prediction and require great contrivance and good fortune to support a win by Smith.

There are other rivals, however, about which this is not true. There are incompatible explanations of the raw data that would underwrite the prediction as well as C', or nearly so. C_4': "Jones is out of money" or C_5': "Voters have finally come to see the real Jones, and they hate him." These diagnoses would be as good news for Smith as the original one.

The upshot of all this, of course, is just another reminder. In one of these complex, non-diagnostic schemata it is possible to dramatically change the diagnostic part and not hurt the overall argument. It's something to keep in mind.

RECOMMENDATION

Casual observation reveals that an absolute majority of arguments aired in public are for recommendations: We ought to stop smoking, should or should not raise taxes, definitely should do what we can to protect the ozone layer. And since recommendations are, for the same reason as predictions, not diagnostic conclusions, our diagnostic skills and apparatus must be brought to bear on them indirectly, if at all. It turns out that evidence for recommendations may be diagnostically compounded in a way rather like that set out in the previous section. But *recommendation* is a much richer notion than *prediction*, so the ways in which evidence may be brought to bear on recommendations are more complex. Complicating our apparatus here will be well worth the trouble, however, for the great assistance it provides in schematizing difficult arguments.

The most common way for evidence to be brought to bear on recommendations is through arguments that appeal to good consequences. This is a very frequently used form: You (I, we) ought to do something (x) because it will have desirable[5] consequences (y). You ought to stop smoking because you'll feel better and live longer; we should protect the ozone layer because it shields us from harmful radiation. Schematically,

Main Argument

S_2 $x \rightarrow y$

S_3 y is good.

C   We (I, you, somebody) ought to do x.

Evidence, then, may bear on C through diagnostic tributaries supporting either S_2 or S_3.

Arguments like this do have one other qualification lurking in the background, and it will be worth brief notice before we proceed. The qualification is that *other* consequences of x will not be bad enough to wipe out the advantage of having y. Good-consequence arguments usually concern themselves with one consequence, or a small number of consequences, and assume that the rest are irrelevant or under control. And this can be wholly unproblematic: There is no great worry, for example, that other consequences of an ozone layer will be so bad as to outweigh its advantage as a radiation shield. But when the matter of other consequences is important, it can be added to the schematic form and considered along with everything else.

[5]For our purposes, avoiding bad consequences will just be a way of having good ones. So we may use the same form when a recommendation is made because it avoids bad consequences.

S_2 $x \to y$

S_3 y is good.

S_4 Bad consequences of x do not outweigh y.

C   We should do x.

Indeed, sometimes the force of S_2, S_3, and S_4 together may be simply put: The net impact of x will be good. But more frequently we will get at the net impact by direct appeal to specific consequences; so the schematized form will be more generally useful.

Diagnostic tributaries may be constructed on any or all of the three supporting statements, of course, and can be of any imaginable form. We may, for instance, accept someone's testimony as adequate evidence for all three in some circumstances. But there are two specific tributary arguments—one for S_2 and the other for S_3—that are worth examining in some detail.

Evidence for a Causal Connection or Mechanism

The most natural application of diagnostic induction is to S_2. The schematic $x \to y$ will have to be read in slightly varying ways depending on the application (x causes y, increasing x increases y, doing x will bring about y, and many others). In each case, however, we will need some reason to think there is a causal connection between x and y—and one with a particular direction. We have already seen in great detail how diagnostic arguments support conclusions like this. So where S_2 is in need of support, the picture will look like this:

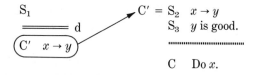

And the tributary will be one of the causal forms we discussed in Chapters 3 and 4.

This represents merely the bare bones, of course. Actual cases will make all sorts of particular detail relevant at each step. So let us exercise the form a bit to see the ramifications.

Illustration. Suppose a friend recommends that I change the way I water my lawn during the hot, dry summer months. She suggests that I water it early in the morning rather than in the evening as is my practice. The reason she gives is that the lawn will look better if I do. Looking better is presumably a good consequence, so we have our standard form:

S_2 Watering earlier makes a lawn look better.

S_3 A better-looking lawn matters to me.

C I should water earlier.

Now suppose further that I am unwilling to accept my friend's statement of S_2 as adequate support. I ask for some evidence: How does she know S_2? She replies with a correlation: Of all the lawns in the neighborhood, the ones watered early are uniformly better looking than those watered later in the day. So the tributary on S_2 is a standard correlation-to-cause argument.

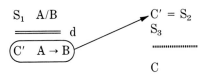

Since we are concerned with a single tributary, we may collapse this complex picture into a single, two-step argument as we did in the previous section:

$$S_1 \quad A/B$$
$$= \qquad d$$

$C' = S_2 \quad A \rightarrow B$
$\quad\;\; S_3 \quad B$ matters to me.

C I should do A.

With the argument in this compact form, it is easy to flesh out the diagnostic step with background allowing us to support a particular direction of causal influence. The whole argument might read as follows:

S_1 Lawns watered earlier uniformly look better than those watered late.

S_1' A lawn-destroying fungus thrives in lawns left wet at night when the weather is warm.

$$=== d$$

$C' = S_2$ Early watering makes a lawn look better.

S_3 Looking better matters to me.

....

C I should water earlier.

There clearly are some circumstances in which this argument would be cogent and convincing. But it is more useful to notice how this schematization would structure disagreement. If I did not buy the recommendation on the basis of my friend's reasoning, this structure will productively focus all of the likely disagreements. It contains places for new information that will either patch up the old argument or replace it with one for another conclusion. Let us examine three of these.

A. Rival Explanations.   I may suspect the diagnostic step. I may think a common cause is a better account of the correlation. People who lavish attention on their lawns like to get it out of the way early in hot weather. And since it is important to water before spraying and weeding, early watering becomes part of a fastidious routine. But it is the spraying and weeding and other fastidiousnesses that make the lawns look so good, not the early watering. Normal mortals, not so devoted to their yards, can't be bothered, and they end up watering later in the day. This account undermines the recommendation by suggesting that early watering, by itself, would not have the consequence my friend employed in the argument. This rival may not settle the matter—probably won't, in fact—but it shows how we may use our diagnostic skills and apparatus in an argument for a recommendation.

B. Costs and Benefits.   Obviously, there may be a question about just *how* good the consequences are in step two. I might agree that how the lawn looks matters to me, but insist that it does not matter *enough* for me to get up early to water it (presuming for the moment that early watering does help). This is just another way to raise the "other consequences" point: It is always relevant to weigh up all the costs and benefits if there are several. In this case I might judge that to me the value of a good-looking lawn is so slight that achieving one does not justify even a small change in my schedule. For someone else it might be otherwise.

C. Good for Whom?   In the example we are following there is little question about who the good consequence is good for: me. My friend is appealing to my interests in a simple prudential suggestion about how to rearrange my schedule. This issue can be very difficult to resolve in other cases, however. When someone argues for the use of videotape replays to decide close calls in football, it is usually unclear who is to benefit from it. There are several different constituencies who might view the change very differently: the offense, the defense, the officials, the owners, the fans, the networks, the game in the abstract, and society at large. The argument will go differently depending on whose perspective we adopt.

Standard Subform.   One very common step in grounding $x \rightarrow y$ involves first establishing that the *absence* of x causes (or is causing or has caused) the *absence* of y. Standard notation is

$$\sim x \rightarrow \sim y$$

This may be the natural diagnostic conclusion, for instance. And from this it is often relatively easy to move to

$$x \rightarrow y$$

If we can establish that raising the speed limit caused an increase in highway fatalities, then we will have provided some reason to think that reducing the limit will bring them back down. If bad dental hygiene increases tooth decay, then we may expect good hygiene to reduce it. So also for my lawn. If we find that watering late in the day breeds a fungus, then shifting to an earlier schedule should at least reduce the problem.

But there are many cases in which going from $\sim x \rightarrow \sim y$ to $x \rightarrow y$ is problematic and requires some further argument. It may be, for instance, that Charlie gained weight because he stopped smoking (eating used up his excess nervous energy). It could well turn out, however, that when he tried to lose weight by taking up smoking again it did not work because his new-found eating habits proved too deeply ingrained. So sometimes a separate argument will be required to go from $\sim x \rightarrow \sim y$ to $x \rightarrow y$.

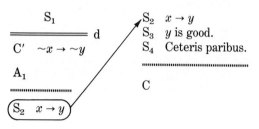

This will not always be required: Sometimes the move will be too obvious to need much support. But it is always good to consider the *possibility* that simply reversing the cause will not reverse the effect. Lowering the speed limit might not lower fatalities, for instance, if special measures to enforce the new law are not taken.

Detailed Illustration.   Let us use what we have learned to help us schematize the argument in a complicated passage. The following is a paraphrase of letters received daily by editors across the country. Because it attempts to deal with a complicated and controversial social matter in a few short paragraphs, effort will be required to keep our own views from affecting the schematization. Our two-step form can aid in providing a charitable rendering.

> Editor,
>
> Social commentators commonly blame our epidemic of lawlessness on poverty. The problem with this analysis is that we have always had poverty, worse poverty, poverty unmitigated by recent social welfare programs, but we have never developed the level of crime we now experience. I think the current wave of crime and vandalism results directly from the decline in moral and religious training at home and in the schools: training that must begin when a child is very young.
>
>   The abolition of prayer in the schools is perhaps the biggest factor. When I was a child attending a one-room country grade school, we began the day by reciting the Lord's Prayer and the Pledge of Allegiance and singing "America." Today I doubt that most children even know the Lord's Prayer.

My parents told me to always mind and respect my teacher, and that if I was spanked in school I would be spanked again when I got home. I was reared with a respect for authority, a trait sadly lacking in today's youth.

I strongly empathize with those teachers who truly care about the moral training of their young charges. They are dropping out in ever increasing numbers, unable to cope with the stress. Disrespect is the major culprit.

Unless we reestablish the moral training of our youth, we are doomed to live in a declining civilization.

> Signed,
> Depressed Former Teacher

The aspect of letters like this that undergraduates find most confusing is the form of the last sentence: They sometimes see the argument as a simple prediction about our future. But this would miss the whole point of the letter, which is heavily *evaluative*. Depressed Former Teacher is not simply working out future ramifications of the human condition's stable properties. She is talking about good and bad consequences of actions we presumably have some control over. This is a sure sign that the argument concerns what *ought* to be done, not simply what will happen in the course of time. Furthermore, the predictive part is *conditional* (we will get y only *if* we do x). And since x (moral training) is something we have some control over, this is a kind of $x \to y$ that fits neatly into standard recommendation form.

Finally, *unless* is something of a flag term. As used here it has the force of a warning (or even a threat), and this fits better into an evaluative picture than a simply predictive one. For all these reasons the conclusion of DFT's letter is best rendered as a recommendation[6]:

C   We should reestablish (or, perhaps, dramatically increase) the moral training of our children, both at home and in school.

---

[6]This is actually to adopt an artificially optimistic posture on purpose. A pessimistic reading like this would apply the argument in terms of deserts: "We deserve the lawlessness we are suffering," for example. Sometimes this will be a more accurate reading but, given a choice, we will always opt in this text for the better-humored version. The pessimistic schematization is always easier than the optimistic one in one respect: It need not project into the future. So if we can manage the latter, we can usually get the former as a matter of course.

Before we turn our attention to the rest of the schematization, one other general remark about the conclusion will be useful. DFT's conception of moral training clearly contains heavy elements of religion and respect for authority. This may or may not fit with your own view of such training. That need not matter. All we must bear in mind is that the phrase "moral training" in the schematization is meant to capture DFT's view. We are trying to schematize *her* argument. Nothing absolute need hang on the words. When commenting on the argument later, we may want to add "in DFT's sense" occasionally for clarity.

The rest of the compound form may be dealt with more easily. For the diagnostic step DFT offers a phenomenon (crime wave) that needs explaining and some background on poverty that suggests one explanation (lack of moral training) is better than another (poverty). A negative causal connection is offered in support of a positive one (see pp. 249–250), and S_4 is presumed as usual. So all we need do is omit the illustrative material and we have the schematized argument:

S_1 Lawlessness has increased.

S_1' Poverty has not increased.

S_1'' Moral training has declined.

$$\overline{}\quad \text{d}$$

C' Increased lawlessness is due to the decline in moral training.

S_2 Increasing moral training will reduce lawlessness.

S_3 Reducing lawlessness would be good.

S_4 Ceteris paribus.

C We should increase moral training.

DFT would almost certainly think this a fair paraphrase of her argument. If it is, it would helpfully focus much of the controversy that has surrounded these issues for years. Objections to DFT's conclusion have usually consisted in objecting to either the truth of one or more of S_1, S_1', S_1'', or S_4 or the step from C' to S_2. Our purpose here, however, is merely to schematize the argument as plausibly as possible. Our compound form has helped us do that.

Anecdotes. In a standard variation on this form, evidence is offered in an anecdote. We are all inclined to draw general morals from particular experiences, and arguments to this effect often show up in print.

> Dear A.C.,
>
> When my oldest boy was killed in an automobile accident, his younger brother seemed hardly to notice. In his peer group it is uncool to cry: There is a lot of pressure to be macho. A few months later, on his thirteenth birthday, the boy suddenly became self-destructive, as though filled with rage at himself. We have sought professional help, but he refuses to cooperate with the therapist.
>
> Please encourage your readers to grieve openly when they lose someone close. Bottling up your emotions is dangerous.
>
> Signed,
> Father of a Troubled Child

First, notice that the diagnostic step is both clear and crucial to the moral that FTC draws. He clearly takes his son's early lack of emotion and later self-destructiveness to be traces of bottled-up grief. If a better account of the former were that his younger son actually did not like his brother, was glad he was gone, our view of the self-destructiveness might well be changed and the recommendation revised. So casting anecdotal evidence diagnostically has the useful effect of suggesting rivals to our understanding of what's going on in a particular case. And this can be useful in structuring our thinking on the matter.

Our main interest in this letter, however, is that it draws a general conclusion from anecdotal evidence. This adds another step to our (still linear) compound argument form, which helps explain the bad reputation anecdotal evidence has in some places.

Since the recommendation is aimed at all of us, the good consequences offered in argument must be for people in general, not just for the boy in the anecdote. Although pretty obvious, this observation exposes FTC's presupposition that his younger son is more or less typical of people in general, at least in this one respect. If he is a representative member of the species, then the argument flows along untroubled by the narrow evidence. But if he is not, the puzzling behavior may be explainable by something peculiar to the kid, some idiosyncrasy—and that would ruin the argument. So, when the diagnostic step centers on an anecdote, we must add a representativeness line to the schematization. It may sometimes be easy to decide, but it will always be crucial.

S_1 FTC's younger son displayed no grief when his older brother was killed.

S_1' He suddenly became self-destructive on his next birthday.

S_1'' Expressing grief would embarrass him among his friends.

=== d

$C' = S_2$ The younger son's self-destructive behavior was due to his not allowing himself to express his grief at losing his brother.

A_1 The kid is typical of us all in this respect.

S_3 Avoiding the causes of self-destructiveness is a good thing.

S_4 Ceteris paribus.

....

C   We should all allow ourselves to express our grief openly.

The reason anecdotal evidence is sometimes disparaged is that, in finding support for A_1, we will often find evidence for (or against) C that is far stronger than that in an isolated anecdote. If we do a study on whether people in general torment themselves for bottling up grief, we will overwhelm the anecdote with other, better evidence. So if representativeness is in question, we might best simply dispense with the anecdote.

While all this is true, there will nevertheless be times when the representativeness of an anecdote will be secure enough to be helpful. Sometimes, against the right background, the relating of an anecdote will appeal to your own experience in a way that makes its point uncontroversial.

When you start jogging you have to beware of drivers turning right. When I first started I was nearly killed several times because I failed to notice they were all naturally looking *left*, wholly unaware of my rapid approach to the crosswalk.

There will be many cases like this. The representativeness line in the mnemonic should help us separate the useful anecdotes from the merely interesting ones.

The Need for Remedies

The second place our diagnostic skills and apparatus may bear systematically on recommendations is on y all by itself[7]: on the very possibility of a good consequence. In the last few sections, our "good consequences" (y) always turned out to be the correcting of something bad ($\sim y$), even though that was not required by the form. In this section we will again restrict our attention to those natural cases: The good consequences we examine here will always be the avoiding of something bad. The reason to do this is that diagnostic arguments can be used to show simply that something bad is happening. Instead of showing us *how* to remedy a bad circumstance (as on pages 246–252), a diagnostic argument can bring evidence of something to remedy. Our evidence may simply show that there *is* a crime wave and not connect it to anything else. In this way a diagnosis may concern the evaluative part of the argument, instead of the conditional prediction.

Since S_1 and S_2 are concerned with the remedy, with the conditional prediction, it is best to connect our new diagnostic tributary to S_3. A slight change in our understanding of S_3 is all that is necessary. Instead of "$\sim y$ is bad" ("y is good"), we make it "$\sim y$ is what's going on, and that is bad." Instead of "Lawlessness is bad," S_3 would read "We have a crime wave going on, and that's bad." This is merely an evaluative diagnosis, no remedy suggested. Because the word *crime* is itself evaluative, we can normally omit the explicit evaluation and just say "What we have here is a crime wave." The evaluation is understood.

More controversial will be arguments that something has happened at somebody's unintended expense or that somebody has accidentally suffered as the result of our doing something else. Tax reform may prove unexpectedly burdensome to one group of citizens; academic programs may accidentally suffer in a school's push to become NCAA champions. Diagnoses like these often provide grounds to seek out remedies: provide a start for a good-consequence

---

[7]Refresh your memory by looking at the Main Argument schematic on page 245.

argument supporting a recommendation. Of course, it's only a start, because we must still find a remedy (S_2) and check to see whether it has other consequences worse than the ill it seeks to redress (S_4). But these consequences may be handled as they were in the sections following page 246. The novelty is in grounding S_3 in a diagnostic argument.

It may strike you that notions like *suffering, expense,* and *burden* are not purely diagnostic here, that they come from applying external standards to our pure understanding of how things work. Perhaps they do, but that does not affect the point of this section. Standards we already have can make diagnostic argument relevant to S_3. These arguments are clearly useful when what counts as bad is clear. We sometimes agree that if $\sim y$ happened (or has happened), it would be a bad thing. A diagnostic argument may then provide reason to think $\sim y$ is what happened: It is the best account of the traces.

For example, everybody would doubtless agree that a dramatic increase in "near misses" between private and commercial aircraft would be a bad thing. And the argument that we have had such an increase would naturally be diagnostic. We might reach that conclusion, for instance, as the best account of a sudden increase in near-miss reports (after carefully considering rival accounts attributing the increase to new technology that makes detection easier or to greater vigilance inspired by a recent mid-air collision). A more interesting argument of the same form would hold that a dramatic increase in close calls is required to account for a *steady* rate of reports, in light of draconian new penalties imposed by the FAA on pilots involved in any reported near miss. Schematically,

S   The monthly rate of reported near misses has not changed over the past year.

S'   Three months ago the FAA instituted the policy of grounding both pilots in every reported near miss until an investigation of the incident is concluded.

S"   Pilot reports are the only evidence of near misses currently acceptable to the FAA.

=== d

S_3 We have experienced a dramatic rise in the incidence of near misses in the last three months.

So we have something to remedy. To get a recommendation we need a remedy (conditional prediction, S_2) and reason to think it achievable without awful drawbacks (S_4). Each of these may have diagnostic roots as well, so the eventual picture might look something like this:

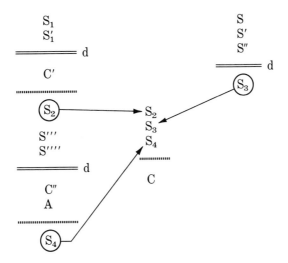

Illustration.   Of course, even if every line in a schematic argument is controversial the schematization still may be useful in organizing the controversy. Such an argument was offered by an eminent baseball commentator a few years ago. It concentrated on S_3, but S_2 and S_4 raise interesting questions as well.

> For two decades, the central affliction of big-league baseball has been its sagging batting averages. Last year, the cumulative National League average stood at .248, and the American League at .239. These are figures to be taken seriously by any baseball fan or baseball magnate not just because they indicate that the game is declining in pleasure and energy but because they suggest that today's big-league stars are less capable than their famous predecessors. It is this unspoken belief that has the most serious effect upon the game's national popularity, and yet it is probably false. In every sport where comparable performances can be fairly measured—track and swimming come to mind—the modern athlete regularly and overwhelmingly exceeds the best marks recorded twenty or thirty years ago. There is no reason to assume that the strength and capabilities of contemporary baseball players are an

exception. The hitting drought, then, is almost certainly due to a number of technical alterations in the game—night baseball, bigger ball parks, bigger infielders' gloves, the slider, the size and strength of today's pitchers, and the vastly increased and more effective use of relief pitchers. The redress should be minimal and precise—a further alteration of the strike zone, a livelier baseball, a more visible baseball, a shaving of the dimensions of the plate. By some means, baseball must bring back its long-lost hero, the .350 hitter—who is, in all likelihood, the same deserving young slugger now struggling so earnestly to maintain himself at .275.[8]

The S_3 tributary looks like this:

S   Major league batting averages have declined in recent years.

S' The capability of athletes in general seems actually to have increased lately.

S" Many recent technical alterations in the game have been tough on hitters.

== d

S_3 Batters have been unfairly burdened by recent developments in baseball.

This (S_3) is, in the author's view, something in need of remedy. He suggests several compensatory changes, the effect of which he takes to be too obvious to need argument. S_4 is assumed, as usual; so we have the following argument:

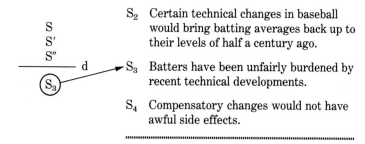

S_2 Certain technical changes in baseball would bring batting averages back up to their levels of half a century ago.

S_3 Batters have been unfairly burdened by recent technical developments.

S_4 Compensatory changes would not have awful side effects.

C   Baseball should adopt technical changes to raise batting averages.

[8]Roger Angell, *Five Seasons* (New York: Simon & Schuster, 1977), p. 86.

Since there is only one tributary, we could write all this in the linear-compound form developed earlier simply by reversing S_2 and S_3:

$$
\begin{array}{c}
S \\
S' \\
S'' \\
\hline\hline \quad d \\
S_3 \\
S_2 \\
S_4 \\
\cdots\cdots\cdots \\
C
\end{array}
$$

This would be a perfectly acceptable schematization, even if we decided to complicate it with tributaries on S_2 and S_4.

Now, every bit of this argument is controversial. The diagnostic step itself, S_2, S_4, and even other aspects of S_3. The aim of this section has been simply to show how compound schematizations can help structure our reasoning in a complex and subtle controversy. But the baseball example may be used to display one further feature of good-consequence arguments. Just as we discovered in our examination of prediction, some of a diagnostic conclusion's rivals may underwrite the same recommendation the original conclusion did. You can get a diagnostic step wrong in such a way as to not damage the overall argument. It is one more thing you have to check.

Consider the possibility that the diagnosis in this case is wrong and that dropping averages are due to dilution of the talent pool. There are many more teams now than fifty years ago and many high-paying jobs in other sports attracting talented athletes away from baseball. So it might be that the average level of batting talent in baseball *is* lower than in the past. Would this undermine the recommendation? Not necessarily. More hitting might well have good consequences for fans, owners, television networks, sponsors, and the general perception of the game, even if it is not aimed at correcting an unfairness.

DIAGNOSTIC CONCLUSIONS

Predictions and recommendations cannot be the conclusions of simple diagnostic arguments because of the kinds of statements they are. They do not directly explain trace data. That is why we must create elaborate compound schematics to express their support. It turns out, however, that perfectly good diagnostic statements will sometimes have to have their support cast in compound, basically non-diagnostic form too. This occurs when the evidence we have simply contains no traces of the particular conclusion we wish to support. Once again, it may contain traces of *something*, just not of the ultimate conclusion, our central concern. And this can happen to a conclusion even if it is the kind of statement that might have been supported directly by a diagnostic argument, had we found the right sort of data.

Consider the Jones family's worry that daughter Jane is near-sighted. They may share this worry because she is not doing well in school, seems to miss assignments written on the blackboard, and squints when looking at distant objects. All these are traces of nearsightedness, and the family could use a diagnostic argument to express its reasons for thinking Jane myopic.

S_1 Jane is not doing well in school.

S_2 She misses assignments on the blackboard.

S_3 She squints at distant objects.
$$\overline{\qquad\qquad\qquad\qquad\qquad\qquad\qquad}\quad d$$
C   Jane is nearsighted.

C would explain S_1, S_2, and S_3, although eye-test results (which would also be trace data) would be more conclusive.

We may, however, have reason to think Jane myopic even if we knew none of these things nor anything else that was a trace of her nearsightedness. Our reason might be background information on her family, for instance. We might know that most members of Jane's family, for at least three generations, have worn glasses from a very early age to correct myopia. This provides some reason to expect that Jane too is myopic, but Jane's nearsightedness will not explain why other members of her family need corrective lenses. So the argument is non-diagnostic.

S_1 For generations most of Jane's family has suffered from nearsightedness.
$$\overline{\qquad\qquad\qquad\qquad\qquad\qquad\qquad}$$
C   Jane is nearsighted.

Now we might explain *why* we take S_1 to be a reason for C by interposing a diagnostic step, just as we have before. We may take the family history to be explained genetically. The history would provide traces of a certain genetic makeup.

S_1 (Family history of nearsightedness.)

== d

C′   Jane's family harbors an especially severe version of the genetic makeup responsible for myopia.

....

C   Jane is myopic.

This argument does not support the conclusion as strongly as the trace data of an eye test, for example, but it does ground a reasonable expectation. Arguments of this form will be useful surprisingly often.

Illustration

Consider the following dialogue:

> Smith: I'm going down to the Post Office to pick up a package they couldn't deliver on Friday.
>
> Williams: You can't get your package today; the Post Office is closed.
>
> Smith: How do you know? Were you there today already?
>
> Williams: No, I wasn't there, but the Social Security Office was closed when I stopped by this morning; and if they are closed on Monday it must be a federal holiday.

Williams' argument that Smith cannot pick up his package has the same form as the one just constructed for Jane's myopia.

S_1 The Social Security Office was closed when I stopped by there this morning.

S_2 It is Monday.

== d

C′   Today is a federal holiday.

A   The Post Office is part of the federal bureaucracy.

....

C   The Post Office is closed today.

C does not explain any of our data, but we nevertheless have some evidence that it is true. Compound form helps us display our reasoning in such a case.

DEDUCTIVE MAIN ARGUMENTS

One role we found for deductive arguments in Chapter 2 was to provide helpful structure for otherwise messy inductive reasoning (see Chapter 2, page 54). The illustration we used there was a deductive main argument with inductive tributaries. One or more of the tributaries may be diagnostic, of course; and this provides another way in which our diagnostic machinery may be used in compound form:

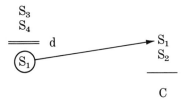

The example we discussed in Chapter 2 was an argument for the charge of embezzlement:

S_1 The defendant had limited authority to write checks on company funds.

S_2 That authority did not extend to using those funds to cover his personal expenditures.

S_3 He did direct company funds into his private account for the purpose of vacationing in the Bahamas.

___

C   The defendant embezzled money from his employer.

In this example, S_3 is an obvious candidate for diagnostic support. The evidence we would have for it would be copies of checks, testimony on conversations, recorded plans and travel arrangements, and the like. S_3 would be offered as the best account of all those things. The defendant's diverting money for that purpose explains the checks, conversations, and plans. So this much of the reasoning would have the form

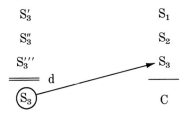

Non-Diagnostic Conclusions

In the compound schematizations we examined for predictions and recommendations, the main (bottom) argument may sometimes be cast deductively for one purpose or another.[9]

C'   A storm front is moving in our direction.

S_3 Storms like this normally sweep unabated across our area within twelve hours.

A   This one will develop in the normal way.

_____

C   It will rain here sometime in the next twelve hours.

This is pretty obviously deductive. If it doesn't rain within twelve hours we will be forced to give up something above the line. Either the storm did not develop normally or we do not understand normal development properly. No rivals are compatible with the support.

Casting the main argument this way may be useful for locating misunderstandings or disagreements or for structuring investigations. Whenever it is important to provide the main argument with some form, deduction is always available. Whether it will be useful or not will depend on the case and on the purpose for which form is sought. All the cautions of Chapter 2 apply.

A NOTE ON COMBINING ARGUMENTS

Several aspects of this chapter raise the issue of combining the force of different arguments for the same conclusion—or for incompatible ones. Say we have a diagnostic and a non-diagnostic argument for C,

_____

[9]Look again at page 50ff of Chapter 2 for a discussion of how this might be useful and how not.

and we want to know the net or combined support they provide. We can usually determine the support, but there is no mechanical way to combine the different implicit questions that different arguments usually have. It takes ingenuity and attention to the details of the different contexts. We might try to rework various arguments on the I.Q. "Is C true?" but this often undermines our judgment by requiring plausibility estimates we are not very good at making.

Sometimes matters of scale are paramount. Support offered by one argument is of such a kind and order that it makes the support offered elsewhere all but irrelevant. Jane's eye-test results are so impressive that the family history becomes a mere curiosity, for example. If the two conflicted, you would simply ignore the genetic argument. In general, the best advice is to choose a suitable main argument about which to cluster tributaries and then try to work all the relevant information into that picture.

STUDY GUIDE FOR CHAPTER 5

1. An inductive argument is not diagnostic if it has no trace data—that is, if its conclusion does not explain any of the support. In one type of *non-diagnostic argument*, the conclusion is a prediction. Since a prediction is about what is going to happen in the future, there are no traces yet left behind to explain.

    (a) Although arguments for predictions are not diagnostic, they generally rely on our diagnosis of what is happening now: We argue (diagnostically) that *this* is the best explanation of *that*, and then we argue (non-diagnostically) that something will happen because our diagnostic conclusion is true. (For example, every time I go to class I get a headache. From this correlation, I conclude (diagnostically) that going to class causes me to get headaches. I predict that today during class I will get a headache. It is clear that my conclusion that I will get a headache in class today does not explain anything and so is not diagnostic. But it is also clear that this non-diagnostic conclusion is based on the diagnostic conclusion that going to class causes me to get a headache, which explains all the terrible headaches I've been having since kindergarten.)

    (b) We can schematize arguments for predictions as *two-step non-diagnostic arguments* (not to be confused with two-step testimony arguments, which *are* diagnostic):

$$
\left.\begin{array}{l} S_1 \\[6pt] S_2 \\[6pt] S_3 \end{array}\right\} \quad \text{trace data and background}
$$

$$
========================= \quad d
$$

C'   Best explanation of trace data

....

C   Prediction

(The step from C' to C is non-diagnostic, we know, but we leave undecided whether it is inductive or deductive; hence the dashed line.) Breaking the argument into two steps allows us to see how the reasons we have for a prediction, and our ability to make predictions, may rest on our diagnostic skills; it also allows us to see where the argument might be weak and where it can be attacked. If there are more plausible explanations of the trace data, or if there are hurdles for the diagnostic conclusion, then the prediction may be undermined.

(c) Sometimes a diagnostic C' will yield a prediction directly, as schematized above. But usually we will find it useful to mention explicitly some assumptions we make in deriving prediction from diagnosis—an assumption of stability, for instance, or one of normalcy. For example, in the weather forecast argument on page 242, we predict that it will rain here today from the diagnostic conclusion that a storm front is moving in our direction (which is the best explanation of S_1 and S_2). But to make this prediction, we assume that the storm front will develop in the normal way or, in other words, that it will behave like other storm fronts that have moved in our direction. This assumption is also a point at which the non-diagnostic argument might be attacked: If there is reason to believe that this storm front is *not* like other storm fronts, or that it will change soon, then the prediction that it will rain here sometime today may be undermined. The argument about normalcy may of course be diagnostic too.

2. Probably the most common non-diagnostic argument is an argument for a recommendation. That I or you or we *ought* to do something is obviously not an explanation of anything, and since I or you or we haven't yet done what we ought to do, there are no traces yet of what we have done.

(a) But just as predictions may rely on diagnostic arguments, so also may recommendations. Again, breaking up the argument into a diagnostic step and a non-diagnostic step allows us to see whether there are any weaknesses in the diagnostic step. Any more plausible rival conclusion we find for the diagnostic step might undermine the recommendation and allow us to conclude that we ought not to do whatever is being recommended, after all.

(b) Someone who makes a recommendation assumes that the consequences of following the recommendation are good. If I recommend that you give up smoking because smoking shortens your life expectancy by ten years (a diagnostic conclusion), then I am assuming that it would be good to live ten years longer. (In this case, as in most other arguments for recommendations, I am actually making a much stronger assumption—that living ten years longer outweighs the pleasures you get from smoking. This sort of assumption can be faulty in many ways: if the costs of following the recommendation outweigh the benefits of following it, if the "good" produced by following the recommendation is actually not good, or if the beneficiary is unclear.)

EXERCISES

1.   Gift of Learning

Dear Editor,

I read with interest the recent *Times* editorial and letters about the tragedy of Los Angeles public school students. I've been waiting patiently for someone to reveal the most obvious reason why Johnny can't read, write, do math, or much of anything education-wise. Alas, my wait has heretofore been in vain.

I'm from the East, so maybe we have bizarre ideas back there, but I always thought that education begins at home. All babies (even animal babies) are born curious and have an instinctual desire to gobble up learning. If a child must wait 6 or 7 years to start learning in school, the inborn need has all but dried up from lack of use.

My parents read to me, sang the alphabet and math tables with me, and showed me how to print letters and numbers as we played together. Not until later did I realize what wonderful gifts they gave me; not just the immeasurably valuable skills of reading and writing, but the priceless love of learning. Without this, all the education in the world would have done me little good.

I know we live in a liberated time, with everyone intent on doing his/her own thing. But if parents put as much time into showing their kids what a joy learning can be as they devote to criticizing "the system," maybe test scores would rise and illiteracy would disappear. And maybe parents and their kids would have something to share with each other, and start communicating again.

ANNIE CAROLINE SCHULER
West Hollywood

    a. What tells you Annie Schuler's argument is not diagnostic?

    b. What tells you that there is likely to be a diagnostic step somewhere?

    c. What diagnostic conclusion does Annie Schuler interpose?

2. Every single student to come in for help in the past week has misunderstood the concept of trace data. We somberly infer from this that nobody yet has gotten the point: We'll have to start over.

    a. Schematize this as a compound, non-diagnostic argument.

    b. Give a rival conclusion to the diagnostic step that would undermine the non-diagnostic step.

    c. Why does your rival in b undermine the non-diagnostic step?

3. There is an increasingly well-known correlation between cholesterol levels in the bloodstream and heart attacks: More people with high cholesterol levels suffer heart attacks than do those with lower levels. This correlation has led many physicians and health organizations to recommend that those of us with elevated cholesterol levels should take pains to reduce the cholesterol content of our diets as a prudent, remedial step.

    a. Taking elevated cholesterol levels to be A and the heart attacks to be B, which of the four basic causal accounts is the above recommendation most likely based on? (That is, which A/B relationship do the recommenders seem to be assuming: A causes B, B causes A, common cause, or chance?)

    b. Schematize the argument in compound form.

    c. Describe a diagnostic-step rival from one of the other three categories. Provide enough detail to actually *explain* the correlation. (If necessary, tell a brief story.)

    d. If your rival in C were true, what effect would that have on the recommendation? Explain.

4. Eleanor Langen paused briefly on her walk from the bus stop to gaze sadly at the majestic shade trees she had known since her youth—or what was left of them. Soon none would remain to shade her walk on hot summer days or cast stark silhouettes against a gray winter sky. Six or eight had died each summer for the past few years, and now nearly half of the original stand was gone. Eleanor was convinced the mysterious disease could be stopped if the city would just take the problem seriously. But she was sure it wouldn't: She had already wasted hundreds of

268 *Chapter 5/Evidence (2): Secondary Diagnostics*

hours chasing through the municipal bureaucracy, trying to find a responsive agency.

a. What evidence does Eleanor have that the shade trees will all soon be gone?

b. Schematize the argument for this prediction in simple two-step, non-diagnostic form. (That is, use the linear-compound form on page 241.)

c. State one or two important assumptions required in the second step.

d. Provide a rival for the diagnostic conclusion that, if true, would undermine the prediction.

e. What new information would make the rival you provided more plausible than Eleanor's diagnosis?

5. In the middle of a writing exercise with her fifth-grade class, Mrs. Lippencott heard a strange roar and the windows began to rattle. Ever since coming to California she had worried about how she would react when this happened; now she would get the chance to find out. "It's an earthquake, children," she said with only a touch of panic. "We all had better get under our desks until it is over."

a. Schematize Mrs. Lippencott's argument in compound form.

b. Identify the trace data in the diagnostic step. Why is it trace data?

c. State a rival to the diagnostic conclusion that would undermine the recommendation.

d. Provide some new information that would elevate the rival you provided to the top of the plausibility ranking.

e. Is the information you provided trace data or not? Why?

6. Southern California has not had a very large earthquake (in the neighborhood of eight on the Richter scale) in more than a century. It is therefore likely that that area will have such an earthquake in the relatively near future.

a. Structure this predictive inference as a simple two-step, non-diagnostic induction. (That is, use the linear-compound form on page 241.)

b. How does this structure help you explain why a similar prediction cannot be drawn from the observation that South Dakota also has not had a very large earthquake in over a century?

7. Boxing Linked to Brain Damage; Ban Urged

Brenda C. Coleman

CHICAGO (AP)—Boxing is "an obscenity" that should be banned in civilized countries because it causes brain damage to thousands of fighters, the editor of a medical journal says.

"Some have argued that boxing has a redeeming social value in that it allows a few disadvantaged or minority individuals an opportunity to rise to spectacular wealth and fame," Dr. George D. Lundberg said in an editorial in today's issue of the *Journal of the American Medical Association.*

"This does occur, but at what price? The price in this country includes chronic brain damage for them and the thousands of others who do not achieve wealth, fame or even a decent living from the ring."

The editorial accompanied a report by medical researchers who examined 40 former boxers and concluded that all fighters—not just battle-hardened professionals—risk debilitating brain atrophy, or deterioration.

The study recommended active boxers get regular neurological examinations, including CT scans, which are computer-enhanced X-ray pictures of the brain.

But Dr. Edwin A. Campbell, medical director for the New York State Athletic Commission, disputed both the editorial and the usefulness of such tests.

"I've been a party to [brain damage research]. . . . But frankly it doesn't conform to reality," Campbell said by telephone from New York, where boxing safety standards are among the strictest in the nation.

Campbell argued that boxing provides thousands of young men with a way to develop themselves physically, intellectually and psychologically. He said it seldom produces the punch-drunk stereotype.

But Lundberg disagreed.

"No prudent physician could have watched the most recent debacle mis-match on Nov. 26, 1982, between Larry Holmes and Randall "Tex" Cobb and believe that the current boxing control system is functioning," Lundberg said.

A professional boxer, 23-year-old South Korean Kim Duk-koo, died Nov. 17 of brain damage after being knocked out five days earlier by Ray "Boom-Boom" Mancini.

"Boxing is wrong at its base," Lundberg said. "In contrast to boxing, in all other recognized sport, injury is an undesired by-product of activity.

"Boxing seems to me to be less sport than is cockfighting; boxing is an obscenity. Uncivilized men may have been bloodthirsty. Boxing, as a throwback to uncivilized man, should not be sanctioned by any civilized society."

Dr. Ronald J. Ross, one of the study's authors, recommends a boxer be required to have a medical "passport" showing when the boxer last fought, whether he was knocked out, and the date of his last medical exam and CT scan.

Last summer, the American Medical Association issued several recommendations.

They included creating a national computer registry of boxers to keep track of injuries and won–lost records, giving ring physicians authorization to stop bouts in progress, restricting fight sites to those with neurosurgical facilities nearby and requiring advanced life-support systems at ringside.

Characterize the dispute between Lundberg and Campbell using a two-step, non-diagnostic argument. There seems to be disagreement at both levels of the schematization: Say something about each.

8.   The Brain: Use It or Lose It, Professor Says

LOS ANGELES (AP)—Research on the brains of old rats indicates that elderly humans should keep their brains stimulated to delay the mental aging process, a scientist says.

"Keep using it or lose it," said Marian Diamond, a 55-year-old neuroanatomy professor at the University of California at Berkeley. "I mean, it's as simple as that old cliché.

" . . . We are challenging the isolation of the elderly by saying that the brain has this potential to stay healthy during aging if given a stimulating environment," said Diamond.

"People can keep their brains stimulated with crossword puzzles, pottery or politics," she added, "just so long as it's something to keep the mind stimulated."

Diamond, who has researched rats for two decades, is not hesitant to extend the conclusions of her study of rat brains to humans because "a nerve cell is a nerve cell is a nerve cell. . . . They are similar in rats and man."

Her most recent research involved 900-day-old rats, an age she said corresponds to 80- to 90-year-old humans.

All the rats spent most of their lives in dull, uninteresting cages. But at the age of 766 days, Diamond moved some of them to special "enriched" quarters—cages inhabited by as many as 12 fellow rats and equipped with toys that were changed daily.

She said this experimental group of rats also got "tender loving care. We held them a lot, and we just sort of gave them a little more attention."

The control group of rats spent their days in standard cages, with no toys and no more than two companions.

Then all the elderly rats were killed. Careful examination of their brains showed that the cerebral cortex averaged 6 percent thicker in rats that lived in an "enriched" environment compared with those in standard cages. The brains of the "enriched" rats also contained 9 percent less of an aging pigment called lipofuscin than did the brains of the regular rats.

"The point is, a nerve cell is designed to receive stimuli, and we have found that it will respond positively to those stimuli at any age," said Diamond. "We actually show that it will increase its dimensions. . . . We found the most change in the brain when the toys were changed daily. The old rats were really curious about what was coming next."

Working closely with rats, Diamond said she gets to know them well.

"Some are mean and nasty, some are quite sweet—just like with people," she said.

But she draws the line at chumminess and doesn't give her rats names.

"No, no," Diamond said, "I wouldn't want to do that."

a. Schematize the argument in this article as a compound, non-diagnostic argument for the conclusion that "Activity and companionship slow the aging of the human brain."

b. What (reasonably cautious) difficulty might be raised with the second-step assumptions?

9.   Keep the Penny?

Late in 1984, an 8-year-old, female Japanese spaniel was brought to the University of Arizona's veterinary diagnostic laboratory. The dog had been trembling for three days, and seemed to be constipated.

Clinicians spotted in an X-ray what appeared to be a tiny, flattened figure eight in the dog's stomach, and surgically removed two pennies that were stuck together. The 11-pound pet died five days after the operation.

Zinc Poisoning Case

In an interview, Dr. Gavin L. Meerdink, the university veterinarian who performed the post-mortem, recalled a colleague's bewildered reaction when Meerdink asked the age of the coins: "He said, 'I don't have any time for your sick humor,' and I said, 'Well, if they're after 1983, you may have a case of zinc poisoning.'"

In fact, the Arizona veterinarians detected zinc contamination in the dog's liver and other tissues, and Meerdink informed the Treasury Department of the findings. Shortly after that, then-Rep. Eldon Rudd (R-Ariz.), noting the troubles of his state's copper industry as well as the potential risk of zinc poisoning, introduced legislation to put more copper back into the penny. The bill did not pass, however.

According to Meerdink, zinc dissolves more easily in stomach acids than copper does, and there is a tendency for it to "start bubbling up from the mint mark" on the newer penny, when exposed to acid in the laboratory.

The Mint stands by its coin, however. It says there has been only one similar incident involving a human—a baby—and that the penny was removed with no harm done.

"We don't see this as totally risk free—nothing is," said George Hunter, the Mint's assistant director for technology, "but we consider the risks extremely small."

Representative Rudd's introducing legislation may be framed as a recommendation: "We should put more copper back into the penny."

a. Ignoring his concern for the state's copper industry, schematize Rep. Rudd's argument for this recommendation as an argument from an anecdote.

b. Provide a rival for the diagnostic conclusion.

c. What difficulty in the second step is raised by the last two paragraphs?

10.   Shorter Term

Dear Editor,

Another week has gone by and more people have been killed in robberies. Robbers kill their victims because the penalty for robbery is almost as great as that for murder. The only reasonable solution is to cut down the penalty for robbery to something significantly shorter than the murder penalty—perhaps eight months in jail. Then there would be no incentive for robbers to kill their victim.

ANDREW RUBIN
San Bernardino

a. Schematize the argument in this letter in compound, non-diagnostic form.

b. Which steps are most problematic? Explain.

= 6 =

TEMPTATIONS
OF CONTROVERSY

A Budget of Caveats

Overview

Our objectivity can suffer when we argue about topics on which we have deep personal convictions. We then express ourselves badly and mislead ourselves and others about the soundness of our reasoning. In this chapter we examine some common temptations and provide guidelines for avoiding the worst of them.

INTRODUCTION

We seldom stir ourselves to create an argument, or to criticize one, unless we feel strongly about the issue it treats. (Exercises in a reasoning class offer an exception to this, of course.) Strong feeling sometimes tempts us to say things too boldly, however, and we are led to ignore important subtlety on which much may hang. In this chapter we develop some *characterizational reminders*, to supplement the structural ones that have occupied us lately. The aim will be to learn to avoid some common traps we fall into when formulating an argument, or a criticism, in the heat of controversy.

These traps are of seven kinds, which divide naturally into two groups. The first group (fallacies of construction) concerns mistakes that tempt us when we're constructing arguments. The second treats temptations that arise primarily when we're criticizing arguments.[1] The three major resources that will guide us through the hazards of

---

[1]You may certainly construct an argument in criticism, in which case you would be open to both kinds of temptation simultaneously.

controversy here are the principle of charity, bare-bones schematization, and diagnostic form.

FALLACIES OF CONSTRUCTION

Begging the Question

We begin with one of the subtler fallacies, because it is in many ways useful to begin with a challenging case. In its most common formulation, I have begged the question if I simply presuppose the conclusion I am trying to support, if in my argument I simply assume my conclusion is true. But while this explanation captures the spirit of the difficulty, it is hard to apply accurately without some assistance. We might argue, for instance, that all deductive arguments must be question-begging, since the conclusion is actually contained in the support. Certain aspects of diagnostic procedure may seem impugned as well.[2] But that is not the intention at all: Nothing very general is at issue here. The aim of this section is to isolate a specific, illicit appeal to the conclusion in an argument. An example will help clarify what counts as illicit here.

A standard sort of example, which occurs regularly in letters to editors, is the following.

Dear Editor,

There seems to be decreasing respect for religion and faith in Almighty God in our country today. Those who shirk religion, and deny God's very existence, will surely regret that choice when they face their Creator on Judgment Day.

It is fairly plausible to read this letter as offering an argument—a reason—for believing in God.

S₁   Unbelievers will face bad consequences on Judgment Day.

C   They should believe in God.

This is an especially simple version of the recommendation form we discussed on page 244ff of Chapter 5. However, all of us know

[2]This will be examined explicitly on pages 286–287.

the sort of context in which an argument like this will arise. And in such a context, the only person who would accept S_1 is somebody who has already accepted C. So the argument begs the question: It can convince only those who are already convinced.

A better formulation of the fallacy is this: I have begged the question if I support a conclusion with a statement that would not be accepted in the context by anyone who did not already accept the conclusion. In Chapter 1 we pointed out that one object of reasoning is to treat disagreement by working from areas of agreement. Having a flag for question-begging should aid in the task. It focuses attention on the context, on what someone needing an argument would accept and what not. This can be a useful reminder when we are overwhelmed with enthusiasm for a conclusion.

Begging the question is nothing very formal or general; it is more a matter of conversation, of understanding people, and of people's understanding. This is why deductive arguments are not automatically question-begging. Deductive support may contain the conclusion in a way that is not at all obvious. Someone rejecting C might have no objection to the support. So the semantic unpacking that shows the argument to be deductive can be genuinely convincing.

Loaded Descriptions

One reason to begin with the topic of question-begging is to introduce a discussion of loaded descriptions. A description is loaded if it contains an evaluation (good or bad) that not everyone would share. *House* and *hovel* may both be used to refer to a dwelling. The difference, in a standard context, is evaluative. "They live in a house" is simply descriptive. "They live in a hovel" puts down the dwelling. Whether *hovel* is a *loaded* description (as opposed to being merely evaluative) depends on whether it is contentious. Loaded descriptions are not merely evaluative—they are controversial, disputed evaluations.

When we are embroiled in controversy, we naturally tend to see only the other side's descriptions as loaded. Ours seem to be simply good sense. So events often generate matched pairs of descriptions. What one side sees as terrorism the other sees as a long overdue reprisal raid. Some see prudent defense; others see nuclear blackmail. Some see a homeless victim of social inequity, others a welfare loafer. Confiscatory taxation versus paying for essential services.

Profit motive versus corporate greed. The list could be extended indefinitely.

This natural asymmetry in human perception may result in bad feeling, calumny, assault, murder, war, and other hostilities beyond the scope of this text. But it is also the world's most fertile source of question-begging arguments; so a cautionary reminder is appropriate here. When you advance an argument on a controversial topic, you can easily end up with a question-begging, loaded description in the support. If you use an evaluative term that only one side of a controversy would find acceptable, the argument is then irrelevant to anyone on the other side.[3]

A standard example would be something like this:

S_1 Dr. Smith has, by his own admission, performed abortions for several years.

S_2 Abortion is murder.

C   Dr. Smith should be stripped of his license and sent to jail.

This argument would be wholly worthless for convincing Dr. Smith himself, or anyone on the pro-abortion side of the issue. For they would simply reject the characterization in S_2. That is the evaluative issue at the heart of the controversy. If you wish to reason with those on the physician's side, you must come at it from some other direction. For them, this argument begs the question.

False Dilemmas

Loaded descriptions can damage our reasoning in another way too. When we have a strong opinion on a topic, we are often tempted to oversimplify the available alternatives—the possible choices—to make all positions but our own seem undesirable, even silly. We dismiss all options but our own under a loaded description.

> Are we going to offer a solid, traditional education or run slavishly after every curricular fad that comes along?

[3]Note that this does not mean such an argument is always useless. It may make a useful point for someone not offended by the description. Whether a question is begged, recall, depends on the context.

This is the standard dilemma-form argument for a recommendation:

S₁ P and Q are the only options.

S₂ Q is obviously bad/wrong/silly.

―――――――――――――――――――――――――――――――――――――

C   We should choose P.

But on important matters the alternatives are never simple, the choices seldom easy. This bit of academic diatribe dismisses all innovation as fad, for instance, and that is surely unreflective. It may be that a traditional education is better than a faddish one, but those are clearly not the only options. The alternatives are too boldly drawn: The dilemma is a false one.

Other argument forms may be victimized by this move as well, and the loaded term is sometimes not so easy to spot.

> Do you realize that you spend the first two days of every week working for the government? You don't start working for yourself until sometime Wednesday morning.

This is a cute device for dramatizing the amount of your pay that goes for various taxes, and sometimes it is simply this. But it contains the suggestion that the time spent "working for the government" is clearly *not* for yourself—simply wasted—and if this suggestion is pressed, the contrast is mischaracterized:

S₁ You spend two-fifths of the week working for the government, not yourself.

―――

C   Forty percent of your salary is wasted.

Government is acting as a loaded description here, suggesting that what you pay in taxes cannot also be for yourself. But much that is financed by tax revenue is of great value to all of us: social security, national defense, schools, roads, and fire protection to name a few. The contrast, again, is more complicated than the terms suggest.

This false dilemma may also be used in a recommendation-form argument:

S₁   You spend forty percent of the week working for the government, instead of yourself.

S₂   This is an intolerably high percentage of your income to simpy throw away.

━━

C   Taxes should be substantially reduced.

The same remarks apply. Whether reducing taxes will be in your interest is a very complicated business: It depends on what services are cut as a result and on the nature of indirect economic impact as well. The "government versus yourself" contrast obscures all this in a tempting but outrageous way.

CRITICAL FALLACIES

Straw Men

A straw-man argument is what you get when you use the principle of charity upside down. Instead of making an argument as strong as possible before criticizing it, you make it artificially weak and easy to make fun of. Typically, the weak formulation does all the critical work. The resulting argument is so obviously silly it requires no further attack: It falls of its own weight. Straw-man criticism is just uncharitable paraphrase. The charitable paraphrase of an argument is A, but you represent it as B, which is substantially weaker; and this destroys the value of the criticism. It is as simple as this, but we all fall into the trap occasionally.

For a crude, introductory illustration, consider the father's argument in Chapter 1, for taking the coast route rather than driving through the mountains. The charitable—that is to say, plausible—schematization of that argument would read,

[A]

S₁   The snow in the mountains will make driving unpleasant and perhaps risky.

S₂   The coast route is snow free, and it has some beautiful scenery.

━━

C   We should take the coast route.

We can all imagine a context in which someone might respond to Dad's argument by saying, "Who's afraid of a little snow?" This could, of course, simply be rude repartee or a rejection of S_1 as false. But let us suppose it is neither of these things, but rather a criticism of the argument under a hostile paraphrase. It would be saying the argument really only came to

[B]

S_1 There is just a little snow on the mountain roads.

S_2 The coast road is snow free.

....

C   We should take the coast route.

The criticism consists in simply substituting weak argument B for stronger one A and hence is a waste of time if you are interested in how good the reasons are for driving up the coast. (In conversation, Dad might retort, "That is not what I said and you know it.")

It might be, of course, that the coast scenery is not beautiful and there is not enough snow to make driving unpleasant. But if you have reason to take issue with the support, the thing to do is say what that reason is: Make an argument, produce your authority. To attack an argument by merely paraphrasing it badly is to joust with a straw man.

There will naturally be times when you will be able to gain social or political advantage by flailing away in public at an artificially weakened argument. This is not our concern here. If we have interest in the reasons—in reasoning—to attack a straw man is a waste of time and energy. Nevertheless, straw men come in so many guises, and are occasionally so tempting, that it will be worthwhile for us to look at some variations on the basic theme.

Perhaps the most common way to weaken an argument is to inflate its conclusion, to make it harder to defend. If you hold the reasons constant and exchange the conclusion for one needing greater support, you have weakened the argument. When this happens in paraphrase, you have constructed a straw man. Reacting to the father's argument about the snow level by saying "Every time it snows we should go look at the ocean—is that what he's saying?" would do just this. Dad's conclusion was simply the following:

C   We should drive up the coast route (given our current plans and the present snow level).

So if we substituted

C′   We should drive up the coast whenever we must travel north and the snow level reaches 3500 feet.

we would get a far weaker argument using the same support. We could weaken it further with

C″   We should drive up the coast whenever the snow level is down to 3500 feet (even if we don't have a trip planned).

And this would still be far stronger than the argument would be with

C‴   We should go look at the ocean whenever it snows.

So using C‴ would turn a decent argument into a worthless one: It would create a straw man.

For a real example, look for a moment at the recycling argument on page 12 of Chapter 1. To criticize that argument as "being opposed to burdening small businesses with the details of recycling programs" would be to attack a straw man. The author may be opposed to all involvement by small business in such programs; but her letter argues for a far more modest and easily defended position. It opposes one particular recycling plan. For that conclusion the argument presented is much stronger.

Testimony arguments are obviously very sensitive to this maneuver. The support offered for a statement is sometimes simply that somebody believes it: She offers her judgment, based on her understanding of things. And as we have seen, this can be strong support indeed. But it is also quite vulnerable to straw-man formulations. For a slight change in our understanding of a statement can make a big change in the competence necessary to underwrite it. When a meteorologist forecasts snow down to the 3500-foot level, anything within a few hundred feet (either way) normally counts as getting it right. That degree of accuracy is both very useful and a sign of great skill. So if I criticize the forecast as badly supported by noting that this forecaster missed by fifty feet last time—or even a hundred feet usually—I am attacking a straw-man version of the testimony argument. I am invoking standards that are neither intended nor useful. It is the worst sort of charity violation.

Illustration. Some time ago a California legislator argued for a repeal of the 55-mph speed limit, primarily because it was so widely disregarded. Opponents countered by accusing the legislator of defending the very general position

C_s Whenever a law is violated it should be repealed.

This is such a laughable view that it needs no refutation. But it also makes the argument a straw man. Many other, more easily defended positions would be quite adequate for the legislator's purpose. One, which is still too tough, would be

C_s' Whenever a law is routinely violated by a majority of those having an opportunity to do so, it should be repealed.

This would be far easier to defend than C_s, since it would not require repeal of most criminal statutes.

Even this would preposterously inflate the legislator's intent, however. Most legislation has peculiar features that make peculiar support necessary, and speed limits are an extreme case. Choosing an exact velocity to impose on highway traffic involves striking a balance among safety, convenience, energy consumption, noise, and the like. It also involves a kind of arbitrariness unlike anything in the laws against murder, rape, and burglary: The last five or ten miles per hour are nearly impossible to justify objectively. So a venerable procedure has always been relatively subjective: Let the traffic set its own speed. In the absence of special hazards, the speed at which the average driver feels comfortable is an important consideration. So the kind of support a speed limit needs will be systematically different from many other kinds of law. The legislative conclusion therefore can and should be very specific:

C   The general 55-mph speed limit should be repealed.

The argument could then focus on specifically relevant costs and benefits, undistracted by straw-man generalities. Although C is far easier to defend than C_s, or C_s', it is difficult enough to occupy the legislature.

Proof

The notion of proof plays a curious role in public debate. Sometimes we talk as though we require proof, when all we need is good reason.

> What proof do you have that new taxes will (or won't) send the economy into a tailspin?

Here, the demand for proof is just a straw man. Public policy decisions always involve some gamble on consequences. The best we ever get ahead of time are good reasons one way or the other. So the unanswerable demand for proof here is irrelevant to our reasoning. Choice rests on the best reasons we can find.

Reasoning in practical contexts seldom admits of—or waits for—proof. The demand for proof is very frequently in the service of a forensic straw man. Yet we are sometimes genuinely unclear about how strong the reasons must be for a certain purpose. How much uncertainty must be removed before you scrap the old car, initiate criminal prosecution, or send in troops? As with anything else, we may reason about this by constructing arguments and explanations using what we *are* clear about—and learning new things where necessary. Cheap rhetorical tricks may win a point, but they get in the way of understanding.

When we are clear about all this, however, we commonly yield to the opposite temptation: the view that in practical matters you can never really prove anything. While probably less destructive than its opposite, this view is also an unfortunate bit of rhetorical excess. It is an overreaction we may avoid with a little care.

Mathematics and formal logic have clear and settled criteria for accomplishing proof. Manipulating the algorithm in a certain way, and thus achieving a certain result, counts as proving it. The clarity of this decision procedure sometimes encourages us to insist on those criteria in everything, including everyday reasoning about life and legislation. But the formal/mathematical criteria are not even coherently applicable to practical reasoning, which leads to the view that, in practical matters, we can never prove anything.

If this is the source of the confusion, we can avoid it by remembering that proof, like precision, requires different standards in different contexts. The notion of proof originated in the circumstances of our everyday lives, and it has a clear and useful role to play there still. When someone asks for proof of something—or denies that it can be proved—they need not be abusing the words. They may be making a very specific kind of point.

As we have noted, a proof is a very strong argument, a very good reason for something. That is why failing to prove something is not so bad sometimes. But very strong arguments are possible; practical proof can be achieved. The criterion of proof, in practice, is the *reasonability* of doubt. If evidence is strong enough to make doubt unreasonable, then it counts as proof. If the evidence falls short of this, you do not have proof. This is simply what is known as the "reasonable man test." If a reasonable person would still have some doubt, then the evidence is not adequate as proof. On the other hand, if support is so strong that doubt would be evidence of unreasonability, then proof is adequate. This criterion has clear application occasionally.

In some cases, what counts for and against a claim is so clear that application is easy. If I say my horse is taller than yours, or that I can play a Bach suite all the way through on my cello, I know just what to do if someone says "Prove it." I measure the horses and play the suite. If, following agreed-upon procedure, my horse comes out taller, that proves it. If I get all the way through without faltering, that proves I can play the suite.

Other cases are more interesting, however. Take the claim by a Pennsbury student that Pennsbury's football team is better than Morrisville's this year. We may have evidence that clearly falls short of proof: a ten-pound-per-lineman weight advantage, for instance. This is imposing, but it is not proof. Morrisville may have a better coaching staff and a more talented backfield, and the extra weight could be unexercised fat. However, had the teams already met twice, and Pennsbury won each game by more than one touchdown, the argument would be far stronger. But it would not yet be proof. Knowing nothing else about the two teams, for you to bet on Morrisville in a third contest would be silly. But football is a game of breaks; and the better team's losing two of two is not unheard of. So doubt can still be reasonable.

Proof would come with convincing victories in adverse circumstances, for example. Suppose Pennsbury had won the two meetings 40 to 0 and 28 to 6. And while Morrisville had been at full strength both times, Pennsbury's team had been decimated by the flu for the first game and had fielded reserves for most of the second half of the second game. Were nothing otherwise unusual about the contests, this would establish the Pennsbury student's case. Doubt would now be unreasonable: As a practical matter, what more do you need?

A further complication is worth mentioning, however. In many circumstances, the reasonability of doubt will depend not only on the weight of the evidence, but on what is at stake as well. Sometimes the consequences of a mistaken judgment are so stark that it is not unreasonable to hold out for greater than normal assurance. Accordingly, in such cases standards of proof will be higher. For example, if I balanced my checkbook using two quite different methods and got the same result, we would normally say I had adequate proof of the balance. If something enormous hung on the result, however—say an eccentric relative has tied my inheritance to my having a certain exact balance on a certain day—then it would be reasonable to check it more elaborately and more carefully. I might even want to call in expert help, just to make sure. And since it takes a stronger case to make doubt unreasonable, it is correspondingly more difficult to provide what we would call proof. To this extent, then, the concept of proof is tied not only to the strength of the evidence, but also to the purposes of the argument. What is adequate proof for some purposes is not for others.

If we are sensitive to the needs and possibilities of practical contexts, we may safely use the notion of proof in formulating everyday argument and criticism. When the unreasonability of doubt is the issue, proof may actually be the most useful tool to exploit. The practical criteria take into account both what we know and what is at stake. It is important to resist the temptation to impose more formal criteria, which are insensitive to our practical concerns.

The Charge of No Evidence

We have dubbed a diagnostic inductive argument "sound" if, on the evidence presented, one rival account is clearly better than the rest and that one is offered as the argument's conclusion. The conclusion of a sound diagnostic argument will be the preferable account of the trace data, and those data will raise hurdles for other accounts. This is so even if the best account is far from established, possibly not even very good.

In our common talk about evidence, the concept of soundness is reflected in the following way. Normally, if we can produce a sound argument for a conclusion, C, we capture this fact by saying *we have some evidence for C*. Put another way, when we say we have some evidence for C, frequently what we mean is that we have some data that are best accounted for by C. It may not be a *lot* of evidence—which is to say the account may not be very *good*. But if it is the best account of something, then we have some evidence for it.

If we know that a satellite's orbit is sinking dangerously close to the atmosphere and the satellite is due to pass over northern Canada tonight, then this evening's widespread reports of a fireball over Baker Lake constitute evidence that the satellite has fallen back to earth. The evidence is far from conclusive, of course; at this stage the fireball still could be a meteorite or, perhaps, some other satellite. But the best bet is that it is the satellite everybody is so concerned about. And that is why we call the fireball evidence of the satellite rather than of something else. In the absence of our special background information, the fireball would quite reasonably be taken to be (evidence of) a meteorite. *That* would be the best account of it. But as things stand, the streak in the sky is evidence of a falling satellite—and a specific one at that.

The semantics of "evidence" is important here because we commonly ignore it, or abuse it, in some circumstances. The problem arises most frequently in the pronouncements of public officials, especially in statements designed to avert responsibility or allay public fears. During the swine-flu vaccination program, for example, there was a well-publicized incident in which three elderly patients died shortly after being vaccinated at one clinic in Pennsylvania. The deaths raised some general fears, which the officials involved were anxious to quell, about the safety of the program. But what the officials said was that there was *no evidence* that the deaths were linked to the vaccination program. Given the important feature of evidence-talk sketched above, this is a confusing—nearly incomprehensible—thing to say in the context. The whole reason for the announcement, the cause of the fears, was the publication of something reasonably taken to be evidence of that causal connection. Given what we know about the human body's reaction to vaccination, it would not be surprising if frail, older people were sometimes not able to survive the treatment. Against normal background, the best account of the striking correlation between vaccinations and death in this incident seems clearly to be some causal connection. In short, the published correlation simply is (some) evidence of a causal link between the two.

The most charitable reading of what the officials meant by saying there is no evidence is that they knew something that was not common knowledge and that this private information promoted some other account (some form of the null hypothesis) above the naturally suspected one. But if this *is* what they were trying to say, they did it in a spectacularly inept and misleading way. To avoid the appearance of foolishness—or deceit—they should have at least told us that they were privy to something we did not suspect that would certainly change our plausibility estimate. The best thing—or at least the clearest thing—they could have done was to reveal their little secret: to tell us what they knew and what account of the correlation is recommended. As it stands, they should forgive us if we suspect they were trying to get away with something—to divert attention using the famous mindboggling-obfuscation ploy, hoping the whole thing would blow over before anybody caught on.

Other examples of this same kind of pronouncement are even more clearly public relations gambits and should be treated in the same way. When tobacco company spokespeople say there is no evidence that cigarette smoking causes cancer, they have the responsibility to show why some other account of the correlation is better. It might be that we have the direction of causal influence wrong, or that pure chance is a better bet than we think. But again, given normal background, these other hypotheses have substantial difficulties to overcome: The orthodox view is a far better account. In the context, the cancer/smoking correlation simply *is* (some) evidence for the thesis that smoking causes cancer.

The Charge of Circularity

One way to accuse an argument of question-begging is to call it "circular." The circle metaphor represents the argument as ending up in the same place it started out: with the conclusion. This metaphor is easily misapplied to diagnostic arguments, however; it is yet another tempting mistake that deserves our attention.

Notice first that many things we might call "starting out with the conclusion" do not beg the question—may, in fact, be perfectly legitimate. Entertaining a conclusion, for instance, can begin an inquiry, which results in an argument for that conclusion. Or you may begin with C to discover whether you have any interest in pursuing the argument. In constructing an argument you may begin with C to make sure it is carefully formulated for its purpose. And when you present an argument, it is good practice to present C first just to let everybody know where you are headed. None of these beginnings fallaciously *presupposes* the conclusion. Each uses it in a wholly unobjectionable way.

Moreover, we may even *presuppose* a conclusion without begging the question or reasoning badly at all: It depends on how we go about it, what we are up to. We may presuppose a conclusion *for the sake of argument*, for instance. We may assume it is true to see where it leads or where it leaves you: to think through the consequences. Something like this takes place in all diagnostic arguments.

Before we can decide on the sound conclusion, we must generate a plausibility ranking. To do this, in general, requires trying out each rival on the trace data to see which one handles the entire collection best. In a way, we assume a rival is true to see how well it fits. This procedure is sometimes mistaken for the question-begging kind of presupposing of a conclusion. At this stage of the text you should be adequately armed to avoid that confusion as soon as it is pointed out.

One case requires special emphasis, however. Sometimes we can find only one rival worth serious consideration. I find automatic transmission fluid on my workshop floor. I remember that I swapped vacuum modulators earlier in the day, and the old one doubtless had some fluid left in it. I must have dripped some on the floor as I carried it to the trash. I pull the suspect from the trash and a few drips fall from it as I do. Case closed. That's where the fluid on the floor came from. No other explanations are worth considering. Much of our diagnostic reasoning is like this. Only one suspect, one hypothesis, comes close to accommodating all the data. And sometimes this is a perfectly good plausibility ranking. We may know the subject well enough to know that the next best bet is some outrageous conspiracy theory: *any* conspiracy theory. All the other rivals are so bad as to not be worth formulating. But since you try out only a single rival, such a case is more easily confused with question-begging: You assumed THE conclusion (if only to try it out on the traces).

The fact that we find only one rival worth considering does not make the diagnostic procedure fallacious, of course. But it does have a danger: We place all of the weight on our general understanding instead of on explicit comparison of rivals; yet we are generally better at making the comparisons. This is something we must keep in mind. But it is easier to keep in mind—and more possible to treat intelligently—if we do not confuse it with question-begging.

STUDY GUIDE FOR CHAPTER 6

1. There are some very common ways in which our own strong commitments can mislead us when we make or criticize an argument. These common mistakes are usually called "fallacies." The point of this chapter is to help the creator and the critic avoid such fallacies.

    (a) One common fallacy in creating an argument, called *begging the question*, is usually described as presupposing the conclusion one is trying to argue for; but it is better formulated as supporting a conclusion with a statement that would not be accepted by anyone who didn't already accept the conclusion. When someone gives a question-begging argument for C, his reasons for believing C will not be accepted as reasons for believing C by anyone who does not already believe C.

    (b) One way to beg a question is to use a *loaded description* of some disputed matter. If an argument concerns whether something is good or bad, then descriptions of it must remain fairly neutral if they are to be acceptable to both sides.

    (c) Related to giving loaded descriptions is the fallacy of *false dilemmas*. When we construct a false dilemma, we give a loaded description of one option (bad) and a loaded description of another option (good), suggest that these are the only two options, and think that we have argued that the second option is the only reasonable one. But, of course, things are always more complicated than this.

2. We can also commit fallacies when we try to criticize arguments. We can characterize arguments badly, or we can criticize an argument for not meeting wholly unreasonable expectations. In order to avoid such critical fallacies, we must employ the principle of charity and be aware of the sorts of standards an ordinary argument must meet.

    (a) A *straw-man argument* is an attempt to criticize an argument by giving a very weak characterization of the argument. One common way of constructing a straw-man argument is to inflate the conclusion beyond the intentions of the author. The author argues for a specific conclusion, which might seem reasonable, but the critic accuses him of arguing for a very general and hard-to-support conclusion (arguing for the repeal of all laws that are ever violated rather than for the repeal of the 55-mph speed limit, for example). Of course, if we abide by the principle of charity, we will not commit the straw-man fallacy.

    (b) Sometimes, we commit a critical fallacy when we claim that the author of an argument has not *proved* her conclusion. Mathematics and formal logic have a fairly clear and agreed-upon conception of proof, but this conception concerns only deductive arguments. That the vast majority of arguments in practical reasoning are not deductive might lead to the view that practical arguments don't prove anything. But the conception of proof in formal matters should not be confused with our very useful everyday conception of proof. One proves one's case in court (and in other practical matters) when one has eliminated all reasonable doubt. Accomplishing this requires striking a thoughtful balance between the amount of evidence and what's at stake; but it is something we are all competent to do in familiar circumstances.

(c) As we saw in Chapter 3, when C_3 is the best explanation of some trace data, those traces provide evidence for C_3: some reason to prefer it to its natural rivals. Conversely, to say there is *no evidence* for C_3 is to say there is nothing C_3 explains best—nothing C_3 seems required to explain. This sometimes places a special burden on someone who wants to deny there is any evidence for some particular C: that burden is to give us a better explanation of the things C seems to best explain. Just saying "there is no evidence for C" in such a case will often seem empty and defensive and will suggest that the critic doesn't really know a better one.

(d) The last critical fallacy, the *misplaced charge of circularity*, is a way of charging an argument with question-begging when it doesn't deserve the charge. If the argument is genuinely question-begging (that is, if the support cannot be accepted by anyone who doesn't already accept the conclusion), then of course this charge is not a fallacy. But sometimes it is perfectly legitimate to *start out with* the conclusion: for example, when one is accepting a conclusion "for the sake of argument," to see where the conclusion leads, or when one is testing rival conclusions to see which is more plausible. In these cases one is not begging the question, just investigating it.

= 7 =

LANGUAGE

Skills and Concepts

Overview

As reasoning becomes more abstract, it increasingly involves us in questions of language: the terms we use to formulate our thoughts. Our examination of practical reasoning has, perhaps not accidentally, provided a pair of tools ideally suited to helping us at this more abstract level. They are the DIAGNOSTIC APPARATUS and the CHARITY PRINCIPLE. In this chapter they will guide our exploration of some deceptive properties of language; they will allow us to unravel some common confusions about language and help us appreciate its vast natural complexity.

INTRODUCTION

In Chapter 6 we saw some of the ways in which our reasoning can become tangled in the language we use. Sometimes differences are magnified by our words, and understanding suffers as a consequence. The descriptions we find natural may mislead everybody else. For this reason, and for others as well, our thinking sometimes turns to the properties of language itself. We find ourselves brooding about meaning, concepts, and the implications of what we say. If all my life-signs disappear temporarily, am I dead temporarily, or is death permanent by definition? Is a tomato really a fruit, not a vegetable? Must I be able to define my terms? Why? When? Which terms? And what counts as an adequate definition? What sort of thing is the meaning of a word? Of a sentence? Can I fail to understand what I mean by what I say?

These are rather abstract questions. They do not directly concern the objects and events of our daily lives, but rather the conceptions we use to talk about them, to refer to them. The worry is not about dying, but about the concept of death; not about a particular tomato, but about the concept of fruit. The question is abstract; it's about what *counts as* dead, fruit, meaning, definition.

These are deceptively tricky questions, about which intelligent people have disagreed deeply for the entire history of recorded thought. Their difficulty derives from the same source as their fascination: the almost unimaginable intricacy of natural language. As a practical tool for communication, our language has evolved, has developed its network of properties, from the impulse humans have to express our interests on an infinite variety of topics in an immense number of different contexts. Natural languages (we will be dealing exclusively with English, to the extent that that makes a difference) develop like ancient cities, without much urban planning. Many of their characteristics have arisen directly in response to local needs and random accident. There is something like a gridwork of paths; but parallels break down, the pattern is distorted here and there by historical accident and local geography, and there are many small patterns within the larger one.

How is it, then, that we handle this tool as well as we do? If it is all that complicated, why is communication often so easy, conversation so effortless? The answer, of course, is that we have guided the development; the language has been shaped by our needs. We are competent to handle it because the language that arises naturally out of human commerce is one that works: works with human skills and human interests in the practical circumstances of our lives. The language is tailor-made to fit the jobs that commonly need doing. It works, for us, in spite of its staggering complexity, because we had so much to do with its design: it is a custom fit.

But talk *about* the language itself has been a relatively small and feeble part of its development. The topics on which we (and the language) have evolved great competence are the matters of life and death, love and hate, pain and pleasure, ends and means of our daily lives. Making our way in the world seldom requires us to confront questions of semantics, definition, and concepts: that is, to talk about the language itself. If someone does not understand what we say, we do not talk about the misunderstanding; we rephrase it, say it again differently. Even when we do talk about it, nothing much hangs on the talk because there are so many ways to communicate—to straighten out misunderstandings. The basic theme is trial and error.

So one reason that abstract matters of concepts and semantics can remain unresolved for centuries is that little (else) of practical consequence hangs on them. I may be completely confused about what sort of thing a meaning is, or whether purposes are causes, and never miss a meal, a bus, or a day on the job. But there is another, more important reason for the intractability of such disputes. It is that, as with any great natural skill, the limits of our competence with language are often hard to see: We can get in over our heads without noticing it. Sometimes nothing warns us that we are using words in a way our training and experience have not prepared us for. We can stop making sense and simply fail to notice.

We are unprepared to talk on many topics, of course. Very few of us, on a moment's notice, could profitably lecture on laser holography, the panic of 1836, *Paradise Lost*, or the Peloponnesian Wars. But each of these matters has its own peculiar vocabulary, which gives all sorts of clues that the topic is exotic and may require special care and training. But when the exotic topic is the working of the language itself, we seldom get such warning. The words are all too familiar. The questions look just like the everyday ones we *can* handle. "Is death permanent?" and "Can causes come after their effects?" look rather like "Is titanium weldable?" and "Can earthquakes come after grandmother dies?" But they are not. They are not alike in just the way that tests our competence and good judgment. The first two questions naturally entangle us in the intricacies of language that we are scarcely prepared to articulate. Our common experience goes only a very little way toward helping us with such questions. If we wish to address them we have to proceed slowly, cautiously, and with a strong sense of the practical purposes for which language has developed its characteristics. Its practical value is the first thing to suffer when we treat language clumsily.

So why bother? Why spend a chapter treating abstract matters of language and concepts if they do not matter in our daily lives? The answer is that they *do* matter in our lives; they just do not matter much for breakfast or shopping for shoes. They do not matter much in the vast array of workaday contexts in which language does its practical work, communicating our mundane interests. But as soon as our interests become intellectual and articulateness becomes a value, then all these abstract matters do become relevant to our lives—our intellectual lives.

We are naturally curious about the workings of our language, partly just because it is fascinatingly intricate, but partly because the intricacy reveals something of the human intellect. An obvious fact of university life is that thoughtful people do think and talk about abstract matters of language and concepts all the time. Nearly everybody I have engaged in conversation on college campuses over a quarter of a century has had opinions on—often *strong* opinions on—a whole variety of abstract conceptual issues. Issues ranging from whether a whale is a fish, or sociology a science, all the way to what it means to say that these are conceptual issues.

So the question of how to reason about such matters is not silly or irrelevant: It arises all the time. All human reflection invites abstraction to some degree or other. The project of this chapter is to develop our understanding of language, and our linguistic skill, in an effort to guide our more abstract reasoning. And the diagnostic apparatus we have now mastered will play a key role in this task. It will allow us to see complexity as the natural product of our human interests; and it will help us tie abstract conceptions to their concrete employment as tools for practical communication.

DIAGNOSTIC BACKGROUND

Our use of language is perhaps the single most valuable application of our diagnostic skill. When we understand what someone has said, we have interpreted their words in a certain way: We have made a diagnosis. To communicate with each other we must grasp the significance of trace data, some of which are words. And the background we require to do this is partly our understanding of the language, but it may include anything and everything else as well.

Sometimes we fall on the right interpretation effortlessly, instantly, without thinking about it:

Would you pass the potatoes one more time, please.

But occasionally we must work on it:

I think the table has drifted off its stop a little, don't you?

Unlike the first example, this sentence does not bring to mind an obviously best interpretation; perhaps you can't think of any reading, plausible or implausible. Since there are no unfamiliar words here, the background on which we must draw to understand this sentence will include much outside the language itself. It would naturally include details of the circumstances, including something about the speaker, as well as our general knowledge of people and their interests. If some gestures went along with the sentence, they would help us reach an interpretation by providing more trace data: Our reading would have to account for the gestures as well as the words.

S_1 Words (sentence).

S_2 Gestures, tone, expression, etc.

S_3 Circumstances.

S_4 Background.

=============================== d

C   Interpretation (of the sentence).

Even when we understand immediately, of course, the pattern is diagnostic. Rival interpretations are never impossible in any strong sense, just implausible or outlandish. And that plausibility judgment is the one we are skilled at making, sometimes instantaneously. But, like any diagnostic enterprise, it requires attending to all kinds of detail in the circumstances, not just the words before us. Suppose the person requesting "potatoes" at dinner had earlier embarrassed herself by thinking the turnips were potatoes, which inspired some good-natured joking around. She had then, in this spirit, twice asked for the turnips by pointedly calling them potatoes. If I have been engrossed in another conversation, and have missed all this, my linguistic skill will trick me (naturally and immediately) into placing the wrong interpretation on her words when she turns to me, points toward the turnips, and says,

Would you pass the potatoes one more time, please.

Even if the turnips were right in front of me, and the potatoes elsewhere, I might reject the right reading of her words because that plausibility judgment is so intimately tied to background I lack. I may even explain away her gesture toward the turnips as a mannerism unrelated to the message.

A CLOSER LOOK AT PERCEPTION

Understanding what people say, coming to see the significance of their words, is like any other perceptual recognition. So it will be useful to extend our discussion of human recognition skills, which we began in Chapter 3, before plunging directly into their most difficult application. When I recognize something, I place an interpretation on some perceived traces. I see the thing in front of me as a crosswalk or a person, a cumulus cloud or a run-down tenement; or I may hear a car stop out front or smell the coffee brewing; or I may recognize a *specific* person, a *particular* concerto, or *my* car. In doing these things I offer an account of traces, of a certain pattern. I implicitly reject other accounts in order to accept the one I do. This isn't abstract art, it's a crosswalk; it's not the sprinklers going on, it's the sound of a car pulling into the driveway; not a mannequin, but a fellow student.

To make this judgment reliably, I naturally must be skilled at noticing the right patterns. But in thinking about perception we tend to invest too much in the traces and ignore the crucial, sometimes overwhelming role played by background and circumstance. I recognize a crosswalk because it is on a city street. The same traces in another place may indicate something else entirely or be wholly meaningless—or they may actually be abstract art. In another case I may recognize something as a person—in part because that thing is in a classroom. The same sleepy form in a department store window could well be a mannequin.

Perceptual competence depends as much on understanding the setting in which trace data occur as it does on noticing the right traces. For we are making a plausibility judgment, choosing the most plausible interpretation; and, as we have seen many times, slight changes in the non-trace data can radically alter the ranking. In other words, we can tell what something *is* from what it *looks like*, but only against the proper background. And this is true for even very familiar objects. When I recognize my car in the parking lot, much of the effortless certainty of that perception stems from knowing where I left it. With that background I can recognize it at night, in bad light, from a silhouette and a few highlights. Of course, that means I can be wrong, can be fooled. Somebody could have swiped mine and substituted a nearly identical one, and I may not notice until I try the key. The available traces would be the same. But my (background) understanding of human motivation and the institutions surrounding cars and parking lots will normally drop that rival from serious consideration. Automatically.

Our perceptions are not infallible, of course, but they do guide us very well in dealing with the world's complexity. And they guide us so well because they are keyed to both kinds of evidence. What I might lack of one kind can be made up in the other category. If my background makes one rival overwhelmingly likely, I can manage a recognition with just hints of trace data. But if an interpretation is antecedently implausible, far more trace data will be required to secure it. If my gaze falls on my car parked in broad daylight at the curb in New York City, but I left it at a curb in Los Angeles this morning, I might not even take notice. If I did, I would certainly shrug it off as a twin. Quite a lot of data would be required to get me to see it as my own car, to see that it *is* my own.

Articulation

As we hinted in Chapter 3 (page 119ff), the effortlessness of our perceptual skill, and the tie that skill has to our general understanding, has a frustrating consequence: inarticulateness. Like those of any great skill, its workings are often mysterious even to the supremely competent. Just as the major league batting champion cannot—need not be able to—say anything helpful about how he swings a bat, I cannot say how I recognize my brother in a crowd or a voice over the phone. Of course, we can say something: medium height, light hair, no glasses; or man's voice, woman's voice, tenor or baritone. But this is not enough to identify anybody. When I spot my brother in a crowd, I am responding to detail of movement and physiognomy of which I am not even consciously aware. He just looks (walks, acts) like my brother. I would recognize him with hair dyed black and glasses.

We are so skillful because we are sensitive to a complex network of traces and background. Much of its value lies in its tying together wisps of detail that we haven't even vocabulary to list separately, if we did notice them separately, which we ordinarily do not. So we are inarticulate about the very traces on which our skill rests; and this sponsors a skeptical worry. How can we trust our perceptual judgment if we are not even aware of the traces we are responding to? How can we rely on our instantaneous interpretation when we do not know just what we are interpreting?

As for any good, effortless, inarticulate skill, the answer is that we rely on it because it works. But it is easier to understand what counts as *working* for other skills (swinging a bat, playing a concerto, or walking) than it is for perception. Our perceptions (of contact, music, or moving) are what tell us the other skills work. What do we fall back on to tell us our perception is working? This is a reasonable question and deserves brief treatment.

We develop simple perceptions—reliable, instantaneous diagnoses—where there is a rich, continuous flux of trace data: where there are always new traces relevant to our latest plausibility judgments. Here, bad judgments naturally betray themselves and the diagnostic net is quickly self-correcting. After our skill develops and matures, this same feature constantly reassures us, testing our judgment in the next wave of information. If we misidentify a voice over the phone, the conversation usually cannot go on very long before something tips us off to the confusion. If we think there is water on the road ahead, driving on to the suspected area naturally brings more relevant data. The unceasing flow of such experiences tells us our (unarticulable) skill really works. It also gives us some sense of the limits of that skill.

We may, of course, *become* articulate about a perception. Nothing (except time, effort, and an understandable lack of interest) prevents our developing a vocabulary for this sort of thing. We might try selective disguises on my brother to see what features I require for an identification in various settings. But nothing like this is required for someone to have a reliable perception, a genuine skill.

In fact, studying a skill can sometimes damage it. Batters may worry themselves into slumps by trying to improve a swing that already works. Virtuoso violinists have lost some of their natural technique after opening schools for children. This is known as the centipede effect. The name comes from the mythical centipede who was once asked how he managed to coordinate all those legs in such a wonderful way as he walked. Puzzling over this, he was struck by the fact that he did not himself understand how he did it. As he thought it over he became more and more confused about the sequence of motions, until, when he tried to walk, he could not manage it, so boggled was his mind at the task.

Worry about the centipede effect need not prevent us from studying our skills. But it does raise a caution: Some skills work best when not reflected upon. So if we do study them, we must take care not to damage them.

Inference

To survive, and make our way as well as we do, requires that our senses process a lot of data quickly and accurately. Simply living trains us to notice certain patterns and gives us the experience necessary to understand their significance. Sometimes we do all this instantaneously: recognize something in a simple perception. Other times we must agonize through the comparison of rival possibilities in an explicit diagnostic inference. But there is no sharp division between the two activities. How fast we make a diagnosis is simply a function of our skill, our training, and the breadth of our understanding.

This is why matters that once required diagnostic inference can, with familiarity, become simple perceptions. When I first started gardening in a hot, arid climate, for example, I was puzzled and frustrated that parts of my lawn would turn brown and ugly without warning. Some investigation supplied an explanation: The underlying granite is close to the surface in these places, causing them to dry out more quickly than the rest of the lawn. Since those spots now had my attention, I soon discovered that I could tell when they were drying out, a day or two before they would start turning brown. The grass would change its appearance in the very pattern that would soon turn brown if I let it. The change was subtle, and hard to describe, but easily detectable if you were looking for it. And the appearance could be brought back to conform with that of the rest of the lawn with just a little water. I had become able to see grass wilting. A diagnostic inference had developed into a simple perception. I can now recognize immediately what before I had to infer, figure out.

The development of perception out of inference is such a natural part of our experience that we scarcely notice it. When we move to a new place, for instance, it takes a while to get used to the new sights and sounds. The new impressions may at first create a dazzling welter. But we soon begin to distinguish patterns in the confusion, and we gradually figure out what lies behind them. After a time, many of these diagnoses simply become comfortable perceptions. We simply recognize the lights of a car coming through the alley, the sound of an upstairs neighbor running in place, the drip from a loose downspout when it drizzles at night.

If the human capacity to convert complex diagnosis into simple perception seems unimpressive in a mundane setting, it is striking when it derives from special training or exotic experience: when the resulting perception is not one we easily share. With repeated experience, radiologists have come to be able to simply see tumors, aneurysms—all manner of pathological conditions—on X-rays; a quarterback can read a new defensive alignment instantly; a mechanic can hear piston-slap; a shepherd can pick out a sick animal by eye at a distance. In all sorts of ways, human beings train themselves to know what something looks like (sounds like, etc.) so they can recognize it instantly. When the setting is right.

Understanding perception in this way does more than simply display its diagnostic credentials, however. It also gives us a ready-made strategy for recovery and repair when perception begins to fail or becomes controversial. We may then treat it in a full-blown diagnostic investigation, thinking up rival interpretations, ranking them, looking for relevant new data. If I get to the car in the parking lot and my key does not fit in the lock, a question is raised about my perception of the car. Could I (my interpretation of the traces) be wrong? I then look for further traces that might distinguish my car, and I look around to see if another like it is parked nearby. New data, new rivals: Everything in Chapter 3 applies naturally.

LINGUISTIC SKILL

Our ability to instantly recognize familiar patterns in well-understood settings is the superskill we use in the task of communicating with each other. It is what enables normal conversation to be so effortlessly successful and what allows subtle, complicated sentiments to be understood at all. In the rest of this chapter we will employ the insights of the previous section, and of earlier chapters, in an effort to understand this great skill (without damaging it). This background will help us come to grips with language as we use it in practice, and with some of its fascinating detail. It will allow us to develop helpful characterizations of some of the key properties of language, detect places where our skill might fail, and help us make our way when it does.

Understanding and the Principle of Charity

Understanding what someone has said is our general recognition skill at work. Our effortless interpretation of words in reading and conversation is a kind of perception. It is distinguished from other recognitions by two features: the traces it interprets and the particular background it requires for their interpretation. The traces contain *words* and—in the sequence of words—patterns. The required background is familiarity with the *practices* and *conventions* of a language-using community. These two features, and the range of possibilities they allow, are what make language so important to our lives.

The feature of perception that is most dramatically important for understanding language is the role of SETTING. Deep and intimate familiarity with surrounding circumstances, and with relevant background, is what allows us to interpret traces accurately and quickly. This is as true when the traces are words as it is when they are shapes and colors.

The setting for language is usually called CONTEXT. The context in which a sentence occurs is crucial to our understanding of the sentence in the same way that the setting in which a perception occurs is crucial to the perception. This is most obvious in cases like the request for potatoes we examined a short while ago. But the point is general: To understand any sentence, we must have or imagine a context, because any arrangement of words may have many interpretations. "I missed my plane" can mean I was late getting to the airport, but it might also be how I discovered my workshop had been burglarized. Virtually every sentence is like this. The message it conveys depends on where it is found.

Part of the context is itself linguistic, a matter of language. Familiarity with the right vocabulary, syntax, and local dialect is indispensable to understanding. For our purposes, however, the substantive context, the part outside the language, will be of greater consequence. Almost anything in the environment and in our background can make a key difference in our understanding of what someone has said. To even begin to grasp the sense of

Give me an oh-three, and make it snappy.

or

I think the table has drifted slightly off its stop, don't you?

We must be intimately familiar with certain matters of substance. Given that familiarity, communication can be effortlessly successful.

Without it, almost nothing comes through.

Even sentences that seem clear when "out of context," such as

The cat is on the mat.

are so only because they readily suggest a context. This last sentence makes the sense it does because our general understanding of pets and floors places it in a typical domestic setting. But with a little imagination, we could conjure up an atypical context in which this same sentence naturally expresses some other, perhaps exotic, sentiment: a bulldozer at a blasting site, for instance. Just as for any other sentence, the best account of it—the most reasonable interpretation—depends on the context.

All this provides some insight into the principle of charity. As it is found here, charity is not just a rule for critical paraphrase and argument analysis; it is an essential part of our linguistic skill. It is the rule we follow automatically in interpreting language: Choose the most plausible reading in the context. As we have seen, this is indispensable to communication, and it is our skill.

Charity is so natural a part of our reading and conversation that we hardly ever notice it. It allows us to pass things off as slips of the tongue, typographical errors, bad grammar, dialect, or butchered language and still get the message—at least sometimes. Like perception in a familiar setting, communication has trouble failing if the context is well understood. We often know so well where the conversation is headed that we need only hints from the words themselves. A half-completed sentence, or an imprudently candid inflection, can easily reveal more than intended. The context, and our plausibility judgment, will do almost all of the work.

At the other extreme, when the context is unclear, the text obscure, interpretation becomes a diagnostic investigation governed by the same principle: Make the best sense possible, given everything we know. Reading documents from long dead civilizations invariably requires us to dig out substantive details of the culture. Even if we know the vocabulary and structure of the language, many passages remain obscure until we understand the practices and preoccupations of the people for whom it was intended.

We usually need to be reminded of the principle of charity only when our skill begins to fail, when we get in over our heads. But this happens all the time when reasoning becomes abstract.

Talking, Writing, and the Principle of Empathy

Even though complex and subtle, our ability to understand language is not our most impressive linguistic skill. Even more challenging is our ability to *create* it: to talk and write. When young, we invariably understand a great deal before we can actually produce even elementary sentences. As we age we find writing far more difficult than reading; and the same experience is repeated when we attempt to learn a second language. This contrast is absolutely typical throughout our perceptual experience, wherever we find a recognition skill paired with a performance skill. Recognizing my car is easier than sketching it; recognizing a Mozart sonata is easier than playing it.

Performances are harder to master than recognitions for all sorts of obvious reasons. Muscles and coordination must be trained in order for us to speak, write, or play a sonata; choices must be made about how the performance should go. But there is one *special* burden we shoulder in producing language that has a direct impact on our reasoning. To create intelligible language, an author (speaker, writer) must constantly see things from the perspective of the audience. Since your words will be given their most natural interpretation in the context, you must string them together with sensitivity to that context. If you want to say P, you must put words together so that P will be the best interpretation of them in that context. This mutual understanding underpins communication. I understand what you say only because I assume you said what you did *because* I would understand it the way I did. If this relationship breaks down generally, so does communication.

We might call this requirement the principle of empathy; and it too is usually trivial because we abide by it so naturally. Becoming competent speakers and writers simply requires us to become skilled empathizers. We can communicate our interests only to the extent to which we become good at judging what interpretation others will place on our words.

Taking Responsibility for Our Words

The principle of empathy bears directly on our reasoning because it determines what our words may be taken to *imply*. Part of "placing an interpretation on words" will consist in simply taking for granted many unspoken things required by the context. Like the setting of any perception, the context required for a shared interpretation will contain a vast amount of detail, most of which must remain unmentioned if communication is to be possible at all. So we are automatically and inevitably responsible for what will be taken for granted, for the natural implications of our words. And this is ordinarily unproblematic, because what we take for granted is, or should be, too obvious to mention. (We have discussed all this before in Chapter 3, page 97ff.) Our mutual understanding determines the common ground of what is too obvious to mention.[1] Empathy requires the speaker to mention everything that is not too obvious to mention; charity requires the listener to take for granted that this has been done.

Again, normally this is no problem. An overnight guest walks into the family kitchen at breakfast time and someone says, "There's toast, hot coffee, and milk in the refrigerator for cereal." In any normal context these words have a clear implication: The guest has been given permission (encouraged, actually) to help herself to breakfast. So if, when she sits down with her toast and coffee, the speaker remarks, "Hey, I didn't say you could *have* any," it is certainly a little joke. Simple incompetence is a very long shot (and abnormal contexts have been ruled out). At this level we all have a pretty good command of what our words imply.

Difficulties usually arise only when we practice deception, when we try to wriggle out of plain implications through legerdemain. And then it is important just to understand the consequences and who is responsible for what. Consider a subtler case. I explain to you that I missed yesterday's important meeting because my mother died. If you take my words seriously, I know perfectly well you will think my mother had *just* died and I could not attend because of circumstances immediately following a death in the family. Either I was too grieved to function or I was needed at home to pull things together, or support the rest of the family, or some such thing. That would naturally explain why I had said nothing beforehand. So if it turns out that my mother died years ago—but made my inheritance contingent on observing the anniversary of her death by staying home all day, and that was the story behind my absence—then I may be

---

[1] Recall that without this we don't talk. But none of this is to suggest that there are any topics we absolutely cannot disagree about and still understand each other. We simply cannot disagree about everything at once. For every topic some things—different things, perhaps—will have to be taken for granted—held constant, as it were. And the people on both sides of a conversation must understand what they are.

accused of deliberately misleading you. I have abused the language. Specifically, you have a natural inclination to put the charitable interpretation on my words, and I have used it to trick you into believing something false.

Nor can I avoid the charge by pleading that what I said was "strictly" true. For in the context what I clearly and knowingly *implied* is just false. I used the wrong words to express myself. I violated the principle of empathy. The right words, ones without clearly false implications, were that I felt obliged to observe my little ritual. And this is monumentally different from what I did say. So if there is a sense of "strict truth" in which what I said was strictly true, it is just as reprehensible as plain falsehood. It was as shabby as any made-up excuse. Worse, if I systematically ignore false implications like this, if I abandon empathy, other people will stop taking my words seriously: I will begin to lose my place in the human conversation. People who know me will not know what to make of my words, will not know what to take for granted. I will cripple my ability to communicate.

The Requirement of Significance.   Perhaps the most pervasive and fundamental application of charity in the use of language is to understand the *motivation* behind the words we use. To grasp what someone says, we usually must have some sense of why he said it, what practical human significance it might have. We understand the words in part because we understand why somebody would want to say or ask such a thing then and there. "Hand me a screwdriver, please." "Is it raining?" "The cat is on the mat." To understand these sentences, we naturally place them in (sketchy) contexts in which they have some human significance. If we cannot do this, we have trouble understanding what has been said.

> For this arrangement, molecules count once and desperately depressed people twice.

Even if the words in this sentence are familiar, we do not understand what has been said until we see its significance, see why it was a significant thing to say.

So a substantial component of our automatic charity consists in viewing others' statements as significant. If we cannot find a significant interpretation, we conclude that something has gone wrong.

Either we do not fully grasp the context, or the author has made a slip of the tongue or does not understand the language or, perhaps, is babbling incoherently.

Unfortunately, sometimes the best explanation is deception. Politicians and advertisers occasionally resort to statements that have clearly false implications when interpreted as significant remarks—as they naturally will be—but that may be defended by appeal to the shabby notion of "strict" truth we used above. That is, their statements may be construed as true only if stripped of the natural significance every competent language user would charitably give them.

Advertising agencies quite commonly run afoul of the significance requirement when plugging their client's product in flattering comparisons. Perhaps the gaudiest instance of this was an ad a few years ago for a medium-priced family sedan. It ticked off traits the sedan shared with famously expensive cars—an interior dimension with the Rolls Royce, front wheel drive with the Cadillac Eldorado. These are shaky enough, but significance collapsed altogether when the car was compared to the Aston Martin. The trait it shared with this exotic sports car was independent front suspension: "Independent front suspension, like the Aston Martin Vantage coupe."

The difficulty here is that virtually all cars, for years, have had independent front suspension. It is as common as door handles and headlights. But since most people do not know much about how the wheels are hung on their cars, they naturally are inclined to take the comparison with the Aston Martin as significant. Even the skeptical among us would have a hard time believing that anyone would say something as fatuous as

It has left and right headlights like the Ferrari Testarossa.

But the comparison of suspension systems is just as silly. So the advertising ploy openly offended the presumption of significance. The only reason to mention the similarity in this context was that it was flattering to the less expensive car. This implication is certainly why the similarity was part of the ad. And it is grotesquely implausible to suppose the advertisers did not know the comparison was trivial. In short, the ad was dishonest.

Once again, the claim may be defended by appeal to the reprehensible notion of "strict" truth. The sedan in question did have independent front suspension, and in that respect it did resemble the expensive sports car. There is no need to review the emptiness of this defense. The common appeal to such defenses in advertising and in politics goes a long way toward establishing the radical claim of some social critics that the institutions surrounding those activities undermine and subvert language itself. The presumption of significance is an important part of what makes language work.

MEANING, DEFINITION, AND CONCEPTS: THE JOBS WORDS DO

The second aspect of perception that will directly aid our understanding of language, and our linguistic skills, is our inarticulateness about it. Part of this too rests on the role of setting: The complexity of our background and our grasp of circumstance makes it hard to say just what it takes, how much we need, to identify something. But another part is the subtlety of trace data to which we are sensitive. We have no way to describe human faces, for example, to the degree of accuracy we can differentiate by eye. And even if we did, even if we developed a splendidly detailed physiognomic vocabulary, we would still have to develop a new skill to use it. We would have to start attending to detail that now escapes distinct notice.[2] This might or might not damage the skill we investigate in this manner; but one thing is clear: Articulating a perception is very different from simply *having* one. The two things require different skills, different training. And they are useful for vastly different purposes.

All this applies undiluted to language and linguistic skills. Linguistic recognition (including that in empathy) is a skill we learn on the job, by trial and error, against the complex tapestry of our understanding of things in general. And we end up with a spectacularly complicated ability, about the workings of which we can say very little. Just how we know what words to use to say what we want, just what we need in order to understand a sentence—these are questions as awkward and difficult as how I recognize a voice over the phone or my brother in a crowd. The competence that gets us through life is in *doing* these things, not in talking about *how* we do them. We have as little opportunity to develop our articulation skill for language as we have for any perception.

---

[2]Forty-three different kinds of eyebrows, for instance, and a whole taxonomy of hairlines. A way to register relative placement of eyes, ears, and mouth would also be indispensable.

One distinguishing feature of language, and linguistic perception, misleads us about this, however. It is that language—communication—naturally breaks itself up into units (words) in a way unlike other recognitions. This breakup suggests that we *can* articulate our linguistic skill, routinely, by dividing it into simple elements and analyzing the elements. We know what words mean, and we simply assemble those meanings into more complicated messages: That's how we do it; that explains our skill; that counts as an articulation.

This destructively misleading picture of how language works gains some support from a natural but mistaken view of dictionaries. We have all experienced the extreme variability in the assistance a dictionary provides: Sometimes it helps a lot, sometimes very little, and a great deal depends on how much we understand to begin with. Nevertheless, we can sometimes talk ourselves into the view that what a dictionary provides are simple, clear "meanings": independently clear building blocks that we simply assemble into a recognizable sentiment. Thus everything we understand has a ready-made articulation.

The problem with this picture is that there is just enough "right" about it to deceive us. It contains a hint of insight (about which more later), but that hint tricks us into thinking about language in a way that damages not only our reasoning, but the skill itself that we misapprehend. Before we can appreciate the insight, we must examine and set aside some of the illusion it creates.

Words

Our natural inclination to focus on words when examining language need not be destructive. If we proceed with care, pay close attention to what we do with words when our competence is great—in the practical contexts where they are hard at work—we can learn much that is valuable. We can study our skill without damaging it.

Our main task is to replace the deceptively oversimple picture of words, meanings, dictionaries, and the like with a more adequate one. Central to this will be to develop a robust sense of what sort of thing a meaning is. Words play many different roles in our sentences, do all kinds of different jobs in communication. Some, like *Nixon*, may refer to specific things (e.g., an individual); some, like *table*, may stand for certain *kinds* of things; others represent more abstract properties and relationships, such as *blue*, *underneath*, and *nuclear*; but some, like *if*, *of*, *might*, *yes*, *would*, and *never* do not properly stand for or refer to anything at all: They just play certain important roles in our sentences. Some words, such as *I*, *you*, *us*, and *me*, depend on who says them; others, like *this* and *that*, sometimes depend on gestures and the position of the speaker. More important, the same word can do one job in one context and a completely different job in another. The word *table* does three different jobs in "dinner table," "table the motion," and "table of contents."

Lumping all these different things under "meaning" tends to obscure the rich, variegated texture of language and our skills. So in the following discussion we will speak alternately of the job, role, or employment of a term, rather than its meaning. Talk of meanings is perfectly fine, of course, so long as we can avoid thinking of them as more discrete and uniform than they are. But, as a rule, sticking with slightly unorthodox talk of jobs and roles will better guard against our falling into the wrong habits of thought.

We may think of learning a language, then, as mastering the different jobs words can do. But the jobs themselves are every bit as complex and subtle as the shapes and colors in vision. This is why mastering them is a matter of trained recognition and empathy. We use our perceptual superskill to match up words and settings (contexts) to make their employment clear. So even though language is broken into words, our skill with it is scarcely easier to articulate than any perception. We learn the jobs, and learn to employ terms, the same way we learn to see and hear things generally: We pick them up, in practice, by keeping our eyes and ears open. We can become competent without *ever* seeing the description of a word's job, role, or kind of employment. We master the basics of our native language long before we first see a definition or a grammatical rule. Our skill is in simply choosing and recognizing words in contexts. We are not very skilled at writing dictionaries and grammar books.

The most striking illustrations of all this may be found in our basic vocabulary. We all know perfectly well what *if* means, for example, but we would have a hard time trying to say anything at all helpful about what it means. Similarly for *the, and, of, to*, and a host of others. Our ability to handle these words in their usual jobs is so great that the question never arises. It is not even clear what sort of description somebody would want. So it is quite possible to be wholly inarticulate about the job of a word we are thoroughly familiar with.

About less basic vocabulary, by contrast, we are usually not completely speechless: We can often say something or other about a word's job. But what we can provide are not general descriptions of the word's role in our language, but rough-and-ready hints about its employment in particular cases. For this is all we need in practice, all we ever *get* to practice. When a question arises naturally about what a word means, it invariably concerns a specific puzzle about the specific details of a particular context. So general characterizations are much less useful than rough-and-ready hints.

If someone asked "What does *clock* mean?" the prudent thing to do would be to discover the sentence in which it occurred. Without that, all we could say would be something general like

A clock is a device for telling time; it tells you the time of day.

And whether this would help would be a matter of luck. For, as general as it is, it does not capture many common features of the word's role in our language. *Clock* is often a verb, for instance, as in "I clocked you at 75 mph back there, buddy." And though someone might figure out from the formula above what the verb means, the formula does not describe it. Nor does it even cover all common uses of the noun. To understand "The sticks seemed to move like the hands of a clock," we must think of one particular kind of time-keeping device. Digital clocks and sundials will not help.

Our competence is in understanding, in handling all these jobs in context. A general job description would be a formula that would generate them all, anticipate all particular questions.[3] For common, useful words it is hard to imagine such a formula. But doing so is, in any case, unnecessary. We can have absolute command of the use of a word and not know its general job description. We may, of course, be able to *generate* one by studying skillful application of the word in many different settings. But that is another issue for another time.

One way to put all this is to say that we may know perfectly well what a word means and yet may not be able to *say* what it means— not be able to say very much about what it means in general. This should make us cautious about the overworked admonition that we "define our terms." The request for a definition may, of course, simply be a request for help with the detail of a particular case. And when this is so, the request is a perfectly reasonable one. But if the

---

[3]This is why dictionaries are sometimes unhelpful. The entries there can anticipate only the most common questions and difficulties. My puzzle may be too unusual to bear mention. The *Oxford English Dictionary* tries to be more comprehensive than other dictionaries in this regard and, as a result, uses up five or six feet of shelf space.

request is for a general rule, one that covers many distinct contexts, then it is almost always unreasonable: neither obtainable nor particularly useful. We hold out for such a rule only under the influence of the misguided picture of language we are trying to overcome in this section. And one reason to dispense with that picture is that it encourages us to demand something we cannot have and do not need.

Moreover, the demand for general definitions can lead to something far worse than just wasting time: It can damage our skill. For all we can come up with on the spur of the moment are crude, hip-shot definitions. But the crudeness is usually hard to see. So we may force our usage to conform with the crude description, destroying much valuable subtlety. We can cripple language by misunderstanding our skill. For example, the following is a typical spur-of-the-moment gloss:

A: What does *thoughtful* mean?

B: *Thoughtful* means "full of thought, something that shows a lot of careful thinking."

If we take this too seriously, we may find ourselves objecting to a grateful old man's thanking a youngster for being so thoughtful in offering him her seat on a crowded bus. "That doesn't take any thought. An idiot could have done it. She probably did it more out of reflex than anything else." But, of course, the job the old man gave *thoughtful* simply *is* its standard one in the context. Its role in this context does not require a lot of thinking, just thinking of someone else. The hip-shot gloss is, as always, inadequate to the complexity of the word's job.

A large part of our skill lies in recognizing standard cases in appropriate contexts. Our ability to discern subtle differences among contexts endows this skill with a complexity that hip-shot definitions are bound to miss. Linguistic recognition, like the familiar physiognomy of a friend, simply defies casual articulation.

Evidence of Understanding.   To be perfectly clear: None of this means you cannot explain what you mean by a word. The point is that the only explanations we should expect to give are not very general. Practical help with the particular details of a specific context is all we can manage—and all we ever need when someone asks, "What do you mean by *X*?" Normally, such a request for clarification is prompted by a specific confusion and does not require that we re-count all the contextual detail and complex variations found in a general description. An adequate reply will treat the specific problem that gave rise to the question, ignoring clearly unproblematic parts of the job. We may almost always presuppose *some* understanding.

A: "You have two days to respond after the notice has been posted."

B: "What do you mean by *posted*?"

A: "I mean on the bulletin board outside my office."

This reply treats only one small aspect of the job done by *posted* here. To understand the reply, the questioner must already know a good deal about what *posted* means and have an intimate familiarity with the context. But he certainly would: The question is not likely to arise in this form unless he met these conditions. The reply is just what is required.

This issue is part of the larger and more important issues of knowing when we understand what has been said, and, conversely, knowing when we have been properly understood ourselves. How do we tell? Sometimes it is easy, sometimes not, but its form is diagnostic. When questions arise, we may appeal to the diagnostic underpinning of our skill, just as we do with general perception.

Because language is a practical tool, it naturally lends itself to practical test. We may easily arrange things to turn up traces best explained by a particular linguistic competence, or its lack. To test whether a preschooler knows what *blue* means, we arrange activities in which many different colored objects are used. If he reliably retrieves or indicates the blue ones when we request it, we gain strong evidence that he knows what the word means. We may drop rival accounts down the ranking ladder by using similar objects—for instance, ones differing only in color. Having several blue objects available—differing in texture, shape, and configuration—will have the same effect. After a while, competence with *blue* is the only plausible account of the systematicity in his behavior.

Tests of young children are relatively difficult cases, however, because we can presume only a primitive grasp of the substantive context. Trace data may be far subtler and (hence) more persuasive when we are dealing with a mature language user, one alive to more contextual detail. I am helping a neighbor work on her car, and I ask, "Would you hand me the $\frac{3}{8}$-drive ratchet with a $\frac{5}{8}$ socket on it?" If she successfully carries out the instruction, that alone constitutes strong evidence for her command of a substantial amount of language. If she fails to understand any of the important words in that sentence, it is unlikely she will respond properly. In conversation we are constantly giving and receiving evidence, manifesting traces of linguistic competence and understanding. Gestures, facial expression, and tone of voice provide an immense amount of relevant data.

As with perception generally, part of our confidence is due to the self-correcting nature of the diagnostic network: to the *absence* of certain traces. Serious misunderstandings are revealed almost immediately by the rich flux of data against a familiar background. In conversation it yields bizarre responses ("Socket? I don't see anything electrical here."). In reading and listening, the sequence of sentences becomes strange, perhaps incomprehensible. Comic routines are based on this (Who's on first? No . . .). Misunderstanding can seldom be carried very far before silliness tips it off. In normal conversation, evidence of understanding is commonly overwhelming.

The possibilities afforded by conversation encourage another kind of test as well. Instead of using indirect tests that appeal to simple tasks and responses, we can sometimes demonstrate our understanding by giving attention directly to the language itself. To discover if someone understands a certain sentence, we can ask him to reformulate it: say the same thing in different words. His ability to formulate a second sentence counts as evidence that he understood the first. To discover whether he understands what job a word is doing in a certain sentence, we can ask him to say the same thing without using the word.

This last kind of test sometimes leads us to think we must be able to describe a word's job to show that we know that job. But it should be clear by now that *saying* what a word means (or does) is only *one* thing among many that we can do to show we know what it means. Furthermore, in this endeavor, what counts as saying what a word means can fall far short of a detailed job description. Sometimes, giving a very rough synonym will do; other times, a bit of allegory or onomatopoeia is required.

"Do you know what a ratchet is?"

"Yes, it's that mechanism at the end of the rather fat handle that makes a clicking sound and allows the handle to free-wheel in one direction."

This is a rough-and-ready description of what *ratchet* refers to in the context, but it is perfectly adequate as evidence of understanding.

The earlier brief exchange about *posted*, then, should be understood in a way something like the following. The question "What do you mean by *posted*?" expresses some unclarity about what job *posted* is doing in the previous sentence. The reply is adequate in the circumstances because it supplies just enough data to deal with that specific unclarity: to make a specific point clear.

So we may appreciate the singular value of words without falling into destructive oversimplifications about how language works. We may know what words mean without imagining our skill in this to be casually articulable. A couple of reminders will help us avoid the temptation to backslide on this point.

1.   When a word is unclear, don't ask for a definition. Ask for help: something, anything, to aid your understanding.
2.   If you wish to be reassured that your audience is following you, don't ask for a meaning. Look for evidence of understanding.

Concepts

Talk of concepts can be useful for all sorts of purposes. Sometimes we are simply interested in them: the concept of justice or cause, of democracy or the family, of life, or of an afterlife. We also talk of people having different concepts *of* justice, say, or of democracy or afterlife. We may also think of the relationships between them— between the concepts of cause and explanation, for instance, or between democracy and capitalism.

This is not the place to investigate the concept of concept, but since we have talked of concepts, conceptions, and conceptual relationships, it is worth mentioning a direct connection they have with the study of this chapter. The concept of X is closely related to the meaning of the word X. This works best for nouns, as in the listing in the preceding paragraph; but we may adapt any part of speech to concept-talk by using a derivative noun or a noun phrase (concept of artificiality, for example, or of destructiveness or implication). So, with this proviso, concepts are closely related to the jobs or roles of words in the language.

Nevertheless, when we talk of the concept of X we are almost never interested in anything like the entire role of X in the language.

Which part or aspect we are concerned with, however, will depend on our interests of the moment, on details of the context. Looking at the relationship between two concepts, X and Y, will focus our attention on the way two jobs interrelate. Perhaps looking at certain features of the job done by X will help us better understand the one done by Y. In any case, the admonitions about meanings apply equally to concepts. That we have a clear concept, say, of explanation does not mean that we can describe it at all helpfully. Describing or analyzing concepts is a complicated and tedious business. It is worthwhile only if you have certain deeply abstract interests. Otherwise, we can obtain all the help we ordinarily need in using concepts without describing them in any detail. So once again, if you are puzzled, don't ask for the concept. Ask for help!

SOME KEY PROPERTIES OF THE JOBS WORDS DO

If we appreciate our linguistic skill as basically diagnostic, like perception, we can then come to grips with some common features of language that might otherwise seem mysterious, even dangerous. The richness of natural language allows genuinely stunning ambiguity and wildly imaginative flights of metaphor; it naturally generates intractable borderline cases and nearly imperceptible shades and nuances in the jobs words do. We may easily doubt the human capacity to handle it all safely. But at the bottom of the fascinating complexity lies our finely honed ability to detect intricate and subtle patterns when they are presented in the right setting, against the right background. This is what makes our general inarticulateness unproblematic. It can help us with particular details as well.

Ambiguity

A large number of common words[4] in English—and every other natural language—routinely perform several distinct jobs. Some will be related, like the two jobs of *table* in "dinner table" and "table the motion." But some will be wholly unrelated: The *can* in "can of chicken soup" bears no plausible relation to the *can* in "Can I go now?" In each of these cases, the different jobs are in different parts of speech; but that is not always the case for a word's different jobs.

[4]*Word* here may be either a written shape or a spoken sound, and the same points may be made about the spoken or written language.

The word *pen*, for instance, is a noun in both "fountain pen" and "pig pen."

A casual look through any competent dictionary reveals that a surprising percentage—perhaps a majority—of the words in our common vocabulary require two or more entries. The different entries nearly always indicate different jobs: sometimes only slightly distinct, but often quite unrelated. Occasionally the proliferation of entries will astonish us—even though we are competent to handle them all. One of the most striking examples is the word *take*. My small dictionary lists thirty distinct entries under *take* with as many as seven subheadings under the numbered entries. A look down the list reveals very few exotic jobs; most of them are quite familiar. Yet most of us are surprised to find such a common word doing so many distinct jobs.

We are surprised for the same reason that finding so many is unproblematic: In most normal cases, the potential ambiguity is effortlessly resolved by the context. Both in performance and in recognition, we are very skillful at selecting the right job for the context. We are so good at it that we never think to list all the problems that would arise if we were not. In most normal contexts there is simply no question of what job *pen* does in

The pig is in the pen.

Nobody would confuse it with the job normally done by *pen* in

The ink is in the pen.

Talking about pigs on the one hand and ink on the other supplies enough substantive context to resolve the question effortlessly.

Notice that we could, by supplying an unorthodox context, reverse the jobs done by *pen* in those two sentences. Being less orthodox, however, the case requires more elaborate description. Suppose Pete and Charlie are entering a pig-decorating contest tomorrow, and one of the ways they plan to decorate old Greased Lightning is with indelible ink pinstriping. Pete shows up late, after Charlie has everything set up in G. L.'s pen, and asks Charlie what he did with the indelible ink. Charlie, of course, says,

The ink is in the pen.

and presto, *pen* has changed jobs.

Ambiguity is not always resolved so completely or easily, of course. Sometimes the context is unclear, or not well specified, and then we may fail to understand, or may actually *mis*understand, the job of a crucial word. This issue was addressed directly on pages 310–313. The remedy is usually to provide a bit of context explicitly: whatever will help. The point of this section is to draw attention to how frequent such misunderstandings would be were it not for our sensitive and sophisticated use of context.

As an exercise, before going on, describe a context that would give *pen* its other job in the sentence "The pig is in the pen." This will test your understanding of the last few pages.

Subtleties.   Variation in the employment of a word may be extremely important even when it is not dramatic, however. What we have been referring to as a single job here may, when examined more closely, turn out to be a tight cluster of related jobs. This too is largely unproblematic in practice, because familiar, well-developed contexts will support very fine distinctions. And these fine distinctions reveal a further range of commonly unnoticed features of our linguistic skill.

Suppose a story read,

The speaker paused briefly for a sip of water, cleared his throat, and continued in somewhat better voice.

The context makes it quite clear that the speaker is a human being. In the following sentence, the word *speaker* does a closely related job, though it refers to an inorganic object:

The coffee on the dashboard spilled directly into the radio speaker.

It is important to recognize that these two jobs are far less distinct than the different jobs attributed earlier to *table*, *can*, and *pen*. *Speaker* is doing something closer to the same kind of job in these two cases. Still, the distinction is clear and unproblematic for nearly everybody. In fact, it is not very subtle at all.

Increasingly subtle shades may be found in the following examples. Consider the job of *light* in

Please turn on the light.

I wear light colors in the summer.
Gotta light?

or the job of *take* in

Take a card.
Take your seat.
Take a rest.

or the job of *bench* in

park bench
piano bench
work bench

The communicative significance of these words—and most words—changes more or less subtly from context to context. But since we learn how to use (and understand) these words in the very contexts in which these distinctions are drawn, we have no difficulty handling the subtlety. Our skill *is* in the application, and these are the applications. Virtually all the common words in our vocabulary may be made to behave in the way *bench, take,* and *light* do in these illustrations. Our ability to do this with words is part of the reason language is the valuable tool it is.

As an exercise, pick a common verb and write three sentences in which it is doing distinct but closely related jobs. (Easy ones are *play, pass,* and *pick*; others you might try are *grow, write,* and *head.*)

Contrast

The significance of some words varies in a relatively systematic way from context to context. This is so, for instance, when part of a word's job is to draw a certain kind of contrast. When the word *red* is used to designate a color, the actual hue properly called *red* will vary from case to case, depending on what it is contrasted with. Consider

red Georgia clay
the little girl with the red hair
red sky at morning (sailors take warning)

The actual hues referred to by *red* in these cases are quite distinct; and none of them would be labeled *red* in a paint catalog or on an ordinary color chart. Nevertheless, the chromatic significance of *red* is perfectly clear in each case, primarily due to the contrast implicit in the context. Red clay is typically a kind of purplish-brown. But when set next to the whites, grays, blues, and tans of other clays, the ruddy contrast is clear. *Red* is quite unambiguous given the limited possibilities. A few years ago, when Yamaha first imported motorcycles into the United States, they offered three colors: red, white, and blue. In a paint catalog, the red they offered would be described as a kind of metallic burgundy. Nevertheless, in the context *red* was perfectly appropriate. If you asked the salesman for a red one and he said they didn't make a red one, he probably deserved to lose the sale.

Similarly with red hair and red skies: There is a sense in which the color would be better described as brown or orange or vermilion, or any number of colors other than red. But in the context the contrast is clear. Only Charlie Brown would try to explain to the little red-haired girl that her hair was not really red, but rather a kind of burnt orange.

A similar observation can be made about *open* in "The door is open." In some contexts the contrast is with *shut*: "Johnny, did you shut the door when you left the house?" "No, Mom, I thought you wanted to air the place out after the breakfast disaster." But when someone knocks on a closed door, we commonly say "Come on in. The door's open." Here the contrast is with *locked*, not with *shut*.

As an exercise, defend the use of *book* in the expression "book of stamps," against the protest that it is not really a book at all.

Comparisons.   Closely related to contrast is the relatively systematic contextual variation of comparative terms. The primary job of one entire class of terms is to specify a relative degree or magnitude of something. The relativity of the comparison entails that these terms lean rather heavily on the substantive context for much of their significance. Such terms usually come in pairs: *large, small; expensive, cheap; tall, short; heavy, light; near, far; bright, dim;* even *good* and *bad*.

What is expensive for a meal is cheap for a car; and what is expensive for a car is cheap for a house. Furthermore, what is cheap for a house in some suburbs of Washington, D.C., might be outrageously expensive, even for a house, in a small town in eastern Oregon. So, even when we know the price of something, to know whether it is expensive we must know the appropriate comparison. And sometimes the comparisons are quite specific.

In general, appropriate comparisons include not only the kind of thing in question, but many other features of the substantive context as well. A very tall man may nevertheless be a very short forward in the National Basketball Association. And that same man might have been a tall forward in the NBA twenty years ago. Comparative terms like *tall* have a built-in contextual place-holder: a variable component that must be filled in by contextual detail before the term is applicable.

As an exercise, use the word *firm* in three different contexts in which what counts as firm differs but only by degrees.

Indeterminate Ranges and the Borderline Case

In the ordinary sense of the terms, rocking chairs are furniture and reading glasses are not. It will be convenient here to introduce a little jargon to talk about this contrast. Let us say that, in its ordinary job, the word *furniture* applies to rocking chairs but not to reading glasses. Further, let us use a kind of engineer's artifice and talk of the contrast as being between positive and negative applications. If a word applies to a case, the application is positive; if it does not, we will call the application negative. A rocking chair, then, would be a positive application of *furniture*, reading glasses a negative application. If a case fits a job in the context at hand, then the application is positive; if it fails to fit, it is negative. In the usual context, the application of *automobile* to Ford sedans is positive; to grandfather clocks it is negative.

Virtually any job done by any word exhibits this feature. The basic value in any job is to draw a contrast between positive and negative applications of the term in that role. *Green* applies positively to leaves, negatively to blood, when it does its normal chromatic job in normal circumstances. *Book* applies positively to things on the shelves of my library, negatively to blizzards and wine bottles (again: usual job, normal circumstances). Sunrise applies positively at dawn, negatively at noon.

The point in belaboring this observation is to note that such things are commonly matters of degree. Dawn *gradually* turns into day, green *fades off* into blue, fat becomes slim by *imperceptible stages*, things *slowly* die. Standard cases gradually fade off into less standard ones; jobs apply less and less clearly, by degrees. This much is perfectly clear of *green, fat,* and *dawn* and only slightly less so of *death.* But the same point can be made for the usual jobs of a surprising number of words: With a little imagination we can describe (if not actually create) a rich spectrum of cases that provide gradually less and less clear applications of the word in any particular job. To take a very simple example, in one familiar context the jobs done by *chair* and *stool* contrast with each other, the major difference being that a chair has a back while a stool does not. Accordingly, if we take a standard, armless chair and whittle away at its back, it will gradually become a less and less clear example of a chair: The term *chair* will apply less and less clearly. When the back is gone it will not be a chair at all in the sense we are considering. For many chairs, what we have left will be a funny-looking stool—one we could turn into a chair by putting a back on it. (This is not to say that in some contexts the word *chair* could not properly apply to the funny-looking stool. But when it does it will be doing a different, usually more complicated job than it is here.)

The reason to emphasize the gradualness with which positive application fades off into negative is to draw attention to the troublesome area in between. Even if we are perfectly familiar with the job in question, expertly competent to handle its application in standard cases, there will often be a substantial range of cases "in the middle" about which our judgment is emphatically uncertain. These cases are not clearly positive applications, but they are not clearly negative ones either. Actual physical processes connecting contrasting states provide the best illustrations of this. As a man loses his hair he gradually becomes bald. But there is no precise point at which *bald* suddenly applies. At the beginning of the process it applies negatively: The man is not bald. At the end of the process it applies positively: The man is bald. But, in the normal case, there will be a number of days or weeks or months toward the end of the process in which it is simply unclear whether *bald* applies yet. Both positive and negative applications are misleadingly categorical: The most comfortable choice is to decline both. This is called a borderline case.

All manner of developmental processes exhibit borderline cases in the application of certain characterizations, especially if those characterizations are pressed when we would normally withhold them. As we gain weight we eventually become fat, but there is no precise point at which the term suddenly applies. Putting together pieces of wood, we eventually construct a chair, but there is no precise point at which the term *chair* suddenly applies. As we age, we eventually become adults . . . and so on. To say there is no point at which a term suddenly applies in a spectrum of cases is just to say that in a range of these cases the term's application is *indeterminate*. In a range of cases the term does not clearly apply positively and does not clearly apply negatively. Between a full head of hair and the Telly Savalas look lie a number of configurations for which the application of *bald* (in its normal job) is simply indeterminate. These are borderline cases of baldness.

As a practical matter the existence of these indeterminate ranges—the fuzzy borderline areas in any job's application—is virtually guaranteed by the perceptual nature of our linguistic skill and by the way natural languages result from its operation. We simply learn to recognize standard cases in application, learn to tell when a context is close enough to standard to allow the words to do the jobs expected of them. We simply learn to make this judgment—inarticulately, but exceedingly well. So if we gradually run through a spectrum of increasingly less standard cases, this judgment is gradually undermined.

This is a misleadingly harsh way to put the matter, however. The existence of semantic indeterminacy, of fuzzy borderlines, is not a problem; it is not something that needs correction. A word's job is useful if it draws a distinction between *some clear* cases. The presence of some clear positive applications and some clear negative applications is frequently sufficient to make the job worth keeping. The fuzziness in other cases is just the inevitable consequence of the way we give words jobs to do: something easily tolerated that allows us to give words interesting jobs. All the examples we have been discussing are like this. The job we give *blue* is useful not because we can positively or negatively apply it to everything whatever, but because it clearly applies to some things we care about. The job we give *bald* is useful because of the way it distinguishes between Telly Savalas and, say, Teddy Kennedy. To be able to make that distinction, we are quite willing to put up with the whole range of indeterminate cases in between. The same kind of thing may be said of *fat*, *chair*, and the rest.

Moreover, the location and nature of the fuzziness itself often has valuable significance. The way a positive application tapers off into a negative one usually indicates something important in the nature of the subject matter—the concepts. The fact that the application of *blue* becomes *gradually* less and less clear as we move down the spectrum toward green is an important aspect of the concept of blue. There is no point at which suddenly there is no blue left at all; it just fades out gradually. It is part of the nature of color mixing: It is in the concept.

Furthermore, and finally, in conceding that a range of cases is indeterminate for one word's job, we do not foreclose the possibility of speaking clearly about those cases. We simply must use different words: That range will not be indeterminate for every word. Between blue and green are some clear blue-greens. Between fat and normal lie *overweight, stocky, chubby,* and, perhaps, *pudgy*; between Kennedy and Savalas go *thinning hair, balding,* and *bald spot.* On borderlines we simply avoid the troublesome characterization altogether. The ability to recognize borderlines and handle them is a sign of linguistic maturity. "Well, it doesn't look much like a chair yet, but I wouldn't be surprised if that's what he's making," or "I'm not sure you would call the injury severe, but it was bad enough for her to have to go to the emergency room to have it checked."

We may simply summarize this discussion as follows. Let us use the letter X to stand for any word doing a particular job. Now we ask of anything plausible the question "Is this X?" (e.g., "Is this [guy] bald?").[5] It will be apparent that most X's require (at least) three distinct answers to cover all the cases: "yes," "no," and "unclear."[6] Ask of every injury "Is it severe?" Ask of every tie "Is it blue?" Ask of every person "Is he or she fat?" Ask of every hump in the earth "Is this a mountain?" In virtually every case, answers will fall under

[5]The question may be refined slightly to "Is this *an* X?" for nouns and "Is this *to* X?" for verbs—but the simpler form will do for each so long as the appropriate articles and prepositions are put where they belong.

[6]One complexity is worth bearing in mind. A case may be borderline for *one* of X's jobs and still be clear for another. Furthermore, the mere fact that a case *is* a tough one for one of X's jobs will sometimes be enough to slide X into a slightly different one, in which the case is clear. Some borderline reds, for instance, will clearly fall under *red* when it refers to a general ruddy contrast. So when somebody uses an unqualified *red* to refer to a tough case, it will often simply be taken to refer to a general contrast. This is a natural application of the principle of charity: finding the most plausible interpretation for the words in the context.

In discussing borderlines we will be primarily concerned with what happens when we do *not* change jobs in such a case. The semantic indeterminacy results when a single job confronts a spectrum or array of cases. Explicit notice of this may help you avoid some confusion.

each of the three headings, even when X marks something perfectly clear in its standard applications. This is a natural and easily tolerated consequence of our basic linguistic skills. We find it enormously useful to give jobs to words that are clear in some interesting cases, even though they fade off into fuzzy indeterminacy elsewhere. We avoid problems by avoiding the categorical use of the word except in clear applications.

As an exercise, describe a context in which the word *two* (as in the number two) is indeterminate between positive and negative application (that is, a clear borderline case of cardinality or twoness).

Metaphor

Our ability to use and appreciate metaphor is one of the most valuable aspects of our linguistic skill.

> The road was a ribbon of moonlight.

Words and phrases that have developed their standard jobs in one context, in one set of applications, will sometimes be of great value when simply transferred into a novel context and directed to an unusual subject (when we talk of character assassination, for instance). By dragging their old, familiar associations—and perhaps some conceptual apparatus—with them into the next context, metaphorical expressions frequently organize our perception of the new subject in a helpful way. Communication is made easier.

Sometimes the message is simple. Geologists say the moon is geologically *dead*; we talk of a *shower* of shooting stars, *green* recruits, throwing some *light* on a topic, and a *photographic* memory. Driving instructors speak of traffic lights as *fresh* or *stale*, depending on how long they have been green. In each of these cases the value of the metaphorical expression is modest but clear. And the clarity is, once again, traceable to our grasp of the substantive context. For when we drag a familiar term and all its associations into a novel context, some of the old associations will not make the transfer; part of the old, standard job does not fit the new subject. But normally the part that doesn't fit is so clear from the context that confusion is nearly impossible. Nobody expects a shower of shooting stars to get him wet, nor a dead moon to decay; and anyone caught tasting a traffic light to see if it is stale would be joking—or deranged. A clear context will rule out these gaffes just as naturally as it will rule out the wrong job for *pen* in the expression "fountain pen."

These same considerations allow the development of more ambitious metaphors, which are sometimes stunning in their ability to capture a complex perception or a subtle insight.

> Writing is, for most, laborious and slow. The mind travels faster than the pen; consequently, writing becomes a question of learning to make occasional wing shots, bringing down the bird of thought as it flashes by.[7]

Similarly, characterizing the sky as sullen or a marriage as stormy may capture the desired mood better, more clearly, than any less metaphorical description. Our ability to make this sort of transfer, to use a word's job in one context to help organize our understanding in another, is just one of the human skills that language exploits to become the powerful tool it is.

Furthermore, as language evolves and words take on new jobs, many of these jobs will be old metaphors that were so useful they simply became another regular job for the word to do. The metaphor dies. We may even forget the original connection. The verb "to jackknife"—referring to what a semi-trailer rig will occasionally do when the driver loses control of it—doubtless originated as a metaphor. When the rig "jackknifes," it folds the way a jackknife does. But the term's popularity ruined it as a metaphor. Jackknifing simply *became* what a semi-trailer rig does when it folds up in a skid. People who have never seen a jackknife know what the verb means.

Thus languages expand and develop. Something of the same sort has happened to many other terms. "Guinea pig," "sitting duck," "butterfly stroke," "insulation," "bucket seat," and "high" (as in intoxicated) are all dead metaphors: dead as a result of their usefulness. Only the good die young.

As an exercise, write a sentence using a common word metaphorically. (If you need help, try *key* or *toothless* or *burn*.)

Equivocation

We are now in a position to see how our natural preoccupation with words can damage our reasoning if we hold too crude a picture of how the language works. When we express ourselves, we choose the

---

[7]E. B. White, *The Elements of Style*, 3rd ed. (New York: Macmillan, 1979).

words we do because of the jobs they have—for what they signify. And we have explored many subtle and complex ways in which the significance of a word—and any statement it is part of—can vary with minute changes in the setting. Unarticulated, often unnoticed, contextual detail determines the relevant contrast, comparison, metaphorical thrust, shades and nuances. And this can mean *everything* to the message delivered by our words.

If we fail to grasp this, we can come to think that the content of a message resides in the words themselves, and that to capture it all we must do is hold on to the words. But this is like carrying water in a sieve. The content is given only by words *plus* context; and contexts are harder to hang on to than words. Our empathic skill is the ability to recognize a context and choose the words appropriate for it. We are far less skilled in generating contexts to make a set formula say something in particular.

So if what you have to say is the least bit subtle, the following admonition is worth bearing in mind:

To say the *same thing* in a different context typically requires different words.

The comfort of familiar words can deceive us about this. But if we identify a sentiment too closely with certain specific words, the words become icons more than tools; saying them becomes something like a ritual. And a ritual, mistaken for something else, can mislead both author and audience.

The ease with which context can change enough to make a difference is well displayed in the Russell-mansion argument we examined at the end of Chapter 2. Simple charity makes it hard for the word *criminal* to have the same job in both S_1 and S_9. Hence using the same word throughout the argument is dangerously deceptive. (Stop here and briefly review that argument [page 77ff] from the perspective of this section.) The heading of this section is the word we used there to label the trouble caused by the slippery word *criminal*: equivocation. Any time a word slips from one job to another in a way that undermines our reasoning or our understanding, equivocation occurs.

Because so much of our linguistic skill is inarticulate, however, it is often hard to *explain* what has gone wrong even after we spot an equivocation. So let us walk through two examples—one easy, the other more subtle—to get some practice in articulating equivocations.

First case. An officer of an unnamed board of education, embroiled in a heated controversy, concealed a tape recorder in her purse and secretly taped the proceedings of a closed meeting. The meeting had been closed to the public in order to permit candid discussion of a sensitive issue at the center of the controversy. When the tape recording was revealed, those who had voted to close the meeting complained that the officer had surreptitiously frustrated the will of the board's majority: The recording of a closed meeting violates the spirit and the purpose of closure. But the officer protested that since she was officially the board's recording secretary, what she had done was fully within the responsibilities of her office.

This, of course, is something of a pun; but since somebody seems to have taken it seriously, to have been misled by it, it deserves the heavy title "equivocation." What a recording secretary is responsible for is just the minutes: a skeletal, stylized, usually discrete record of a meeting's business. So the job done by the term *recording* in the expression "recording secretary" does not automatically license the *tape* recording of anything, let alone a closed meeting. This defense involves the confusion—or perhaps the intentional conflation—of two distinct but related jobs of the word *recording*: an equivocation.

Second case. Reacting to the government's antismoking campaign, a tobacco company spokesman once said,

> Since we have not *discovered* the cause of cancer, how can anyone say that *smoking* causes cancer?

The question is rhetorical, naturally: The implication is that nobody can. If we knew that smoking causes cancer, then it would appear mistaken to say the cause of cancer remains undiscovered. But the appearance is deceptive. For the job done by *cause* when used with the definite article (*the*) in this context is subtly but crucially distinct from the job it does in the simple, relational statement "*x* causes *y*." When scientists inquire into *the* cause of cancer they are looking for something very general, for some physiological account of malignancy in animal tissue. They want to understand the organic, chemical, possibly molecular sequence of events that leads to the strange cell behavior we know as cancer. They want to understand this sequence of events independent of the particular physical event triggering it, and perhaps even independent of its location in the body.

By contrast, when we say that smoking (or too much sun, or ingesting nitrosamines) causes cancer, we are talking about the triggers, not the physiology. The point has been covered elaborately in Chapters 3 and 4: We have a correlation between smoking and lung cancer that must be explained by a causal connection between the two. We know enough to rule out reverse-cause accounts as implausible, leaving us with "smoking causes cancer" as the best of the rivals. We can discover all this without understanding anything at all about *how* smoking causes cancer. And this is just what we have done. We have learned a great deal about cancer's triggers, while remaining largely in the dark about the underlying physiology.

So the spokesman's gambit involves an equivocation. His first clause is true only of the underlying physiology: That is what we have not yet discovered. But he wants, by using the same word (*cause*), to trick us into thinking he has rebutted the claim that smoking can trigger malignant cell growth, which he has not.

As an exercise, use the vocabulary developed in this last example to respond to the following complaint that might have been lodged during the building of the Panama Canal: an equivocation.

> Since we have not yet *discovered* the cause of malaria, how can you say that *mosquito bites* cause malaria?

EXERCISES

1. A: "Did you enjoy the concert?"

   B: "Well, I did and I didn't."

   A: "Why would you say a thing like that? It can't be both: What you've said is simply self-contradictory."

   a. What did B probably mean by her reply?
   b. Use the principle of charity to explain to A why his response was both silly and rude.

2. Explain how the principle of charity is at work in our use and understanding of metaphor. Use an example.

3. Suppose a teacher who knows you well encourages you to take an intimidating advanced course, saying "I know if you try hard enough you will pass." You devote yourself to the course, work at it night and day, but still fail. When you complain to your advisor that she was wrong, she defends herself by saying "I wasn't wrong; you just didn't

try hard enough. Had you tried hard enough to pass you *would* have passed: That you failed simply shows that you did not try hard enough."

Explain why the teacher's reply is puzzling, and explain what interpretation we probably should place on it, by appeal to the requirement of significance.

4. Consider the following conversation.

> Sue: Martha, do you know what "yes" means?
>
> Martha: Well, roughly, it means "I agree."
>
> Sue: That doesn't really cover all the cases, does it? For instance, suppose you asked me if I was going to the store, and I say "yes," that would make perfectly good sense. But if I had said "I agree" that would have been silly, wouldn't it? There is nothing to agree *to*.
>
> Martha (testily):   Of course, I can't give you a perfect dictionary definition on the spot.
>
> Sue: Then you don't really know what the word means, do you?

Does Martha know what *yes* means? Explain why you think so, or why you think not.

5. A: I've decided to cut class today in sympathy with the protest, but I sure don't want to.

   B: Baloney! You're cutting class of your own free will. If you're doing it voluntarily you're doing it because you want to—that's true by definition.

   A: That's not so. We sometimes do things we hate to do, but that doesn't make them involuntary. I didn't want to go to my niece's piano recital—I knew I would hate it—but I went anyway, just to keep peace in the family.

   B: That's just it. Your wanting to keep peace in the family outweighed your not wanting to hear the kid play. So the net effect was that you *wanted to go*. That's why you went. It's always like that: You do what you want to.

Does A misunderstand what *want* means? That is, did he really want to go to the piano recital? Was he using words incorrectly in saying he didn't? Explain why you think so and why B might respond as he did. (Hint: You might relate your answer to the discussion on page 306ff of this chapter.)

6. An old puzzle asks, "If a tree falls in the forest when nobody is within earshot, does it make a sound or not?" This is a puzzle because our natural temptation to articulate our linguistic skill (to *say* what a sound is) prevents us from thinking clearly about the matter, and we find problems with all the natural solutions or answers. Is sound what you hear, or is it just waves in the air, or must it be both? Write a short essay explaining why it is unhelpful to address this puzzle by trying to figure out, in the abstract, what a sound is. Suggest a better treatment.

7. A: I just bought one of those talking cameras. It's really a blast. Would you like to hear it say something?

   B: You don't have a talking camera, just one that selects among simple, prerecorded messages. It's crazy to call that "talking."

   Supposing A to be sympathetically disposed, how might he explain to B the job *talking* is doing in what he said (that is, explain why it isn't crazy to call the camera's sounds "talking").

8. The word *can't* (as in "I can't do it") is commonly a contrast term. It says that something or other is not possible, but its force will vary from context to context depending on the *kind* of possibility the circumstances make relevant.

   a. Give an example of two sentences in which *can't* signifies different kinds of constraint or impossibility. Provide enough context in each case to make the contrast clear.

   b. Explain B's misunderstanding in the following exchange.

   A. I'm sorry to give such short notice, but I'm afraid I can't come to your party. We were just about to leave when my daughter fell out of a tree and broke some bones. I'm just now leaving for the hospital and I thought I'd call before I left.

   B: Gee, I hope she's all right. But, really, you shouldn't say you *can't* come—nobody is forcing you to take her in. You've just *decided* to: It's purely voluntary. I'm sure it's the right decision—I'd do the same thing. But you shouldn't say you *can't* come when what you mean is you *won't* come.

9. Illustrate the comparative nature of *same* and *exactly* (that is, display the contextual variation in what counts as the same and what counts as exact).

10. a. Use the noun *window* metaphorically.
    b. Use a common verb metaphorically.
    c. Use the verb *to die* as a dead metaphor.

11. Customer: We need a small tree for our yard—something that will mature under eight feet, preferably with branches nearly to the ground.

    Nursery employee: That's not a tree. What you want is a shrub, a large bush. Trees start at fifteen feet.

    Carefully explain what's wrong with the nursery employee's response.

12. On one tempting reading the following bumper-sticker slogan contains an equivocation:

    When guns are outlawed only outlaws will have guns.

    Explain the equivocation.

= 8 =

A BUDGET OF TEMPTATIONS

Some Perils of Abstract Reasoning

Overview

The understanding of language developed in Chapter 7 may be used to provide our reasoning with some very specific guidance. In this chapter we exploit that understanding to help us deal with ambiguity, vagueness, and the hazards of exaggeration. The aim will be to do this with a sensitivity that allows us to preserve the functional complexity of language we have documented in our exploration.

INTRODUCTION

When our abstract reasoning becomes entangled with an oversimple picture of how language works, we are sometimes led to fire words from their established jobs and even occasionally create special new jobs to substitute for the old ones. Such casual, badly aimed revision, as we should now be able to appreciate, has great destructive potential. If we misunderstand the functional complexity of the architecture, we may think we are purifying it by snipping off parts that don't fit an oversimple picture. And this can easily damage immensely useful structures that exist simply because they respond to human needs and complement our skills.

This is not to deny that the language contains forms that are sometimes befuddling, or otherwise objectionable, or even that the cure is ever to purge the language of an institution. But our befuddlement is almost always better addressed by simple explanation, reformulation, attention to contextual detail. And when radical surgery *is* required, the rationale is uniformly more modest than we like to believe. It is almost never a profound conceptual matter.

331

When we find ourselves in a reformist mood, enthusiastically firing words from their jobs, we must try to keep a grip on a central observation of the last chapter. Common words do many different jobs in different contexts—some dramatically distinct, some closely related, others only shades apart. And all this variety is both useful and completely within our normal competence. We begin to feel uneasy with the normal range of jobs words do only when we misunderstand our skills, especially our appreciation of substantive context. Insecurity then drives us to think words should be restricted in one way or another. We generate damaging myths about how the language should work. Perhaps the most prevalent and disruptive of these is the view that one job in particular is the only one really right for a certain word. This is called the myth of one proper use, and it has a number of sources.

THE MYTH OF ONE PROPER USE

In general, the fact that a word has an established job in a certain context creates an enormous presumption in favor of keeping it. The job will nearly always have arisen because we have found it useful, and our understanding of the context will normally allow us to distinguish this particular job from others the word might have. In some contexts, *thoughtful* does mean something like "full of thought" or "heavily cerebral"—not unexpected from our simply putting *thought* together with *ful*. But, as we noticed in the last chapter, *thoughtful* frequently registers a kind of considerateness largely unrelated to the intensity of thought involved. Just why we find this a useful job for *thoughtful* to have is difficult to articulate, as is so much of our handling of language. But we do find it useful, and it is wholly unproblematic in its normal contexts. There is no reason to fire the word from either job. It does them both quite well.

What, then, makes the myth of one proper use so attractive to intelligent people? There are two major sources: misunderstanding historical possibilities and misunderstanding the technical language of science.

Etymology and Components

Studying the historical development of a word (its etymology), or noticing that is is composed of certain component parts, can sometimes help us understand how that word came to have some of its jobs. It can even help us understand those jobs better. Knowing what an accordion is helps us understand what an accordian pleat is; knowing that *tweet* is used to refer to the high-pitched sound of common songbirds makes it easier to understand the job *tweeter* is given in stereo systems; and understanding that *fenestra* is the Latin word for window might help us understand how *defenestration* could be a form of homicide.

Struck by the value of this useful device, we are sometimes tempted to turn it into a pedantic rule: a rule determining what job a word should have and, more destructively, which ones it should not. Unfortunately, language does not work this way: Many of the jobs words would be given if this "rule" were used are ones they do *not* have, and many that they do have are ones they would not get on this "rule." We are occasionally inclined to press ahead nevertheless, determined to reshape the language the way it "should" be according to our "rule": firing words from their established jobs and rehiring them for others.

But all this neglects both the essentially practical foundation of language in human communication and the fragile complexity of our linguistic skills. Once a word has established itself in an important, useful job, we are almost never wise to try uprooting it and replacing it with something else. (The rare exceptions will be touched on shortly.) The best thing is usually to thank our lucky stars that some word has the job we need, learn it, and use our skill with contexts to make the subtle points we must. Our ability to handle specific jobs in well-specified contexts allows us to grasp what has been said without concern for weird components or incoherent etymology. Exotic histories are sometimes worth mentioning as curiosities, but they should not interfere with our talking to each other.

A striking illustration of this may be found in music. When a part (or an instrument) is referred to with the word *obbligato*, it means that the part (or instrument) is mere accompaniment and may be omitted if desired. This is so in spite of the fact that *obbligato* is an Italian word meaning "obligatory"—which sounds as if it should mean just the opposite of what it does. Music dictionaries admit that the evolution of the word into its current paradoxical use is confusing and most likely involves a simple mistake somewhere along the line; but this is just an explanation, not an objection. The term has been accepted among composers and performers, and it does the job satisfactorily. If the paradoxical history is mentioned at all, it is mentioned only as a curiosity.

Consider an easier case. The blackboard in my office is green. That fact has encouraged some people to argue that it should not be *called* a blackboard. Blackboards, they say, should be black. It might be mentioned in passing that the color of most things the protesters would allow to be blackboards is slate gray, not black. But this is not the crucial point here. The crucial point is that in offices, classrooms, and the like, *blackboard* unproblematically refers to all kinds of different writing surfaces suitable for use with chalk. Within a substantial range, the color does not matter much. The job of *blackboard* in "The blackboard in my office is green" is perfectly clear in the context for normal English speakers. And that is all we can ask of words and their jobs. The fact that all blackboards used to be black— or at least gray—is an interesting historical curiosity; but it is not a good reason to take away one of the jobs *blackboard* currently does quite satisfactorily in a range of useful contexts.

So, once again, breaking up a word into components (like studying its historical roots), although sometimes useful, does not provide a reliable guide to the jobs that word has. It is important to resist the temptation to scrap great chunks of a language and rework it in the hope of making this procedure more helpful and more reliable. The way in which a language evolves and words get their jobs is very complex and subtle: It is shaped by our entire network of perceptual and linguistic skills. Hence what jobs a word gets is only partly controlled by any one consideration, such as ancient roots or simple composition. The primary task of language is clear communication of mundane human concerns in practical contexts. Our sense of elegance and concern for transparent etymology is of secondary importance. What matters for practical, human communication is primarily that a word's jobs be clear and useful in specific contexts. And the job of *blackboard* in classrooms and *obbligato* in music—and many other words with strange or paradoxical histories—is perfectly satisfactory from that point of view.

As an exercise, describe how you would sympathetically try to talk somebody out of the view that *fireplace* has to mean any place there was a fire.

Science

Because a word, or one of its forms, has a particular job in science or technology, we may be tempted to think that other jobs this word has are inferior, *un*scientific—even illegitimate. For instance, in elementary thermodynamics it is common to distinguish three modes of heat transfer, three ways in which heat may be transferred from one thing to another: conduction, convection, and radiation. Conduction occurs when a warm body (or substance) is placed in contact with a cold one; convection occurs when heat is moved by currents set up in a liquid or gas; and radiation is the transfer of heat from a warm body to colder surroundings (or vice versa) through electromagnetic waves—commonly infrared radiation. Considering this technical terminology, some people (often, high school science teachers) have argued that it is silly, or even mistaken, for us to use the word *radiator* to refer to the radiator of a car. This is so, they argue, because the heat transfer provided by a car's radiator is accomplished almost entirely by conduction and convection, an insignificant fraction of it being due to radiation.

But once again this perspective involves a misunderstanding of language and its many practical tasks. Knowledge of the three modes of heat transfer, and even of their application to automotive cooling systems, is very interesting and useful in some important contexts. But this does not remotely recommend that we fire the word *radiator* from its established job in other (non-thermodynamic) contexts. The everyday use of *radiator* is both clear and practically valuable in these contexts, and its practical value is enough to grant it job security. That the automotive job of the word *radiator* ignores a technical distinction is irrelevant. "I need a new radiator cap." "Would you flush the radiator while the car's being serviced?" "The mess on the garage floor is due to my leaky radiator." The job of *radiator* is clear in each of these sentences; none of them would be improved by our carping about conduction and convection.

Furthermore, as we should expect, our skill in grasping substantive context will easily allow the word *radiator* to do different jobs here without confusion. A person familiar with thermodynamics has no trouble getting his car's cooling system fixed. And when a physicist reads "An ideal black-body is the optimum radiator of heat," she does not think of fins, pipes, and antifreeze.

As an exercise, write out a brief explanation of what motivates the following (assume it is said seriously): "That insect your sister was complaining about wasn't an insect at all—it was a small spider. Insects are a very specific kind of six-legged arthropod. Spiders are in a different classification altogether: They're arachnids, and they have four pairs of legs."

The Contrast: Genuinely Objectionable Uses

What, then, would justify firing a word from an established job? Are not some jobs inherently damaging to communication or thought? It is interesting to notice how modest even the best-looking cases are. We are so good at using context to make subtle distinctions, and so adept at finding the best interpretation of someone's words, that even the most offensive barbarisms seldom deceive us longer than momentarily. Consider, for example, a standard journalistic abuse of the word *refute*. Suppose a headline reads, "GM Chairman Refutes Union Charges." The union has charged that GM is an immensely wealthy organization that can easily afford the new contract proposed by union negotiators. Very often in such a case, what the GM executive will have said will be something like this:

> The union spokesman fails to understand our predicament. This has been an extremely slow sales year; our profit margin is very small compared to past years. We simply cannot afford the union's lavish demands: They would be out of line in a good year; this year they are just impossible.

In normal circumstances (which we will assume), this statement falls embarrassingly short of being a refutation of the union's charges. The GM chairman has *denied* the charges—emphatically—and has sketched the outlines of an argument for his denial; but he has *not conclusively established* his position. He has said the union charges are false, he has argued that they are false, but he has not *shown* them to be false: He has not refuted them. There is an enormous difference here between saying and showing.

Now this much is so obvious that the attentive reader immediately realizes that the headline writer has misused the word *refute*—has given it a job that is not (yet, at least) in the dictionary. It is terribly implausible to suppose the writer actually thought that what the GM executive said was conclusive, that it did provide a refutation. So we automatically adopt the more plausible interpretation: He is giving *refute* a nonstandard job. Perhaps he thinks it means an emphatic denial, or a plausible denial, or some support for a denial, but he simply cannot realize it means a conclusive denial, a knock-down argument. That is staggeringly implausible on its face. So even here, when a word is given a job it does not even have yet, and one fraught with dangerous and misleading possibilities, we are capable of understanding an author's confusion and compensating for it—enough, at least, to understand what was said. We can rewrite the headline ourselves. "Oh, what he meant to say was 'GM Chairman Emphatically Denies Union Charges' or, perhaps, 'GM Chairman Argues Union Charges Unfounded.'"

The point of all this is not to license the barbaric bastardizations that find their way into print. It is to show how careful we must be in saying why we wish to deny a job to a certain word. The above case is one of the clearest possible. There is all the reason in the world to fight the sloppy handling of *refute* by journalists. There is all the reason in the world to resist letting *refute* do the job given to it by the headline writer and even to fire it if it gets that job. But the reason is *not* that we cannot tell the jobs apart in practice or that we usually misunderstand what was said. Our skills are too good, too resilient, too difficult to trick for that. All we can offer is some modest but reasonable speculation about the future of our valuable linguistic institutions—something that we are not very good at and that will not support grand generalizations. Something like the following:

> Look, giving *refute* two closely related but incompatible jobs in very similar contexts is asking for trouble. It will doubtless make talking about such things more difficult than it is already, and it will increase the possibility of confusion. And since we already have words or phrases that do exactly what the headline writer above wanted *refute* to do, it seems reasonable to stick with the current array of jobs these words do.

This is about as strong as such an argument can get; and given that the journalistic abuse has not yet found wide acceptance, it is a very strong argument indeed. Once a job is deeply ingrained in linguistic practice, however, the case is much more difficult to make. Innocence is hard to recover.

There are other reasons to fire words from certain jobs—or at least to resist using them. But these are largely personal or social reasons and have next to nothing to do with our ability to communicate clearly. Some words we might not want to use simply because to do so is a sign of illiteracy. *Ain't* and *irregardless* are perfectly clear in application, for example, but are usually avoided in literate contexts. We might want to argue that *irregardless* should be fired from its job because it is just an embarrassing conflation of *irrespective* with *regardless*. But embarrassment is all we can plead here, not unclarity. We usually know what people mean when they use it.

Similar objections may be raised against clichés and hackneyed phrases. For a whole variety of social and personal reasons they are likely to be offensive, which sometimes is a very good reason to avoid them. We often wish what we say (and write) to be not just clear, but pleasant, and achieving this requires as much effort as does achieving mere clarity. But as important as they are, these considerations are beyond the scope of the present discussion. Trying to understand what allows an expression to be clear and valuable in a certain job is enough to occupy us here.

EXERCISES

1. Suppose someone had talked himself into believing that *valuable* (always) meant "able to be valued" because of the way the word could be broken into components. Everything that has been or could be valued by somebody is thus valuable; nothing could be called worthless (meaning "not valuable") that might be of some value to somebody.

   Explain as sympathetically as you can what has gone wrong.

2. A: The widow who lives next door to me is incredibly unselfish. She's always giving her time and money to help other people. She took in an entire family of homeless people during that cold snap last winter, even though she's on a rather tight budget herself.

   B: That's not unselfish: She gets a kick out of it. She does it because it makes her feel good. It's self-interest, really.

   Take B's argument here to be that if you do something in your own interest, that is enough to show that it is a selfish thing to do.
   a. What is wrong with this position?
   b. What about the word *selfish* may have attracted B to this view?
   c. How might you talk B out of it?

3. Explain the confusion of contexts most likely responsible for the following:

   You should never call fever and runny nose *symptoms* of a cold; they are actually *signs* of a cold. Physicians reserve the word *symptom* for subjective indicators, for how a patient says she feels.

4. A: Did you know that Venus is both the morning star and the evening star?

B: It's silly to call Venus a star at all. It's actually a planet, not a star. Stars produce their own light; the planets merely reflect the sunlight falling on them.

Write a short essay about what has gone wrong here. Say something about what distinguishes the contexts in which *star* does its broad, everyday job from those in which it does its narrower, technical job.

5.   A: I finally attended a real, live symphony concert last night, and I actually enjoyed it. I never expected to like classical music so much.

B: You shouldn't call that classical music. Musicologists distinguish classical periods in serious music from romantic ones; and that music last night was all from the late nineteenth century, which was a romantic period. Brahms and Mahler are, strictly speaking, romantic composers, not classical ones.

Briefly explain B's misunderstanding.

6.   It is sometimes said that the tomato is a fruit, not a vegetable. This is based on the fact that the fruit of a plant is the part that contains the *seeds*, as the tomato does.

Write a short essay explaining the confusion most likely responsible for this suggestion. (This case is actually trickier and more complicated than any of the previous examples.)

PRECISION AS A VICE

Recall that the jobs we give words to do will naturally have fuzzy borderlines in their application: ranges in which their application is indeterminate, neither positive nor negative. This is an inevitable consequence of our skill and the way words get their jobs. And we have seen that the existence of indeterminate ranges is not just harmless, but often a valuable aspect of the job.

We nevertheless find ourselves strongly tempted to tidy up the fuzziness, to draw in sharp boundaries, to reform the language by making it more precise. We will say things like "I define *fat* as anything more than twelve pounds overweight," or "Any gash greater than one inch in length will be called *severe*," or "Let us make the blue/green division at exactly 5500 angstroms on the monochrome scale." Intended as reform, this tidiness is as destructive as any other reform; so it will be useful to examine our temptation here, to understand its source, and to formulate a strategy for dealing with it.

A Model of Useful Precision

It is legitimately useful to draw a sharp distinction more or less arbitrarily in a spectrum of cases when a practical purpose makes that arbitrariness unimportant. Say you are sending three busloads of schoolchildren to have a group picture taken. It is important that the children arrive roughly in order of height so they can be arranged in a reasonable time. So you divide them into three groups: tall, medium, and short—one group for each bus. There is no sharp distinction in the groups between tall and medium-height or between medium-height and short. Nevertheless, when the first bus is full the next child in line counts as medium-height for your project. Similarly, when the second bus is full, the next child in line counts as short. Where you draw the line depends on extraneous things like the number of seats on the bus, the chance distribution of heights in the group, and whether you start with the tall end of the class or the short. It matters very little, however, since the task is semantically very modest. You have not sharpened up the jobs done by *tall*, *medium-height*, and *short* in English. You are not saying that *tall*, for example, simply means "over five foot three" (the tallest kid on the middle bus), even in this context. You have merely made a convenient division in a group of children by giving these terms arbitrarily precise jobs *in this specific context*. You can get away with it because the arbitrariness does not matter here and because you are doing no damage to the valuable jobs those terms do elsewhere.

This model may be in the back of our minds when we turn our attentions to less benign purposes. When we do intend to sharpen up the jobs themselves—to say that *fat* just *means* more than twelve pounds overweight, for instance, or that blueness simply stops at 5500 angstroms—we may think what we are doing is just like allotting the kids to the buses. The two are not alike at all, of course; the model merely disguises from us the sad and silly consequences of revising language in this way. But the disguise often works—it's a tricky point—so it will be worth examining in some detail.

Borderline reform may be motivated in two distinct ways. It may come simply from a genuine desire to purify language; but it may also result from an attempt to grapple with some particular issue of substance. The dangers and damage differ somewhat depending on which kind of case it is, so we will treat the two motivations separately.

Retrospective Reform: Destructive Self-Deception

We sometimes react with frustration when an important question falls on a borderline case. Something really important hangs on the question: Is she dead? Are we in a recession? Am I fat? Is it a human being? Are those the blue ones? The key terms in these questions (*dead, recession*, etc.) all have broad areas of indeterminacy, in which they do not apply either positively or negatively. So when we are asked about such a case, the answer will come up "application unclear, case indeterminate, question undecidable." The importance of the underlying question may then encourage us to force the issue. "Well, dammit, it's too important to remain unclear. I'll *make* it clear: I'll draw in a line to *decide* whether it's human, she's dead, I'm fat, and the rest."

It is here that our impulse to revise the language most damages our reasoning. For it allows us to deceive ourselves about what is going on by keeping the words the same and moving their jobs around. It is the most egregious form of equivocation: It guarantees a trivial result. You can get any answer you like with this method, which makes any answer worthless.

The whole reason you chose the troublesome word was that it did the right job (*human, recession, fat*, etc.); it asked the right question. The word itself, the orthography, how it sounds—these are not important: The job is why you chose it. So you do not want to change jobs, for that changes the question. The whole exercise is motivated by the importance of the original question.

The defensive reaction at this point contains the deception. We are tempted to say, "Well, it's not much of a change, is it? The clear cases remain; I've just tidied up a bit in the middle." It is tempting to think the change itself is trivial. But it is not. The consequences, for both the issue at hand and the language itself, are disastrous. This cannot be stated too strongly.

As for the reasoning, for the issue, note that the old job does not tell you how to choose a new one, cannot tell you *where* to draw the line. An infinite number of new jobs are usually possible. Since either answer (positive or negative) is wrong on the old job, and either one could be right on a new one depending on where you draw the line, you simply have to choose. You choose from among the possible new jobs, and in doing so you choose an answer for the question. And that ruins it. The change, far from trivial, *completely* determines the answer. The old job is wholly irrelevant to the answer; *all* that is relevant is the tidying up. So the "reasoning" is just sleight of hand: It distracts us with a flourish about answering a particular question and then sneaks in a different question to get the kind of answer it wants.

The isolated damage to our reasoning is perhaps less than that to the language itself, however. For the change is seldom trivial. Sharpening up the fuzzy edge of a common word's job alters the language as an instrument of practical communication. Changing to clearly positive cases that were not clearly positive, and to clearly negative cases that were not clearly negative, is a fundamental change in our conception of the job: one that would result in communication failure at crucial junctures if adopted without notice.

A:　"Get me the two blue ones and the green one."

B:　"But I see only one blue one and two that are kind of blue-green."

A:　"Oh, I draw a sharp distinction between blue and green. One of the blue-green ones is over the dividing line, so I call it green; the other two are on the blue side."

B:　"Well, how was I supposed to know that? If you play around with the words you can't expect to communicate clearly."

Moreover, as this conversation illustrates, we can usually express what we wish in the fuzzy area without reforming our concepts. We do this by simply avoiding the indeterminate characterization ("blue") and using the linguistic resources already available ("kind of blue-green").

Not only does borderline reform risk confusion for very little gain, it usually entails substantial loss as well. Much of value in the old job is lost in the revision. That is obvious when precision comes at the expense of great oversimplification, as it does in the reforms of *fat* and *severe* suggested above. The normal job given *fat* concerns not just weight, but height and build as well. Adding 12 pounds to the frame of someone who is 4 feet, 11 inches and normally weighs 98 pounds is significant; adding 12 pounds to the average NFL tackle is negligible. Furthermore, the distribution is crucial. If it is all in the middle, *fat* might clearly apply in its normal job; if it is distributed all around on the frame, it might clearly not apply. To fire *fat* from its old job and give it the new, precise one, we sacrifice whole dimensions of the old job; and it is not clear that we gain anything at all. We can always say "12 pounds overweight or greater" without changing anything. We need not steal *fat* from its old job to do it. Exactly the same point may be made of *severe*. Its normal job takes into account not just the length of a gash but the depth, location, and associated trauma—all very useful aspects to have lumped into one job, even if it does have a fuzzy edge. The fuzzy edge may be handled in the usual way.

But these are easy cases. The matter is more subtle when precision does not rip whole dimensions from the old job. Consider *blue*. Suppose we draw the dividing line near the middle of the blue-greens (however we determine the middle). The change wrought thereby in the job done by *blue* is fundamental. For part of the old job is to point out that hues near the new sharp line do not quite fit. Some hues that will be just plain blue on the new conception definitely are not just plain blue on the old. Furthermore, ones that will not be blue at all—namely, those just over the line on the green side—definitely do have some blue in them on the old (i.e., normal) conception. In other words, the fact that it fades off gradually toward green is part of our conception of blue: The taper is an essential part of the job, a valuable aspect to which we appeal all the time. And it is lost in the reform. So although cases like this are subtler than *fat* and *severe*, reform can be just as destructive.

A General Strategy for Borderlines.   How, then, should we handle these cases? Is there a general strategy for reasoning near borderlines that will help us avoid the pitfalls? Yes, of course there is; but it requires carefully disentangling the semantic issue from the substantive one. On a borderline, the first thing to do is *concede the irresolvability of the semantic issue*: recognize that the question does not have a clear answer. Then try to express your underlying concern in different terms: What would we have done with an answer had we been able to get one? Frequently a new way to express the underlying substantive issue will leap right out. It may then be dealt with unencumbered by borderline semantics. Let us look at some easy examples.

We ask, "Is Uncle Charlie bald yet?" and the answer comes up "unclear." So we must consider why we wanted to know. Let us say we asked the question because we had not seen him in a long time and wanted to be sure we would recognize him. In this case we might seek a description of Uncle Charlie's hair in different terms. Whoever responded "unclear" to the first question should be able to say something more specific about just how Charlie's hair had thinned; and this information might help us recognize him even better than had we gotten a clear answer to the original question. In this way we may deal with the underlying substantive concern that originally motivated the question while bypassing the troublesome question itself.

In another case a legislator asks an economist, "Are we in a recession?" The economist may reply, "Well, it's hard to say. Several indicators are severely depressed, but some others are about normal; one or two are actually a bit better than normal. It's a tough case. I don't really know what to say." All the signs of a semantically indeterminate case. What should we do when the best estimate we can get is "uncertain"? Examine *why the question was asked in the first place.* Suppose the legislator asked because he wanted to know whether to support some legislation designed to stimulate the economy. He (or the economist) might be able to deal with the pros and cons of *this* issue, without taking on the tough semantic nut offered by talk of recession. The economist might say, "Well, with inflation running at 13 percent I wouldn't recommend stimulating legislation even if we were in a recession." On the other hand, he might offer, "We should not wait for a recession to begin stimulating the economy. Selective tax cuts would probably ward off a recession without creating undue inflationary forces." The point of this example is not to offer economic counsel. It is to show how we can deal with an underlying substantive issue without resolving the indeterminate semantic issues originally offered as its expression. Divide and conquer. Separate the substantive issue from the irresolvable semantic one if possible. Then deal with the substantive issue in whatever way you can.

Consider a more difficult illustration. In the years immediately before World War II, some international airlines would fly passengers to island and coastal locations in flying boats. These were relatively ordinary, high-winged passenger planes, except that the bottom was hull-shaped; they could land and take off from water and hence had access to places without airports. Howard Hughes' *Spruce Goose* is an example of such an airplane. Suppose we ask the question "Is a flying boat a passenger ship?" in a nautical context.

This is a useful example for our purposes because, in attempting to answer the question, we are pulled in both directions. On the one hand, there is something strange about calling a flying boat a passenger ship. The things usually referred to by that phrase in this context are ocean liners: craft much more seaworthy than flying boats and constrained to travel on the water. On the other hand, a flying boat does have many important features in common with more normal passenger ships. It has a modestly seaworthy hull and is designed to transport passengers or cargo across vast expanses of ocean. It needs a dock to load and unload. And in some circumstances it might even be pressed into water-bound service: taxiing passengers from one dock to another. In fact, were oceans mostly shallow—say, like the Everglades—ships generally might have evolved into something like flying boats, using air rather than water as the medium of propulsion, perhaps even using an airfoil for stability.

This example illustrates the most typical and perhaps most frustrating kind of borderline case. The great majority of jobs we give words are like the job *passenger ship* usually does: They are useful because, in the course of our lives, they have innumerable clear applications—both positive and negative. We normally handle them effortlessly and unproblematically. We are seldom tempted by troublesome applications. Consequently, when a problematic application first tempts us we are easily frustrated—sometimes even piqued—because it does not fit effortlessly under one application or the other. New possibilities opened up by technological advance or social change are frequently the culprits, raising possibilities and combinations not imagined previously.

Whatever the cause, our best strategy upon encountering such a case is to concede its irresolvability. Neither positive nor negative application is happy without qualification. So, once again, ask, Why do we want to know whether a flying boat is a passenger ship? What made us ask? Is there some underlying issue that may be resolved without forcing the semantic one? Let us suppose the answer is yes. What raised the question was the wording of a charter. A flying boat had landed in a harbor, taxied up to a dock, and unloaded its passengers—whereupon the authorities in charge of the harbor had demanded a fee for use of the dock. But the airline protested that the harbor's charter specified that only *passenger ships* using the facility were required to pay a fee; and since a flying boat is not one of those, it is exempt. Now if we are right in classifying a flying boat here as a borderline case of a passenger ship, then it is no more clearly exempt from payment than it is required by the charter to pay: Neither answer is right. This is an important point: Neither side wins on a borderline. This is why the issue is still to be resolved in different terms.

A standard appeal, when the letter of the law is unclear, is to intent. If the charter's intent was to place the burden of maintaining the harbor on those benefiting from its use, then we might appeal to this in resolving the substantive issue. The flying boat is making the same use of the harbor that a normal passenger ship would, so unless some equally weighty consideration can be found to argue against treating it as one would a normal passenger ship, the airline should be required to pay. This is the kind of resolution you often can find when you look past borderline semantics to the underlying issue.

Prospective Reform: Diminishing Our Resources

We have seen that *retrospective* reform is self-deceptive. Answering a question by sharpening a borderline is semantic legerdemain. It involves changing the question, equivocating on the crucial term. Furthermore, the answer that comes up is semantically arbitrary. We may draw in a sharp line on either side of the case we have; we may devise either answer: yes or no. If there is some underlying substantive concern that inclines us to *want* one of these answers rather than the other, then it is far better—and more honest—to deal with that substantive matter directly and forget about pushing the semantics around.

Prospective borderline reform raises more complicated issues. If we are trying not to answer a question already asked but to change the language for the sake of *future* questions, then no reasoning (outside the language) will be at risk. But, in practice, the simple sharpening of a borderline is unlikely to be helpful, even in framing future questions. It is unlikely to add to the linguistic resources at our disposal. In fact, as we have noticed already, the net impact of such a sharpening can easily be to impoverish the language. For we always lose something of value in the old fuzzy job: sometimes a whole dimension, sometimes just valuable "taper." And often the gain in precision is pointless, because other terminology is already available to handle the case in question with greater precision.

This last point cannot be overemphasized. When we need to speak precisely about weight, for example, we always have recourse to pounds and ounces. When we need precision about what time of day it is, we may consult a clock. If we ever need great precision in talking about hair loss, we can simply count follicles, or square inches. We can even talk about minute variation along the monochromatic scale by appeal to exact wavelengths of light. And, we can, of course, do all this without firing *fat* and *slim*, *dawn* and *dusk*, *bald*, *blue*, and the rest from their practically valuable, though fuzzy-edged, jobs. We can have the best of both worlds: the precision when we need it, the complexity of more basically perceptual predicates when that is more valuable.

This last way of putting the matter displays yet another hazard of casual borderline reform, even if it is intended only prospectively. When we sharpen up the jobs of useful common words like *fat*, *bald*, and *blue*, the newfound precision is usually impossible to use in just those contexts in which we need the job. The value of many practical jobs that words get lies partly in our easy access to them. The reason we appeal to the normal jobs done by *fat*, *slim*, *blue*, *bald*, *dawn*, and *chair* is that casual inspection is often adequate to tell whether or not the jobs apply to something. Normal conversation benefits outrageously from having them around. When we attempt to apply these words in new, sharpened versions of their jobs, the newly imposed precision will often be lost in our uncertain grasp of the application. Normal people in normal contexts simply cannot tell very accurately how many pounds overweight I am or what wavelength radiation is entering their eyes. If being bald is losing exactly 87.4 percent of one's hair, there will be a whole range of cases in which we cannot be sure without counting, which in practical contexts is simply impossible (not to mention silly and rude). In such cases the fuzziness that used to be part of the job will now inhabit the application. So sharpening up the fuzzy borderline does not even eliminate indeterminacy; it merely transfers it from job to application.

As a final note on this topic, it is worth pointing out that most subjects contain inherent limits past which it does not even make sense to ask for increased precision. A frequent observation in the last few pages has been that if we wish more precision than the words we are using allow in their normal jobs, we can always rephrase the issue in different, more precise terms. If *fat* and *slim* won't do, we can switch to pounds and ounces. But in nearly every application, precision, even in appropriate terms, may be pressed past a certain point only at the expense of substantial arbitrariness. It is senseless to ask for my weight in micrograms, because it varies thousands of micrograms every minute due to scrapes, cuts, and evaporation (minus) and accumulation of environmental debris (plus). It is similarly senseless to ask for the length of my house in microinches. This is only partly because the irregularity of the stucco is several hundred thousand microinches. The unevenness of the walls and asymmetry of the whole structure are far greater than that. And variations due to temperature, wind pressure, humidity, and seismic jiggles must also be accommodated. To give an answer accurate to microinches would require arbitrarily distilling a number out of all this. And any number within a million or so of it would be just as good.[1] My house does not have a length to that degree of precision. The most helpful, even the most accurate, answer I could give would be so many feet, plus or minus an inch or two.

Equivocal Fuzziness: Effective Borderlines

The borderline applications we have been examining are all reasonably intersubjective: In practical contexts, all competent language users would have reservations about roughly the same range of cases. Doubtless this is because the difficult cases of things like *fat*, *blue*, and *bald* arise as frequently and neutrally as the clear ones. We all get lots of opportunity to develop a common sensitivity to the indeterminable area and appreciate the value of the taper.

Some borderlines are not so tidy, however. Some jobs taper off into areas in which cases never or seldom arise. Some have ideological commitments affecting their application in various ways. Still others are subject to parochial influences of local culture or commerce. For a variety of reasons our perceptions may not coincide on

---

[1]The number might be useful for *something*, of course. Its change might be used to monitor important physical changes in the structure, or it could be used to compute an exact property tax rate. But its usefulness does not show that it is the length of my house; it just shows it is useful. We might coin a new phrase "tax-roll length of my house" to stand for a specific function of precisely determinable lengths of walls and things. But this would be a new job and would deserve a new term here. It would not be the length of my house.

This is, in a way, just one more reflection of the arbitrariness of resolving borderlines. Figured down to microinches, length is semantically indeterminate when applied to large, coarsely constructed objects. (It is even indeterminable when applied to carefully machined blocks of steel, but less elaborately so.) We may sharpen up the borderline however we please: From the point of view of the job done by "length," any possible answer is as good and as bad as any other.

the tough cases. As a result, the nature of a job—the significance of a word—will vary in small but systematic ways from person to person or place to place.

Although this is a kind of ambiguity, it differs importantly from the kind we discussed earlier, in which a word's different jobs were quite distinct. Here the jobs overlap almost completely: We find substantial agreement on application to the clear, standard, common, easy cases. Differences arise only in the troublesome middle ground that is the subject of this section. One person's tough cases are another's easy ones, and perhaps vice versa. But the essential reason to separate this kind of ambiguity from the sort discussed earlier is that resolving the difficulties to which it leads is, unsurprisingly, very much like resolving any borderline case problem: Find the underlying issue and treat it in different terms.

The most innocent example of deviant borderlines might be something like this. Virtually all of us would unproblematically agree on the clearest application of *lawn* in the job that word has in landscaping. A lawn would be a plot of grass. A front yard covered with desert weeds—spurge, Russian thistle, wild poppies, oxalis— would not be a clear case of a lawn, even if the weeds were kept down with a mower. A yard of weeds would be a difficult case: rather like a lawn in important respects, but distinct from it in perhaps the *most* important respect. Yards of weeds and wild flowers are, at best, borderline lawns. Yet it is easy to imagine a community in which grass is unusually difficult to maintain and in which as a result virtually all the residents grow whatever will survive and keep down the dust in the yards surrounding their homes. It would be quite natural in such a community to jimmy the semantics a little and refer to the weed-covered yards as lawns. The community might adopt this as orthodox usage. A borderline lawn for most of us would simply be a lawn for them, which is a way of saying they have a different conception of "lawn." But the difference is not dramatic; it is very subtle. And it is common enough to be accorded special treatment if we can bring to bear what we have learned in this section.

Of course, the lawn example is so innocent that no interesting reasoning problems are likely to arise from it. Only when something important seems to hang on the equivocal characterization do interesting problems arise. When our personal commitments move the indeterminate areas around, then characterizational issues generate heat. Is a Toyota Celica a sports car? Is *Rhapsody in Blue* classical music? Could a robot be conscious? When a substantive dispute centers on such a question the best strategy is to discover what it is, express it in terms all parties can agree on, and deal with it independently of the semantic controversy. In other words, as long as the semantic disagreement falls in our "troublesome middle area" it is best to regard the entire area of disagreement as semantically indeterminate and treat the dispute as though it concerned a standard borderline case, as illustrated below.

One such controversy currently raging concerns whether or not a (human) fetus is a human being. For many people the case is borderline: There are pulls in both directions. But others have decided it one way or the other; and because the case is bound up in personal, religious, and ideological issues, hostility has focused on this disagreement, and the case has caused some very hard feelings. It will accordingly make a good illustration of the recommended strategy.

Consider a familiar argument:

S₁   The deliberate killing of an innocent human being by another person is murder.

S₂   A fetus is a human being.

S₃   Abortion is the deliberate killing of a fetus.

C   Therefore, abortion is murder.

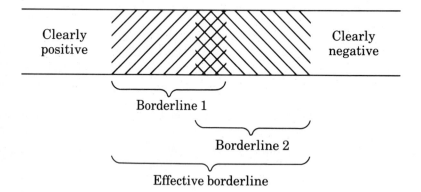

If we accept the supporting three statements, the argument is pretty good.[2] It is clear in the context that *fetus* refers to a human fetus, that fetuses are presumably innocent, and that abortions are carried out by *persons*. So the pieces of the argument fit together in the proper way. But not everyone subscribes to the clear truth of all three statements. In particular, huge controversy rages around the second. And if the second goes, so does the argument. What to do?

Consider for a moment two people whose conception of *human* differs very slightly, but just enough to cause them to disagree about this statement. A accepts it, while B thinks fetuses are only borderline human beings and hence withholds clear assent. They give *human* slightly different jobs, which show up only in tough cases like this. Notice how silly (or self-deceptive) it is to try to resolve a substantive matter by pushing the semantics around.

Assume, reasonably, that the underlying substantive issue concerns how we should treat abortion, and abortionists, under the law. A offers the above argument to support his view that abortion should be forbidden: We should treat abortionists as murderers. Presumably A and B could agree that the underlying issue is whether or not we should forbid abortion. Now suppose A goes back to his argument and attempts to secure B's agreement by semantic means. Notice what can happen. A will insist that B change the job he gives *human* so that the second statement is true. B relents. Unfortunately for A, this move cannot be isolated from the rest of the argument. For if B had originally assented to the first statement, he did so before he changed the job he gave *human*. So now the first says something slightly different, and he must reassess it. What he is likely to say, of course, is that murder covers human beings only as he *used* to use the term. In its new job, *human being* includes some things the killing of which is not clearly murder as he understands it. His conception of murder is tied to his former conception of *human*, not his new one.

Not yet seeing the futility of attempting a semantic resolution of a substantive disagreement, A might further insist that B change the job he gives *murder*. Let us say that B agrees to use *murder*, as A does, to cover the killing of human beings in the newly agreed-upon

---

[2]In fact, if we merely made explicit a few of the assumptions presupposed in the context of the argument, it would be deductive. Nothing in the following discussion requires such a strict interpretation, however.

application of *human being*. This glues the argument back together: Abortion is murder for both A and B now. But the expense has been to raise a question about the connection between semantic and substantive issues. Before adjusting the jobs done by *human* and *murder*, B doubtless conceded the importance of A's argument because of the connection between its conclusion and the substantive issue. Characterizing something as murder sounded like an important consideration in deciding whether to allow it or forbid it. But now that *murder* has a different job, B may well want to reassess the argument's substantive impact.

Once again it is reasonable to expect B to think that changing jobs vitiates the connection. In *murder's* new job B might well feel not all murders should be forbidden; in its new job some murders are permissible: For B, *murder* drops its pejorative force. What's in a word if you play around with its jobs? The point is that if, for whatever reason, people have different conceptions of *human*, and hence different conceptions of *murder*, it is very likely that they will also have different perceptions of permissible behavior and reasonable social policy. Such perceptions may well be amenable to argument. But, if people understand what is going on, it is silly to expect that moving the semantics around will have much effect on their settled views. They can always keep their views and express them in the new terminology. In any case, *we must avoid the fatuity of moving a borderline to fit our preconception* on some matter, *and then trying to use the adjusted semantics to justify the preconception.*

So we are led inexorably to direct confrontation with the substantive issue: Should abortion be forbidden? It is by no means simple to deal with; it may be beyond general resolution. But any direct consideration is more honest—and offers more promise than semantic sleight of hand.

EXERCISES

1. Some years ago the NCAA declared a student ineligible to play varsity basketball because he had signed a contract to play professional basketball. The case was complicated by the fact that the student in question immediately changed his mind about turning pro, returned to college, and never received any money under the contract. The NCAA argued that the mere signing of a contract gave him professional status; he was therefore, strictly speaking, no longer an amateur, and hence was ineligible to play on an amateur team.

a. What is the semantic issue?

b. What is the underlying substantive issue?

c. What is the difficulty in the NCAA's argument?

d. What strategy might the NCAA have adopted to deal with the case more clearly?

2. Attorney: While my client's husband was in surgery, all his life signs (heartbeat, respiration, etc.) vanished for nearly ten minutes. He was therefore technically dead. According to the law, marriage is terminated by death. So it was perfectly legal for my client to remarry without obtaining a divorce from her first husband.

Prosecutor: Nonsense. Death is *permanent* by definition. The accused's husband did not die—he *almost* died, and "almost" doesn't count in the marriage law.

a. What makes the case a tough one semantically?

b. How might we deal with the underlying substantive issue without forcing the semantics?

3. Explain why it is senseless to ask for the duration of a war in microseconds (millionths of a second).

MISCHARACTERIZED INSIGHTS

Most of us exaggerate for effect now and then. We quite commonly say things like "He hit it a mile" or "I have a million things to do" or "I thought I was going to die" in circumstances in which a literal reading of them would be clearly false. One of the most interesting observations to make about hyperbole like this is that we are almost never misled by it. In normal contexts we virtually always understand exaggerations *as* exaggerations and are able to see through them to the sober sentiment they are intended to express. In saying things like "It was the worst night of my life" or "He is the fattest person in the world" or "It seemed to go on forever" or "I wouldn't take one as a gift," we seldom wish to be taken literally, and that is usually understood. The transparency of exaggeration allows it to form the basis of a great deal of humor; it also assures it a serious role in communication.

The two (humor and communication) are sometimes not independent. When a road tester says "The brakes on this car are so bad you have to count telephone poles to know whether you're slowing down," the two go together. The statement is amusing, but it also expresses some of the frustration—or terror—you might experience driving the car. And this is the communicative task hyperbole tackles best. We exaggerate to express the great degree of something when that degree would be far more difficult to express literally. The terror simply might not come through in the data table's cold listing of 419 feet as the stopping distance from 60 miles per hour. The easy, clear, succinct expression of extreme degree is what we are after when we say of a boring lecture that "It seemed to go on forever" or when the man in the antacid commercial used to say " . . . thought I was gonna die." Literal exaggeration provides clear, graphic expression of just how bored we were or just how bad he felt. This is usually obvious; and this is also why it is usually silly to respond with "Really? Forever?!" or "You didn't really think you were going to die—you would have screamed for help or called an ambulance." No, of course not; the statements are not to be taken literally. Anyone who responds in this way has missed their point.

Our natural tendency to exaggerate for effect does occasionally get us into trouble, however. On some topics and in some contexts we are easily seduced by our own hyperbole. We end up taking it seriously and insisting on statements that are literally outrageous. This happens quite commonly when we try to express abstract insights into the nature of things. The source of the difficulty is, once again, our clumsiness with—our lack of talent for—abstraction. Its awful consequence, once again, is the gratuitous savaging of our language.

Something like this was probably behind the "thoughtfulness" example we examined earlier. When someone says,

> It doesn't take much thought to be considerate; it's stupid to call that "thoughtful."

they seem to be saying something plainly silly, misrepresenting a simple fact about the language. But there is an insight buried here, one that might be put more soberly like this:

> The job held by *thoughtful* concerns the amount or degree of thought in only one narrow context; in one common application it involves simply thinking of others in a certain way.

This more modest formulation lacks punch, however. And we seem to need punch in our insights. It is a debilitating addiction.

As a start on detoxification, it is useful to compare this case with an unproblematic exaggeration like "I've got a million things to do." This is hyperbolic for "I'm very busy." On any orthodox way of counting, even when I am very busy, the distinguishable things I have to do may come to six. But saying "I've got six things to do and that will more than use up the day" does not capture the panic and dead-run preoccupation of the pending schedule that "I've got a million things to do" seems to. The difference between these two cases is that, when pressed, we naturally concede that "a million" literally exaggerates the number of things on the schedule, that the exaggeration is for effect. By contrast, we are far more reluctant to abandon the "it's stupid" formulation of the insight about thoughtfulness, even though what it rejects is clearly *not* stupid: It is an absolutely normal complexity in the linguistic duty of *thoughtful*. The difference is doubtless due to the subject matter. Our casual familiarity with things like daily schedules allows us to reformulate the exaggeration confidently with no sense of substantial loss. We are comfortable with the practical equivalence of the two ways of putting the matter. We are not nearly so secure, however, when dealing with something as tenuous and abstract as an insight. Insights are by their nature often elusive and difficult to capture. So when we lose the zing of the exaggeration, we may think we have lost the insightfulness too. The modest formulation seems to demean the insight, seems to suggest that it is not such a big deal after all. So we cling to the overstatement in spite of its ludicrousness, even at the expense of hobbling the language.

The remedy is to recognize that even modest-sounding insights may be important and valuable to us. Modest insights are often all we can hope for on certain subjects; we must learn to appreciate what we can get and not try to blow it up into something it can never be. Unexaggerated insights can have an important impact on our perception and understanding, in spite of their modesty. In fact, accuracy is usually more essential to their value as insights than zing is. So it is worth our time to cultivate some enthusiasm for modest expression here. With a little care we can have the best of both worlds: the insights *and* the linguistic resources we are tempted to destroy on their behalf. To this end, consider another example. A radio commercial declares,

All hypnosis is really self-hypnosis.

Suppose the ad defends this by arguing that successful hypnosis requires the subject's cooperation, and since this cooperation makes the subject a kind of participant in his own hypnosis, it is self-hypnosis. The best that can be said for such a construction is that it is just a bad way to put the point. (It does not matter here whether we agree or disagree with the suggestion: *This* is a bad way to make the point.) For self-hypnosis openly suggests that the subject's partici-pation in his own hypnosis is *active*: that he is doing it himself, that it is his own activity, involving his own technical competence. But this is the very opposite of what happens in most hypnosis: Participation consists in relatively passive acquiescence; the subject does not even know *how* to do it; it requires the active administration of a hypno-tist, of somebody else who knows what to do. To call such cases self-hypnosis is to confusingly mischaracterize a modest insight that may be put much more clearly. In fact, it was put more clearly above in the "defense":

> Successful hypnosis requires the subject's cooperation.

or, negatively,

> You cannot be hypnotized if you resist.

These reformulations express the ostensible point of the original statement without the misleading hyperbole. They are still very interesting, but they avoid the mistaken implications.

With this background you should be able to handle other such cases. If someone says,

> Buddhism isn't really a religion (because it has no supernatural being).

or

> Geraniums are actually weeds (because they'll take the place over if you let them).

the proper reaction is neither to take the statement literally nor to reject it out of hand. If anything hangs on it, you should be ready with a modest reformulation that retains the insight without the overstatement.

All this applies to what might be called everyday insights. Insights from science, on the other hand, are sometimes to powerful, so overwhelming, that the remarks thus far provide inadequate admonition. Scientific insights require special attention.

Underlying Explanations from Science

The various scientific disciplines routinely offer, in their own theoretical terms, explanations of familiar features of our everyday lives. They explain why light-colored clothing is cooler than dark; why tides are higher at one time than another; why the sky is blue; why certain places have more earthquakes than others; why binoculars make objects seem closer; why your ears pop when you change altitude; how camera film registers an image—and countless other things just like these. Such explanations provide the theoretical story underlying things we are all more or less familiar with.

The characterizational difficulty that arises in such cases may be generally described as follows. Call the phenomenon being explained A and the underlying, scientific account B. B explains A. The standard, neutral way to express the relationship between A and B is something like this:

What makes A happen is B.

or, perhaps,

When B occurs, what you get is A.

or, more generally,

When A occurs, what is happening is B.

We have a phenomenon and an explanation, and the two are linked together in some way such as this. The phenomenon, A, is something described in the nontechnical terms of everyday conversation: cooler, closer, blue, pop, earthquake, and the like. The explanation, B, on the other hand, will usually appeal to the theoretical terms of a scientific discipline: radiation, index of refraction, photon, precipitate, geological plate.

Because of this difference in terminology we are tempted, in a whole range of these explanations, to mischaracterize the explanatory insight in the way that results, again, in the destruction of valuable language. Because A is cast in everyday language and B invokes the awe-inspiring concepts of science, we are tempted to think that A is just a crude way of saying B and should be dispensed with. So, in place of "B explains A" we are tempted to offer

A is not really happening at all. What is *really* happening is B.

But this is all a misunderstanding—precisely the misunderstanding behind some of our worst reformist temptations. When B explains A in this way, it virtually never explains it *away*. Thermodynamics explains the relative coolness of light-colored clothing by appeal to its more efficient reflection of incident radiation. But it would be absurd to capture this by saying "Light-colored clothing isn't *really* cooler; it just reflects more of the incident radiation." This would perversely mischaracterize the insight. The sensible way to put it is "Light-colored clothing *is* cooler *because* it reflects more of the incident radiation." When geologists explain earthquakes as elastic vibrations in the earth's crust induced by slippage along a fault, they do not show that there really are no earthquakes, just vibrations induced by fault slippage. That is just what earthquakes *are*. In each case (here, clothing and earthquakes) A and B are two different ways of talking about the same thing, each perfectly satisfactory in its own context. They happen to come together in an explanation, but the explanation eliminates neither one; it simply displays the relationship between them. It is "A *because* B," not "B instead of A."

This is perhaps easier to accept when we notice that the different terminologies in A and B have different kinds of jobs to do, different purposes. The terms of A are useful in our everyday lives, and the terms of B are useful in scientific theory. The jobs of the scientific terms are explicitly crafted to aid in scientific investigation and explanation. The more mundane vocabulary has been shaped and selected to aid in conveying the practical matters of our pedestrian existence. These two endeavors are so disparate it would be astonishing if the same terms, the same jobs, the same distinctions would do for both. The fact that they come together in an explanation is a relatively minor incident in the lives of the various terms involved.

To be suited for practical, everyday conversation, language must be geared to our practical needs, rudimentary physical abilities, largely unaided perceptual skills, and a wide variety of interests other than scientific explanation. This is why we have terms for rather coarse divisions in the visible spectrum of light and rough-and-ready distinctions such as *up* and *down*, *hard* and *soft*, *loud* and *quiet*, *smooth* and *rough*, *bitter* and *sweet*. This is also why we attribute the characteristics we do to the objects we do. The best practical language is whatever helps us communicate our basic concerns clearly and quickly.

The language of scientific theory, on the other hand, is primarily geared to displaying systematic interrelationships among different phenomena in an explanatory way. As a result, some of its most important terms refer to nonexistent idealizations (*mass point, inertial reference, black body, ideal gas*) or to entities the discrimination of which is difficult or expensive or both (*photon, neutrino, wavelength, geological plate, moment of inertia*). As a result, things that are simple to communicate in our everyday vocabulary are frequently beyond our practical ability even to *characterize* in the language of underlying scientific theory. "It smells rather like cantaloupe" or "The best ones are slightly asymmetrical" or "The rich mixture of dissonance and harmony can move you to tears" or "Stay on the main road until the pavement begins to deteriorate, then take the next left: It will be obvious." Sometimes we would not even know how to begin a theoretical recharacterization of such a mundane sentiment as one of these.

But even if we *could* begin, there is usually no point in it. In choosing what to wear, we will sometimes find it useful to understand that light-colored clothing is cooler than dark. It is perfectly clear what this means, as is its occasional impact on our choice. But at this level all that matters is *that* it is cooler, not why. And we do not need thermodynamics for that. Similarly for earthquakes. What normally matters in the conduct of our lives is the shaking and breaking and swaying and toppling, not mechanical models of the earth's crust. In short, we have a phenomenon (A), described in one set of terms, and a scientific account (B), described in another. The relation between these two things is simply that one (B) explains the other (A). We must resist the temptation to think the explanation gets rid of what it is trying to explain.

Note that none of this means the underlying science is of no relevance to our everyday lives. It is. Thermodynamics lies behind much of the technology we depend upon in our work and in our homes. Our growing understanding of plate tectonics will doubtless make life less hazardous in seismically unstable regions. But our gratitude to science for all these things does not extend to vandalizing our conversations by trying to express our interests in a vocabulary designed for a wholly different purpose.

Detailed Illustration.   In this final section we will examine an especially tempting mischaracterization of a basic scientific insight. In the process, strands of argument from several different parts of this chapter will be drawn together and illustrated in a single case. Consider the following exchange:

> A: I got started so early this morning that I watched the sun rise while waiting for the bus.

> B: Don't you know the sun doesn't actually rise? The sun stands rather still at the center of the planetary system; what appears to be the sun's rising is actually the earth's own rotation, gradually bringing us out into the sun's light.

The quick treatment of this would be to point out that B has exaggerated an insight from astronomy, which makes him want to fire *rise* from its normal job in A's sentence. And since everybody understands what A said, there is no need even to restate the point, much less revise our diction here. What is required is a less destructive formulation of the insight.

One such reformulation would be this. If you adopt the astronomer's point of view, and observe the earth from the sun (or from the Milky Way), you would not think of the sun as rising at all. You would see the earth turning in the distance, various parts of its surface coming from the dark side, through the morning terminator, into the light. Looking at things from this perspective will sometimes make them clearer and will benefit communication as well.

This brief treatment is not likely to persuade someone bent on scientifically purifying our language, however, as B seems to be. To make the confusion clear in such a case will require marshaling considerations from earlier sections of this chapter. The aim must be to make obvious how silly it is to adopt an astronomer's point of view in our ordinary conversation: Communication suffers, and for nothing.

The most important things to point out about the exchange between A and B are that they are not doing astronomy and their conversation is not taking place on the sun. The fact that they are chatting casually, on the surface of the earth, is an immensely important feature of the context. In this context the word *rise* is simply part of our institutionalized way of referring to the sun's first coming into view in the morning. It is a normal and natural way of talking about dawn: part of effortlessly successful communication.

By contrast, the astronomer's perspective, and idiom, would be baffling in this context—a substantial bar to communication. If A walked into a roomful of normal English speakers and tried to tell us how early he had gotten up by talking about the morning terminator, most of us would not understand him at all. And those who did would wonder why he put it that way instead of talking in normal English. In other words, A's strange idiom would raise charity problems: It would be a difficulty to be overcome in our finding a plausible interpretation for his words. We would be at a loss to explain his strange choice. "If all he's trying to say is he got up before sunrise, why didn't he just say so?" Mischaracterized insights damage your sense of empathy, undermine your performance skill.

Recall that just why we give words the jobs we do is hard to articulate; and *rise* here is no exception. But the reason is definitely *not* that we are wedded to a discredited astronomical view, as B seems to suggest. Everybody I know accepts a spinning earth as a matter of course. Yet I have never encountered anyone over 15 not competent to handle *rise* in this job. The two are simply not connected. The case is rather like using *lunatic* to mean "insane person." Using the word thus does not commit you to holding discredited theories about the effect of the moon on our minds. In the same way, to read geostatic astronomy into A's words dramatically violates the principle of charity.

We may, of course, speculate about why we find *rise* the natural word to use. Very likely it has something to do with the fact that, as a frame of reference for motion, the earth dominates our lives and our interests, even our interest in dawn. We naturally treat it as fixed, much as we treat the airplane as fixed as we talk of movement inside it during a flight. We may view the sun's rising as we do my walking back through the cabin to the rest room. From the ground's point of view, what I did was slow my velocity slightly and allow the rest room to gradually overtake me. But the additional complication is irrelevant to my practical concern. It would be silly and confusing to use the ground's point of view.

To be perfectly clear: In some obvious contexts the astronomical perspective is appropriate, helpful, even necessary. The task is to be clear about when it is and when it is not. And for most practical purposes it is not. Forcing the exotic perspective on mundane conversation damages our communication, our thought, and even our behavior. In short, the job speaker A gave to *rise* at the start of this section is perfectly clear and wholly unproblematic. It neither affirms nor denies any particular cosmological theory. On the other hand, to use exotic astronomical expressions in this context would be obscure and potentially misleading to nearly everybody. Listeners would wonder why A did not say it in the normal way; and this would raise explanatory hurdles in the path of the interpretation A wished them to place on his words. Empathy fails and communication is jeopardized whenever we lose control of a modest insight.

EXERCISES

1. Each of the following epigrams arguably exaggerates a modest insight. In each case, identify the exaggeration (the suspect formulation) and then express the intended point in more straightforward terms.
   a. Lake Erie is not really a freshwater lake; you can't drink the water, and it kills freshwater fish.
   b. Buddhism is not really a religion, because it does not require belief in a supernatural being.
   c. In California geraniums are weeds; if you don't keep after them they will take the place over: They are the main reason I use weed killer.
   d. An anthology is not really a book, because it does not have an author, just an editor.
2. On pages 338–339 of this chapter you were asked to treat the following cases under the heading of the myth of one proper use. They may also be thought of as mischaracterized insights. Formulate the insight more modestly in each case.
   a. It is silly to call Venus a star; it's a planet, not a star.
   b. If my neighbor enjoys helping the needy as much as she seems to, then her doing so is actually selfish.
3. The categorical bumper sticker

   If guns are outlawed only outlaws will have guns

   may be taken to express a plausible, less categorical insight. What is it?

4. A: Did you notice how blue the sky was this morning? That was the first time in months it has been so striking.

    B: Of course I didn't, and you didn't either. The sky is a fiction: All that's up there is clear air and black space. What happens is that particles in the atmosphere diffuse the sun's light in such a way that the shorter wavelengths from the blue end of the spectrum dominate what reaches your eye on the surface of the earth. It's all an illusion, really.

Write a short essay describing what has gone wrong here. It should include a clear demonstration of both the unproblematic value of blue-sky talk in normal contexts and the silliness of B's proposal to revise our language there; and it should reformulate B's insight to avoid its apparent conflict with orthodox diction.

5. Earlier in this century Sir Arthur Eddington, a noted physicist, popularized a spectacular-sounding statement, which he claimed was an insight provided by physics into the nature of things. The statement was that *there really are no solid objects*. His support for this surprising contention was that "modern physics has by delicate test and remorseless logic assured me" that what we think of as a solid object—a rock, a table, a hockey puck—is *actually* only a swarm of sparsely scattered electric charges: mostly emptiness. The books and papers on my desk, for example, are not supported by the substance of a solid object, but rather by "a series of tiny blows from the swarm underneath." Our belief in solid objects, Eddington complained, is simply a popular myth we cling to out of an ignorance of physics and some innate hardheadedness.

Write a short essay explaining why Eddington's insight is sensationally mischaracterized. That is, by examining the normal contrast marked by *solid object* in our talk about things, explain why Eddington's insight does not show our belief in solid objects to be misguided. Then reformulate the insight from physics more modestly.

6. A: Well, you can't see something that doesn't exist: That's true by definition.

    B: Gee, that sounds too tough. What about the stars we see at night, for example? Astronomers tell us that the light from many of them left so long ago that some could easily have blown up and vanished in the meantime. Some will still be visible to earthlings for hundreds of thousands of years after they've ceased to exist.

    A: Well, you really don't see the star itself, just the *light* from the star, and *that* still exists.

B: But in this respect a star does not differ from any other object: What's in your eye is the light coming from it, not the thing itself. Do you want to say you never really see objects, just the light from them?

A: Yes, strictly speaking you never see objects, just the light.

In this exchange, A begins by mischaracterizing an insight about the job done by the verb *to see* (see hip-shot definitions in Chapter 7) and is then driven to mischaracterize the physics of perception in order to save the original oversimplification. Write a short essay explaining why A's recommendation is misguided. Provide a better formulation of each insight.

7.   Consider the following epigram.

All companies are in the same business: making money.

a.   Explain the mischaracterization or exaggeration (that is, explain what the epigram might be taken to say that is simply false).

b.   Reformulate the insight more modestly.

8.   The following passage suggests that we should change the way we talk about colored surfaces.

Do you realize that surfaces that appear green are not really green themselves but merely reflect the green part of the light falling on them? An ordinary leaf, for example, has a physical property that allows it to absorb all of the incident light except for some of the green, which it reflects back into your eye. That's why it looks green. If the green light were removed from the incident beam, leaves would no longer even appear green—they'd look black. It is silly to call the *surface* green when it is actually just the light.

a.   The revision suggested here is actually rather subtle. Try to describe it—that is, explain what words are being fired from their normal job.

b.   Write a short essay explaining why the revision is misguided, and formulate the insight of the passage in a less misleading way.

Glossary of Important Terms

Argument   the giving of reasons (support) for a conclusion.

Bypassing account   See **Chance.**

Causal account   explanation of a **Correlation** (A/B). There are three types of causal account: forward (A causes B), reverse (B causes A), and common (X causes A and also causes B independently of A).

Chance   non-causal account of a correlation. To make the chance rival plausible, one must sometimes provide a **Bypassing account** of B: There is no causal connection between A and B. Rather, D (something independent of A) causes B.

Competence step   See **Testimony.**

Correlation   when two things (events, series, etc.) happen together. The shortened form for a correlation is A/B.

Deductive argument   an argument whose conclusion is contained in the support and is semantically guaranteed by the support.

Diagnostic inductive argument   An **Inductive argument** whose support contains some **Trace data** and whose conclusion(s) explains some of the support.

Explanatory hurdle   a piece of **Trace data** that a particular conclusion has a great deal of trouble explaining.

Flag term   A term that may help in *schematizing*. Terms like *hence, therefore,* and *so* indicate conclusions; terms like *if, supposing that,* and *since* indicate support claims.

Implicit question (I.Q.)   The question that a practical argument is concerned with. The **Rival conclusions** must be answers to the I.Q.

365

Inductive argument   an argument that is not deductive.

Link   connection between support and conclusion. For a deductive argument, the link is unbreakable; for an inductive argument, there will be degrees of link strength.

Modus operandi considerations (employed in correlation-to-cause arguments)   considerations about the way things characteristically work and the characteristic traces they leave.

Mutually exclusive   See **Rival conclusions.**

Non-diagnostic argument   an argument that does not contain **Trace data** to be explained by rival conclusions. The conclusions of non-diagnostic arguments may be predictions or recommendations.

Non-trace data   information (often background) that makes it easier or harder for a rival to explain the trace data but is not itself explained by the rival conclusions.

Paraphrase   clearer and shorter restatement of a passage of prose.

Plausibility ranking   the ranking of **Rival conclusions** according to their plausibility. The plausibility ranking can change with new information.

Principle of charity   the guiding principle in paraphrasing. This principle tells us to give a passage the most plausible paraphrase the context will allow.

Rival conclusion   a different conclusion to the same argument. Rival conclusions must answer the implicit question and must be mutually exclusive. (That is, they can't give overlapping answers to the I.Q.)

Semantic incompatibility   when two statements contradict one another.

Sincerity step   See **Testimony.**

Testimony (argument)   a diagnostic inductive argument using someone's statement as trace data. Testimony can be broken up into two steps to enable us to consider the author's sincerity separately from his or her competence. (There is a useful schema for testimony arguments on pages 172–73 and a testimony checklist on page 175, both should be memorized).

Trace data   in a diagnostic inductive argument, support that is part of, or a trace of, what happened and hence is something explained by the rival conclusions.

Appendix

= A =

FURTHER ISSUES FROM SCIENCE

The following three news service articles all appeared before the one discussed in Chapter 4. They are presented here in chronological order. As you read them, try to characterize what is going on diagnostically. Note the various rivals that are advanced and the bits of information that are offered as trace and background. Observe particularly which rivals are helped or hurt by the non-trace data, which traces are explanatory hurdles, and how the proponents of a rival try to explain away its hurdles.

1.   New Theory Offered on Death of Dinosaurs

Robert Strand

A team of scientists is proposing that dinosaurs were wiped out 65 million years ago by a spectacular collision of Earth with an asteroid that cast the globe into several years of dust-choked semi-darkness.

This new hypothesis would explain why 75 percent of all living species disappeared at the same time. The idea was advanced Friday at the annual meeting of the American Association for the Advancement of Science.

The most common explanation for the global catastrophe has been that water retreating from the continental shelves caused climatic changes to which the dinosaurs could not adjust.

A recent theory suggests that the climatic changes were caused by a massive invasion of fresh water from the Arctic Basin into the oceans.

But Dale A. Russell, a Canadian paleontologist, told a symposium that no physical evidence exists to support the notion of sharp temperature declines.

The new hypothesis was explained by Luiz W. Alvarez, a Nobel laureate physicist at the University of California. His team has been pondering mysterious deposits of a rare element, iridium, at sites in Denmark, Italy and Spain.

The iridium was laid down in limestone at the exact time of the dinosaurs' demise, and the iridium concentration was 160 times what might have been expected.

Iridium is a thousand times more abundant in meteorites than in the Earth's crust, a fact that suggests the deposits came from an extraterrestrial source.

Alvarez proposed that Earth was struck by an asteroid six miles in diameter that blasted a crater 100 miles wide with the force of 100 million hydrogen bombs.

Such an explosion would have thrown an enormous quantity of dust into the stratosphere where, according to the hypothesis, it remained for several years casting Earth into semidarkness.

Lack of sunlight would have killed plankton in the ocean and plants on land, thus depriving fish and animals of food. Russell concluded from evidence in fossils that 75 percent of all living species, including the dinosaurs, the most intelligent creatures of the time, became extinct.

2.   How Dinosaurs Disappeared from the Earth Again Disputed

Jack Schreibman

BERKELEY—The academic battle over the demise of Earth's dinosaurs is headed for another skirmish as one of the world's leading fossil experts argues the prehistoric beasts died out gradually, and were not annihilated by a sudden, "catastrophic" event.

Paleontology Professor William A. Clemens of the University of California at Berkeley said in an interview that 10 years' research at a Montana fossil site convinces him that the largest creatures ever to walk the Earth became extinct after a cooling period of five million to seven million years.

Clemens, a curator of the Museum of Paleontology at the university, said his view of dinosaur extinction was developed at a site in eastern Montana known as "Bug Creek."

"We've got the most refined record of what happened at that time of any place in the world," Clemens said. "We've got one window to see what happened in a global situation. . . . What we see through our 'window' suggests gradual change" for the immense reptiles that ruled the planet for more than 150 million years.

Clemens presented a paper on his views yesterday at the annual meeting of the Society of Vertebrate Paleontology.

His hypothesis collides with another, backed mainly by geologists, that contends a great earth-girdling cloud of dust was raised by an extraterrestrial body smashing into Earth. The cloud so changed the environment that dinosaurs vanished in the relatively short span—from a few years to over a few thousand years.

Geology professor Walter Alvarez, also of UC-Berkeley, believes a space-born catastrophe killed off the dinosaurs. The theory stems largely from the discovery of iridium in rocks formed during the Cretaceous–Tertiary boundary period, around the time when the dinosaurs disappeared. Iridium is found in asteroids.

Alvarez and others argue that an asteroid smashing into Earth would have hurled so much dust into the atmosphere that the sun would have been blotted out, causing a temporary collapse of the food chain.

In March, Alvarez wrote in *Science* magazine, "We have an enormous amount of evidence showing that an asteroid or comet hit the earth 65 million years ago . . . and was in some way responsible for the extinction of the dinosaurs, and many other kinds of animals and plants."

Clemens says that theory fails to explain the survival of so many other species, including fish, lizards and turtles, and the early ancestors of today's mammals.

"The asteroid hypothesis," said Clemens, "calls for such severe changes in the environment in a matter of a few days, months or years . . . you just expect other kinds of animals to almost totally go extinct. . . . There would have been devastation in the (geological) record, and there isn't."

Alvarez said Thursday he supports the catastrophe theory today more strongly than he did when it surfaced four years ago, and he is convinced "that an impact did occur."

Alvarez said the material his colleague used is not new.

"Bill Clemens appears to be using the same information available (to him) in 1980. . . . I don't see anything new," he said.

Clemens said only two kinds of animals actually died out in the period—dinosaurs and flying reptiles. Marsupials almost became extinct.

Clemens said his evidence indicates the cooling of the Earth, because of the drying of climate-tempering inland seas, forced dinosaurs into devastating migrations, in a futile search for territory and food.

"You get plenty of evidence of extinction from contraction of the ranges, and these big dinosaurs probably needed large areas to maintain the population of the various species," said Clemens.

Clemens suggested it is possible that plant-eating dinosaurs starved because of insufficient food to maintain their huge bodies, and flesh-eating dinosaurs, which dined on them, consequently also perished.

3.   Researchers Debate Cause of Dinosaurs' Extinction

Lee Siegel
Associated Press

SAN FRANCISCO—Scientists debated yesterday the mystery of what killed the dinosaurs, offering conflicting new evidence against the usual suspects: comets, volcanoes, a death star, acid rain and gradual mass extinction.

Dartmouth College geologist Charles Officer said his latest studies of mineral deposits suggest global volcanic activity lasting perhaps 100,000 years—not comets smashing into Earth—killed the dinosaurs and a third to a half of all other organisms 65 million years ago.

"The effects of this intense volcanism would be global cooling, intense acid rain and increased ultraviolet radiation," Officer said during the American Geophysical Union's fall meeting.

"These effects would produce the selective extinctions," both by directly killing exposed animals and by destroying many of the plants they ate, he said.

But Frank Kyte, of the geophysics institute at the University of California at Los Angeles, argued such huge volcanic events were "very improbable" and much of the evidence supports the comet or "asteroid impact theory."

The debate, attended by 500 scientists, reflected an ongoing controversy over whether volcanoes or comets disrupted the climate, oceans and food supply to wipe out dinosaurs, many plants and ocean-surface organisms, even though mammals, birds and ocean-bottom organisms survived.

Some believe either a comet shower or volcanoes would have kicked up enough dust and smoke to plunge Earth into a cold darkness to cause the mass extinction.

However, William Clemens, a University of California at Berkeley paleontologist, said the recent discovery of dinosaur fossils in Alaska shows the creatures could survive in cold, dark conditions.

Scientists on both sides also believe many life forms were killed by strong acid rain, created by either comets or volcanoes.

But Massachusetts Institute of Technology meteorologist Ronald Prinn said his studies show only comet showers could produce acid rain strong enough to cause extinctions.

There also was debate over whether mass extinctions occurred regularly during Earth's history. If they did, it is possible because a so-called "death star" periodically passed through a cloud of comets surrounding the solar system, disturbing their orbits and sending deadly showers of comets toward Earth.

Critics of that theory have argued extinctions did not occur regularly. But Piet Hut, a Princeton University astronomer, said the death star's own orbit could have been altered by other stars.

Clemens said the mass extinction 65 million years ago did not claim its victims simultaneously, suggesting sustained volcanic activity, not a sudden comet impact, was responsible.

Hut replied that new calculations suggest comet showers.

The following articles are not related to the dinosaur controversy. They raise a variety of interesting points. Try to characterize what is going on in them diagnostically.

4.   3.1-Mile Hole Planned for Quake Research

Associated Press

SAN BERNARDINO—Geologists begin drilling the nation's deepest hole for research purposes on the San Andreas Fault today, hoping to unlock some secrets of the formation that has caused many of California's worst earthquakes.

Using a rig that required 70 trucks to carry, the geologists will drill a 3.1-mile hole in an effort to solve a fundamental mystery: If there is friction along a fault, why isn't there also heat?

The hole also will serve as an "ultraquiet observatory" to monitor seismic activity at the fault, according to Mark Zoback, professor of geophysics at Stanford University, who conceived the project.

The plan, funded by the National Science Foundation, calls for drilling nearly two miles into granite to extend an existing 1.2-mile borehole near the fault at Cajon Pass.

Researchers particularly hope to resolve the "stress–heat flow paradox," an apparent contradiction between faulting theory, stress measurements and thermal observations at the fault.

At the San Andreas fault, where the Pacific and North American plates are slipping past each other at a rate of 1.2 inches a year, frictional resistance should generate significant amounts of heat, according to fault theory and laboratory measurements, Zoback said.

Yet more than 100 temperature measurements taken near the fault show no frictional heating.

The experiment also will provide information on the effect of earthquakes in the fault zone and may help long-term earthquake prediction, Zoback said.

Earthquakes occur when the earth's brittle outer layer moves suddenly—up to 10 yards at once—to catch up with the more gradual motion of the lower layers.

5.   Researchers Find Evidence of 1812 Quake

                              Doug Beeman
                            Press-Enterprise

SANTA BARBARA—The San Andreas Fault ruptured in a devastating earthquake near Wrightwood in 1812, but scientists say the finding raises more questions than it answers about Southern California's earthquake patterns.

"We're raising the uncertainty of our knowledge," said Gordon Jacoby, a scientist with the Lamont–Doherty Geological Observatory at Columbia University in New York.

Historical accounts recorded several earthquakes in Southern California in 1812, including one on Dec. 8 that caused a part of a mission to collapse at San Juan Capistrano.

Scientists had assumed that the Dec. 8 earthquake occurred along a fault near the coast of Southern California because most of the reports of the earthquake came from areas near the coast.

But Jacoby and two other scientists—P. R. Sheppard of Columbia University and Kerry Sieh of California Institute of Technology—now believe that earthquake occurred along the San Andreas Fault. They base that conclusion on tree ring cores taken near Wrightwood.

The 5-millimeter cores of older trees near the San Andreas Fault show wide bands of growth through the year 1812. The following year, and for many years after that, the tree rings are bunched closed together, suggesting a "long and painful recovery for the tree," Jacoby said.

Jacoby said scientists took core samples from enough trees to conclude the sudden drop in growth was caused by a devastating earthquake.

The findings were made public yesterday at the annual meeting of the Seismological Society of America at the University of California, Santa Barbara.

Jacoby said a similar drop in tree growth is observed in the tree rings after 1857, when the San Andreas ruptured in a devastating earthquake between Parkfield in Monterey County and the Cajon Pass.

Jacoby and Sieh said they also have found much sketchier tree ring evidence of the 1812 San Andreas earthquake.

Sieh, who has done extensive research into the rate at which earthquakes occur along the San Andreas Fault, said the tree rings could indicate that the fault ruptured along the very southernmost portion above San Bernardino and through the San Gorgonio Pass. Scientists have said the southernmost portion of the San Andreas may be ready to rupture in a major earthquake, based on the belief that the last such earthquake occurred in early 1700s.

But Sieh also said the finding could mean that the section of the San Andreas from the Cajon Pass to Central California breaks in a much more irregular way than previously believed.

Another theory is that great earthquakes along the San Andreas occur in clusters, Sieh said. By putting the location of the 1812 earthquake along the San Andreas Fault, it may mean that the granddaddy of California's seismic faults ruptured in three great earthquakes within 100 years of each other—1812, 1857 and the 1906 San Francisco earthquake.

6.   Fallen Meteor Supports Theory of How Life Began

Associated Press

PASADENA—Analysis of a meteorite that fell on Australia in 1969 supports a hotly debated theory that the chemical building blocks of life on Earth came from deep interstellar space, a scientist said yesterday.

Researchers long have known that meteorites, including one that fell near Murchison, Australia, 18 years ago, contain amino acids, which are organic chemicals needed for the formation of life.

But many scientists argue that the chemical building blocks of life already were available on Earth after its formation 4.6 billion years ago, and there was at most a negligible contribution from meteorites or asteroids that struck the planet.

Scientists at the California Institute of Technology and Arizona State University analyzed the hydrogen in amino acids and fragments of such acids taken from a sample of the Murchison meteorite. They found unusually high levels of a heavy form of hydrogen named deuterium.

Because deuterium is rare on Earth but much more common in gas clouds in interstellar space, the analysis suggests the amino acids, or at least the simpler organic chemicals that formed them, came from space beyond our solar system, said Caltech geochemist Samuel Epstein, principal author of the study.

If these building blocks of life were present not only on Earth or in space within our infant solar system but in space between the stars, the chemicals might also have been "a possible source of life in other solar systems."

Epstein said his study was published in April in *Nature*, a British science journal.

7.   Moon Formed in 24 Hours, Computer Figures

C. Eugene Emery, Jr.
Providence Journal

Using one of the nation's most powerful computers, researchers in Massachusetts and New Mexico have found evidence that the moon was created when an object the size of Mars struck a blow against Earth 4.5 billion years ago.

The computer simulations have shown that the cataclysmic encounter created the moon in less than 24 hours.

If true, the discovery would explain the differences in composition between Earth and its moon, and explain why the moon is so large compared with its parent body.

The discovery coincides with new evidence that has cast serious doubts on the three traditional theories of the moon's formation.

One previous idea was that the moon came from the same material that created Earth. According to this concept, Earth began spinning rapidly when it was still molten, its spin fast enough to make a ring of material form around the planet. That material then condensed to form the moon.

But scientists have always had trouble explaining how our planet could have begun to spin so rapidly and then slow down so dramatically after the chunk of material was flung into orbit. In addition, the theory could not explain why the moon's orbit is not in line with Earth's equator.

A second theory was that the moon was formed elsewhere and was captured by Earth's gravity.

But test rocks brought from the moon by the Apollo astronauts showed that Earth and the moon have similar ratios of three types of oxygen (oxygen-16, oxygen-17 and oxygen-18), which is strong evidence that both bodies formed at the same spot in the solar system.

The third theory, given the most weight in the past and seemingly supported by the oxygen measurements, was that Earth and the moon formed together, much as double star systems form elsewhere in the galaxy.

That theory has not been able to explain everything.

One problem has been that Earth and its moon contain vastly different amounts of iron, something you would not expect if the two bodies had formed side by side. A little over 30 percent of Earth's mass is composed of iron, an amount slightly higher than the ratio found in meteorites. By comparison, less than 2 percent of the moon is made of iron.

The moon also seems to be deficient in many of the lighter elements common on Earth.

The reason scientists could not choose among the three competing theories, said A. G. W. Cameron of the Harvard–Smithsonian Center for Astrophysics in Cambridge, Mass., "turns out to be because none of them are correct."

The theory that the moon was formed by a collision—which Cameron refers to as the "big splash" theory—was first formally proposed in 1975 by William Hartmann and Donald Davis of the Planetary Science Institute in Tucson. The main reason it was popular was that the old theories had too many flaws.

The new evidence for the impact theory comes in computer simulations done by the Cray XMP supercomputer at the Los Alamos National Laboratory in New Mexico. The XMP is capable of doing up to 400 million calculations each second.

A supercomputer was needed because the researchers had to calculate the gravitational interaction of just over 3,000 individual particles used to make up Earth and the Mars-sized object. Because every particle has a gravitational attraction to each of the other 2,999 particles, each step in the simulation required about 5 billion calculations. It took the computer about 20 hours to do each simulation.

Only when the researchers ran the simulation with a mass of 14 percent did a moon-sized object evolve with all the right characteristics.

Scientists think the collision occurred 50 million to 100 million years after Earth started to form, when the planet was still molten and some large objects left over from the creation process continued to roam the solar system.

Here is what they think happened:

As the Mars-sized object, traveling at 23,760 miles per hour, passed near Earth, the interaction of gravity pulled the two objects even closer together.

One minute and thirteen seconds later, the object has begun to deform, with some of its surface material beginning to hit Earth's molten surface. The grazing impact comes minutes later.

At eleven minutes after the initial encounter, a massive chunk of Earth's outer layer has been carved away and nearly half of the Mars-sized object has been sheared off by the impact, creating 5,000-degree temperatures.

Twenty-six minutes later, an observer standing on Earth's surface would have seen a wall of granite and iron rising 8,000 miles into the heavens as the remains of the object stream off into space and swing around the planet.

Over the next half hour, much of the lighter material begins to fall back to Earth. The iron core of the object, now separated from the lighter material, remains intact, orbiting the planet. But it doesn't remain in orbit for long.

An hour and eight minutes later, the iron has coalesced into a single chunk and begins falling toward Earth, striking the planet four hours after the initial encounter.

Fifteen hours later, what's left in orbit falls together to form a molten mass destined to become our moon.

Appendix

= B =

ANSWERS TO EVEN-NUMBERED EXERCISES

CHAPTER 1

2. b. [It is useful to treat the second part of this exercise first.] This article is hard to paraphrase because there is some tension between the first two paragraphs. The first (abetted by the headline) seems to question *whether* alcohol has a beneficial effect; the second grants the good effect and says the question raised is with our understanding of its mechanism. To include both points charitably requires downplaying the tension and perhaps employing some ambiguity of expression.

   a. A paraphrase meeting this condition would be something like this:

   > A study has found alcohol to have no effect on a particular blood protein, which raises some questions about alcohol's beneficial effect on the cardiovascular system.

   This paraphrase is complex enough that it might better be rendered as a main point and a secondary one.

   Main Point: A study has found that the healthier hearts of moderate consumers of alcohol are not due to alcohol's stimulating the production of a cholesterol-fighting protein, as was previously thought.

   Secondary Point: Alcohol is not a substitute for exercise.

   c. The substance of the article is arguably exhausted by the main point above. We may omit the motherly advice as being the product of journalistic condescension: The writer did not want to appear to encourage alcohol consumption.

4. a. S_1 Both pilots unemotionally acknowledged the presence of another plane.

S_2 There was plenty of time between acknowledgment and collision to allow them to avoid each other.

S_3 Neither made any attempt to avoid collision.

C   A third plane near the two rapidly approaching aircraft was situated so that each pilot thought *it* represented the danger to be avoided, but clearly it represented a threat to neither plane.

b. S_1 Ivan Potter's car crashed through a freeway guardrail and rolled into the adjoining field.

S_2 Examination of Ivan's corpse at the crash site revealed no broken bones or external injuries.

C   The crash occurred because Ivan had died at the wheel.

c. This passage registers an objection and makes a threat, but contains no argument: Nothing is offered in support of anything else.

d. S_1 Most of what AJS imports are fountain pens.

S_2 Every fountain pen imported by AJS is defective.

S_3 Most of what AJS imports is from China.

C   At least one fountain pen from China is defective.

e. (Charitable reconstruction)

S_1 For president, there is little reason to prefer any one of the major-party candidates to the others.

S_2 A "none-of-the-above" space on the ballot would allow people to participate in an election and express their opinion without flattering some candidate with a least-of-evils vote.

C   The ballot should contain a "none-of-the-above" space.

6. S₁ A badly beaten body was found in the library at midnight.

S₂ The butler was seen sneaking out of the library just before midnight.

S₃ When interviewed by a police investigator later that night, the butler appeared frightened and gave an implausible account of bloodstains on his cuff.

C   The butler did it.

8. The first thing to do is read the article to get a sense of its conclusion. Here it jumps right out at you: Holding a president to a single six-year term (hereafter, SSYT) is a bad idea and should not be adopted. This conclusion will guide our paraphrasing and schematizing.

Next, letter the paragraphs and briefly paraphrase the substance of each as it bears on the above conclusion. (In the following list, explanatory commentary is added where it might be helpful, but the commentary is not part of the paraphrase.)

a. Introduction. (Comment: The first paragraph merely explains that the issue is important, so nothing in this paragraph will appear directly in the paraphrase.)

b. Bell and Connally have proposed SSYT.

c. It has been proposed many times before.

d. Something must be wrong with it for it to have failed so many times.

e. SSYT is worth reconsidering only because of the eminence of Bell and Connally.

f. One reason offered for SSYT is that it would improve administration by decreasing the distraction of politics.

g. Another, related reason is that depoliticizing the presidency would increase general confidence in government.

h. The reasons offered in paragraphs f and g assume that re-election politics demeans the presidency and undercuts a president's leadership.

i. (i) The assumption in paragraph h is false.

   (ii) SSYT would decrease a president's accountability for his acts. (Comment: "Not increase" here is sarcastic. If SSYT merely left accountability alone it would not be worth mentioning. Broder quite understandably takes the decrease to be partly obvious, and his concern with it surfaces again in paragraph k.)

j. (i) Shortening its maximum term would (probably harmfully) shorten an administration's planning focus.

   (ii) Removing it from politics would reduce its influence with Congress.

k. Removing a president from politics would encourage him to ignore public opinion.

l. Broder's summary, with conclusion explicitly restated.

To organize all this into a schematic picture, it helps to pull the points together under general headings. Most of the column is devoted to rejecting proponents' claims for SSYT. These fall naturally under two headings: efficiency and confidence. If we call these S_1 and S_2, Broder's accountability point is S_4 and the historical observation in paragraphs c and d is S_5. Schematically,

S_1 SSYT would damage a president's ability to administer by reducing his influence with Congress and shortening his planning focus.

S_2 SSYT would reduce confidence in government by making it easy for a president to ignore public opinion.

S_3 SSYT would reduce a president's accountability for his policies and actions.

S_4 SSYT has been rejected dozens of times before.

C   SSYT is a bad idea.

We may now account for each paragraph as follows:

S_1 is j(i) and j(ii), but laces together the content of f, h, and i(i) as well.

S_2 represents k and i(i), but does so by way of g, h, and i(ii) as well.

S_3 is k and i(ii).

S_4 uses most of e and d.

C is the rest of d, restated in l.

This omits a, b, e, and part of l. But that is just as we should expect, since they fall into clear padding categories. a, b, and e are introductory, and the omitted part of l restates generally the thrust of what has gone before.

10. S_1 The cost of the damage and injury caused by uninsured motorists is unfairly borne by those who carry insurance, by way of the higher premiums they must pay.

(Comment: Note that charity requires toning down derisive exaggerations like *scofflaw, contemptuous,* and *deadbeats*.)

12. a. Conclusion: The dogs were set on Dorsey for fighting practice. (Note: "Dorsey feels that . . ." is not part of the conclusion; he is not trying to support a claim about his feelings.)

   b. The dogs attacked, backed away, looked toward the school as though responding to somebody there, and attacked again. (Note: This is far stronger than saying merely that Dorsey got the feeling that somebody was directing them. Charity requires the stronger formulation.)

   c. The dogs were terriers, the type used in dog fighting.

   d. S_1 Dorsey was attacked by two terriers of the type used in dog fighting.

      S_2 After attacking, they backed off, looked toward a nearby school as though responding to somebody, and then attacked again.

      C The dogs were set on Dorsey for fighting practice.

(Comment: From the conclusion Dorsey drew, it is even plausible to suppose he recognized the dogs as fighting terriers. So this schematization is not absurdly charitable.)

14. a. S_1 Differences in size, handling, and braking make the separation of car and truck traffic important to safety.

   S_2 Trucks guzzle fuel at higher speeds.

   ....

   C   Freeway fast lanes should be reserved for cars.

   b. First paragraph: The first sentence is C; the rest is padding (introduction and context setting).

   Second paragraph: Elaboration of C.

   Third paragraph: The first sentence is a quick synopsis of S_1 and S_2. The next sentence is padding (useful aside). The rest is an elaboration of S_1.

   Fourth paragraph: The first sentence is S_2. The second is padding (illustration). The third is a restatement of C.

CHAPTER 2

2. a. Deductive.

   b. The most natural recasting is simply to drop the insupportably general S_2.

   S_1 All the important economic indicators are good.

   ===

   C   The short-run future of the economy is rosy.

   c. Such an item of information from the past destroys the support offered by the deductive casting: It shows that S_2 is false, and a deductive argument with false support provides its conclusion with no support at all. On the other hand, economic indicators can by themselves provide strong inductive support for a projection even if they are right only most of the time. So a single exception will affect the strength of their support hardly at all.

4. a. Inductive.

   b. This one's easy to get out of. A lurid scandal could hurt Dilworth's popularity so badly that the outnumbered Democrats could defeat him; or another very popular Republican, running as an independent, could draw off enough votes to cause a non-Republican to be elected. Anything like this could defeat Dilworth without giving up anything in the support.

c. and d.

(i) You might make it deductive, as we have before, by adding the recursive generalization:

   S_2 When a Republican runs in an overwhelmingly Republican district, which has elected only Republicans for years, he (or she) always wins.

But this is certainly false, and since the inductive version is actually pretty strong, it is clearly preferable to this recasting.

(ii) You might try something subtler.

   S_2 Whenever this (S_1) is the case, only a lurid scandal can prevent Dilworth's victory.

   S_3 There will not be a lurid scandal.

But again, S_2 is false.

(iii) You might try adding to the list of things that could defeat Dilworth (death, competing Republicans, apocalypse), and then ruling all of them out in S_3. But the list would be very long, and hard to complete, so instead you might try to come up with a summary characterization.

S_2 Whenever this (S_1) is the case, only something weird or unusual can prevent Dilworth's election.

S_3 Nothing weird or unusual will happen.

Adding these two support claims to S_1, we get a deductive argument closer in plausibility to the inductive one. Still, the plausibility of S_2 depends on what we count as "weird" and "unusual." A competing Republican may be neither. As usual, much effort and imagination is required to create a semantic trap that even approaches the plausibility of the corresponding inductive argument.

6. S_1 The jury deadlocked 11–1 for conviction.

   S_2 One juror was consistently late.

   S_3 He referred to witnesses who did not testify.

   S_4 He did not believe officers.

   C The mistrial was due to one juror's making up his mind before deliberations.

   a. Inductive. There is obviously no semantic conflict between the aberrant juror's behavior and his voting for acquittal. S_1, S_2, and S_3 might have been due to bad bus connections, a bad memory and a traumatic arrest, respectively. Moreover, the possibility that the lone dissenter made up his mind *during* deliberations is also compatible with the support.

   b. and c. The only easy way to make this deductive is to add the following recursive generalization:

   S_5 Whenever a one-vote mistrial occurs after a consistently late juror, who disbelieves officers, refers to non-testifying witnesses, the mistrial is due to a juror making up his (or her) mind before deliberations.

   S_5 is clearly silly, so the inductive casting, which provides at least some ground for the conclusion, is stronger.

8. S_1 Two dogs attacked Dorsey, backed off, looked toward a nearby school as though responding to somebody, and then attacked again.

   C The dogs were set on Dorsey for fighting practice.

   a. The argument is obviously inductive, because so many other possibilities are compatible with Dorsey's description of what happened. The dogs might have been momentarily distracted by something at the school that had nothing to do with fighting practice; or they might really have been responding to somebody, say, a terrified owner who had lost control of them and was trying to dissuade them without exposing himself to wrath and lawsuit. And so on.

c. and d. To rule out all these possibilities semantically, we would have to add a generalization like the following:

S_2 When dogs behave as Dorsey describes, it has always been the case that they were set on the victim for fighting practice.

Since S_2 is certainly false (a single case in which dogs behaved as described, but were not using their victim for fighting practice, would refute it), the inductive formulation, as modest as it is, will provide Dorsey's conclusion with greater support.

10. [See Ch. 1, answer 6, above, for schematization.]
   a. Who committed the murder? (Note: This question obviously might be relaxed in the course of McSweet's investigation, but that it was murder is clearly presupposed in the passage.)
   b. Inductive. The butler can get out of it in a multitude of ways without contradicting the support, though most of the ways will be implausible. Both the blood on his cuff and his nervousness may have been due to a different murder he's hoping McSweet won't discover. Leaving the scene of the other murder, he ducks into the library when he hears someone coming—only to find another body. When all seems clear he tries to sneak out of the library unnoticed, but he is observed.
   c. and d. The only readily accessible deduction would employ the recursive general premise:

S_4 Whenever a butler is seen sneaking out of a room in which a brutally murdered body is soon to be found, implausibly explains a blood stained cuff, and is nervous under police questioning: the butler is the murderer.

This, of course, is a pointlessly risky thing to add to the support package. The inductive rendering captures our reason to suspect the butler far better than anything with S_4 in it.

12. a. C_2 Johnny's breathing difficulty was due to an allergy to dogs, and his dog died while he was in the hospital.

   C_3 The difficulty in Johnny's lung was due to some other obstruction, which came out with the brick.

(Note: C_1, "Johnny was faking asthma for sympathy," is not a rival if we keep the implicit question.)

b. and c. These are both pointedly compatible with the support, which shows that the argument is inductive.

d. and e. We can make the argument deductive by adding the following:

> S_4 When a long-standing breathing difficulty clears up soon after a toy brick—which had been in the victim's lung for some time—is removed, it is clear that the difficulty was due to the brick.

S_4 is actually fairly plausible, due to its narrow focus: It applies to very few cases. Nevertheless, the inductive version of the argument better represents the evidence package. First of all, the inductive argument is *very* strong, so there is little to be gained by any recasting. But more importantly, S_4 seriously misrepresents our understanding of the matter. We know there are other possibilities that cannot be ruled out categorically (as S_4 does). We understand the strength of the case because we understand how implausible are the ways out of the conclusion, given the data. The plausibility of S_4 depends on how many similar cases there have been (and will be). This is something we do not know and need not discover to evaluate this argument.

14. S_1 Kaussen's death was by hanging.

S_2 Authorities have ruled out foul play.

S_3 Kaussen was in financial trouble.

S_4 He had been acting strangely.

C   Kaussen committed suicide.

a. How did Gunter Kaussen die?

b. (i) Kaussen hanged himself by accident.

(ii) Kaussen was murdered (by being hanged).
(Note: Foul play [e.g., murder] is not eliminated *semantically* by the authorities' finding. Death by anything other than hanging conflicts with S_1, however.)

c. Kaussen was poisoned (the hanging was faked).

d. The fact that b has an answer shows that the argument is inductive: There are rival conclusions that are compatible with the support.

16. a. S_1 Skeleton of URMM was found hanging over the door of a wrecked car at the bottom of the cliff.

    S_2 He had been missing for six months.

    S_3 Crash site is far enough from habitation for crash to have gone unseen and unheard.

    C   URMM died in an automobile accident.

(Alternate formulation of C: URMM died when his car left the road and went over a cliff. Being more specific, this would expand the list of rivals somewhat and yield a different exercise.)

b. C_2 URMM was murdered, put in his car, and the car pushed over the cliff.

    C_3 URMM died when he slipped and fell down the cliff and got tangled up in an old car wreck.

    C_4 (Borderline case) URMM committed suicide by driving off the cliff. (You might want to say this is a rival because it shows that the incident was no accident. Nevertheless, it is a perfectly good idiom to say that a certain percentage of traffic accidents are suicides; that is, traffic accidents don't have to be accidental. So there are pulls in both directions.)

c. How did URMM die?

d. (What we need here are cases in which URMM did not die in the crash.

    C_5 URMM died at the wheel (and then went over the cliff).

    C_6 URMM survived the crash but was incapacitated and died of exposure (or animal attack, etc.).

(Note that C_4 fits about as well or as badly here as it does in b.)

    e. All the rivals offered above are compatible with the support.

    f. The argument is inductive.

18. a. The question addressed in the next-to-last paragraph is some version of "Why weren't the flaps and slats deployed?"

    b. The three rivals mentioned are these:

       (i) The flaps and slats were not deployed because the crew decided they were not needed.

      (ii) They were not deployed because the crew forgot about them.

     (iii) They were not deployed because of a mechanical malfunction—one possibly overlooked on the preflight check.

    c. This last rival, (iii), seems to suggest two distinct possibilities:

       (i) A mechanical malfunction with some sign or manifestation that would have alerted the crew, had they noticed it.

      (ii) One with no such warning manifestation.

    d. (i) This short paragraph suggests that we allow the possibility that the data recorder's indication was wrong. The most idiomatic way to expand the I.Q. to cover this possibility would be this:

        Why were the flaps and slats not deployed, or, at least, why did they appear not to have been?

      (ii) Any rival that explains the reading as being due to a malfunctioning data recorder would be acceptable.

CHAPTER 3

2. a. What happened to the missing sheets?

    b. C_1 The teaching assistants lost them.

    c. C_2 Some (enough) students took more than one from the stack.

       C_3 Some sheets spontaneously disintegrated.

    d. The original argument is not sound, because another rival is more plausible on the information given.

e. After class, a number of homework sheets are found blowing around on the lawn between the philosophy department office and the classroom. The new ranking would be

C_1

C_2

C_3

4. a. C_1 Sweden's nationwide inspection program has increased vehicle life in that country.

 b. One good rival would be

 C_2 Advances in rustproofing techniques have been responsible for the increased vehicle life in Sweden.

 c. It is very hard to say, which means it is not *clearly* sound, for there are so many factors that could have had an impact: Besides rustproofing technology, changes in snow-removal procedure, escalating costs of new cars, and the price of fuel could change things enough to account for a difference of a few years. It nevertheless seems plausible to suppose the inspection program had some impact.

6. a. S_1 The scoop arm of *Viking I* stopped responding to commands during a series of operations on the surface of Mars.

 S_2 When a simulator on Earth performed the same sequence of operations, its arm was jammed by a pin.

 S_3 A simple operation caused the simulator's pin to fall out.

 S_4 When *Viking I* was instructed to perform the same simple operation, the arm again functioned normally.

 S_5 A television camera on *Viking I* subsequently spotted, on the ground below, a pin just like the one that had jammed the simulator arm.

 == d

 C_1 The scoop arm on *Viking I* had been jammed by a pin.

 b. C_2 The arm stopped against a martian boulder (not visible on TV), which was later nudged out of the way by the arm or moved by a marsquake or some such thing.

        C_3 A Martian was just having fun with the lander and grabbed the arm, holding it still until it stopped struggling.

  c. C_1

      C_2

      C_3

  d. S_6 Earlier videotape shows that the pin was on the ground before the scoop malfunctioned.

  e. S_7 When *Viking I* is returned to Earth the pin is still in place, and dirty scrapes and gouges are found on the arm just where a boulder might have jammed it.

  f. C_2

      C_1

      C_3

8. a. C_1 Studying longer will not improve your grades very much.

    (Alternative formulation: The amount of time you study does not have much effect on your grade.)

  b. Several studies have found that students reporting long hours of study have grade point averages only slightly higher than those reporting much less time studying.
(Alternative formulation: Several studies have found very little correlation between G.P.A. and reported study time.)

  c. (Note: Rivals must be incompatible with C_1; so they must explain why the studies show so little variation of G.P.A. with study time, in spite of the fact that study time *does* have a substantial impact on grades.)

      C_2 Smart students (or well-organized ones) need to study less to reach a certain G.P.A. than those who are less smart (or less well-organized).

      C_3 Students taking harder courses need more study time to attain a certain G.P.A. than those taking easier courses.

  d. It may be that students systematically misrepresent their study time. (Incomprehension, e.g., may make study time seem longer than it really is; or poor students may be embarrassed by how little they study and so exaggerate when asked.)

   e. Why do grades change so little with such large differences in reported study time?

10. a. It was a suicide.

   b. C_2 She was unintentionally killed during a mugging in a nearby town, and her body was dumped where it was found. Her car was stolen by the muggers, who happened to be involved in a flaming crash, just up the embankment from where they dumped the body.

     C_3 At night, and in the fog, she was unable to see how steep the embankment was; so when she stepped over the guard rail in her attempt to flee the developing inferno, she stepped off into space.

   c. Their inference is not sound.

12. a. A change in the preoccupations of recent college graduates he has interviewed.

   b. The materialism implicit in television advertising.

   c. The number of hours the average household watches TV, the years during which TV began to saturate American life, and the nature of TV advertising.

   d. S_1 About 1975 the central preoccupation of American college graduates in job interviews shifted from the nature of the job itself to pay and benefits.

     S_2 Starting about 1975, college graduates had lived from infancy in households dominated by TV.

     S_3 The empty materialism of TV advertising overemphasizes rewards, breaking the connection with the work necessary to get them.

————————————————————————————— d

     C   Television has had an unhealthy effect on the way American college graduates think about work.

(Comment: Obviously, many variations on this schema are possible. The point of each would be to show Garrett marshaling some background information to help his conclusion explain a particular trace.)

14. a. (i)   That the jaw of a European rat and the tooth of a Euro-
              pean pig were found together on the north coast of Haiti.

    (ii)   That charcoal in a typically European well on the same
           site was dated to the late fifteenth century.

    (iii) The strontium level in the tooth.

  b. C_1 The site was the location of a fort built by Columbus after
             the *Santa Maria* ran aground in 1492.

  c. C_2 The site was occupied by some other early Spanish
             explorers.

     C_3 The traces came from several different episodes, including
             later Spanish imports.

     C_4 Archaeological hoax.

  d. The fact that the pig grew up in Spain: It explains the stron-
     tium level in the tooth, and it is explained by the researchers'
     hypothesis about the site.

  e. The main argument is this:

     S_1 The jaw of a European rat and the tooth of a European pig,
             both unknown in Haiti before Columbus' arrival, were
             found together on the north coast of that country.

     S_2 Charcoal in a European-style well on the same site was
             dated to the late fifteenth century.

     S_3 The pig grew up in Spain (near Seville).

     S_4 The *Santa Maria* ran aground somewhere in the West
             Indies in 1492, and records have Columbus building a fort
             on land nearby.

     S_5 Columbus sailed from a port in Spain (near Seville).

     == d

     C_1 The site in question is where Columbus built his fort.

     The tributary argument is this:

     S_6 Strontium in the bones and teeth of a plant-eating ani-
             mal reflects the composition of the soil where the animal
             grew up.

S_7 The strontium level in the pig's tooth matches that in the soil near Seville, Spain.

─────────────────────────────── d

S_3 The pig grew up in Spain (near Seville).

So the overall structure would be

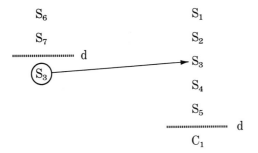

f. Non-trace data are the following:
   (i) That the rat and the pig in question were unknown in the New World before Columbus' arrival there.
   (ii) The *Santa Maria* grounding story.
   (iii) That Columbus sailed from a port near Seville.
   (iv) That strontium in teeth and bones reflects soil composition.
   (Note that much else is presupposed, but not offered explicitly as data.)
   So S_1, S_4, S_5, and S_6 contain non-trace data.

16. a. Rivals:

   C_2 Neither pilot took seriously the warning about another plane; each issued a perfunctory acknowledgement to placate the ground controllers.

   C_3 The pilots were, with calm determination, settling a long-standing grudge in an aeronautic joust.

   C_4 The controls of both planes were mysteriously locked, but both pilots happened to have extremely impassive personalities.

   C_5 There was a third plane, but only one of the pilots saw it, and he mistook it for the one he was to avoid. The other pilot was an abject incompetent who wouldn't have recognized an imminent collision with the earth itself and whose calm acknowledgement merely signaled stupefying ignorance.

b. Trace data:

T_1 The lack of emotion in the pilots' voices.

T_2 The failure to attempt an avoidance, in spite of the adequate time.

C_2 accommodates T_1 and T_2 together by offering the conclusion that the pilots did not think a collision was imminent.

C_3 accounts for them separately—T_1 by making the pilots calmly determined, T_2 by making the collision intentional.

C_4 explains T_1 with stoic pilots and T_2 by appeal to locked controls.

C_5 is more complicated. It breaks both T_1 and T_2 in half and accounts for the actions of one pilot as in C_1 and the other in a new way. T_{1a} and T_{2a} are explained because the first pilot thought there was no danger of collision (hence his unemotional response and failure to swerve to avoid the collision). T_{1b} and T_{2b} are explained as the product of simple ignorance of the danger.

c. and d.

C_3 might be so elevated by our uncovering a history of growing antipathy between the pilots, finding a copy of the schedule and rules for an airborne joust, and observing partisan throngs on the ground watching the proceedings with intense interest. The first of these three items would be background information; the second and third would be trace data.

C_2 would rise to the top if it were found that air traffic controllers in that area are famous for issuing collision warnings rather generously, even when the danger of planes coming close to one another is only very slight by normal standards. You might wish to add that the crews of both aircraft were intimately familiar with local controllers and had remarked on the fatuity of heeding their advice on collisions. All this would be non-trace data.

18. a. The argument is inductive, since the youth could have, compatibly with the supporting statements, gotten the plague from an intentional injection; and the squirrels could be dying from something else.
    b. It is diagnostic, because the conclusion is offered in explanation of S_1 and part of S_2.
    c. S_1 and S_2 contain trace data, as explained in b.
    d. Both the habits of blow flies and the disease-carrying capacity of fleas are non-trace data, since neither is explained by the conclusion or its rivals.
    e. See a.

20. (Consult the schematization offered in Chapter 1, question 6, above.)
    a. and b. S_1, S_4, and S_5 contain the traces. C_1 and its rivals are trying to explain why the arm stopped (S_1) and how it came to start up again (S_4); somehow to explain the pin on the ground (S_5); or explain it away as irrelevant.
    c. S_2 and S_3 do not contain traces, since they concern a wholly different event from the one C_1 and its rivals are trying to explain. They are explaining what happened on Mars, not on Earth; but what happened on the simulator obviously *helps* C_1 account for what happened on Mars.

    d. C_2 The arm was stopped by a martian boulder.

    e. Hurdle for C_1: A pin is in place in the arm when *Viking I* returns to Earth.
    f. C_1 can account for this (though not plausibly): Pranksters intercepted the returning probe and inserted a pin in the arm.

22. a. I.Q.: What kind of animal carcass are these?

    b. C_1 Dogs

       C_2 Coyotes

    c. C_2.

    d. C_2 better explains the stomach contents, and perhaps the deftness of the skinning as well.

24. a. Where is the T.A.?

    b. S_3, S_4, and S_6 are the traces to be explained. S_1, S_2, and S_4 offer useful background to help in the explanation.

    c. S_6 and, to a lesser extent, S_3. (Recall that explanatory hurdles are always trace data: something hard to explain.)

    d. (Add to C_2): The T.A.'s officemate also has office hours at this time. (Alternatively: The T.A. took a call in the main office that turned out to be an emergency at home. She did not return to her office before leaving.)

26. a. S_1 Richard Talada died of carbon monoxide poisoning (in his apartment).

      S_2 Two weeks earlier his wife died mysteriously (of pneumonia).

      S_3 A bird's next was found in the furnace flue.

      S_4 Carbon monoxide is a by-product of LP gas combustion.

      S_5 The furnace had been malfunctioning.

      S_6 The investigators who found the nest thought it blocked the flue enough to cause a carbon monoxide buildup.

    b. S_1, S_2, S_5, and S_6 are the traces. The first three are easy: The nest blocking the flue enough to cause a CO buildup could explain the two deaths, as well as why the furnace was heating so poorly. S_6 is trickier: C_1 being true can explain why competent investigators *think* it's true (had it been a small nest in a large flue, they would not have suspected it). This kind of trace is treated in great detail on pages 161–63 of Chapter 4.

    c. Talada's son's not dying when his mother did is a hurdle for the bird's nest conclusion because this conclusion has some trouble explaining it. (This rival must take on added complexity to account for the other traces and this fact too.)

    d. This hurdle raises the general possibility that something more complicated is going on—that Mrs. Talada did not die of CO poisoning. This is not a very serious possibility at this stage, because there are many ways to explain her son's survival. One is by appeal to peculiarities of the circumstances (e.g., height and location of crib, or local ventilation).

28. a. S_1 Men began to die (nine years) earlier than women some (twenty-five) years after they abandoned suspenders in favor of belts.

   S_2 Men in the Andrus family have never worn belts, and they live, on average, just as long as the women in the family.

   S_3 Men from the Midwest tend to live longer, and fewer of them wear belts.
   .... d

   C_1 Wearing a belt interferes with your digestion.

   b. All are traces. C_1 is offered to explain the longevity of men from the Midwest; the fact that, in the Andrus family, men live as long as women; and why male longevity is currently shorter than female.

   c. Andrus suggests that part of the Andrus family trace data may be explained by clean lungs and religion. This weakens the support for the digestion thesis provided by S_2.

   d. The argument would be weakened if it turned out that men from the Midwest who wore belts lived as long, on average, as those who did not. This would be trace data: an explanatory hurdle for the belt theory.

30. a. S_1 The metal parts of an electrical adapter, found at the site of a fire in Plymouth Tower, were pitted and burned away.

   S_2 The plastic parts had melted away.

   S_3 A temperature of 2000 degrees Fahrenheit is required to pit copper.

   S_4 The fire was not that hot.

   S_5 Electrical shorts can generate temperatures of 2000 degrees Fahrenheit.
   .... d

   C_1 A short circuit in an electrical adapter caused the Plymouth Tower fire.

b. S_1 and S_2 are trace data: They are explained by C_1.

c. S_3, S_4, and S_5 are relevant, but not traces: They help C_1 explain S_1 and S_2.

d. C_2 The fire was started by someone smoking in bed.

e. A maintenance man says that, on an inspection tour through that part of the tower a week before the fire, he saw an adapter, just like the one in question, all melted and pitted.

CHAPTER 4

2. a. A is an automobile accident. B is Ivan's death.

  b. The fact that Ivan suffered no broken bones or external injuries detectable by competent examination.

  c. This favors the direction B → A, because it is so hard to explain on A → B, which is the only other plausible candidate.

  d. Had Ivan been talking with someone on his car telephone at the time of the crash (momentary panic, then sounds of crashing, then silence), A → B would have been more plausible. (Alternatively: Autopsy shows a fatal internal hemorrhage, due to a physiological defect but doubtless triggered by mild impact with the steering wheel.)

4. a. A is for solar flare. B is the satellite's failure (silence).

  b. A → B is offered as an explanation, which suggests that A and B, as characterized above, are being taken to be the correlates.

  c. The most plausible rivals would fall into the chance category.

    C_2 The satellite failed due to a defective part; the defect in the part was wholly unrelated to the solar flare.

6. a. That they happened the same night.

  b. It suggests that the quake caused the collapse.

  c. A is the earthquake. B is the collapse of the outbuilding.

  d. Of the remaining categories, chance is most plausible, since the other two categories are virtually unheard of and are difficult to imagine or contrive.

e. C_{2B} Vandals knocked the building down with a bulldozer.

f. Caterpillar tracks all over the site and across the debris. (Note that termites and other causes of structural weakness are naturally part of the earthquake rival. To make them into bypassing accounts would require special care.)

8. a. A is graduation from Yale. B is earning substantially more than an average income.

   b. A → B.

   c. It could be that, if your family is wealthy enough to send you to Yale, wealth by itself may guarantee you higher than average earnings after graduation. This would be a common cause account, with X being family wealth.

   d. If a study found that Yale graduates from wealthy families earned much more than the Yale average and those attending on scholarship much less, that would help the common cause account described above.

   (Now ask yourself this: If the study found no difference, what *other* common cause account might it suggest?)

10. a. A is being a heavy coffee drinker. B is suffering coronary artery disease.

    b. A → B.

    c. The second paragraph offers some possible reverse and common causes. Excessive coffee consumption may, for example, be part of a lifestyle that includes fatty foods and little exercise. And it may be that fatty food and lack of exercise, not the coffee, are what cause clogged arteries.

    d. (i) If by varying only the coffee—keeping diet and exercise uniform—a study found that high coffee consumption correlated with *less* heart disease, that would be TRACE DATA in support of the above rival.

       (ii) If experiments on animals showed that coffee reduced the level of harmful cholesterol in the animals' blood, that would be non-trace data supporting the same rival.

12. a. A is watching more television. B is doing less well on achievement tests.

    b. A → B.

    c. Given the correlates, reverse-cause accounts are nearly inconceivable, but common-cause explanations are easy to construct.

C_2 Certain personality types hate school (and hence do poorly on achievement tests) and are independently drawn to television watching (which does not hurt achievement).

C_3 Some teachers may assign very little homework, which causes their students to do poorly on achievement tests and (independently) provides more time for television.

  d. If we found that the many hours of TV watched by the underachievers was legitimately educational (NTD), and that cutting back on it tended to drop achievement scores (TD), some common cause would be a better bet than a simple $A \to B$.

14. a. That daily bathing in a hot spring is what keeps the monkeys in Hokkaido's botanical gardens healthy.

  b. A is a daily hot bath. B is being healthy.

  c. (i) It might be that monkeys are selected for the botanical garden on the basis of health: Those looking as though they may be ill with a contagious disease or in need of observation are confined to cages. So all the naturally healthy monkeys end up with access to a hot bath, which is denied the sickly ones. In this case healthiness would explain the baths ($B \to A$) rather than vice versa.

    (ii) It could be that being unconfined is a common cause. This rival would say that confinement causes monkeys to be disease prone and also explains their not taking hot baths. It is the fresh air and exercise (and perhaps diet) available in wandering the botanical gardens that make unconfined monkeys healthy. Baths are an irrelevant accompaniment.

  d. If the stream dried up and the unconfined monkeys got even healthier, the common cause rival would be promoted to the top of the ranking.

16. a. S_1 Researchers have found a correlation between moderate drinking and less than average hardening of the arteries.

    S_2 Alcohol has been found to increase high-density lipoprotein (apolipoprotein).

    S_3 High-density lipoprotein reduces the fatty plaque that causes heart disease.

d

C   Moderate alcohol consumption reduces the risk of heart disease.

b. S_1 offers the definitive trace: correlation explained by the causal connection offered in the conclusion (A → B).

S_2 is background offered in support of the direction of influence alleged in the conclusion.

c. The tributary argument is this:

S_4 When daily drinkers abstained from alcohol consumption, their high-density lipoprotein levels fell; and when they resumed drinking, the levels rose again.
══ = d

S_2 Moderate alcohol consumption raises the level of high-density lipoprotein in the blood.

So the overall structure would look like this:

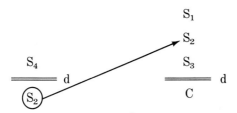

d. The trace in the tributary is the correlation between alcohol consumption and high-density lipoprotein levels.

e. This one is slightly tricky, because you have to separate the consumption of alcohol from the activities surrounding it. It may be that what effects high-density lipoprotein levels is not the alcohol itself, but other things (diet, anxiety) that change when a daily drinker abstains for a time. So participation in the experiment could be a common cause. Abstaining leads to lifestyle changes that reduce high-density lipoproteins and also (naturally) to lower consumption of alcohol, which has no effect on them.

The subtlety of this last rival lies in keeping it distinct from a complicated version of the A → B rival. For if it is not the *effort of abstaining*, but the effects of the (lack of) alcohol itself, that cause the lifestyle changes, this case would not be a common cause, but rather a direct one. It would not be the simple physiological story suggested in S_2, however, but another rival.

18. a. A is a hearing loss (disorder). B is a criminal behavior.
    b. $A \rightarrow B$.
    c. Hearing loss creates communication difficulties leading to a loss in self-confidence, which inclines a person to unacceptable behavior.
    d. (i) Socioeconomic conditions might provide a common-cause account. It might be that how and where you grow up determines the hearing hazards you are exposed to and independently inclines you toward or away from a life of crime.
       (ii) If gunfire and tense situations are threats to hearing, a reverse-causal account might be suggested. A life of crime could lead to hearing loss through elevated exposure to gunfire and tension.

20. a. A blizzard (A) correlates with the crashes (B) to suggest $A \rightarrow B$.
    b. What we all know about blizzards suggests that it is tough to fly a helicopter in one (visibility, turbulence, etc.).

    c. S_1 A/B

       S_2 It is tough to fly a helicopter in a blizzard.
       === d
       C   The blizzard caused the helicopters to crash.

    d. (i) The most plausible rival is chance. A mechanical failure unrelated to the blizzard causes one helicopter to crash into the other, disabling them both. (Groundfire would work here too.)
       (ii) A bizarre common cause would be for a cargo plane full of silver nitrate, destined for a cloud-seeding operation elsewhere in the conflict, to collide with the helicopters, causing them to crash and releasing the chemical, which causes the blizzard instantly.
    e. If the aircraft were designed to fly safely in blizzards, and both pilots were experienced in such conditions, the chance

rival would look much better. It would also help the common-cause rival, but much less.

22. a. S_1 Mr. Slegel and Dr. Rumack said that tea drinkers should not be worried by the Mississippi woman's reaction to Comfrey tea.

      S_2 Mr. Slegel is chairman of the company that sells the tea. Dr. Rumack is director of a poison center.

$$================================= \text{ d}$$

      C_1 Tea drinkers should not worry about Comfrey tea.

b. Mr. Slegel's testimony, at least, might be better explained as an attempt to mitigate the awful commercial consequences of the publicity. This would be explanation by appeal to something other than the truth of the statement, and hence a C_2 rival. The plausibility of this account is raised by the fact, mentioned in paragraph 2, that the episode had already forced cancellation of a company stock offering.

24. a. S_2 The statement was made at a closed team meeting (not at a pep rally) in response to a suggestion that the team try some risky experimentation in early season, non-conference games.

      S_3 The coach has a reputation for being candid about his team's prospects, even when to do so is painful. (This would make C_1 a clear favorite for Stage I.)

      S_4 The coach is confident that the team can go undefeated.

      S_5 The team is defending NCAA champion, has lost no starters from the previous year, and is currently ranked first in the coaches' poll. (This could be used in Stage I too, to show what the coach said was not crazy to believe.)

      S_6 The coach has had a number of undefeated teams, in all but one of which he has expressed great confidence early in the season. He has invariably had a realistic assessment of his poorer teams. (This would make C'_1 a good bet for Stage II.)

b. C_2 would be a better bet if we changed S_5 and S_6 as follows:

      S_5 The team is coming off a mediocre season, with a number of regulars returning, but with many new faces too.

S_6 The coach seems genuinely able to believe what's necessary for the sake of team morale. Nearly every season recently has disappointed his announced expectations.

c. To elevate C_2':

S_2 The statement was made at a pep rally.

S_3 The coach has a reputation for sacrificing candor to inspiration and seems to think a constant, fatuous optimism is part of his job.

26. S_2 The salesman is salaried (not on commission), successful (doesn't particularly need the sale), and a good friend of the customer he made the statement to.

S_3 He also has a reputation for almost painful honesty.

S_5 The engine has a disturbing knock at some speeds and leaves a trail of smoke when starting out from rest.

S_6 The salesman is a mechanical incompetent who is famous for being overly impressed by a clean, shiny exterior.

28. a. The sampling procedure explains the sample property (small metal pieces) quite independent of the nature of the population. This procedure would end up with small pieces of metal no matter what else the population contained.

b. If the metal pieces were wet, say, or dirty or stained in a certain way, we could more reliably attribute these properties to the population as a whole. For there is no strong connection between these properties and being ferrous (what a magnet will select). If all the little iron pieces in a box are wet, for example, the most plausible explanations of the wetness will not limit it to those pieces; it's a good bet that much else is wet too.

c. Anything that would sample by grasping (like pincers) or scooping would break the natural connection between procedure and small pieces of metal. So if a procedure of that sort came up with nothing but small metal pieces, one pretty good explanation of the sample would be that the box contained nothing but small pieces of metal.

30. a. The sample is chosen by motivation to return the ballot.

Whoever feels strongly enough about the issue to go to the trouble of sending the ballot in gets into the sample.

b. and c. It might be that a marginal student, who feels threatened by the proposal, would be more strongly motivated than the average student to return the ballot. That such a student might also be more likely than the average student to vote "no" would jeopardize representativeness.

d. There are many ways. Most straightforward would probably be to randomly choose 15% of the student body from a registration list and make an effort to contact each one.

32. a. The dangers are that an isolated penitentiary may draw its population from an atypical background or environment and that this atypical attribute is connected with hearing loss. This is just the sort of connection between sampling procedure and sampling property that makes a sample unrepresentative.

b. Gather more relevant data. Background showing the Parchman inmates to be more or less typical of prison populations would be relevant (and would support the researcher's conclusion). But further trace data from other states and other regions of the country would be more convincing.

CHAPTER 5

2. This case presents evidence that something needs to be remedied in support of a recommendation. So it is closely parallel to the baseball example in the text. (Since it has but one tributary, we can use linear-compound form with S_2 and S_3 reversed.)

a.   S   Every student to come in has misunderstood the concept of trace data.

———————————————————————— d

$C' = S_3$ Everybody in the class misunderstands the concept of trace data.

S_2 Starting over would remedy this.

S_4 Starting over is better than any other remedial strategy available.

C   We should start over.

b. S'_3 Understanding the concept of trace data is so obviously crucial that nearly everybody who misunderstood came in for help.

c. Given the modest assumption that coming in for help does some good, it is possible, if S'_3 is the right account, that almost nobody is left in the dark about trace data. So there would be little or nothing to remedy: The recommendation would be pointless.

4. a. That six or eight have died each summer for the past few years.

   b. S_1 Six or eight of a majestic stand of shade trees have died each summer lately.

   == d

   C'   The trees are suffering from some mysterious disease.

   A_1 The city refuses to take the problem seriously.

   ....

   C   All of the trees will soon be gone.

   c. Besides A_1, it might be worth mentioning that Eleanor is assuming that no other kind of agency, public or private, has responsibility for or interest in saving the trees. A less interesting assumption is that the trees won't be cured naturally through some accident or quirk of nature.
   (Note: One thing that is definitely not an assumption at this stage is that the problem with the trees is a disease. Eleanor does not assume this; she infers it: That is what the diagnostic step is all about.)

   d. C''   The grove has been losing members of its original, ancient population, providing room for second- and third-generation trees to prosper.

   e. Eleanor's grove is substantially the oldest of such trees in the city; and none of the other groves—including some nearby— is suffering serious disease or mortality problems.

6. The trick here is to see that some kind of diagnostic picture is interposed between observation and prediction to make the prediction seem reasonable.

a. S_1 Southern California has not had a very large earthquake in more than a century.

== d

C′ The local fault system is locked together quite firmly, thus (temporarily) preventing the slippage that produces earthquakes.

A_1 When this locking happens, stresses build up within the fault system and eventually become more than the locked rock can resist.

A_2 Along the main fault system in Southern California, this process takes about a century.

....

C Southern California will soon have a very large earthquake.

b. The difference lies, of course, in the diagnostic step. The best explanation of the recent absence of great earthquakes in South Dakota is not a locked fault system. It is the basic lack of seismic activity in that part of the world: The earth's crust is boringly stable beneath South Dakota. So, recent quiescence will not lead to an earthquake prediction there, with any plausible set of assumptions.

8. a. You have substantial discretion here in how you characterize the diagnostic rivals and hence in how much you pack into the first step. A middling austere diagnosis would be something like this:

S_1 Rats that, in the last sixth of their lives, had more attention, companionship, and things to do had substantially thicker cortexes and substantially less aging pigment in their brains than did rats confined to normal, impoverished environments.

== d

C′ The activity and companionship were responsible for the difference.

To get from this to the non-diagnostic conclusion, you must bridge two gaps in the second step: the one between physiology and aging and the one between rats and humans.

C′   In rats, activity and companionship thicken the cortex and reduce the brain's aging pigment.

A_1 A thinning cortex and accumulating aging pigment either constitute or are closely related to the deleterious aspects of aging.

A_2 Human brains resemble rat brains enough for all this to apply to us.

C   Activity and companionship slow the aging of the human brain.

(Comment on assumptions: A_1 is clearly implied by Dr. Diamond's comments; A_2 is intended as a charitable paraphrase of the "a nerve cell is a nerve cell" remark.)

   b. What counts as stimulating activity for human beings (e.g., reading, working crossword puzzles, reminiscing) is sufficiently distinct from the activity of rats that it may involve neurons differently enough to damage the analogy.

10. a. S_1 Many people are murdered during robberies.

d

C′   (The explanation of this is that . . .) The penalty for robbery is very nearly the same as that for murder.

S_2 Reducing the penalty for robbery would (therefore) reduce the incentive robbers have to kill their victims.

(S_3 and S_4 are presumed.)

C   We should reduce the penalty for robbery.

   b. Both S_4 and the diagnostic step are problematic against normal, everyday background.

    (i) It is conceivable that, in the violent, panicky circumstances of a robbery, a robber's actions are not very sensitive to long-run consequences. Reflex and short-run preoccupations may be the overwhelming causal factors in robbers murdering their victims. In this case C′ would not be a plausible explanation of S_1.

    (ii) Increasing the penalty for murder—or for murder during a robbery—may achieve the desired result better.

CHAPTER 7

Page 317

Examples using *plan* and *pass* would go something like this:

Play. a. We can't play football here until the field dries.
       b. Emily learned to play the cello before she was ten.
       c. I just don't know what card to play.
       d. Everybody's sick, so Johnny doesn't have anybody to play with.

Pass. a. The accident occurred when I tried to pass the car ahead of mine.
       b. The quarterback was trying to pass the ball too much this afternoon.
       c. You should simply allow remarks like that to pass without comment; it is always a mistake to become defensive.
       d. Tom was arrested for trying to pass a bad check.
       e. It hurt so much I thought I might pass out.

Page 319

  a. Whip the cream until it is firm.
  b. Make sure the gelatin is firm before removing it from the molds.
  c. The bridge sagged because they installed the heavy cross-members before the concrete was firm.
  d. After the quake, the pattern of cracked walls revealed where the earth was not firm.

Page 324

Examples for the suggested words would be these:

  a. He seems to think that that essay award is a key that will admit him to any college in the country.
  b. The bill is well intentioned but toothless: It contains no enforcement apparatus.

c. The golfer is out there burning up the course. (Alternatively: When you get involved with somebody like that you always get burned.)

Even-numbered Exercises

2. Metaphor exercises our natural charity perhaps as much as anything in language. For, first of all, when an expression is used metaphorically, a literal reading of it will usually be obviously false, or just non-sensical. We say "he put all his eggs in one basket and got burned for it"; yet there were no eggs, no basket, and no fire. So we look around for a more plausible reading and find a clear but modest metaphor.

    Second, we can usually find many different ways to work the metaphor in a context (many metaphorical eggs, baskets, and burnings) if we try. But charity has us settle on the obviously sensible reading if there is one. There may not be one, of course: Metaphors can be difficult, opaque, or inept, like anything else in language. The fact that metaphor is *sometimes* clear and helpful is the marvel: And this depends crucially on the rich diagnostic plausibility judgments captured in the principle of charity.

4. Of course Martha knows what *yes* means. Her obvious competence in English would provide overwhelming evidence for that view even had she not attempted to address the question directly. Her response to the question, moreover, adds strong evidence for the same view (that she knows what it means: It's a pretty good attempt, even though far from complete.) The jobs done by words in our basic vocabulary are far too complex to be interestingly describable on the spur of the moment—or even after much reflection and research. If we held out for this standard, nobody could be said to know what most words mean. The answer to "Do you know what *yes* means?" (or most other common words) would be "Of course not," and nobody would be silly enough to ask the question. (Do you know how much Mount Hood weighs—exactly?)

    But that isn't what the question asks (when it is being used sensibly). It asks whether you *understand* what the word means, not whether you can describe that understanding. So the answer to the question is often "yes"—although it is sometimes "no" and we can frequently tell which it is without asking the person directly.

6.   (Sample essay) The puzzle arises perhaps because our first hip-shot is inevitably an oversimplification: Sound is what you hear, a sensation in your head. This leads to the unhappy conclusion that the tree falling in an unpopulated forest makes no sound because nobody's there to hear it, to have the sensation. So we flee to another hip-shot: Sound must be vibrations in the air. The tree makes those even when nobody's around. We like that better, but it suggests that people who lived before acoustical physics didn't know what a sound was—and that seems wrong. What to do?

    The first thing to do is stop shooting and try to get a grip on the context. For, as you should expect, context determines everything. Sometimes it will be sensible to think of a sound as (to say a sound is) a sensation, sometimes as vibrations, sometimes both, sometimes neither. And this will depend on the job done by the verb *to be* (*is*) as much as on the word *sound* itself. Sometimes we will need to distinguish between properties we sense auditorily (harmony, loudness, pitch, harshness) and those we find through analyzing the vibration (frequency, amplitude, and more complex mathematical properties of harmonic motion). Other times it will be useful to run them together (to say that pitch just *is* frequency, for instance).

    In most of our dealing with sounds we do not know, and do not need to know, anything about the relevant properties of the underlying physical mechanism. What we recognize in a sound, or enjoy in music, are details of pitch and harmony that were known long before the discoveries of acoustical physics. We would neither recognize nor enjoy (in anything like the same way) the vibrational analysis if it were set out before us. So in these usual contexts what we characterize as sounds aren't vibrations, even though sounds are the manifestation of vibrations. (For more discussion on this distinction, see pages 357–62 of Chapter 8.)

    When we're dealing with acoustic design, however, or trying to understand sound propagation or any of a number of similar things, it will often be useful to run the two sets of properties together (e.g., pitch with frequency). In such a context, *sound* may refer naturally to the vibrations or indifferently to both sets of properties.

    So how does all this apply to the tree in the forest? Can we just look at the context and find our answer? Of course not; that is what created the puzzle in the first place. There's not enough context provided to guide us. That's precisely why we're left hanging in limbo among the possible alternatives. And this is what generates frustration, tempts us to savage the language. Alternatively we may say the problem lies in the fact that the context is *abstract*: emphatically not a practical one. And this cuts our linguistic skills free from their foundation. The requirement of significance cannot help us here.

The words *sound* and *is* do all sorts of jobs, depending on what needs doing. If nothing in particular needs doing, then all you have are lots of possibilities—nothing in particular. The example has been explicitly contrived so that nothing of human significance seems to hang on what we say. So in the normal sense, it simply doesn't *matter* what you say. Say what you wish.

That, in the abstract, is the solution to the puzzle. But our frustration is concrete and usually is not relieved by anything on this level. To regain our composure, shake off the centipede effect, it always helps to exercise our skill a bit: change the circumstances, consider similar cases, and see what might be at stake, what human significance the words might have.

Consider the broken lamp on the fireplace hearth, knocked off a table during last night's burglary. Did it make a noise when it fell? You bet it did. Does it matter whether the burglars were deaf? Not at all. The way the words work in this context, whether or not the breaking lamp made a sound is not in the least affected by who or what was around to hear it. A deaf burglar's worry would not be whether the lamp *made* a noise; it would be whether anybody heard it.[1]

We might want to say, then, that the contrast between making a sound and not making a sound is, in this context, partly subjunctive. The lamp made a sound in this sense if it *would* have been heard by a suitably placed listener—even if it was in fact not heard by anybody. But saying this does not require knowing anything about the underlying physics. We've known that about sounds forever. Even if I knew nothing of vibrations in the air, the possibility of deaf burglars doesn't make me wonder *whether*

---

[1] It is, of course, possible to worry about whether the lamp made a noise when it broke. But that would be a different worry altogether. We might suspect, for example, that the lamp was made of rotten foam rubber that fell into deceptive-looking pieces on the hearth.

the lamp made a sound when it broke. I wonder only whether somebody heard it.

So our temptation in the empty forest to require that sounds *be* vibrations so that we can make sense of unheard sounds gets the matter backwards. We accept vibrations as the explanation of sound only *because* they make it plain how the sound can be independent of a hearer. When we first learn of the vibrations we are not *troubled* by the fact that they can exist in the absence of an ear to be vibrated. We don't react hesitantly or skeptically, as though we're just discovering something new about sound (my God, it must have made a sound even though the house was empty). No, that was already part of our understanding. Physics would have to account *for* it; meanwhile we could count *on* it.

8. a. (i)   If I don't make this sale I'll lose my promotion, and I just can't allow that to happen.

    (ii) They think something's happened to my spine! I can't wiggle my toes.

    (iii) You can't buy liquor on Sundays in this state.

   b. The first thing to be clear about is that there is nothing wrong with A's choice of words. Her meaning is absolutely clear, and her use of *can't* is not just standard but almost mandatory here. Had she said *won't* instead, it would have been obscure and puzzling to sensitive language users.

   B's misunderstanding is doubtless a version of the myth of one proper use. The picture of *can't* as some sort of physical constraint or inability has damaged his linguistic competence, obscuring from him the rich complexity of the job the word does so effortlessly in our conversation. We might try to talk him out of it by pointing out our skill with contexts, as we have done in this chapter. But it may require remedial exercise as well. (When I ask if you can come, I'm only inquiring about your schedule and priorities, not asking you to anticipate whether you will be in traction or held at gunpoint.) Some cases of this affliction are almost intractable, however.

10. a. "Window of opportunity" is a common metaphor. A less shopworn example would be "Although he was confined to his room, the daily newspaper gave him a window on the world."

   b. When she opened the old address book, one name leaped out and hit her right in the face.

   c. We never did discover what caused the engine to die.

12. The equivocation is on othe word *outlaw*. The slogan seems *plausible* only if *outlaw* does one job, but its intended threat materializes only if it does a different one. The slogan is effective in registering the threat of gun-control legislation only because *outlaw* refers specifically to robbers, rapists, and other criminals, on the prowl, out to do you harm. But for the statement to be plausible, *outlaw* must do a much broader job: One would become an outlaw in this sense merely by breaking the (proposed) law against owning guns. Then anyone who did not give up his firearms would be an outlaw, and only outlaws would have guns. But most such *outlaws* would not be the scary folks normally conjured up by the word, and the threat is no longer clear and compelling.

In short, the threat is clear only if the statement is implausible; and the statement is plausible only if the threat is not clear. You can't have it both ways.

CHAPTER 8

Page 335

In normal conversation, calling something an insect is wholly insensitive to what kind of arthropod it is, even to whether or not it is what life scientists call an arthropod. It means, roughly, "bug." The fact that *insect* has a valuable job in biological taxonomy is interesting, but that job is easily distinguishable from the more mundane job it has around the house and in everyday life. The context makes it perfectly clear that the sister in question was using *insect* in its everyday sense, not its technical one. Objecting to her choice of words makes it look like the objector thinks the technical job is the only proper one for the word. This misunderstanding is what we have called the myth of one proper use.

Pages 338–39

2. a. A's word choice is flawless. All A is attempting to say is that the widow gladly makes sacrifices to help other people; and that is precisely what is captured by *unselfish* in this context. B seized on the *gladly* part as demonstrating that the sacrifices were in her self-interest, and presumably it does. But good will is crucial to the job done by *unselfish* here. If she gave of herself only grudgingly, bitterly, by having to be

shamed into it, her act would not be unselfish at all. The clearest cases of unselfishness (as intended here) are ones done happily—and hence plausibly in the doer's self-interest. This is doubtless what B misunderstands about the job *unselfish* does here, and what the myth of one proper use encourages.

b. B may be a victim of the powerful temptation to think we can tell what job a word has simply by looking at its component parts and how they fit together. *Self-ish* might sound like it simply covers all self-interest considerations, and hence *un*-selfish behavior would have to be something not done in your own self-interest. Some such construction is doubtless at the bottom of B's argument. But to accept this account is to fall prey to the tempting but simple-minded view of language we should by now be able to dispense with. *Unselfish* does not always mean "not in your own self-interest"—perhaps it does not ever mean quite that; but in any case, that is not the job it has in the sentiment A is trying to express.

c. (Sample essay) Frequently, the best thing to do in cases like this is to examine the *contrast* naturally drawn in the context. We may perhaps best see B's underlying misconception by looking at selfishness. Selfishness has, to be sure, something to do with self-interest. But the lesson of Chapter 7 is that even rough characterization of the jobs familiar words do requires careful attention to actual applications. And the clearest example of selfishness is something like taking all the meat from the platter at dinner, butting into a line ahead of those who have been waiting, or refusing to drive three minutes out of your way to help a colleague who needs a ride to work. In none of these cases is the selfish behavior always or clearly in the interest of the selfish person. Eating all the pork chops, for example, is frequently not in the gourmand's interest all by itself. But even if some clear advantage does accrue from such gluttony, it seldom outweighs the social and physical consequences it normally brings down upon the glutton's head. For very few of us is the pleasure of another chop or two worth the hostility, contempt, and other opprobrium that normally result from such an act. But that does not show taking the pork chops was *not* selfish. The concern with one's self that is manifest in selfish acts is quite typically narrow, blatant, and shortsighted and hence rather likely to end up not being in the selfish person's best interest. This is why *selfish* is such a powerful term of reproof.

The self-interest B attributes to A's neighbor is, by contrast, reflective, subtle, all-things-considered. Her behavior—her sacrifice—may be in her own self-interest, but it is *not* due simply to a narrow, shortsighted preoccupation with herself. This is the important contrast, and this is why her behavior does not fit the reproving job given *selfish* in this context. When *unselfish* is used in the way A uses it, it is intended as an honorific term—a term of praise. But the praise is not for doing something harmful to oneself. Just the opposite: It is for the gladness of self-sacrifice: precisely what makes B question the term. For whatever reason, we as human beings naturally appreciate people who are genuinely pleased to be helpful and charitable. It is very useful to have words to capture this appreciation: *Unselfish* is one that does.

4. (Sample essay) Calling Venus a star in this context is perfectly clear and wholly unobjectionable. What's silly is thinking we must fire a word like *star* from its everyday job simply because science has used it to mark a technical distinction. In its everyday employment,[2] Venus is one of the stars: sometimes the morning star, sometimes the evening star, often the brightest star in the firmament. What modern astronomy has discovered is that there is a huge and striking difference in the physical makeup of the various bodies that dot the nighttime sky, particularly in the nature of their illumination. Some are rather like the sun, others are more like the moon, especially in the latter respect. But nothing in this discovery—as important as it is—says we should not have a word referring indifferently to all the venerable dots in the night sky, lumping them all together when the astrophysical distinctions are unimportant. That is, science gives us no reason to fire *star* from its long-established job, the one it has in expressing sentiments like "Aren't the stars beautiful tonight?" It would be a pedantic embarrassment to add "Yes, and the planets too!" The distinction is gratuitous here: *Star* covers them all.

---

[2]Actually, astronomers often employ it in this "everyday" job even when they do astronomy. They speak of the parallax of the fixed stars, presumably contrasting with the "other" ones. And Kepler titled his earth-shaking treatise *De Motibus Stellae Martis.*

In fact, because they are brightest, the planets—what the Greeks called the wandering stars—are the stars we talk about most often. Besides the morning star and the evening star, they include the only stars visible during the day (if you look hard enough), namely Jupiter and Venus. The planets are what Cassius refers to when he tells Brutus that the fault lies "not in our stars, but in ourselves . . ." In smoggy climates, the planets often constitute a majority of the stars visible at all. So when astronomers use the word *star* to *contrast* with *planet*, it should be clear they are using it to mark a technical distinction of little relevance to much of our common talk about stars. The distinction is enormously important in some contexts, of course; but this fact, as should be transparent by now, provides no reason at all to rob us of the useful job done by *star* in less technical circumstances. The choice of terms to mark the astronomical distinction is, as always, relatively arbitrary. There is little about the word *star* that makes it singularly appropriate for this astronomical job. Astronomers might just as well have used the word *sun* (as one Greek suggested, long ago) and characterized the revelation as discovering that most of the stars are actually *suns*. But they did not: They used the word *star* to make the distinction. And so we have to be just a bit more careful about the context when we use that word, so we understand which of its two closely related jobs it is doing at any moment.

This case reflects the risk we take whenever science commandeers an established, nontechnical word to do an important, technical job, especially when the old job somehow suggests the new one. It invites confusion; it tempts us to fire the word from its original job, simply because it is not the technical one. Science is unlikely to stop pirating established terms to mark its exotic distinctions; and as long as we are adequately sensitive to the subtly different jobs words can do in subtly different contexts, we may encourage science in this practice. Scientists do nevertheless bear a special responsibility in this enterprise: to take some pains not to rob us of a useful concept just to have a flashy or suggestive way to make a scientific point. If, following the currently jocular idiom of microphysics, the next subatomic particle is named the "smithereen," we may soon be faced with

You didn't really blow it to smithereens, just to bits and pieces and fragments and splinters.

It would be a sad loss, and one we could avoid simply by resisting the myth of one proper use.

6. (Sample essay) The confusion displayed here is a version of the myth of one proper use: the insistence that the word *fruit* do its technical, scientific job in an especially inappropriate context. Perhaps the best way to see this is to hark back to the notion of contrast we discussed early in Chapter 7. Sometimes a central feature of a word's job will be the contrast it draws, and that contrast can change from one context to another. Ignoring (or misunderstanding) the contextual variability of contrast is a major source of reformist misadventure—and is neatly illustrated in this case.

Seeds make the tomato a fruit only in botanical taxonomy. There the fruit of a plant is a structural part playing a key role in reproduction. In this sense *fruit* contrasts with *stem, leaf,* and *root,* for example, but it does not contrast with *vegetable. Vegetable* is not on the list of structural parts of a plant. A tomato is "the fruit *of* the tomato plant," as opposed to the leaf, stem, or root of that plant. But there is no "vegetable *of* the tomato plant." So in the sense in which tomato is a fruit, it is not a fruit as opposed to a vegetable.

When *fruit* does contrast with *vegetable,* it is performing its nontechnical, nontaxonomic job. This is the one it commonly gets at mealtime, in kitchens, and at produce counters. Here *fruit* has something to do with taste—and hence what kind of salad it goes into or whether it is right for dessert. And in this sense a tomato is not a fruit; it is a vegetable. Tomatoes do not go into fruit salads, but rather the other kind. Tomato juice is not a fruit juice. The tomato is one of the eight vegetables in "V8." All sorts of things that are fruits in structural taxonomy are vegetables in grocery stores: squash, cucumbers, eggplants, and beans, to name only a few. Furthermore, some things that are not structural fruits, such as rhubarb, count as fruit in that word's other job.

None of this should be surprising. Words do many different jobs, and the context is generally up to the task of sorting the right one from the wrong ones. Usually we do this effortlessly. Only when we misapprehend our skills—or are in the grip of the centipede effect—do problems arise in normal contexts. Then the task is to regain the skill, not spread the affliction. If you ask for fruit juice and the waiter brings tomato juice, saying a tomato is after all a fruit, you have been badly treated and might consider not leaving a tip. If you order a fruit pie and he brings a pizza, he is just in the wrong job: He should seek safer employment.

Page 353

2. a. This is a tough case simply because it does not arise very often. It is a possibility we have had to take seriously only with recent advances in medicine. For most of our history, when life signs disappeared for even a very short time, they did not return. We quite reasonably used—and still do use—life signs (heartbeat, breathing, reflex) as criteria for issuing D.O.A. certificates in emergency wards. Institutions such as marriage and life insurance have reasonably neglected the possibility of recovering lost life signs because the possibility has been so remote.

When we get so little chance to exercise semantics in an area like this, it will naturally give rise to indeterminacy of the kinds discussed in this section. Equally competent users of English will disagree about whether the case is positive or negative, and many will feel strong tugs in both directions. So this case cannot be settled by appeal to what the words mean: It is simply an unclear case of death. The matter must be resolved some other way.

b. The most plausible "underlying" appeal here is to the obvious rationale of the death provision in the marriage contract. The point of freeing a person to remarry on the death of his or her spouse is that the dead spouse is no longer available to participate in the marriage and no longer around to care about its existence. But this is emphatically not true in the case we are considering. If the marriage contract were amended to cover the temporary loss of life signs, it certainly wouldn't be to allow remarriage for such an occurrence.

So appeal to an underlying, substantive resolution would, while not taking the prosecutor's hard line on permanence, nevertheless come down on that side of the issue. If the woman wants to remarry, she first needs to get a divorce.

Pages 362–64

2. a. Isn't it interesting that the brightest objects in the nighttime sky, such as Venus and Jupiter, don't generate their own

light, but merely reflect that of the sun; whereas all the
fainter objects are actually distant suns, some much bigger
and brighter than our own.

   b. My neighbor's unselfishness is in her own best interest. (It's a
wise charity that rewards itself so handsomely.)

4. (Sample essay) B's retort makes it sound at first like the problem
is with *blue*. But there is no question that something is blue; the
question is *what*? B seems to think it can't be the sky, roughly,
because there isn't anything up there to call sky. So we're left
with the physics of diffraction.

But once again, a reasonable insight tempts us to hobble our
diction, to fire words from perfectly clear and useful jobs. The
insight is that the sky is not a surface, so its having a color isn't
going to be like a wall's having a color. But none of this remotely
recommends giving up talk of the sky, or its color: these words
convey something absolutely clear and straightforward almost
without exception. Saying the sky is blue—attributing blueness
to the sky—is an absolutely reliable way to direct other people's
attention to something we occasionally wish to share our perception of.

That attribution tells us where to look and what to look for,
and most of us get the hang of it right away: Intersubjectivity is
easy to achieve. The fact that it is hard to give a characterization
of the sky from some points of view is indeed interesting, but it
raises not the slightest difficulty for the bulk of normal talk about
the sky. All that talk requires is a competent eye and common
interest. To translate it all into the underlying physics would be
gratuitously puzzling, sometimes even worse than that.

> After the crew has been confined below decks for two days by an
> insanely raging storm, a sudden lull tempts the first mate to pull
> himself off the debris- and vomit-strewn floor and up the four
> steps to the door to the deck. He struggles with it briefly, gets it
> open, sticks out his head, and gasps, "My God, Captain, there's
> blue sky out here."

The message is clear, and worries about the objective nature of
the sky and the paths of light rays are clearly beside the point.
For the captain to respond with speculations about diffusion and
wavelength would be evidence of delirium. The mate should
assume command.

6. Let's begin with a reformulation of the two insights, and then weave them into a story about what has gone wrong and how we might learn something from the temptation exposed here.

The linguistic insight is that the verb *to see* is a success word: You can't see what didn't happen. That is, if X didn't occur, then, as a matter of how the language works, you didn't see X occur. You may have thought you saw X, but you didn't—it must have been something else.

The insight about perception is far more modest. It is simply that direct observation involves light coming from an object entering our eye and creating an impression or image.

(Sample essay.) The job done by *see* in the usual run of contexts simply does apply to objects and their behavior, not to light. What we see are cars and people and movies and fireworks. Being able to talk about our perceptions in this simple way is constantly useful, and largely unproblematic. Usually we gain nothing by alerting everyone to the underlying optics. (In this respect the case is similar to that of *sunrise*.) I saw Mary Ann at a party last night. Suppose I tell somebody that and he responds, "You know, what actually happened was that some photons from a nearby incandescence bounced off Mary Ann, passed through the lens of your eye, and obliterated themselves against your retinas in just such a way as to form an image of Mary Ann." What to say? It looks like he just missed the point of my remark. True, photons were whizzing about, but when it was all over, what had happened was that I had seen Mary Ann. That is all I wanted to say. If he was not interested in who I saw at the party he could simply have said so.

One thing is clear, however. His response in no way suggests I did *not* see Mary Ann: It offers an (unsolicited and rudely irrelevant) account of what probably took place when I did. That the account has light doing interesting things inside my eyeball is no reason to change the job of the verb *to see*. We can describe those things without destroying any valuable linguistic institutions; and the normal job of *see* in this context is too valuable to give up. In that (normal) sense I did *not* see the light itself; I did not see anything in my eyeball—that would require mirrors and magnifying lenses. What I saw was Mary Ann. The ordinary job of *to see* is to help me articulate this fact. Recognizing familiar objects and actions is something we are all pretty good at; and it is something we often wish to convey. That is enough to justify having some linguistic institution to enable us to convey it. That institution in English is the usual job given *see*.

Yes, of course seeing has something to do with light and with eyes. But exactly what it has to do with them is irrelevant most of the time. In fact, we are much better at telling who or what we saw than we are at saying just what happened to the photons. Physicists may even change their minds about the photons, and it will not affect the content of our casual recognitions one scintilla. The valuable but mundane jobs common words do are insulated from scientific discovery in just this way.

What about stars, then: Do they raise any special problems? Yes, they do, but only rather minor ones, which may be dealt with soberly. Scientific discoveries were involved in determining the celestial distances and light velocity that revealed the great time lag in our perception of stars. And this is important in characterizing that perception. But it does not *undermine* it. It does not mean that we do not see the stars. The time lag affects only a verb tense in the characterization of what we see: We see the stars not as they are, but as they used to be. And for most practical purposes even this distinction is not very significant.

Celestial cases actually afford the best illustration of how unimportant time lags—and other complexities—are to direct perception. When *Voyager I* passed close to Jupiter, for example, it allowed us to see detail on that planet's surface which had been invisible from Earth. But what counted as seeing involved digital coding, more than an hour-long trip across the solar system, decoding into still photographs, electronic and photographic enhancement of the image, and construction of a movie out of the stills. In the end we were able to see the counterrotating bands of clouds, the turbulence around the giant red spot, even an erupting volcano on one of Jupiter's moons. And we can describe all this—surface perceptions as well as underlying science—clearly and in great detail, without jettisoning any basic linguistic institutions.

Seeing involves marshaling our estimable visual competence to recognize objects and phenomena. But the underlying character of the marshaling—the exact process of recognition—can be varied and complex. None of the simple pictures captures all that is valuable in it. So when someone appeals to a tempting oversimplification to fire our perception vocabulary from one of its central tasks, we can sympathize, but it is silly not to resist. I knew the storm front had passed through last night when I was able to see stars through my bedroom window. Objecting that I did not really see the stars, just their light, simply misrepresents a valuable chunk of the language.

Up to this point, firing *see* is rather like firing *sunrise* from its job at dawn. In each case a scientific fact appears to recommend the firing of a useful expression because the practical operation of language is misunderstood. For "sunrise," the protester demands we substitute some astrophysical circumlocution. Here, A demands that we substitute "see the light from" for the simpler "see." Practical communication is made more difficult and less certain by each of these artifices; and the exercises have been designed to show there is no need to suffer the inconvenience and take the risk. When properly understood, existing linguistic practice is perfectly adequate to its mundane but important tasks. The firings were hasty and ill considered.

But the two cases differ in one essential detail. Any astrophysical locution we substituted for *sunrise* would merely be unusual and perhaps theoretically exotic. It would be unnecessarily puzzling and cumbersome, which of course is bad enough, but it would be only that. The problem is much worse for *seeing*. The expression A wants us to substitute for *see* already has a job to do in this context, a *different job*. This makes the substitution more than just strange and puzzling: It makes it openly misleading.

When we normally speak of seeing the light of or from some object, our seeing the light specifically *contrasts with* seeing the object itself. We often see the light when the object itself is out of view. We see the moonlight on the patio while the moon is out of sight overhead. We see the torchlight on the cave walls, but not yet the torch. We see the beam of light from the flashlight when the instrument itself is lost in the black. This is why "see the light from X" is such a particularly unhappy substitute for "see X" in this example. "See the light from X" already has a job in this context; and not only is it different from the job given "see X," but one of its major features is its *contrast* with the job of "see X." To give "see the light from X" the job formerly held by "see X," in addition to its other miseries, obliterates this useful contrast too. What is being fired is not just a single expression, but a contrasting pair.

(A different sample essay) From another perspective, we may reasonably take A's original statement, the one that launched this discussion, to be a partial job description: an attempt to capture one aspect of the job done by *see* in this context. Claiming that it is "true by definition" suggests a concern with language itself. That would also explain the character of the exchange with B that follows the remark. If we adopt this plausible interpretation, the entire preceding discussion simply traces the dangerous temptations of such hip-shot descriptions. Before seriously examining language at work, we may find inconceivable the suggestion that quick, general job descriptions usually miss important detail. So we abandon the detail in defense of the description, and we destroy valuable parts of the language. This sounds enough like what A did to justify pursuing this interpretation one step further.

Given what we have learned about language, "You can't see what doesn't exist" certainly has the ring of a beguiling oversimplification. It is too stark, too categorical, to hope to capture an accurate connection between the jobs of *see* and *exist* in their workaday contexts. But it does capture something of interest. There is something obviously valuable in A's original observation, and possibly this is what drives A to defend it at such absurd lengths. If A had understood how hard it is to capture such semantic detail *accurately*, he might have defended it in a more plausible and less destructive fashion. Specifically, it may be defended as a helpful oversimplification that we may fashion into something more accurate (and *less* simple) by adjusting it for contextual nuance. Let us see how this might be done.

First of all there are some contexts, concerning certain kinds of subject matter, in which we may simply accept the substance of A's original statement: You can't see what doesn't exist. In a famous short story by James Thurber, a man claims to have seen a unicorn in his garden. When he tells his wife, she replies, "The unicorn is a mythical beast," properly taking this to reject her husband's claim. She feels no need to spell it out in further detail, simply because we do, implicitly, accept A's counsel here. Mythical beasts do not exist, and you cannot see in your garden beasts that do not exist. For you to see one in your garden, it would have to *be* there, and it cannot do that unless it exists. But all this is so obvious there is no need to say it.

We must be careful in applying this principle in other cases, however. For all it does is point out that, in this kind of context, the content of a perception must be a *fact*. That is, if we are wrong about what we say we see, then we did not see it—we only *think* we saw it. And this *is* an important feature of the job *see* does here. The word simply does not apply when its object is a mistaken diagnosis.

In the run of normal cases this requirement presents no practical problem whatever. As we noted in Chapters 3 and 4, we are very skilled at an enormous range of mundane diagnoses. Our confidence that we saw X happen is often very good reason to think X happened. Some special circumstance is usually required to overthrow this kind of perception. As long as we understand this, and as long as we stay well within the limits of our perceptual competence, we may comfortably identify seeing X with thinking we see X. The point is only that we must give it up when someone produces good reason to think X never occurred. The nonexistence of unicorns rejects the husband's claim only because it shows that what he saw could not have been what he *said* he saw. Whatever it was he saw in the garden, it was not a unicorn. The content of his claimed perception is not a fact.

But none of this shows that the fact must occur *at the same time* as the perception. The umpire calls the runner out at second: He says he saw the shortstop tag him before he reached the bag. But in slow-motion replays, from three different angles, we see the runner's foot touch the bag before the ball is even in the shortstop's glove. Umpires are usually right, but this time we've got him. And we've got him because of what *we* saw, even though we saw it long after it happened. In the quiet of a comfortable study we see the runner begin his slide, the dirt start to fly, the jolt as his spikes dig into the bag; we see the white blur snap back the infielder's glove; then everything disappears in an explosion of dust. We see it over and over until we can recognize the trajectories of individual dirt clods from several perspectives. Our perception is better than the umpire's because of the enormous advantage afforded by slow motion, different angles, and knowing exactly what to look for. That our perception occurs long after the fact is irrelevant: It is a perception, and a very good one. (It too may be undermined by further evidence, of course—even further perceptions; but that is enough of a long shot to be reasonably disregarded until something raises our suspicion. In this it is like any other of our best perceptions.)

Something similar is going on when we see turbulence around Jupiter's red spot. Elaborate electronics and a substantial time lapse do not count against our perception. What matters is that we get it right, and the electronic complexity is crucial to our doing that. The electronics are designed specifically to complement our visual skill in the way required to aid our judgment. The result, of course, is that the turbulence we see is taking place not at the instant we see it, but hours or even days before. As long as we get it right, the job *see* does in this context fits the case perfectly, just as it does the instant replay.

Were we able to see surface detail on the star we began with, that case would be like Jupiter's. But we cannot. Of the star, all we see is *it*. And this actually makes it simpler—because the facts we are to get right or wrong are merely its existence and its direction from earth. So long as the light reaching us now did leave a real star out there in roughly that direction some time in the past, the perception we now form using that light counts as seeing the star. Naturally, we see it as it was then, not as it is now; but that seldom makes any difference in the practical contexts in which we talk of the stars. (It makes a lot of difference to physicists and cosmologists; but they see far more in the light than we do just using our eyes.) In this particular context we *can* see things that do not exist any longer; we just cannot see things that never did exist in the first place.

8. (Sample essay) The trick here is to recognize how profound a change is being proposed in our language. The words being fired from their jobs in our talk of colored surfaces are *is* and *have*, two of our basic, workhorse verbs. We are not to say that a surface *is* green, but merely that it *reflects* green light: This is a fundamental change in the way we talk about the properties things *have*. For it is hard to treat colors differently from many other properties. The effects of such reform would be far-reaching—devastating, and, as always, for no good reason.

The argument against firing *is* and *have* from their jobs here is the same appeal to our skills and interests we have made whenever this temptation arises. These are the normal terms we use to refer to obvious chromatic features of our environment, usually without any problem whatever. And in the vast run of contexts the underlying physics is so monumentally irrelevant to the practical point of the reference that muddying up our diction with electrodynamic theory is inexcusable.

A: Charlie just bought one of the ugliest cars I've ever seen. It's mostly a revolting pea-green, with a brown tufted vinyl top.

B: Don't you know that the part that appears pea-green is not really that color at all? It just differentially reflects that part of the spectrum. . . .

B's retort is impertinent; in most settings it would be simply rude. Its tone is reproachful, yet it adds nothing to the ostensible topic of Charlie's taste in cars. A might reasonably write the conversation off as unsalvageable, wondering just how he pushed the wrong button in B's brain.

This is the short treatment, which is adequate if the centipede effect hasn't a strong grip on you. If it has, a more detailed look at the jobs done is required. We may come to see the irrelevance of electrodynamics only by demonstrating how unproblematic these jobs are and how natural it is for these verbs to have them.

The job we give to *is* and *has* (the verbs *to be* and *to have*) in talking about colored surfaces is simply basic predication—one of the fundamental moves in any language. When we say that a car is unstable on rough roads, we attribute the property of rough-road instability to that car: This is to predicate the property of that car. Similarly, we attribute beauty to the sunset when we say the sunset is beautiful; we attribute coolness to the evening when we say the evening is cool; we attribute cleverness to Linda when we say Linda is clever. We could have formulated these sentiments using the verb *to have* as well: The car has a rough-road instability, and so on. It is in this way that we attribute a property to a surface when we say it is blue, has the color blue.

But to think that this is incompatible with discoveries in physics about colored light is to misunderstand predication. It is to misunderstand the wide variety of things that can count as properties and the range of circumstances in which we sensibly attribute these properties to things. We attribute beauty to the sunset when we say the sunset is beautiful. But this is not to *deny* that it has something to do with the clouds—even though they are not explicitly mentioned. "Yes, of course, it's the clouds too; they're all part of it." Talking about a beautiful sunset is simply our way of referring to the whole colorful business. And this way of doing it is normally transparent: nothing could be clearer. Like so much about language, predication—the attribution of properties to things—has many subtle features we can easily ignore, easily miss the importance of—features that are a product of our overriding concern with practical communication.

Much of simple predication is dominated by a single practical purpose: *to direct someone's attention to something in a way that will allow the other person to share our perception of it*. This helps explain both why we choose the property we do and why we attribute it to the thing we do. The "thing" provides an object for attention; the property provides a way of attending to it. Minutely different contexts, containing minutely different aims and interests, will attribute the same property to a variety of different things, and a variety of different properties to the very same thing, all depending on the perception we wish to share. We attribute the instability to the car because we are making a road test of the car, and we have discovered something about the car that readers will find useful. If somebody objects, "It's not really the car that's unstable, it's the motion," he has missed the point of the message. In a way it *is* the motion, but in another way it's the car, and the car is what is important here. All we mean in saying the car is unstable is that it reliably exhibits an unstable motion under certain conditions. The different attributions are compatible with each other; they just have distinct uses, make different points.

We attribute beauty to the sunset because that directs attention to the phantasmagoria on the western horizon produced by the setting sun. To object that it is not the sunset but the clouds is to miss the simple point of the attribution. Clouds can be beautiful in many different ways, times, and places. To speak of the beauty of the sunset is to direct our attention to one of these: one time, one place, one way of being beautiful. Terribly useful; wholly unproblematic.

So it goes for colors too. In attributing colors to surfaces, we are simply directing attention to a feature of those surfaces that most of us find obvious and interesting in normal conditions.

What is striking—and obvious—about the car is its hideous pea-green color; this is what reflects on Charlie's taste. The underlying electrodynamics is neither obvious nor of much interest in practical conversation. It is a boring distraction in discussing automotive aesthetics.

Attributing the color to the surface is in its way rather like attributing the beauty to the sunset and the instability to the car. The car has the property "rough-road instability" even though it manifests itself only when the car is traveling above a certain speed on a rough road. The surface has the property "blue" even though it manifests itself only when the surface is illuminated in a certain way. The criterion for having the instability is moving in a certain way on rough roads. The criterion for having a certain color is appearing a certain way to normal observers in normal sunlight. That is all it is for the surface to *be* that color. It is not that the surface is not really blue but rather merely reflects the blue light falling on it. It *is* blue *because* it differentially reflects that part of the spectrum—just as the sunset is beautiful (in part) because of the patterns in the clouds.

The overriding point here is that if we fire *is* and *has* from their normal predicating jobs in this case because of something in electrodynamics, then we could just as plausibly fire those verbs from that job in an enormous range of other cases too. It is not the car, it is the motion; it is not Linda, it is what she said; it is not the sunset, it is the clouds. And it is not even the clouds, but rather the light patterns. But besides offering us the inconceivable task of rebuilding vast, devastated chunks of English, this counsel neglects the hard-won insights of Chapter 7—namely, that languages primarily are practical tools for communicating our normal, mundane interests; and anything that helps get that done more easily, more clearly, more certainly is not just legitimate but welcome: something to be celebrated.

Before we leave this example, one other point deserves mention. Even more boldly than in the previous exercise, what is being fired here is not simply a pair of verbs, but a pair of contrasts. We normally contrast the color something *is* with the color it *appears to be*, due, say, to abnormal local conditions.

This suit is really dark blue, although in this light it appears to be black.

Given the run of normal, human interests, this is a useful thing to be able to say on a variety of different occasions.

> If you paint the part between the beams light beige it will appear white, while not glaring back at you as a pure white would.

But adopting B's counsel and firing *is* and *has* from their predicating jobs here would make these sentiments more difficult and complicated to express. For we could no longer speak of something's actually *being* blue, or being beige or being pure white, but only of it's *appearing* to be blue or black or green, etc., under a variety of conditions. Instead of saying the suit is blue but appears black, we would have to say that the suit that now appears black *would* appear blue under certain *other* conditions that we might then go on to specify. But it would be very difficult to say exactly what the conditions are under which a blue suit appears blue. So we would doubtless fall back on some formulation such as "normal conditions": normal observers, normal illumination, against a neutral background, some such thing.

But the elaborate conditional circumlocution "would appear blue to a normal observer in normal illumination against an appropriate background" merely comes to what we usually express by simply saying it is blue. And in most conversations we would gain nothing by substituting the cumbersome ellipsis.

> Charlie just bought a car that a normal observer in ordinary sunlight against a neutral background would find appears to be a nauseating pea-green.

Certainly nothing in electrodynamics can make this a reasonable way to talk. The car does not just *appear* to be ugly: It *is* ugly. It is ugly because of its color: It is a nauseating pea-green. The sentiment is clear; nobody misunderstands what is meant; and underlying physical theory adds nothing whatever.

COPYRIGHTS AND ACKNOWLEDGMENTS

The author wishes to thank the following for permission to reprint the material listed.

ASSOCIATED PRESS   For the following news articles: "Medfly Officials Suspect Hoax," "Smoke-filled Air Said Hazardous to Non-smokers," "Researchers Debate Cause of Dinosaurs' Extinction," "How Dinosaurs Disappeared from the Earth Again Disputed," "Tooth Decay Might Be Limited by Saccharin," "The Brain: Use It or Lose It," "Boxing Linked to Brain Damage; Ban Urged," "Fertilizer Link to Lou Gehrig's Disease Under Study," "Rat's Bone Is Clue in Hunt for Columbus' Fort," "Vandalism Cited in Train Derailment," "Woman Made Ill; Herb Tea Recalled," "W. German Landlord, Deep in Debt, Kills Self," "Study Time Affects Grades by Very Little, Study Finds," "Blast Levels Camarillo Packing Plant," "Disease Link Seen to Water Heaters," "Dogs May Have Eaten Dead Woman's Body," "Man Suspects Dogs Were Set on Him for Fighting Practice," "Beneficial Effects of Alcohol Questioned," "Holdout Juror Halts Porno Trial," "El Niño Chances Diminish," "3.1-Mile Hole Planned for Quake Research," and "Fallen Meteor Supports Theory of How Life Began." All reprinted by permission of the Associated Press.

RICHARD BLUE   For Letter to the Editor, "Free Agents," from the *Los Angeles Times*, October 6, 1987. Reprinted by permission of the author.

DAVID J. BRODER   For "Move by Bell and Connally to Limit Term of President Rejected a Long Time Ago." Reprinted from *The Washington Post* by permission of the author.

THOMAS M. CONDRAN   For Letter to the Editor, "On the Road," from *Road and Track* Magazine. Reprinted by permission of the author.

DR. PATRICIA FROSTHOLM   For Letter to the Editor, "Arts Center's Empty Seats," from the *Los Angeles Times*, December 27, 1987. Reprinted by permission of the author.

J. C. GARRETT   For Letter to the Editor from the *Los Angeles Times*, October 7, 1987. Reprinted by permission of the author.

HEMET NEWS   For "Skeleton, Car Wreck Found in Mountains," *Hemet News*, January 19, 1987. Reprinted by permission of *The Hemet News*, Hemet, CA.

KNT NEWS WIRE   For "Studies Link Coronary Artery Disease, Coffee Drinking," printed in the *Boston Globe*, and "Study Links Drinking to Less

INDEX

A 8
B 9
C 0
D 1
E 2
F 3
G 4
H 5
I 6
J 7